THE
ODYSSEY

Homer

COLLINS
CLASSICS

Harper Press
An imprint of HarperCollins*Publishers*
1 London Bridge Street,
London SE1 9GF

This edition published 2011

A catalogue record for this book is available from the British Library

ISBN-13: 978-0-00-7420094

Printed and bound by CPI Group (UK) Ltd, Croydon, CR0 4YY

Mixed Sources
Product group from well-managed
forests and other controlled sources
www.fsc.org Cert no. SW-COC-001806
© 1996 Forest Stewardship Council

FSC is a non-profit international organisation established to promote the
responsible management of the world's forests. Products carrying the FSC
label are independently certified to assure consumers that they come
from forests that are managed to meet the social, economic and
ecological needs of present and future generations.

Find out more about HarperCollins and the environment at
www.harpercollins.co.uk/green

Life & Times section © HarperCollins Publishers Ltd
Gerard Cheshire asserts his morals rights as author of the Life & Times section
Classic Literature: Words and Phrases adapted from
Collins English Dictionary
Typesetting in Kalix by Palimpsest Book Production Limited,
Falkirk, Stirlingshire

10 9 8

History of Collins

In 1819, millworker William Collins from Glasgow, Scotland, set up a company for printing and publishing pamphlets, sermons, hymn books and prayer books. That company was Collins and was to mark the birth of HarperCollins Publishers as we know it today. The long tradition of Collins dictionary publishing can be traced back to the first dictionary William published in 1824, *Greek and English Lexicon*. Indeed, from 1840 onwards, he began to produce illustrated dictionaries and even obtained a licence to print and publish the Bible.

Soon after, William published the first Collins novel, *Ready Reckoner*, however it was the time of the Long Depression, where harvests were poor, prices were high, potato crops had failed and violence was erupting in Europe. As a result, many factories across the country were forced to close down and William chose to retire in 1846, partly due to the hardships he was facing.

Aged 30, William's son, William II took over the business. A keen humanitarian with a warm heart and a generous spirit, William II was truly 'Victorian' in his outlook. He introduced new, up-to-date steam presses and published affordable editions of Shakespeare's works and *Pilgrim's Progress*, making them available to the masses for the first time. A new demand for educational books meant that success came with the publication of travel books, scientific books, encyclopaedias and dictionaries. This demand to be educated led to the later publication of atlases and Collins also held the monopoly on scripture writing at the time.

In the 1860s Collins began to expand and diversify and the idea of 'books for the millions' was developed. Affordable editions of classical literature were published and in 1903 Collins introduced 10 titles in their Collins Handy Illustrated Pocket Novels. These proved so popular that a few years later this had increased to an output of 50 volumes, selling nearly half a million in their year of publication. In the same year, The Everyman's Library was also instituted, with the idea of publishing an affordable library of the most important classical works, biographies, religious and philosophical treatments, plays, poems, travel and adventure. This series eclipsed all competition at the time and the introduction of paperback books in the 1950s helped to open that market and marked a high point in the industry.

HarperCollins is and has always been a champion of the classics and the current Collins Classics series follows in this tradition – publishing classical literature that is affordable and available to all. Beautifully packaged, highly collectible and intended to be reread and enjoyed at every opportunity.

Life & Times

Homer and his Works

Homer, to whom *The Odyssey* is attributed, is thought to have been writing at around 800–900 BC, and the poem is thought to mark the beginnings of Western literature, almost 3,000 years ago. Many believe that it could not have been written by one person and that several were responsible for composing the work. *The Odyssey* is essentially a very lengthy poem or, more accurately, a lyric or rhapsody as it would originally have been performed in song in Ancient Greece.

Homer lived on the Aegean coast of what is now Turkey, but was then a part of the Greek Empire. The Ancient Greek cosmology was filled with mythological stories that were taught to children by way of explaining the world around them. All manner of gods and monsters were central to the stories and the Greek islands and mountains served as realms in which different scenarios were played out. Intertwined with the mythology were legendary tales of significant historical characters, loosely based on truth. This all added up to a complex and vast folklore. It was this folklore that Homer, either in the individual or collective sense, drew from in his epic poems, which include *The Iliad*, effectively the prequel to *The Odyssey*. These two works form the foundation for subsequent Greek culture – society would use them as points of reference and guidance, in the same way that many have used the testaments of the bible to instruct their way of life. So it was that Homer's poems became manuals for appeasing the gods and living peaceful and fruitful lives in Ancient Greece.

As for Homer himself, it is a matter of considerable contention between Classical scholars as to whether he ever existed and when. There is very scant evidence available, so it seems likely that he may be a mythical figure, an old father time, grandfather to the nation. As a result any literary works of significance were attributed to him, simply because it was impossible to know who the real author or authors were. As there was a great oral tradition of story telling in Ancient Greece, it is more likely that the epic poems were developed and refined over generations by many orators. Perhaps a politician realized their worth as pedagogic texts and ordered scholars to document them for that very purpose. Or perhaps a master orator, or rhapsode, had them documented, so that his apprentices could travel to different regions of the Greek empire and recite the exact same texts.

The Odyssey

The central character in *The Odyssey* is the eponymous Odysseus. The story is epic in its scope and describes the many heroic deeds and adventures of Odysseus as he attempts to find his way home after the Trojan War. One of the major themes of the work is the play-off between the human qualities known by the Ancient Greeks as *mētis* and *hubris*. In simple terms *mētis* is best described as intelligence and common sense or cunning and guile. *Hubris*, on the other hand, is excessive pride and self-confidence. In essence they are opposed traits – the perfect individual needs to have a measured balance of both in order to avoid failure in whatever life throws at them. The original meaning for the term *nemesis* was the punishment meted out to those who displayed excessive defiance of the gods, which could result from an imbalance of these qualities.

The poem is also fundamentally about the human sense of belonging and homecoming, a theme ubiquitously familiar to all people and one that echoes throughout the poem as Odysseus finds himself in a huge variety of different situations in his quest to return home to his wife and son.

The Structure

The Odyssey, like *The Iliad*, is entirely written in *dactylic* or *heroic hexameter* verse. It has 12, 110 lines. *Dactylic hexameter* describes the rhythmic pattern or meter of the verse, which uses six (*hexa*) units known as feet (*dactyls*) per line. *Dactyl* actually means finger, but is used in allusion to fingers walking the page like feet. The reason for this consistent form throughout the poem is due to the oral tradition of reciting poems in song. It made recitals more entertaining because they were performed rather than being delivered in a dry and monotonous way. However, a great deal of the poetic form has been lost in translation from the Greek to other languages, including English.

THE ODYSSEY

TRANSLATOR'S NOTE

The twenty-eighth English rendering of the Odyssey can hardly be a literary event, especially when it aims to be essentially a straightforward translation. Wherever choice offered between a poor and a rich word richness had it, to raise the colour. I have transposed: the order of metrical Greek being unlike plain English. Not that my English is plain enough. Wardour-Street Greek like the Odyssey's defies honest rendering. Also I have been free with moods and tenses; allowed myself to interchange adjective and adverb; and dodged our poverty of preposition, limitations of verb and pronominal vagueness by rearrangement. Still, syntax apart, this is a translation.

It has been made from the Oxford text, uncritically. I have not pored over contested readings, variants, or spurious lines. However scholars may question the text in detail, writers (and even would-be writers) cannot but see in the Odyssey a single, authentic, unedited work of art, integrally preserved. Thrice I noted loose ends, openings the author had forgotten: one sentence I would have shifted in time: five or six lines rang false to me: one speech seems to come before its context. These are motes in a book which is neat,

close-knit, artful, and various; as nearly word-perfect as
midnight oil and pumice can effect.

Crafty, exquisite, homogeneous – whatever great art
may be, these are not its attributes. In this tale every big
situation is burked and the writing is soft. The shattered
Iliad yet makes a masterpiece; while the Odyssey by its ease
and interest remains the oldest book worth reading for its
story and the first novel of Europe. Gay, fine and vivid it is:
never huge or terrible. Book XI, the Underworld, verges
toward 'terribilita' – yet runs instead to the seed of pathos,
that feeblest mode of writing. The author misses his every
chance of greatness, as must all his faithful translators.

This limitation of the work's scope is apparently
conscious. Epic belongs to early man, and this Homer lived
too long after the heroic age to feel assured and large. He
shows exact knowledge of what he could and could not do.
Only through such superb self-criticism can talent rank
beside inspiration.

In four years of living with this novel I have tried to
deduce the author from his self-betrayal in the work. I found
a book-worm, no longer young, living from home, a main-
lander, citybred and domestic. Married but not exclusively,
a dog-lover, often hungry and thirsty, dark-haired. Fond of
poetry, a great if uncritical reader of the Iliad, with limited
sensuous range but an exact eyesight which gave him all his
pictures. A lover of old bric-a-brac, though as muddled an
antiquary as Walter Scott – in sympathy with which side of
him I have conceded 'tenterhooks' but not railway-trains.

It is fun to compare his infuriating male condescension
towards inglorious woman with his tender charity of head
and heart for serving-men. Though a stickler for the prides
of poets and a man who never misses a chance to cocker up
their standing, yet he must be (like writers two thousand

years after him) the associate of menials, making himself their friend and defender by understanding. Was it a fellow-feeling, or did he forestall time in his view of slavery?

He loved the rural scene as only a citizen can. No farmer, he had learned the points of a good olive tree. He is all adrift when it comes to fighting, and had not seen deaths in battle. He had sailed upon and watched the sea with a palpitant concern, seafaring being not his trade. As a minor sportsman he had seen wild boars at bay and heard tall yarns of lions.

Few men can be sailors, soldiers and naturalists. Yet this Homer was neither land-lubber nor stay-at-home nor ninny. He wrote for audiences to whom adventures were daily life and the sea their universal neighbour. So he dared not err. That famous doubled line where the Cyclops narrowly misses the ship with his stones only shows how much better a seaman he was than his copyist. Scholiasts have tried to riddle his technical knowledge – and of course he does make a hotch-potch of periods. It is the penalty of being pre-archaeological. His pages are steeped in a queer naively; and at our remove of thought and language we cannot guess if he is smiling or not. Yet there is a dignity which compels respect and baffles us, he being neither simple in education nor primitive socially. His generation so rudely admired the Iliad that even to misquote it was a virtue. he sprinkles tags of epic across his pages. In this some find humour. Rather I judge that here too the tight lips of archaic art have grown the fixed grin of archaism.

Very bookish, this house-bred man. His work smells of the literary coterie, of a writing tradition. His notebooks were stocked with purple passages and he embedded these in his tale wherever they would more or less fit. He, like William Morris, was driven by his age to legend, where he found men living untrammelled under the God-possessed skies. Only, with more verbal felicity than Morris', he had less poetry. Fashion gave him recurring epithets, like labels: but repetitions tell, in public speaking. For recitation, too, are the swarming speeches. A trained voice can put drama and incident into speeches. Perhaps the tedious delay of the climax through ten books may be a poor bard's means of prolonging his host's hospitality.

Obviously the tale was the thing; and that explains (without excusing it to our ingrown minds) his thin and accidental characterisation. He thumb-nailed well; and afterwards lost heart. Nausicaa, for instance, enters dramatically and shapes, for a few lines, like a woman – then she fades, unused. Eumaeus fared better: but only the central family stands out, consistently and pitilessly drawn – the sly cattish wife, that cold-blooded egotist Odysseus, and the priggish son who yet met his master-prig in Menelaus. It is sorrowful to believe that these were really Homer's heroes and exemplars.

T.E. SHAW

O DIVINE POESY
GODDESS-DAUGHTER OF ZEUS
SUSTAIN FOR ME
THIS SONG OF THE VARIOUS-MINDED MAN
WHO AFTER HE HAD PLUNDERED
THE INNERMOST CITADEL OF HALLOWED TROY
WAS MADE TO STRAY GRIEVOUSLY
ABOUT THE COASTS OF MEN
THE SPORT OF THEIR CUSTOMS GOOD OR BAD
WHILE HIS HEART
THROUGH ALL THE SEA-FARING
ACHED IN AN AGONY TO REDEEM HIMSELF
AND BRING HIS COMPANY SAFE HOME

VAIN HOPE – FOR THEM
FOR HIS FELLOWS HE STROVE IN VAIN
THEIR OWN WITLESSNESS CAST THEM AWAY
THE FOOLS
TO DESTROY FOR MEAT
THE OXEN OF THE MOST EXALTED SUN
WHEREFORE THE SUN-GOD BLOTTED OUT
THE DAY OF THEIR RETURN

MAKE THE TALE LIVE FOR US
IN ALL ITS MANY BEARINGS
O MUSE

BOOK 1

By now the other warriors, those that had escaped headlong ruin by sea or in battle, were safely home. Only Odysseus tarried, shut up by Lady Calypso, a nymph and very Goddess, in her hewn-out caves. She craved him for her bed-mate: while he was longing for his house and his wife. Of a truth the rolling seasons had at last brought up the year marked by the Gods for his return to Ithaca; but not even there among his loved things would he escape further conflict. Yet had all the Gods with lapse of time grown compassionate towards Odysseus – all but Poseidon, whose enmity flamed ever against him till he had reached his home. Poseidon, however, was for the moment far away among the Aethiopians, that last race of men, whose dispersion across the world's end is so broad that some of them can see the Sun-God rise while others see him set. Thither had Poseidon gone in the hope of burnt offerings, bulls and rams, by hundreds: and there he sat feasting merrily while the other Gods came together in the halls of Olympian Zeus. To them the father of Gods and men began speech, for his breast teemed with thought of great Aegisthus, whom famous Orestes, the son of Agamemnon, had slain.

'It vexes me to see how mean are these creatures of a day towards us Gods, when they charge against us the evils (far beyond our worst dooming) which their own exceeding wantonness has heaped upon themselves. Just so did Aegisthus exceed when he took to his bed the lawful wife of Atrides and killed her returning husband. He knew the sheer ruin this would entail. Did we not warn him by the mouth of our trusty Hermes, the keen-eyed slayer of Argus, neither to murder the man nor lust after the woman's body? "For the death of the son of Atreus will be requited by Orestes, even as he grows up and dreams of his native place." These were Hermes' very words: but not even such friendly interposition could restrain Aegisthus, who now pays the final penalty.'

Swiftly there took him up Athene, goddess of the limpid eyes. 'Our Father, heir of Kronos, Lord of lords! That man Aegisthus has been justly served. May everyone who slaughters a victim after his fashion go down likewise into hell! But my heart is heavy for Odysseus, so shrewd, so ill-fated, pining in long misery of exile on an island which is just a speck in the belly of the sea. This wave-beset, wooded island is the domain of a God-begotten creature, the daughter of baleful Atlas whose are the pillars that prop the lofty sky: whose too are the deepest soundings of the sea. The daughter has trapped the luckless wretch and with subtle insistence cozens him to forget his Ithaca. Forget! Odysseus is so sick with longing to see if it were but the smoke of his home spiring up, that he prays for death. I marvel, my Lord of Olympus, how your heart makes no odds of it. Can you lightly pass over the burnt offerings Odysseus lavished upon you, by the Argive ships in the plain of Troy?'

'My child,' protested Zeus, the cloud-compeller, 'what

sharp judgements you let slip through your teeth! As if I could overpass the merit of Odysseus, who stands out above the ruck of men as much for worldly wisdom as for his generous offerings to the Gods that eternally possess the open sky. It is Poseidon the world-girdler who is so headily bitter against him, for the sake of that Cyclops whom Odysseus blinded, even the god-like Polyphemus, their chief figure and Poseidon's very son: – for his mother Thoosa (daughter to Phorkys, an overlord of the ungarnered sea) conceived him after she had lain with the God under the beetling cliffs. Because of this, Poseidon the land-shaker, though he dare not quite kill Odysseus, at least implacably frustrates his every effort to get back to the land of his fathers. But come, let us put all our heads together and contrive the man's return; then will Poseidon have to swallow his bile. Against the concert of the Immortals he cannot stand alone.'

Athene the clear-eyed, the Goddess, answered and said: 'Father and Lord of all, Kronides, if indeed the ineffable Gods now judge it fit that prudent Odysseus should return, then let us call Hermes, our usher, the killer of Argus, and despatch him straight to Ogygia, the island of that nymph with the lovely hair: to warn her how it is become our fixed act that the dauntless one be allowed to set out homeward forthwith. For my part I shall go to Ithaca and rouse his son Telemachus, instilling some tardy purpose into his spirit, so that he may call his Greek exquisites to council and give check to the mob of wooers besetting his mother Penelope, the while they butcher his wealth of juicy sheep and rolling-gaited, screw-horned oxen. I will send the youth to Sparta – yes, and to sandy Pylos – to ask those he meets for news of his dear father's return: not that he will hear anything, but his zeal will earn him repute among men.'

She ceased, and drew upon her feet those golden sandals (whose fairness no use could dim) that carried their mistress as surely and wind-swiftly over the waves as over the boundless earth. She laid hold of her guardian spear, great, heavy, and close-grained, tipped with cutting bronze. When wrath moved the goddess to act, this spear was her weapon: with it, and stayed by her pride of birth, she would daunt serried ranks of the very bravest warriors. Downward she now glided from the summit of Olympus, to alight on Ithaca before Odysseus' house, by the sill of the main gate. With that war spear in her fist she seemed some traveller seeking hospitality: she had a look of Mentes, a chief in Taphos.

The gateway was thronged with the self-assertive suitors, whose pleasure for the moment was to sit there playing at chequers on the hides of the oxen they had killed and eaten. Round them bustled their criers and nimble pages, some mixing wine and water in the parent-bowls ready to drink, others wiping down table-tops with soft sponges or re-laying them for the next meal, while yet others were jointing huge sides of meat. If the suitors saw her they did not move or look before handsome Telemachus gave sign. He sat despondent in the hurly, fancying to himself his honest father's sudden arrival from somewhere, somehow: and the scatter there would be, through the palace, of these wasters when they saw him stride in to regain men's respect and king it honourably once more over his household.

As he so dreamed amidst the unheeding suitors he became aware of Athene waiting by the threshold; and went straight to her, vexed to the heart that any guest should be delayed at their door for lack of welcome. He clasped her right hand, relieving her of the metal spear, and spoke to her these winged words: 'Accept, O guest, the friendliest greetings. Enter and taste our food: and thereafter make known to us your every need.'

Whereupon he led the way into the noble house. Pallas followed until he set her spear in the polished spear rack beside a high pillar, amongst weapons once used by the long-suffering Odysseus. Then he spread smooth draperies over a throne of cunning workmanship and seated her upon it. For her feet there was a foot-stool, while for himself he drew up a painted lounge-chair in such a way that they were shut off from the suitors. Telemachus feared lest that roistering mob's impertinences might disgust the stranger and turn his stomach against eating. Then too he wished to put some privy questions about his missing father.

A maid came with a precious golden ewer and poured water for them above its silver basin, rinsing their hands. She drew to their side a gleaming table and on it the matronly house-keeper arranged her store of bread and many prepared dishes, making an eager grace of all the hospitality. A carver filled and passed them trenchers of meat in great variety, and set out on their table two golden beakers which the steward, as often as he walked up and down the hall, refilled for them with wine. The suitors swaggered in. One after the other they seated themselves on the thrones and long chairs. Their retainers poured water for their hands, and the maids of the house heaped loaves of bread in each man's table-basket while the serving lads brimmed the wine-cisterns with drink. Every hand went out to the abundance so laid ready.

But when their lusting for food and drink had been assuaged the suitors began to mind them of other things; of singing and dancing, those twin glories which crown a feast. The steward returned with a very splendid lyre for

Phemius, whose hap it was to play the bard for them, under compulsion. He ran his hands over the strings, plucking out an exquisite air, under cover of which Telemachus bent towards clear-eyed Athene and said softly, that the company might not overhear: –

'Honoured stranger, will my words offend? I pray not. They now have their minds easy for music and verse, these suitor-maggots who freely devour another man's livelihood. Freely indeed, without let or fine! Ah, if they did but catch a glimpse of the Master returning to Ithaca, how they would beseech high heaven for the gift of swifter running rather than more wealth in gold or raiment. But alas, his bones whiten to-day in some field under the rain: or the swell rolls them through the salty deep. Yea, he has perished dreadfully: nor would a glow of hope kindle in our hearts if the wisest man on earth told us he was coming home. The sun of his return has utterly gone down.

'Enough of this – instead, tell me, I pray you, and exactly, who you are: of what state and stock? You came, I suspect, by ship; for I am very sure that by dry land you found no road. But what were the sailors who put you ashore in Ithaca, or rather, what did they profess themselves to be? I ask all this in order to satisfy myself that you are really a new-comer, tasting our hospitality for the first time, and not a guest entailed on us by my father: for so great a traveller was he, you know, that our house is honoured by throngs of his acquaintance from every land.'

Then said the clear-eyed Goddess, 'I will meet all these questions of yours frankly. My name is Mentes. My father Anchialus was a noted warrior. I am a leader of the oar-loving islanders of Taphos. I put in here with my ship and crew on our way across the wine-dark sea to Temesa, where we hope to barter a cargo of sparkling iron ore for the copper of those foreign-speaking people. My ship is berthed well away from the city, in Reithron, that lonely inlet which lies below tree-grown Neion.

'Between our families there is a long tradition of friendship and guesting, which father Laertes will confirm, if you ask him: though they tell me that he now comes no more to town, because of the infirmities of his advanced years. Wherefore he buries himself in his secluded vineyard, among his vine-stocks on their ordered terraces: up and down which the old man drags himself, slow step after step, cherishing the grapes, until the feebleness of age once again takes him sorely by the knees. Then he rests, for the old woman, his sole attendant, to wait on him with restoring meat and drink.

'And the reason for my present visit? Because I heard that HE was back. I mean your father: for be assured that the marvellous Odysseus-has in no wise perished off the face of the earth: though it seems the Gods yet arrest him in midpath of his return. And therefore (albeit I am by trade no teller of fortunes, nor professed reader of the significance of birds), therefore I am about to prophesy to you what the Deathless Ones have put into my heart and made my faith: – namely, that the day of Odysseus' coming again to his native place is near. He may be penned within some surf-beaten islet ringed by the wide sea: or some rude tribe of savages may hold him in durance. But only for the time. Infallibly he will find means of escape, though they fetter him in fetters of the purest iron. The man is fertility itself in his expedients. – Now tell me something, plainly, as I have told you. Are you real and very son to Odysseus, you who are so well grown of body? His head and fine eyes you have exactly, as I remember him in our old association; for we were much together in the days before he set out for Troy in the hollow ships with all the chivalry of Greece; since when we have not met.'

Careful Telemachus answered thus: 'Indeed you shall have it very plain, my friend. My mother says I am his son: for myself I do not know. Has any son of man yet been sure of his begetting? Would that I had been the child of some ordinary parent whom old age had overtaken in the quiet course of nature on his estate! But as it is, since you press it, they do name me the child of that vaguest-fated of all men born to death.'

Athene put to him one more question. 'I think when Penelope conceived so goodly a son it was meant that the Gods had not appointed a nameless future for your stock. But give me the straight truth again. What feast or rout of a feast is this which rages about us? What part in it have you? Is it a drinking bout or some sort of marriage? No sodality would be thus indecent. A mannered man now, entering by chance, might well forget himself with disgust at seeing how outrageously they make free with your house.'

Soberly Telemachus answered her again, saying, 'Stranger, since you probe into this also and put it to me, I must confess that our house looked to be rich and well-appointed while my father ruled it as master. But the Gods saw fit to order it quite otherwise when they spirited him away with an utterness beyond example. Had he plainly died I should not have taken it so hardly: above all had he died with his likes on the field of Troy in his friends' arms, after winding up the pitch of battle to its height. For then the fellowship of Greece would have united to rear his funerary mound and the fame of his prowess would have been (for his son) a glorious, increasing heritage.

'Instead we have this instant vanishment into blind silence, as though the Harpies, winged Scavengers of the

Wind, had whirled him into their void: and I am left weeping with pain. Nor do I weep only his pain. The Gods have gone on to invent other evils for my count. Every man of authority in the islands, from Doulichion, and Same, and Zacynthos of the woods, as well as every figure of this rugged Ithaca – all, all, are come wooing my mother. It seems that she can neither reject the horrible offers, out and out, nor accept any one of them. So here they sit, for ever eating up my substance and making havoc of the house. Surely soon they will devour me too.'

Athene heard him out and then said fiercely, 'A shameful tale! Here's a crying need for Odysseus, to man-handle these graceless suitors. Would that he might appear now in the outer gate, erect, helmeted, with shield and two stabbing spears, the figure of a man I saw enter our house the first time we entertained him on his way up from Ephyra. He had been down in his war-vessel to get from Ilus, son of Mermerus, some deadly poison to smear on the bronze heads of his arrows. Ilus feared to affront the ever-lasting Gods and refused him any. So it was my father, carried away by the huge love he bore him, who furnished it. If only that Odysseus we knew might to-day thrust in among the suitors! Indeed their mating would be bitter and their shrift suddenly sharp. However such things rest on the knees of the Gods, whose it is to appoint whether he shall re-enter his halls and exact vengeance, or no.

'Wherefore instead I counsel you to take most earnest thought in what way you shall by your single self expel the suitors from the house. Listen to this plan of mine which I would urge upon you. Tomorrow assemble all the Greek chiefs. Address them bluntly, calling the Gods to witness how you order; firstly, that the suitors disperse, every man to his place; and secondly, that your mother (if her nature yet inclines toward marriage) betake herself to the palace of the mighty man her father. It shall be for them, there, to make the new match for her, regulating rich dues and providing such wedding festivities as befit the alliance of a favourite daughter.

'There remains your personal duty, on which also I have a word to say, if you will hear it. Get yourself a ship of twenty rowers, the very best ship you can find. Set forth in this to seek news of your long-overdue father. Even if no mortal tells you anything, yet who knows but there may steal into your mind that divine prompting by which Zeus very often gives mankind an inkling of the truth. Go to Pylos first and consult its revered Nestor; thence to Sparta where you will find brown-haired Menelaus, latest of all the mail-clad Achaeans to get back from Troy. If you learn that your father is living and has his face towards home, then steel your temper to one more year of this afflicted house. But if you learn that he is no more – that he is surely dead – then return and throw up a mound to his name, with the plenishing and ceremonial befitting a great fallen warrior: after which do you yourself give his widow, your mother, to some man for wife.

'These things first. Yet also it must be your study and passion to slay these suitors in your house, either by fair fight or by stratagem. Childishness no longer beseems your years: you must put it away. My friend (I wish to call you that, for you are man in frame and very man in form), my friend, be brave, that generations not yet born may glorify your name. Consider young Orestes and the honour he has won in all men's mouths by putting to death his father's murderer, the crafty blood-boltered Aegisthus who trapped noble Agamemnon. No more – I must back to my swift ship: its waiting crew will be grumbling because I have delayed them all this weary while. Only a parting word – make it your instant and main effort to do as I have said.'

Heedful Telemachus replied, 'Sir, the kindness of your advice to me has been like a father's to his son: and I will ever gratefully remember it. But I beg you, however urgent your business, to delay your setting out till you have bathed and refreshed yourself. Then go to your ship, spirit-gladdened, with a gift from me in your hand: for it shall be a worthy gift to remind you of me always: some very beautiful treasure such as only great friend gives to friend.'

The Goddess Athene, the clear-eyed, refused him. 'Do not try to hold me. I long to be on the way. As for this token which your friendly interest prompts, let it be mine on the return journey when I can carry it straight home. Choose your richest gift. It shall be matched by what I give you in exchange' – and having so said she went, suddenly and elusively as a sea bird goes; leaving the young man quick with ardour and decision and more mindful of his father than ever of late. Telemachus, as he felt this change come to his spirit, was amazed. The persuasion took him that his visitant had been in some way divine. Accordingly his carriage as he went once more among the suitors reflected God-head.

To that audience the great singer still sang: and they sat round, hanging on the song which told of the woeful return entailed by Pallas Athene upon such Greeks as had gone to Troy. In her upper storey, Penelope, that most circumspect daughter of Icarius, caught rising snatches of the minstrelsy. Her wit pieced these together into their sense. Down she came by the high stairs from her quarters and entered the great hall: not indeed alone, for always two waiting women closely followed her. So, like a stately goddess among mortals, she descended upon the suitors:

to halt there where the first great pillar propped the massy roof. As veil for her face she held up a fold of her soft wimple: and the ever watchful maidens covered her, one on either side. Thus stood she and wept, till she found words to address the inspired bard.

'Phemius,' she cried, 'do you not know many other charmed songs for people's ears? Songs in which poets have extolled the great deeds of Gods or men? Sing one of those, here from your place in the company which will, none the less, sit silently drinking and listening. But this lamentable tale give over: the sorrow of it slowly melts my heart within my bosom; for you tell of the event which has brought down upon me – me above all women – this unappeasable pain. So continually does my memory yearn after that dear head. O my lost hero! whose glory had spread throughout Hellas and Argos, the very heart of the land!'

Telemachus decently cut her short. 'My Mother, why take it amiss that our trusty singer should entertain us as the spirit moves him? I think it is not poets who bring things to pass, but rather Zeus who pays out to men, the Makers, their fates at his whim: we have no cause against Phemius for drawing music out of the hard fate of the Danaans. A crowd ever extols the song which sounds freshest in its ears. Harden your heart and mind to hear this tale. Remember that Odysseus was not singular in utterly losing at Troy the day of his return. There were others, many others, who in the Troad lost their very selves. Wherefore I bid you get back to your part of the house, and be busied in your proper sphere, with the loom and the spindle, and in overseeing your maids at these, their tasks. Speech shall be the men's care: and principally my care: for mine is the mastery in this house.' She, astonished, went back up the stairs, laying away in her breast this potent saying of her son's. But when she had regained the upper storey with her serving women she began to weep for Odysseus her lost husband, and wept until the grey-eyed Goddess Athene cast a pitying sleep upon her eyelids.

Behind her back the wooers broke into riot across the twilit hall, everyone swearing aloud that his should be the luck of lying in her bed: but to them the dispassionate Telemachus began, 'Suitors of my mother and lewd ruffians: – tonight let us forgather and feast: but no shouting, please, to spoil our privilege of hearing this singer with the divine voice. Tomorrow I vote we go early to the assembly and all take seat there. I have to unburden my soul to you formally and without stint on the subject of your quitting this house: and to suggest that you remember your own banqueting halls in which you may eat your own food-stuffs and feast each other in rotation from house to house. But if you deem it meeter and more delightful to waste the entire substance of a solitary man, scot-free and for nothing – why then, waste away! Only I shall pray to the Gods – the ever-lasting Gods – on the chance that Zeus may decree acts of requital. In which case you will all be destroyed in this house, scot-free and for nothing.'

So he spoke: and they curbed their lips between their teeth to contain their astonishment at Telemachus' daring to taunt them with such spirit. At last Antinous, son of Eupeithes, undertook to reply. 'Why, Telemachus, those very Gods must have been giving you lessons in freedom of speech and heady taunting! All the same I doubt Zeus ever making you king of sea-girt Ithaca, even if that dignity does happen to be your birth-right.'

Said Telemachus with restraint, 'Antinous, take not my words against the grain. If Zeus willed it I would assume even that charge ungrudgingly. You imply it is the worst thing that could happen amongst us men? Let me tell you it is not so bad a fate to be King: quickly does a royal house grow rich, and himself amass honour. However, since the mighty Odysseus is dead, surely this headship will fall to some one of the swarm of kings young and old now infesting this land of Ithaca. My determination and aims are bounded by this house – to be lord in it and over its bond-servants whom the triumphant might of Odysseus led in from his forays as thralls.'

Eurymachus son of Polybus then put in his word. 'Telemachus, the question of which Greek shall reign over this island lies on the lap of the Gods. Yet assuredly you shall possess your belongings and have the lordship in your own houses: nor against your will shall any man come and strip you of them forcibly while Ithaca holds an inhabitant. But my good lad, let me question you about that visitor of yours who slipped away so suddenly that none of us had time to make him out. Yet his face was not the face of a negligible man. Whence came he and what country gave he as his own? Where do his kindred live and where are the corn-lands of his family? Did he come with news of your father, or on some business of his own?'

Discreetly Telemachus reassured him: 'Eurymachus, the time of my father's return is long over. I do not now credit any messages regarding him, whatever their source. Nor does any soothsaying take me in: though my mother may at whiles call some noted diviner to the palace and seek sooth of him. As for the stranger, he is a former friend of our family from Taphos called Mentes, whose father was old wise-minded Anchialus. Mentes is a man of authority among the seafaring Taphians.' So he said: but secretly Telemachus was sure of the immortal Goddess. Howbeit the suitors turned to dance and to the enthralling song, making merry while the evening drew down; and they celebrated until evening had darkened into night. Then the longing for sleep took them and they scattered, each man to the house where he lodged.

The mind of Telemachus was perplexedly brooding over many things as he also sought his bed within his own room, which was contrived in the highest part of the main building, that stately landmark of the country-side. Eurycleia the daughter of Ops son of Peisenor, attended him, lighting his way with flaring slips of pine-wood – Eurycleia the trusted, the adept, who, in the flush of her youth, had been bought by Laertes, out of his great wealth, for the price of twenty oxen. In the house Laertes had esteemed her even as his beloved wife, but never dared have intercourse with her, fearing the temper of his wife. Of all the servants it was Eurycleia who most loved Telemachus, for she had nursed him when he was a tiny child. Accordingly it was she who lighted him to his well-built room.

He flung open its doors and sat himself on the couch. There he pulled off his long clinging tunic, which the old woman received into her skillful hands and folded and patted into smoothness before she hung it on the clothes-peg beside his fretted, inlaid bedstead. Then she quitted the chamber, pulling-to the door after her by the silver beak which served as handle and sliding the bolt across by its leathern thong. And there Telemachus lay all night, wrapped in a choice fleece, pondering in his heart how he should compass the journey enjoined upon him by Athene.

BOOK 2

So soon as rosy-fingered morning came forth from the first grey dawn, the beloved son of Odysseus sprang from bed, dressed, threw the sling of his cutting sword over one shoulder, and tied the rich sandals round his nimble feet: stately as a God he stepped out and down from his bed-chamber. On the moment he had called his heralds and told them to sound, with their ringing voices, the assembly amongst the long-haired Achaeans. As he bade, the heralds sounded: and as they bade, the Achaeans assembled speedily. Telemachus waited till all had come together into place and then, tightly gripping his copper-bladed spear, he strode through their throng. For company he had just his two flashing-footed dogs at heel: but Athene poured about his form so significant a glory that upon his approach the eyes of the crowd were held at gaze. The elders yielded him way and in his father's great chair he sat him down.

Debate was opened by honoured Aegyptius, an aged councillor of ten thousand wiles, whose years bowed him double. He was quick to speak because his favourite son, Antiphos, expert with the spear, had gone away with Odysseus in the capacious ships to Ilios, that land of good horses. To tell truth, Antiphos was even now dead, barbarously slain in the vaulted cave by the Cyclops, who had cooked him, too, and eaten him for his latest, and his last, feast. Aegyptius had yet three other sons. One of them, Eurynomus, had thrown in his lot with the suitors; and two kept the house, helping with the husbandry: but the consolation of these did not still the old man's inward aching and outward lamentation for the one who had not returned. Therefore it was that he now rose up and spoke through his tears: –

'Hear now, O men of Ithaca, and attend my words. Never once since the day that mighty Odysseus sailed from us in his ribbed ships, has our assembly met in session. Who is now our convenor? Is some one of the new generation in extreme urgency? Or one of us elders? Perhaps an army approaches, of which a man has had warning and would make us share his certain knowledge? Or is it some matter touching the common weal, which he would disclose and expound? Anyway I judge his zeal timely: may the event turn to his advantage, and Zeus ensure him the good thing for which his soul yearns.' – Thus far: and the dear son of Odysseus rejoiced at the auspicious phrase. The longing to deliver his mind pricked him to his feet in the midst of the gathering. Peisenor the herald, past master by experience of public conduct, thrust into his hands the gavel which gave right to speak: and Telemachus began, addressing himself first to the old councillor.

'Venerable Sir, the man who convened the people is not far to seek. Here he stands, in your eye. I am compelled to action by the burden of my pains. I have no word of any army coming, no advance or exclusive news affecting that or the common estate. The need, the motive, is personal. A two-headed evil has stricken me and struck my house.

I have lost my noble father who was once your king, the king of all present: but also my very gentle father. And upon this harm comes far heavier harm, one which bodes the early wasting of my home and an utter ruin of my livelihood.

'My reluctant mother is plagued by suitors, sons of the leading men in this and other islands. Their honest course would be to interview her father, Icarius, and ask him to fix his daughter's marriage terms and give her to the man he liked or found fittest from among them. But they shrink in a twitter from such plain dealing. Instead they have fallen to haunting our place day after day, at the expense of my sleek cattle. Oxen and sheep and goats must be sacrificed to feast their greed. They gulp our wine – stuff with the glint of sunlight in it – like ordinary drink. Everything is being spent.

'Odysseus, now, was a man who could defend his house against the spoiler: but there is nothing of his build about us. So long as we live we shall remain feebly untrained bodies, incapable of such defence. Not for want of willing: it is strength I lack, to meet this intolerable provocation; the grim, slow sack of my innocent house. Will not a fellow-feeling for people who are living beside you, neighbours, make you share their vexation and ashamedly pity their plight? Pray you, Sirs, begin to fear the anger of the Gods a little, lest they be aghast at the evil already wrought and turn to requite it. I beseech you by Olympian Zeus, and by Themis, in whose justice courts like this are gathered together and, after session, released. No. Rather, my friends, let me be. Leave me to wear myself out with the misery of my own grief. Perhaps Odysseus, the father who was so good to me, in reality hated his panoplied Greeks and did them deliberate injuries; which you now in turn deliberately repay by cheering on my afflictors. Better hap for me, by far, if yours were the appetites emptying my store-houses and byres. For then how soon there would be a counter-stroke! We should go through the city with our tale, clinging as suppliants to all we met, demanding our monies, till everything had been given back. But as it is, you heap up in my heart these irremediable pains.'

So he spoke through his gathering rage: and here, in a gust of tears, he flung the gavel to the ground. The audience were seized with pity and sat still and silent, all of them, lacking face to return angry words to these words of Telemachus. Finally Antinous gave tongue as follows: –

'Your lost temper and haughty lips, Telemachus, conspire to smirch our conduct and link us with disgrace. Yet I tell you it is not the suitors who are guilty, among the Achaeans, but your respected mother, that far-fetched artful mistress. For these three years – nay, longer: in the fourth year now – she has rapt away the wits of the Achaean men. She has led every one of us to hope, given each his privy assurance, let fall little messages: while her heart all this while has been harbouring quite other designs. One trick her subtlety devised was to instal in her apartments a huge loom, and set up on this a fine wide weave; and ever she would say to us, "Sweet hearts, go slow. Allay your burning intent to have me married. The death of royal Odysseus lays on me the duty of completing this linen shroud, to save its gossamer threads from being scattered to the winds. It is for the burial of Laertes, the aged hero: and it must be ready against the inevitable day when fate will pull him to the ground and death measure out his length. If I leave it undone, and in consequence the corpse of this old, once-wealthy man lie bare of cerement, I shall be the pointing-block of every Achaean woman within our neighbourhood."

'So she protested, and our manly hearts credited her tale. Daily she laboured at the vast loom, weaving: but each night she had torches brought in and unravelled the day's woof. Thus for the space of three years she deceived us and cheated the Achaeans: but when the fourth year was wearing through its sequence of seasons one of her maids, who knew the whole truth, told on her. Then we caught her in the act of unpicking the glorious web: and forced her against her inclination to finish it right off. Hear, therefore, Telemachus, the suitors' reply to you: hear and understand it to the bottom of your heart, and all the people of this country with you. Send away your mother. Order her to be wedded straightway, as her father will command, to the man who best pleases her.

'But if, instead, she insists on continuing to wreak havoc among the bachelors of Achaea, then let her do so – at the price. Athene has bestowed on her an armoury of graces (skill in all the housewifely crafts, and such arts and airs as her guileful wit adeptly turns to personal advantage) beyond parallel among the famous beauties of old time: not Alcmene, nor Tyro, nor diademed Mycene could match this Penelope in intriguing charm. Yet, for the time, you shall see that her intrigues are not opportune. The suitors will swallow up your goods and sustenance for just so long as she persists in this frowardness which heaven has let possess her mind. She gains her notoriety: you regret your substance, vainly lost. We shall not go about our business nor go home till she has made her choice and been married to some one of us Achaeans.'

With measured words Telemachus answered him. 'Antinous, in no way can I forcibly expel from our house the mother who bore me and gave me nourishment. Besides, there is my father somewhere in the earth – if he lives – or perhaps he is dead. At any rate, consider the terrible expense if mine were the hand which put her away: I should have to pay back her dowry to Icarius. And to what end? I should be evilly entreated by her father. More evil would fall on me from above, for as she was driven from our door my mother would imprecate against me the dread furies. Also my fellow-men would condemn me out of their mouths. So I shall never stoop to give her such order.

'But listen – you and the other suitors. Do our family affairs jar your sense of niceness? Then get out of my guest-quarters. Arrange to entertain each other from your own resources, turn and turn about among your houses. Yet, if you find it pleasanter and better to go on scathelessly destroying the entire livelihood of a lone man – then go on. Meanwhile I shall be praying to the everlasting Gods, if perchance Zeus may grant that due penalties be paid. For then will our house, unscathed, see all of you destroyed within its walls.'

So did Telemachus invoke Zeus: and the All-seeing, in answer to his prayer, sent forth two eagles from his mountain top. Swift as the storm-blast they flew, wing-tip to wing in lordly sweep of pinions, until they were over the midmost of the many-tongued assembly. There they wheeled in full flight, with quivering, outstretched, strong wings, and glazed down with fatal eyes upon the upturned faces. Next they ripped with tearing claws, each at the other's head and neck, swooping quickly to the right over the houses of the citizens. So long as eye could follow them everyone stood wondering at the birds and musing what future history this sign from heaven could mean.

While they mused came the voice of Halitherses, son of Mastor, an elder of great standing who surpassed all his generation in science of bird-reading and the foretelling of dooms. Out of this deep of knowledge he now held forth: 'Hear me, islanders of Ithaca: hear me out. Especially the suitors, for what I portend concerns them most. Great evils are rolling down upon them. Odysseus will not longer remain sundered from his people. Even now, it may be, he approaches, carrying within him the seeds of bloody doom for every suitor. He will be deadly, too, for many others of us substantial men in this island of the pellucid skies. Wherefore before the event let us devise a plan by which the offence of the suitors shall be removed – unless they forthwith remove their own offence, which, did they study their interests, would be their wiser choice.

'I speak of what I know surely. This is not my first essay in divination. Everything has come to pass of what I prophesied to Odysseus, when that resourceful leader was sailing for Ilios with the Argive host. I foretold that after enduring many disasters and the loss by death of his whole fellowship, he would at the last find himself again made free of a home, where no one knew his face, in the twentieth year from his setting out: and today all this mounts to its fulfilment.'

Him, in turn, Eurymachus son of Polybus denied. 'Come, come, dotard. You will do better to stay at home and prophesy to your children, saving them from this wrath to come. In practical affairs I am the master-prophet. Multitudes of birds flit hither and thither in our bright sunshine: but not all bear messages from heaven. Odysseus, of whom you prate, died long ago and far enough away. If only you had gone and died with him! Then we should have escaped these oracles of yours, and you would not have had this chance of perhaps making future capital for your family by egging on the vexed Telemachus to publish his griefs.

'Yet, I fear, your family will never receive from him the reward you envisage. I am about to speak hardly: but what I say shall surely be. When an elder of long and wide worldly experience prostitutes his stored wisdom to abet a young man's anger; then, in first instance, the consequences are very grievous for the young man, who finds himself impotent to bend his hearers to his will. And secondly, for you too, Ancient, the regrets will be bitter. Upon you we shall lay such fine as will make your heart ache to pay it.

'Now, before you all, I have advice for Telemachus. He must order this mother of his back to her parents, for them to decide her re-marriage and assess the sumptuous interchange of gifts which go with a dear daughter. I assure you that till then the cadets of the Achaeans will not desist from their irksome and exigent wooing. Why should they? We fear no one on earth: certainly not Telemachus with his bluster. Nor are we to be moved by the soothsayings which you, old man, mouth over at us, without end – save to make yourself ever more generally detested. Telemachus' goods shall be ruthlessly devoured, and no fair deal come his way while Penelope thwarts the people in this matter of her re-marriage and keeps us dancing attendance on her, day in, day out; our passions too excited by the chance of winning so admirable a bride to cultivate any of the ordinary women who would make us fitting mates.'

'Eurymachus,' said Telemachus in deliberate reply, 'I will not re-open entreaties or discussion upon this subject, with you or any other arrogant suitor. We have deferred our case, in fullest detail, to the Gods: and made it known to all the Achaeans. Instead, I now ask you for a clean-built ship and twenty rowers to man her. In this I purpose to go round Sparta and sandy Pylos, enquiring after my long-lost father. Perhaps news of his return is to be gleaned from men: or a whisper may come to me from Zeus, whose breath oftenest conveys forewarnings of truth to us mortals.

'If I learn that my father is alive and on his homeward way I can endure this wilful spoiling of my house for yet a space: but if it be confirmed that he is dead and gone, then I will turn back to this loved land of mine and heap up for him a barrow to hold the rich tomb-furniture which is seemly for so grand a name. Afterward I will give my mother to a man.'

He ended and sat down: and there rose from the throng Mentor, the comrade to whom stout Odysseus, on sailing for Ilios, had committed his house; enjoining all in it to be obedient to the old man and in his steadfast guard. Wherefore out of his good heart Mentor protested as follows: 'Give heed, now, men of Ithaca to what I say to you. Here is a warning to all sceptered kings, that they wholly abjure clemency and gentleness, and take no thought for just dealing. Instead let them be harsh always, and unseemly in conduct: for glorious Odysseus, your king and the king of all this people, was like our father in his mildness – and lo! not one of you remembers him. Yet I advance no plaint against these haughty suitors, whose ill-nature has led them into deeds of such violence. Indeed this violence I find not excessive, weighed against their risk. They have staked their heads upon a persuasion that he comes home no more. My complaint is rather against the rest of the people, because you have sat by mutely, without word of denunciation or restraint: though you are very many, and the suitors are but few.'

Leocritus, the son of Euenor, opposed him. 'Mentor, you crazy mischief-maker, why waste breath in pleading that the people stop our nuisance? To make war over a matter of feasting would be outrageous, superior numbers or no superior numbers. Even suppose that your Odysseus of Ithaca did arrive in person, all hot to drive from his palace the noble suitors who have made it their banqueting hall. His wife may yearn for his coming: but in that way she would have small joy of it. In his very palace he would encounter horrid fate if he alone attacked so many of us. You babble vainly. Enough of this. Let all the people return to their employments, leaving only Mentor and Halitherses (because they have long been hangers-on of his family) to deal with this youth's journeying. Yet I fancy he will stay long enough in Ithaca, news-gathering still from his chair: and the project of a voyage come to nought.'

He finished, and the assembly was speedily dissolved, the crowd streaming homeward: while the suitors repaired to the palace of magnificent Odysseus. But Telemachus walked by himself far along the margin of the sea, and there laved his hands in the transparent sea-water before praying to Athene. 'Divine One, hear me! Yesterday you came to my house and told me to venture by ship across the shadow-haunted main, seeking news of my absent father. Now see how the Achaeans, and especially these lustful, bullying suitors, thwart my every turn.'

While he prayed Athene drew nigh. She had put on the appearance of Mentor's body, to the life: and it was with Mentor's voice that she exhorted him stirringly, thus: – 'Telemachus, let not your courage and resource fail you now. In your father deed and word notably marched together to their deliberate end. If your body holds a trace of his temper it will suffice to make this effort of yours neither bootless nor aimless. But if, on the contrary, you are not true issue of Odysseus and Penelope then I may abandon hope of your achieving any purpose. Few are the sons who attain their fathers' stature: and very few surpass them. Most fall short in merit. But surely this time you will not, you cannot, prove fainthearted or base: nor can you have failed to inherit some of Odysseus' cunning. Therefore I have good hope that you will attain your goal. Pay no heed to the advice or intentions of these infatuate suitors. With them instinct and decency are alike at fault; nor do they apprehend the death and black fate hovering over them, to overwhelm them all in a day.

'As for this journey of your heart, it shall not be too long denied you. Because I was a friend of your father's, therefore I am myself obtaining you the fast ship: and I shall be of your company aboard her. For the moment do you go back to your house, and mingle cheerfully with the suitors: while you get ready the victuals. Pack everything securely. Let the wine be in wine-jars and the barley meal (the marrow of men's strength) in tough skins. I will very quickly gather from the town our crew of willing fellows. Sea-girdled Ithaca is rich in ships, new and old. I go to survey them and choose the fittest; which we will presently equip and launch into the open sea.'

So said Athene, the daughter of Zeus. Telemachus, hearing the divine accent, made no delay but returned straight home with his heart-ache, to find the suitor-lords in guest-hall or fore court, where they were stripping the skins off his slaughtered goats and singeing his fat pigs for the cooking fire.

Antinous, with a laugh and loudly calling his name, swaggered up to him and took his hand. 'Telemachus,' said he, 'you have just now given your enmity too free tongue against us. Instead, will you not henceforward banish from your mind these thoughts of doing us hurt and forget your injurious words and eat and drink with us as of yore? Meanwhile the Achaeans will be making quite ready for you all you want in the way of ship and crew, to take you most quickly to hallowed Pylos for news of your august father.'

Well-advised was the reply of Telemachus, as he gently drew his hand from the grasp of Antinous. 'It is not possible for me to dine softly in your too-proud company: to be at ease and merry-make. O suitors, was it not grief enough that in my callow childhood you shore from me so much of my precious goods? Today I am a grown man and hear from others all this tale; and verily my swelling heart prompts me to visit upon you every evil I can contrive, whether from Pylos or in this place. Therefore will I most surely go on my journey: nor shall it be a barren quest, though by your crafty precaution I travel but as a passenger, without ship or rowers of my own.'

The suitors went on feasting their hardest, where they were, till he had spoken. Then they hooted and jeered at him. One graceless cockerell held forth after this strain: 'Really, Telemachus does mean to kill us all. He now hates us so terribly that he may bring back avengers with him from the sands of Pylos or from far-away Sparta. Or perhaps he plans to visit the luxuriant fields of Ephyra, and procure some life-destroying drug to mix into our wine-bowl and cut us all off together!'

And another youth of the same sort cried out, 'I tell you what, if he goes off in the inside of a ship, perhaps he will wander away from his friends, like Odysseus, and get lost. Then what extra work we poor creatures will have, dividing up all his belongings among ourselves. I vote we give the house-property to his mother, for the man who makes her his wife.'

Thus they japed: but Telemachus went from them to his father's store-chamber. Under its high, wide dome lay heaped up the gold and the copper: also great chests of clothing, and an abundance of pleasant-smelling olive oil. Secured against the wall in ranks, stood jar upon jar of old delicious wine, every jar filled with pure liquor, fit for the Gods but awaiting the day of Odysseus' home-coming – if he was ever to come home, through his toils and pains. This treasure-room had swinging double doors, strong and tight, always shut: and between them, day and night alike, there lodged the woman-guardian, old Eurycleia, the daughter of Ops, Peisenor's son. She in her sagacity stood watch over all its wealth.

Telemachus called her into the chamber and said to her, 'Good mother, pray draw off for me in jars some sweet wine: your second best, that which comes next after the very special vintage you are reserving for him, the unfortunate one, godlike Odysseus, in case he somehow tricks death and fate and wins his way back. Fill me twelve jars, sealing each with its stopper. Then run barley meal into stout-sewn leather sacks. Twenty measures let there be, of your well-kerned barley groats. See that no one spies what you do: but heap up all the things together in one place, whence I can fetch them this evening after my mother has gone up to her room in preparation for bed. I am going to Sparta and sandy Pylos, hoping to learn something of my father's return.'

Eurycleia, the foster-mother who loved him, wailed aloud at the tidings and implored him tearfully: 'Alas, my dearest child, why has such a notion come into your head? How should you hope to make your way over the vast earth, you a shielded only son, when your father Odysseus, the descendant of gods, himself perished there very far away, wandering in some place unknown? Further, so soon as your back is turned these men in your guest-hall will think out some evil to overtake you: and thus you will die in a trap, leaving them to share out your goods between them. Instead, do you sit here in your proper place. It is no duty of yours to stray over the desolate sea in search of misfortune.'

Wise Telemachus answered her: 'Be brave, good nurse. This plan did not come to me without the prompting of Heaven. But swear not to breathe a word of it to my dear mother till eleven or twelve days are passed, or till she misses me and learns that I have gone away. I want to spare her beautiful face from being furrowed with tears.' Thus he spoke, and the old woman swore a great oath by the Gods. He heard her swear and seal the oath: and after it at once she turned to drawing off his wine in jars and filling the stout leathern wallets with barley meal, while Telemachus returned to the living rooms and entertained the suitors.

All this time the clear-eyed Goddess was taking thought for the next stages of her plan. In the guise of Telemachus she traversed the entire city and standing by each of her men said her say, exhorting them to muster at nightfall by the swift ship: the ship itself she asked of Noemon, famed son of Phronius, who granted it heartily.

The sun went down into the sea, and the streets grew obscured. Then Athene had the fast ship run down into the water and stowed aboard her all the gear proper to a well-found galley. She had her brought round to the very mouth of the harbour where the picked crew had rallied, every man of them inspired by the grey-eyed Goddess with her own zest.

Athene, steadily pursuing her course, next visited the great house of Odysseus and there poured out upon the suitors a fond sleep and dazed them as they drank, till the cups slipped from their drowsy hands. Incontinently the banquet broke up, as each man struggled homewards to his bed in the city, with a weight of slumber bearing down his eyelids. Then the Goddess called Telemachus to speak with her outside the comfortable halls. She was again Mentor in speech and body. 'Telemachus,' she said, 'your companions, all armed and ready, sit now on the thwarts abiding only your advent. Let us go, and not hold them longer from the journey.'

With the word Pallas Athene went swiftly in the lead. He followed in her track. When they came out on the beach to the ship, there they found the long-haired company waiting at the water's edge. To them Telemachus, their appointed leader, made his first speech: 'Friends, come with me and lend a hand with the rations. I have everything put together, ready, in the house: and my mother knows nothing of our business, nor do any of the house-maids. I have told just one woman out of them all.'

He spoke and led back: and they went with him. They laded everything on their shoulders to the ship and put it away below, as the beloved son of Odysseus directed. Afterwards Telemachus went on board (Athene having preceded him) and sat down in the stern-sheets, quite near where she had seated herself. The crew loosed the after-warps, clambered aboard, and took their seats on the oar-benches.

Then did Athene, the clear-eyed, summon up for them a favouring breeze, a brisk following West Wind which thrummed across the wine-dark sea. Telemachus roused his followers and bade them get sail on the vessel. They obeyed him: the fir mast was raised aloft and heeled through its pierced cross-beams: the stays were rigged and the white sails hauled up by their halyards of pliant cowhide.

The wind caught the sail, bellying it out, and the blue-shadowed waves resounded under the fore-foot of the running ship as she lay over on her course and raced out to sea.

They made fast all the running tackle of the swift dark hull and got out the drinking bowls. These they filled with wine, brim-full, and poured out as offerings to the Immortal Gods that are for ever and ever: honouring especially the clear-eyed Daughter of Zeus: while the ship cleft through the long night towards the dawn.

BOOK 3

Forth from the lovely waters sprang the sun into its firma-
ment of brass, thence to shine upon the Immortals, as also
upon mortal men walking amid the corn-fields of earth;
while the ship drew into Pylos, the stately citadel of Neleus.
There upon the fore-shore were gathered the inhabitants,
doing sacrifice to the Earth-shaker, Poseidon, the dark-
tressed God. Nine congregations they made, each five
hundred strong: and every congregation had offered nine
victims, jet-black bulls free from any fleck of colour, to the
God: in whose honour the leg-bones were now burning
with fire while the assembly ate of the entrails and organs.

Straight towards this beach the tight ship was steered.
The crew brailed up and furled: then moored her. Afterwards
they all issued forth (including Telemachus) in the train of
grey-eyed Athene. She turned to him and said, 'Telemachus,
here is no room for false modesty: no room at all. Have
you not come oversea in quest of your father, expressly to
learn where the earth is hiding him or what doom he has
drawn upon himself? So you must go up straight, now, to
this horseproud Nestor, and make him yield to you the
inmost secrets of his heart. Implore him, yourself, to speak

perfect truth: and then he will not deceive us: for his mind is compact with wisdom.'

The cautious Telemachus protested thus: 'Mentor, how dare I approach him, how cling to him in supplication, when I am all unversed in speeches of subtle appeal? It is only right for a young man to be diffident when he importunes an elder.' The Goddess rejoined, 'Your heart will prompt you in part: and other things the spirit will teach you to say. I think if ever anyone was conceived and grew to manhood with the fostering care of the gods, it was yourself.'

Pallas led on swiftly while she spoke. Telemachus followed her divine steps, till they encountered the throng of the men of Pylos. There sat Nestor amongst his sons, with his followers busied about him, arranging the feast or roasting joints of beef or skewering choice morsels on the spits. Yet no sooner did they spy strangers than one and all crowded forward with welcoming hands, to have them take place in the gathering. Peisistratus, Nestor's son, reached them first. He took a hand of Athene and a hand of Telemachus and led them to fleecy sheepskins spread over the sand of the beach beside the platters, where sat Thrasymedes, his own brother, and Nestor their father. He gave them portions of the beasts' inwards: and pouring wine into a gold tankard he raised it to Pallas Athene, daughter of aegis-bearing Zeus, with these words:

'Offer a prayer, O guest, to our lord Poseidon, upon whose feast you have chanced in visiting us now. And after you have made your drink-offering and prayed the due prayer, then pass the honeyed wine to this your friend, that he may offer: for I deem that he, like you, will wish to supplicate the eternal Gods, for lack of whom the hearts of all the world would go desolate. If I give the embossed cup to you, before him, it is only because he is younger, a man of my own generation.'

Thereupon he put the sweet wine into her hand: Athene was gladdened by the right instinct of the man, who had preferred her in serving the storied golden cup; and presently she uttered to kingly Poseidon all her desire in prayer.

'Hear us, World-girdler, nor refuse, as greedy, our prayers for the gaining of our end. Entail upon Nestor, greatest of his line, as for the sons which follow after him, glory. Give to all in Pylos a bountiful return for these hundred victims they have so largely sacrificed. Grant further that when Telemachus and I go back, it may be with a happy issue to the purposes for which we have sailed here in our swift, black ship.' So she prayed, and all the while was bringing her own prayer to pass. Then she gave the rich loving-cup to the dear son of Odysseus and he repeated her prayer.

By now the others had roasted the flesh-meat of the victims and drawn the gobbets off their spits. Portions were shared out to all: and they ate their fill of the noble spread. But when at last the appetites for food and drink had been relieved, to them Nestor, Gerenia's knight, began to speak: –

'When strangers are fully satisfied with food, as now, it is fair to make enquiry of them and find out who they are. Tell us therefore of yourselves, O guests! Where did your journey over the sea-ways begin? Is yours a business venture, or do you cruise at random like those pirates who quarter the salt waves and risk their souls to profit by what others lose?'

Telemachus was inspired to answer him bravely, being heartened thereto by Athene herself, who wished that he might acquire men's respect through diligence in seeking news of his absent father. 'O Nestor, Neleus' son, chief glory of the Achaeans! You ask whence we come. I will make all plain. We are from Ithaca, that lies below Neion: and our motive, which I now set forth, is personal, not public. I cast about for trace of my father, a man of universal fame, the patient and mighty Odysseus. Rumour has it that in the sack of the Trojan capital he fought by your side. We can tally all the others who served at Troy; or mark just where each one died his grievous death: but Zeus has left the fate of this last man a mystery. No one can say for sure where he was lost – on the mainland, borne down by men who hated him, or in the deep, beneath the waves of Amphitrite.

'Because of this I am suppliant at your knees, O Nestor: begging that you relate his pitiful death, as you saw it with your own eyes, or learned it from the lips of such another waif. His death, I say, for even from his mother's womb calamity had marked him for her own. Do not in pity convey to me smooth things, things gentler than the truth: blurt out, rather, all that met your sight. I beseech you if (when you Achaeans were sore pressed by the men of Troy) my father, noble Odysseus, ever pledged himself to you and fulfilled his bond – that so you now have regard for me and give me the naked fact.'

Then answered him Nestor, knight of Gerenia. 'Dear lad, since you recall to my mind those dreary memories, hear the tale of what we endured in that fatal land – we fierce, ill-disciplined Achaeans; and of what we endured while we strayed after booty over the misty face of the ocean wheresoever Achilles led: as also of our struggles about the great walled city of King Priam. There our bravest died. Aias, the lord of battles, lies there: Achilles himself:

and Patroclus, whose wisdom at the council board was godlike. And there too died my lovely son, the strong, clean Antilochus, who was surpassingly swift-footed and a fighter. Ever so many evils we suffered beyond this count. Mortal frailty could not support the whole story, not though you tarried here for five years or six enquiring into all that the Achaean chivalry there lost. Before the end you would have faded back to your native land.

'Nine years we pegged away industriously, entangling the enemy in every kind of evil trick: and, in the event, hardly did Zeus see it through. With one particular man of us, all that time, no one dared compare himself, aloud, as a master of craftiness: for manifestly in stratagems of any sort the palm was borne off by Odysseus, your regal father – if really you are his son. A strange wonder takes me as I gaze on you: though you have his tricks of speech. One would have sworn that never any lad could speak so like him. See now, all the while great Odysseus and I were together, we never, in council-chamber or in open assembly, spoke to two briefs. It was as if we had a single heart from which we expounded to the Argives, with forethought and ripe council, how they should arrange it for the best.

'Even so we destroyed the tall city of Priam. It was afterwards, when the god had dispersed the Achaeans and we had all gone down to our ships, that Zeus contrived in his heart a sorry return for the Argives, because they had not, all of them, been either upright or circumspect. As for the grisly doom which swallowed so many of them up, it arose from the fatal anger of the grey-eyed Daughter of the Great One, who set dissension between the two sons of Atreus. Wherefore these two chiefs summoned all the host together, indecorously and not by rule, near sundown: and they came staggering with wine, did the strong sons of the

Achaeans, to hear why the brothers so intemperately sounded the assembly.

'Then Menelaus urged that the Achaeans should be mindful only of an immediate return over the swelling horizon of the sea: but in this advice he did not at all please his brother Agamemnon, whose plan was to hold back the host while he offered hundreds of victims in sacrifice to allay that deadly wrath of Athene. The fool: who did not see that she was not thus to be persuaded. The face of the everlasting Gods is not suddenly changed. So did the brothers confront each other in full view, bitterly wrangling: till the Achaeans impatiently sprang up with thrilling tumultuous cry and clang of armour. The opposed councils each found advocates amongst them. Sleep, when it came to us that night, came tossed and broken by hard thoughts of one another; while Zeus aloft brooded over us, quickening the seeds of our iniquity.

'In the morning the faction whereof I was one drew down our ships to the good salt sea. We loaded them with our treasures and our captives, the outlandish, loin-girt Trojan women: while the other faction held back, keeping with Agamemnon, shepherd of the host. We, the journeying half, then set sail and went. Very swiftly did we sail, for the sea in all its hugeness was divinely spread smooth for our keels till we came to Tenedos, where we made sacrifice to the gods as beseemed men homeward bound.

'Yet did Zeus still deny us an unchequered return: indeed he was cruel and for the second time let loose evil dissensions among us. From Tenedos, therefore, some of us turned prow to poop, and rocked off again, back whence they had come. Of these were the party of Odysseus, the myriad-minded, the resourceful, whose judgement veered to favour once more Atrides-Agamemnon.

'For my part I fled away, with a fleet of vessels following me: in my heart I felt that the God was brewing mischief. Diomedes, the fighting son of Tydeus, fled too, and his example carried all his fellowship with him. After we two had gone there pursued after us the high-coloured Menelaus, who found us in Lesbos taking further counsel upon our long voyage: – whether it were best to go wide of cliff-bound Chios, by way of the island of Psyria which we should keep upon our left: or to pass this side of Chios, by stormy Mimas. We asked the god to give us a lead. He answered that to cut across the central sea to Euboea would be our quickest escape from disaster. Then there sprang up and blew a loud following wind, before which the ships scudded fast across the fish-filled ways till they made their landfall on Geraestus in the dead of night. We went ashore and slew many bulls there and burnt their marrow-bones in sacrifice to Poseidon, by token that so great a stretch of open sea was favourably passed. It was no more than four days later that the following of Diomedes, daunter of horses, beached their trim ships in Argos.

'I held on for Pylos, helped thereto by the friendly wind which never once let up on us from the first day when the god caused it to blow. Thus easily, dear lad, did I return home by myself, without learning the fate of the other Achaeans or knowing who was saved and who was lost. What news I have gathered since, sitting quietly in my great hall, that shall you now learn from me without exception, as is your due.

'The Myrmidons, they say, those spearmen, got back in good order under the renowned son of great-hearted Achilles. It was well, also, with Philoctetes, gallant son of Poias: and Idomeneus brought back all his company to Crete: – all, that is, who escaped the war. The sea wrested none from him. Of the fate of Agamemnon, son of Atreus, word must have come, even to those remote fastnesses which are your home, relating the calamity of his return to the woeful fate Aegisthus had schemed for him. Yet Aegisthus paid a reckoning even more terrible. How good it was that a son of the victim survived, and that he should avenge his great father's cruel death upon Aegisthus, the sly murderer! Fortify yourself, my tall and comely friend, upon his example: that your praises may be sung by posterity.'

Telemachus answered him gravely, 'Nestor, son of Neleus, chief glory of the Achaeans: I grant you that young Orestes took the last drop of his revenge; and therefore shall the Achaeans indeed trumpet his fame, for ever and ever. Would that the Gods had endowed me with strength like his, to visit upon the lawless suitors these iniquitous presumptions with which they artfully insult my feebleness. But when the Gods spun the web of fate for me and for my father they made no such blissful provision of power for us. Our part is only to endure.'

Then said Nestor of Gerenia, master of the horse: 'Friend, now you open this matter and make mention of it to me, let me admit that I have heard how your palace is beset by a mob of those who would marry your mother: and that they plot to your disadvantage, in your despite. Tell me, do you willingly yield to them? Or is it that some divine will has made the people of your part to turn against you? Who knows, perhaps one day HE will arrive and reward their violence with violence upon themselves: as he can do equally, whether he come alone or with the might of Achaea at his back. Furthermore, should the grey-eyed Athene single you out to cherish, with the loving care she bore famous Odysseus in the Troad where we Achaeans suffered – never saw I such open affection on the part of the Gods as was there displayed by Pallas, who would stand openly by his side – if Pallas will so love you and vex her heart for you, then may one or two of them be distracted clean out of the idea of marriage!' Telemachus replied sadly, 'Reverend Sir, I do not think this word of yours can live. Your saying is too great. So much too great that I grow afraid. Not all my hoping, not the good-will of the Gods, could bring it about.'

Here Goddess Athene broke in. 'Telemachus, it is unseemly to let such words escape past the barriers of your lips. When a God wishes, it is idly easy for him to preserve a man, even in the ends of the earth. For my part I should choose to be vexed with every sort of pain on my way home, so that I reached there at last and enjoyed my return: rather than get back just to meet death at my fireside, as Agamemnon died through the treachery of his wife and Aegisthus. Yet I grant you that not the immortal gods themselves can for ever shield the man they love from the common meed of death, or continually avert that fatal decree which lays every man prone in the grave at the end.'

Telemachus answered after his wont, 'Mentor, we will speak no more of it. Why harrow ourselves imagining returns for him, when already the Deathless Ones have given him death and the dark which follows it? But see, I wish to change the topic; and ask another word of Nestor, as from one whose rulings and conclusions have final authority. They tell me he has been King for thrice the span of ordinary generations. By this virtue he seems to my gaze almost an immortal himself. So Nestor, son of Neleus, give me more true history – how died that great king, Agamemnon, son of Atreus? By what subtleties of device did Aegisthus snare into death a man so much better than himself? Where was Menelaus in the business, that Aegisthus dared to kill? Absent perhaps, wandering abroad in the world far from Achaean Argos?'

Nestor of Gerenia, the exceeding rich in horses, answered, 'My child, I can tell you the whole truth of it. You have rightly guessed how it would have been had tawny Menelaus, Agamemnon's brother, come back from Troy to find Aegisthus alive in his brother's place. There would have been no corpse to need the kindly rites of burial. Dogs and carrion crows would have torn the carcase to tatters in the open fields beyond the city walls: nor would any of our women have keened over him, so abhorrent was the man's crime.

'We were away, you see, fighting our great fights at this siege, while he, comfortable in the heart of Argos and its green horse-pastures, was ever speaking in the ear of Agamemnon's wife, trying to steal her love. For long she would not abide the foul thing, Clytemnestra the divinely fair, the noble-minded. Besides there was ever at her side the family minstrel, whom Atrides, before he left for Troy, had told off to protect his wife.

'Yet the doom of the Gods linked her with disaster after all. Aegisthus lured the singing man to a desert island and there abandoned him to be a spoil and booty for the birds of prey. Whereupon her lust matched her lover's, and he took her into his house. Many thigh-bones of oxen he burned to the gods on their holy altars: and many dedications of tapestries or gold he made, in thankfulness for the momentous success he had achieved beyond his heart's hope.

'Then we came sailing back together, Atrides-Menelaus and I, fast friends. But at Sunium, the sacred headland of

Athens, Phoebus Apollo shed down his gentle darts upon Menelaus' navigator and ended his life. He dropped dead, with the steering oar of the moving ship yet within his hands. This Phrontis, son of Onetor, excelled all the men of his trade in skilfully holding a ship to her course when squalls bore down thick and heavy. So Menelaus was delayed there, in spite of his anxiety to be moving, till he had given due and rich burial to his henchman. Then at last he got away across the wine-dark ocean, at the best pace of his hollow ships, as far as the steep slope of Maleia. There however, Zeus the far-seeing swept him grievously astray by loosing upon the fleet a blast of piercing winds and monster waves which grew mountainous.

'The squadron was torn asunder. Some ships the God thrust almost to that part of Crete where the Kydonians live beside the streams of Iardanus. When the wind sets from the south-west, a long swell drives in there against the smooth wall of cliff which sheerly fronts the mist-veiled sea, from the furthest end of Gortyn westward to the promontory by Phaestos: where a low reef stems the whole sweep of the tide. Upon this came the half of the fleet. The ships were shattered by force of the waves against the crags: and the men in them narrowly avoided death.

'As for the rest of the dark-prowed fleet, the other five vessels, – they were borne by wind and water to the coasts of Egypt; in which strange region, with its foreign people, Menelaus lingered, amassing great store of gold and goods, all the while that Aegisthus at home was carrying out his dastard scheme. Therefore it chanced that he had seven years of rule in golden Mycenae after killing Atrides: and all the people served him. But in the eighth year there returned from Athens the goodly Orestes to be his undoing. For Orestes killed the traitor Aegisthus, his father's murderer: a son slaying the sire's slayer. After perfecting his vengeance Orestes gave a funeral feast to the Argives over the bodies of the mother he hated and despicable Aegisthus: and that self-same day there sailed in Menelaus of the loud battle cry, laden down with all the wealth that his ships could carry.

'Learn from this, my friend, not to wander from your home for too long, abandoning your property, when there are men rampaging in the house likely to share out and consume all you have: for so you would find your journey to have defeated itself. Yet I exhort, nay I order, you to visit Menelaus who has so newly come home from abroad, from parts so foreign that the stoutest-hearted would despair of ever returning thence when once driven distractedly by storms across that fearful, boundless sea: a sea so vast and dread that not even in a twelvemonth could a bird hope to wing its way out of it.

'Wherefore I would have you visit him, sailing in your own ship with your crew: but if you prefer the road, a chariot and team are at your disposal, with my own sons to guide you to tawny Menelaus, in Lacedaemon the fair. Make your appeal to him with your own lips, for then he will heed and answer truthfully out of his stored wisdom, not thinking to play you false.'

There Nestor ceased: but now the sun was going down and the shadows deepening. So to the company spoke the goddess, grey-eyed Athene. 'Ancient, right well have you told us your tale: but it is time to cut the tongues and mix the wine, that we may complete our offerings to Poseidon and the other immortals: and then must we think of our couches: for it is bedtime. The sun has sunken into the shadow of the world and we should be going, lest we sit unmannerly long at the table of the Gods.'

Her audience approved her. The henchmen poured water on their hands and the serving-boys filled the drinking bowls to the brims with compounded drinks. Then they served round to each a fresh cup. The ox-tongues were cast into the fire, and rising to his feet each man poured his libation in turn. After they had so offered and had drunk of what was left all their hearts' desire, then Athene and godlike Telemachus would have been going back together to their hollow ship: but Nestor stayed them with words of protest: –

'May Zeus and the whole company of the immortals deliver me from your passing by my house, to slight it and sleep in your ship, as if I were a naked, needy man who had at home neither cloaks nor coverlets for the soft sleeping of himself and his guests! Praise be, I have great store of bedding. Never, I swear, while I live shall the beloved son of my comrade Odysseus lie out on the bare boards of his vessel – nor while there are children of mine left in the palace to entertain whatever guests may come under its roof.'

Athene replied, 'Well said, old friend: and Telemachus will do your bidding, as is most fit. Let him even now go with you to sleep in your palace. But my duty is to order and hearten the crew of our black ship by returning to them with our news. You see I am the one man of years in the party. All the rest are young men, fellows in age of stout Telemachus, and they have come with us on this trip for love's sake. Therefore with them I sleep this night through, beside the black shell of the ship: and in the morning I shall push on to the estimable Cauconians, who for no small while have owed me no small sum. Meanwhile let it be your care to send Telemachus, your guest, forward with one of your sons in one of your fast chariots: choosing for him from out your stud two of the lightest footed and deepest chested horses.'

The goddess ended her say, and took flight from them, in the way of a sea-eagle. Astonishment fell on all present and the venerable man was awed at what his eyes saw. He seized Telemachus by the hand, crying his name and saying: 'Friend Telemachus, what fear could one have of your growing up weak or base, when from your youth gods walk with you as guides? Of the great dwellers on Olympus this can be no other than the Daughter of Zeus himself: the Tritonian, the All-glorious: who also was wont to single out your great father for honour, from among the Argives.

> 'O QUEEN, I pray you, be gracious unto us, and bestow upon me a goodly repute amongst men; for me, and my sons, and for the wife I love and honour. And I vow to you a yearling heifer, broad-browed, uncovered, and never yet subjected to the yoke of man. This beast will I sacrifice to you, after I have caused her horns to be covered with pure gold.'

Such was the prayer that he uttered, and Pallas Athene heard him.

Then did Nestor, Gerenia's knight, lead into the fair hall his sons and his sons-in-law; who there in the palace of that most famous sire sat them down, orderly, each on his seat or throne: while the old lord mixed for his visitors a cup of wine which had mellowed eleven years in its jar before the good-wife broke the sealed wrappings and poured it forth. With such drink did the old man have his cup blended: and he poured the first of it to Athene, praying fervently the while to her, the daughter of aegis-bearing Zeus.

The others again made their drink-offering, and drank till their hearts were satisfied. Then the company dispersed, each to his own quarters in search of sleep: but for Telemachus, godlike Odysseus' son, Nestor the Gerenian horselover had coverlets spread on an inlaid bedstead in the coved entry of the house, under its reverberant roof. For company there was Peisistratus with his good ashen spear: Peisistratus, though a tall man who led his rank in the battle, was yet unmarried, and so, alone of the sons, kept his father's house. The old lord slept apart in the depths of the great building, where his lady wife had made ready their couch and its coverings.

Day-break: and the rosy-tinted fingers of dawn crept up the sky. Nestor, knight of Gerenia, left his bed and came forth to sit before the lofty gateway of his house on the smooth platform there built. Its white stones, all smoothly polished, had been the old-time seat of Neleus, that divinely-unerring counsellor, long since subdued by Death, who had gone down to Hades leaving Nestor as warden of the Achaeans to sit in his place and wield his sceptre of power. About him gathered the cluster of his sons, coming from their private houses: Echephron and Stratius and Perseus and Aretus and magnificent Thrasymedes. Also the sixth son, brave Peisistratus came: and they brought goodly Telemachus too, and set him there amongst themselves as Nestor began to address them:

'Quickly, quickly, dear sons, do my bidding, that I may single out from all the gods for reverence, divine Athene, who visited me in the flesh yesterday at the God's solemn feast. Let one of you, therefore, run to the pastures for a heifer to be brought as quickly as the neat-herd can drive her here. Let another hasten to the black ship of largehearted Telemachus and bring up all his company save two. Let some one else bid Laerkes the gilder come, to lap in gold the horns of the victim. The rest of you stay in the house to see that its women busy themselves, laying the tables in our famous hall and arranging seats and a proper provision of fire-wood and sparkling water.' So Nestor ordered and they ran to obey. The heifer appeared from the fields and the crew of high-hearted Telemachus arrived from their swift and goodly ship: also the smith came, carrying in his hands the tools of his smithying by which his art was manifested – the anvil, the hammer and the shapely tongs to work his gold.

Athene, too, came to accept her sacrifice.

Then did Nestor, the ancient knight, bring out his gold: and the craftsman cunningly overlaid the heifer's horns in order that the goddess might be glad when she saw the loveliness dedicated to her. Statius and noble Echephron led the beast forward by the horns. Aretos came out from the living rooms, with a lotus-bowl of water for lustration in one hand and the basket of barleymeal in the other. Thrasymedes, strong in battle, stood ready, poising his sharp axe to cut down the heifer. Perseus held the blood-basin.

Venerable Nestor opened the rite of sacrifice by dipping his hands into the water to purify them: then he began to sprinkle the meal, praying earnestly the while to Athene and casting hairs from the forelocks of the heifer into the flame. Then, after they had joined in prayer and in scattering the heave-offering of grain, suddenly the son of Nestor, ardent Thrasymedes, stepped in and struck. His blade cut through the sinews of the neck, and the might of the heifer was undone. The women raised their wavering cry, the prince's daughters and his daughters-in-law and his honoured wife, Eurydice the eldest daughter of

Clymenus: while the men strained up the beast's head from the trodden earth, that proud Peisistratus might sever her throat.

The dark blood gushed forth, and life left its bones. Very quickly they disjointed the carcase, stripped the flesh from the thigh bones, doubled them in the customary manner with a wrapping of the fatty parts, above and below, and banked the raw meat over them. Then the elder set fire to his cleft billets of wood and burned the offering while sprinkling ruddy wine upon the flames. So the thigh bones were utterly consumed even as the young men tasted the entrailmeat, crowding about their father with the five-pronged roasting forks in their hands. Afterwards they chopped up the rest of the flesh into morsels which they impaled on their points and broiled, holding the sharp spits firmly out to the fire.

During this sacrifice beautiful Polycaste, the youngest grown daughter of Nestor son of Neleus, had given Telemachus his bath, washing him and anointing him with rich olive oil before she draped him in a seemly tunic and cloak: so that he came forth from the bath-cabinet with the body of an immortal. He rejoined Nestor, the shepherd of his people, and took place by his side. The flesh-meat was now ready. They drew it off the fork-points and sat down to dine. Men of standing waited on them, filling up with wine their golden beakers: and when they had eaten and drunken till they would no more, Nestor, Gerenia's knight, again opened his mouth and said:

'Now, my sons, it is time to harness to Telemachus' chariot the long-maned, proud-tailed horses, that he may be upon his way.' So he spoke, and heedfully they hastened to do his bidding. Very soon the swift horses were ready beneath the chariot's yoke. The house-keeper packed in bread and wine which she brought from her stores, together with such dainties as kings, the spoiled darlings of the gods, are wont to eat.

Telemachus stepped up into the stately chariot. Peisistratus, Nestor's noble son, stepped up beside him and gathered the reins into his hands. Then he struck the horses with the whip: and these, glad to be loosed, flew down from the steep crag of the citadel of Pylos out on to the plain: which all day long they steadily traversed, with the yoke nodding to and fro over their necks.

Down sank the sun. The road became blind. They were in Therae, by the house of Diocles, son to Ortilochus, who was own son of Alpheus. With him they rested the night, duly entertained: and at the first red pointers of dawn in the sky they were yoking their horses to the gay chariot for their next stage.

Forth they drove through the court-yard gate past the echoing porch. Again the driver swung his whip: again the willing horses flew forward. Presently they entered the wheat-lands, sign that their journey drew towards its close; with such speed had the horses pressed on. Again the sun grew low and the roads were darkened.

BOOK 4

They came to the country of Lacedaemon, where it nestled among the hollowed hills: and they drove up to the home of famous Menelaus. He was in act of feasting his many kinsmen to celebrate the marriages of his son and of the flawless daughter of his house. The girl he was giving to the son of that breaker of the line of battle, Achilles. It was in Troy that Menelaus first accepted the proposal and bowed his head in agreement that his daughter should go; and now by horses and car he was about to send her to the storied city of the Myrmidons over which her bridegroom was king: for the Gods were causing the fulfilment of the match proposed. As for the son – Menelaus was bringing from the town of Sparta the daughter of Alector to wed his Megapenthes, his strong but only son whom he had got by a slave-woman: for to Helen the Gods vouchsafed no more fertility after she had borne her first adorable child Hermione, who was as fair as golden Aphrodite herself. So they were dining delightedly, these neighbours and kinsmen of the famous Menelaus, under his tall roof-tree. Of the party one was a minstrel who sang divinely to his lyre. As soon as his preluding chords were heard two clowns danced in among the guests and threw cartwheels upon the hall floor.

Just then in the clear space before the house there reined up the chariot and pair of heroic Telemachus and Nestor's distinguished son. Master Etoneus the lively squire of famed Menelaus happened to see them come. He ran through the palace to bear news of them to the Shepherd of the People. Going up close to him he said pointedly, 'Two men are arriving, my lord Menelaus, nursling of Zeus: strangers, but godlike in look as though they were of Zeus' own kin. Tell me quickly, shall we now unharness their swift horses? Or send them on to some proper man for entertainment?'

Ruddy Menelaus flushed in wrath and cried to him, 'You were not anciently such a fool, O Etoneus, son of Boethus! But herein you babble like a fond child, forgetting how many times we two have eaten hospitably in other men's houses on our way back to this palace, where may Zeus for ever grant us surcease from pain! Hasten to take the horses from the chariot of our guests and bring the two riders in to feast with us.' At his order the squire darted back through the hall bidding the other brisk footboys help him. They loosed the sweating horses from the yoke and haltered them in the horse-stalls, throwing down for them a mixed feed of corn and white barley. They propped the chariot against the polished return of the gateway and led the men into the marvellous house.

Upon first sight of this palace of the heaven-nurtured king the visitors paused in amaze. The lustre that played through it was as though the sun or the moon had risen within the lofty dwelling of far-famed Menelaus. They stared round, feasting their eyes: then went to the polished bath-tubs and bathed: or rather, the house-maidens bathed them and rubbed them down with oil, and after swathed them in warm mantles over tunics; fitting them to take place on their thrones beside Menelaus the son of Atreus.

The washing ewer, a goodly golden ewer, was brought to them by its maid-servant who poured water over their fingers into the silver cistern. She arranged a shining table by their side upon which the aged housekeeper put bread and rich victuals in joyful profusion. The butler came with platters of various flesh-meats and placed golden goblets to their hands. Menelaus waved them to his bounty saying, 'Taste of our food and be glad: so that after you have eaten we may enquire of you who you are. In scions like you the fathers' stock has not gone to waste: patently you are of the breed of kings, sceptered god-children of Zeus. The mean people do not sire sons like you.' With this introduction he picked up and passed to them the luscious loin of beef which had come to him as his privileged portion: then their hands duly made free with the refreshments provided.

Later, when their longings for food or drink had been put away Telemachus leaned his head across near the son of Nestor and whispered in his ear, that the others might not catch his words, 'Son of Nestor and joy of my heart, see what a blaze of polished copper and gold and electrum and silver and ivory goes through this echoing hall. Surely the mansions of Olympian Zeus must be like this, one great glory within of things wonderful beyond all telling. I am awed by the very sight of it.'

Fair-haired Menelaus had overheard his whisper. He opened his mouth to them with momentous words. 'Dear children, with Zeus no mortal man can vie. His houses and his treasures are from everlasting to everlasting. On earth – well, there may be a man as rich as myself, or there may not: but it was only after terrible suffering and eight years of adventure in foreign parts that I won home from overseas with this my wealth. I wandered through Cyprus and Phoenicia and Egypt: I have seen Ethiopians and Sidonians and the Erembi in their native haunts: even Libya, where the ewes bring forth their lambs with horns on and bear them three several times in the cycle of each year. No Libyan, be he king or shepherd, goes short of cheese or mutton or sweet ewe-milk, for the udders are full there all the year round.

'Yet, while I was roaming in such places gathering the wealth you note, another man crept privily upon my unsuspecting brother and murdered him; by connivance of his vile wife. Wherefore my rule over all these great possessions gives me no joy. Probably the story will have been told you by your fathers, whosesoever sons you are: for I have notoriously suffered much and brought to ruin a family which had been flourishing and rich in blessings. Gladly would I cut this wealth to a third if so I might repeople our homes with the men who died years ago in the rolling Troad, exiles from Argos the mother-land of horses. For these my men I am always moaning aloud and making lamentation – or perhaps not quite always, for now and then my heart grows suddenly sated with grief: and thereupon my eyes run dry, even as I sit here in our lordly hall. So abruptly does the comfort of tears turn cold and become a surfeit.

'Yet above and beyond all my company do I especially vex my weeping heart for ONE, whose memory makes me utterly loathe sleep and food. No man of the Achaeans deserved so greatly or laboured so greatly as great Odysseus laboured and endured. For him it was written that the outcome should be but sorrow upon sorrow: and for me a distress for his sake not ever to be forgotten while he continues missing and we in ignorance of whether he be alive or dead. Without doubt they mourn him too, old Laertes and self-possessed Penelope and Telemachus, who was no more than a child newly-born, left behind by his father in the house.'

Thus he spoke, and his words moved in the son a longing to bewail his father when he heard mention of his name. A tear splashed from his eyelids to the ground and he lifted up the purple cloak with both hands before his eyes: while Menelaus who noted it guessed the significance and pondered in his heart and head whether he should wait and allow him to name his father: or press him and try his every word by cross-questioning.

While thus his heart and mind debated, Helen, like a vision of Artemis of the golden distaff, came out from her high-coffered, incense-laden room with her women; of whom Adraste carried the graceful reclining-chair for her mistress while Alcippe had her soft woollen carpet and Phylo a silver basket given the queen by Alcandre, wife of Polybus, a dweller in Egyptian Thebes, that richest in palaces of all the cities of the earth. Polybus himself had given to Menelaus two bathing-tubs of silver and a pair of three-legged cauldrons and ten talents in gold: while his wife added for Helen other wonderful gifts, such as a spindle all of gold, beside this silver basket which the maid Phylo now brought in and set beside her. The basket was mounted on a wheeled carriage also of silver and the rims of it were carried out in gold. It was heaped full of the smoothest yarn and across it, at the moment, lay the distaff wound with wool of a woodviolet blue.

The queen sat down in her long chair which had a stool to support her feet: then she began to speak with her lord, asking him all that was forward: 'Do we know yet, heaven-nurtured Menelaus, from their own lips the truth about these two men our visitors? Shall I play the ignorant or disclose what my sure instinct tells me? My heart is so full of it that I must speak and discharge my utter astonishment: for never in all my experience saw I man or woman with so extraordinary a likeness as this lad bears to magnanimous Odysseus. Surely he must be Telemachus, that son he left behind him a mere infant in the house, when for the sake of this worthless self of mine all you Achaeans came up breathing savage war against the town of Troy.'

Auburn Menelaus answered her and said, 'Indeed, now I can see the likeness which you limn. Those are the feet of Odysseus and his hands and the flash of his eye and his head with the crested hair atop. And just now when I was casting my mind back upon Odysseus and recounting the bitter toil and woe he suffered for my sake, the young man suddenly let a salt tear drop from his bent brows and raised up the purple cloak to veil his eyes.'

Peisistratus the son of Nestor took up the reply and said 'Menelaus, Zeus-fostered son of Atreus, leader of the common people, my friend here is indeed the son of that man, the one and only, as you say. But he is very slow-spoken and would be ashamed in his heart on first coming here to pour out a flood of words before you, in whose utterance we two are taking such pleasure as if it were the voice of a god! Therefore did Nestor of Gerenia, master of chariots and horses, send me with Telemachus as guide. For Telemachus greatly wished to see you and be prompted by you to some word or work. Heavy griefs fall to the lot of a home-keeping son whose father is absent, if so it be that he can find no guardian to champion him. The father of Telemachus is still absent, and he lacks men at home to ward him from calamity.'

To which the reply of yellow-maned Menelaus was:

'Wonderful, wonderful! that there should come to this house the son of my most especial friend who endured unnumbered ordeals for my sake. I had promised myself that when Odysseus came he should be embraced above all my Argives: if only all-knowing Olympian Zeus had granted us to return across the salt sea in our running ships. I would have removed him from Ithaca with his goods and his child and all his dependents, and contrived for him in Argos a dwelling place, a house, a city, by emptying completely of inhabitants one of the towns of my lordship which lies round about us. Then continually would we have foregathered here; nor should any force have sundered us, the lover and the enjoyed, before death's black cloud rolled down on us and covered one from other. I think the God himself perhaps envied us that happiness which would have been: at least he decreed that Odysseus, unhappy soul, should not return.'

So spoke he, and his words quickened in them all a longing to weep. Argive Helen, seed of Zeus, burst into tears: Telemachus too and Atrides-Menelaus: nor could the son of Nestor keep dry eyes, for there came to his memory stainless Antilochus whom the glorious son of shining Dawn had slain. Remembering him he said memorably: 'Atrides, that you were fuller of the knowledge of God than any other of mortal men was always the saying of venerable Nestor, whenever in his great house we brought up your name and questioned of you. Yet in this moment, if it be lawful, I would have you take counsel of me. Know that I take no delight in weeping after my supper: and now it is much after supper: the night advances towards the birth of a new dawn.

'Not that I would disclaim the fitness of weeping for any one of the sons of men who has run upon his fate and died. The last homage we can pay to woe-begone humanity is to shear close our hair and let the tears run down our cheeks. See now, I too have suffered loss: my brother who was far from meanest of the Achaeans. It may well be that you knew him. I was too young to meet or set eyes on him: but they tell me Antilochus was remarkable for that he outran other men in his swiftness of foot and fought surpassingly.'

Said fair Menelaus, 'My dear, when you have said so much you have spoken and acted with the discretion of an enlightened man, even were he a generation older than yourself. As the son of such a father naturally you speak with wisdom. It takes no art to pick out the offspring of a man into the texture of whose days the son of Kronos has woven bliss in the marriage bed and in the procreation of fair children. Nestor, to return to him, has had supremely granted him for all his days that he should glide peacefully into old age in his comfortable halls, surrounded by sons well-advised and very adept with their spears. So now we will let be the weeping aloud which before came upon us and remember again our supper. Ho there, pour water once more upon our hands that we may eat! In the morning Telemachus and I will bandy our fill of tales.'

So he spoke: and Asphalion the great man's handiest retainer poured water over their fingers, which they then employed on the rich food set ready. But Helen, of the line of Zeus, called to mind another resource. Into the wine they were drinking she cast a drug which melted sorrow and sweetened gall, which made men forgetful of their pains. Whoso swallowed it mixed within his cup would not on that day let roll one tear down his cheeks, not though his mother and his father died, not though men hacked to death his brother or loved son with the cutting edge before him and he seeing it with his eyes. These drugs of subtle potency had been furnished the daughter of Zeus by the wife of Thon, even Polydamna the woman of Egypt, where the ploughlands excel other plough-lands of earth in bearing abundance of medicines: of which some when compounded are healing and others baneful. Every man of that country is a physician of knowledge incomparable, for they are of the true strain of Paeon the healer of the Gods.

Helen, after she had mixed the Egyptian drug with their wine and bidden them serve it, returned to the conversation and said, 'Menelaus, son of Atreus and godson of Zeus, and you other sons of the great: it is the way of Zeus to dispense good and evil, now to this man and now to that. He is the all-mighty. Your present lot is to feed, sitting in the halls, and to cheer yourselves with tales, of which I will lead off with one that is seasonable, touching a single one of those innumerable adventures of Odysseus; one only, for beyond all my listing or telling were the exploits of that hardy one.

'Marvellous was this adventure which the iron-nerved man conceived and dared to execute in the Troad of unhappy memory to all Achaeans. He punished himself with humiliating stripes and threw a coarse wrap about his shoulders as if he were a bondman: and so went down into the broad streets of the hostile city amongst his enemies, hiding himself in his foreign shape and making believe he was a mendicant, a figure very unlike that he cut in the Achaean fleet. Yet in this disguise he went through the city of the Trojans – and not a soul of them accosted him. But I knew who this man was and challenged him again and again while he cunningly eluded my questions. After the washing and anointing with oil when I was clothing him in new garments I swore to him a mighty oath that I would not declare to the Trojans that it was Odysseus, before he had got back to the swift ships and the bivouacs. Then he told me all the intention of the Achaeans: and get back to them he did, replete with great fund of news, after killing many Trojans on the way with his long pointed sword: whereupon the Trojan women wailed shrilly: but my heart laughed, for now my desire had shifted to get back home, and deplored too late the infatuation engendered by Aphrodite to lead me away from my own dear country, abandoning child and marriage-ties and a lord not poor in wit or looks.'

Fair Menelaus took up the tale: 'Of all these things, my lady wife, you have said what is needful. In my time I learnt the counsel and thought of many brave men, and traversed many countries, but never set eyes on another man as high-hearted as my beloved Odysseus. The sort of deed his bold heart would imagine and dare to do was such an adventure as that carved horse within which all we flower of the Argives lay hidden, with death and destruction our guerdon for Troy. You came to us then, my lady: surely some god prompted you in desire to glorify the Trojans. Godlike Deiphobus had escorted you thither. Three times you circled our packed lair, stroking it with your hands and calling by name upon the leaders of the Greeks. Your voice was the voice of all our absent wives. Myself and the son of Tydeus and stout Odysseus were inside and heard you calling: and of a sooth two of us, Diomedes and I, raged furiously to leap up and call you or quickly to answer you from within. But with main strength Odysseus held us back against our passions. Wherefore all the other sons of the Achaeans were still: save only Anticlus who was about to address you, when Odysseus with his great hands gripped his jaws and held on, thus saving all the Achaeans: until Pallas Athene at last called you away.'

To him staid Telemachus replied: 'Son of Atreus, Menelaus, foster son of Zeus, bulwark of the rank of battle: all the worse is our pain. For this courage did not deliver him from grievous ruin nor would it have availed if his heart had been of unflawed iron. But come now, dismiss us to our beds that we may stretch out and take our fill of the sweetness of sleep.'

At his word Helen of Argos ordered her house-maidens to range beds under the sun-porch, piling them with lovely purple blankets covered smoothly with rugs and thick woollen cloaks on top of all. The maids left the hall, torch in hand, and made ready the beds. Then the usher showed the guests out. So they slept there, in the entry, heroic Telemachus and Nestor's brilliant son: while the son of Atreus lay remote in the great house, and beside him Helen of the flowing robes, fairest of women.

At dawn's first redness in the sky Menelaus of the resounding war-cry arose from bed, clothed himself, belted on a sharp sword and bound gay sandals beneath his lively feet. Like a god he went forth from the married quarters and calling Telemachus to sit by him, greeted him and said, 'What promptings drove you to me, princely Telemachus, here to Lacedaemon the fair, over the broad swelling sea? Public or private need? Confide in me freely.'

Telemachus answered him with advisement. 'Atrides-Menelaus the god-nurtured, pre-eminent when battle is ranged, I come to know if perchance you can give me any rumour of my father. My household is being eaten up and my fat properties ruined. Our home is full of evil-minded men, these inordinately proud suitors of my mother, who ever butcher my numerous sheep and slow swaying oxen with the crumpled horns. Therefore am I come pleading to your knee that you may consent to tell me the story of his pitiful destruction as you saw it with your eyes or as you learnt it from the lips of another wanderer. Indeed his mother conceived him to great misery. Condone nothing and spare me nothing out of misplaced pity: but relate just as much as you saw of him. If the excellent Odysseus my father ever fulfilled word or pledge of his to you in that Troy of unhappy suffering for the Achaeans, then I pray you recompense me now by remembering it and dealing with me as faithfully.'

Menelaus flushed with anger and cried to him: 'The dastards, who would lay their puny selves in the bed of that whole-hearted warrior! It is as if a deer had laid her newborn suckling fawns in a lion's den and gone out searching across the mountain-spurs and green valleys for her pasture. When the strong beast returns to the thicket which is his lair he will fearfully kill those poor intruders: and even such a mean death shall Odysseus deal out to these pests. By Zeus our Father, and Athene, and Apollo! I can remember how once in luxurious Lesbos Odysseus rose up in a rage and wrestled with Philomeleides and threw him strongly: and all the Greeks rejoiced. If only he might confront the suitors with that old strength. How swiftly would fate close on them and turn their nuptials into bitterness! As for these questions you entreat of me I promise you to distort nothing nor let myself speak beside the truth, nor shall I trick you. Yea, not one word will I hide from you or cover up of all that the Ancient of the Sea, the Infallible, told me.

'It was in Egypt. I was eager to return but the Gods delayed me there because I had not perfected their full ritual sacrifice. Ever jealous the Gods are, that we men mind their dues. In the surge that breaks across the mouth of the river of Egypt there lies a certain island which men called Pharos, no further from the land than a laden ship will make in the daylight hours, granted that she has a favouring wind to bluster her squarely forward. In it is a harbour with good landing beaches and clean, deep wells of fresh water, from which, after drawing their fill, men run down the trim hulls into the sea. In this island the gods kept me for twenty days, nor ever did there blow a breath of those sea-breezes which inspire ships to move over the wide ridges of the sea.

'And now would our last rations have been devoured and with them the courage of my men, had not a divinity taken pity on me and been merciful. Eidothea she was, that daughter of stalwart Proteus, the sea's venerable lord. The sad sight of me touched her heart on a time she met me wandering furtively apart from my followers, who daily quartered the island, angling with hooks that they had bent up, for fish to allay the hunger which griped their bellies. Eidothea, however, drawing near called me and put a question: "Stranger, are you foolish or to such a point easy-going that freely you abandon yourself to enjoy the sense of pain? All this long time you are prisoned in the island and put no term to the delay, though the spirit of your company diminishes." Thus she addressed me: and I in my turn replied, "Whatever one of the goddesses you are, let me protest that I am not willingly held here. It would seem that I have transgressed against the immortal gods which are in high heaven. Tell me therefore of your knowledge (for the Gods know all) which deathless one it is who fetters me here and prevents my leaving? Also of my return; how is that to be managed across the swarming deep?"

'So I said: and forthwith the fair goddess answered, "Freely will I inform you, Stranger. This is the haunt of the authentic Ancient of the Sea, Proteus of Egypt, the

Immortal One, who knows the unplumbed ocean-pits and is first minister to Poseidon. Rumour makes him my father by course of nature. If you can but summon strength to lie in wait for him and take him, then he will impart to you how and where and when your course should be and what return you will have, riding over the fishes' element. He will even tell you, heaven-nurtured, if you press him, what good or evil has befallen your homes while you have been wearing this weary road."

'Taking her up I said, "This ambush, Goddess, must be of your designing if it is to succeed; otherwise be sure the old divinity will see or hear something suspicious and avoid my snare. It is pain for mortal man to compel a god."

'The glorious goddess acceded instantly. "Hear then this detailed plan. When the climbing sun has reached the zenith of its sky, even then daily does the unerring Ancient of the Sea come forth from his deep with the breath of the west wind to attend him and drape him in its darkling ripple. He comes out, into the wave-worn caves, and lies him down to rest: while drove upon drove of his seals, bred from salt-water by an ocean-nymph, forsake the grey brine and sleep too around him, bitter-scenting the place because their breathing holds the bitterness of the salt abysses of the sea. Thither I will bring you at the break of day and set you properly in ambush; you and three of your companions, carefully chosen as the trustiest men of your staunch ship. And now I will warn you of all the formidable tricks of this old god. First he will muster his seals, to count them: and when he has fingered them all off and recognized each one, then he will lie down in their midst like a shepherd in the midst of a flock. When you see him settle down, at that moment call up your mighty strength and hold him there, though he will struggle vehemently, desperately, to escape you. In his urgency he will assume all shapes, of whatever things there be that creep upon the earth: and he will turn to water and to flaming heavenly fire: but do you hold to him, unflinchingly, gripping ever the tighter: and at the last he will speak in his own nature and as you saw him when he lay down to sleep. Then indeed, hero, cease your effort and let the old man be: while you ask him which of the gods is angry with you and how you shall return home across the fish-quick sea."

'Having spoken she dived beneath the billows: while I plodded away to the ships drawn up on the beach. My mind as I went was all clouded with perplexities. However I did regain the ships and the sea: and by them we made our supper while immortal night came down. Then we stretched out to sleep with the breaking of the surf beside us.

'At the first red finger of daybreak in the east I was again afoot, pacing the verge of the outstretched sea in most earnest supplication to the gods: then I chose three of the company, the three I could most trust in any undertaking. As for the goddess she had been down into the broad bosom of the sea and brought back from the depths the pelts of four seals all newly flayed. She had thought out a way of deceiving her father, and had dug lying-places in the sand of the sea-shore: by them she sat awaiting us. We came to her side and she made us to lie down in these lairs, where she threw a seal-skin over each form. Then indeed our vigil was like to have been most terrible, so hard to bear was the deathly stench of the sea-born seals. Indeed what man would choose to couch beside a monster of the deep?

'The goddess it was who saved us and refreshed us greatly by bringing to each one of us and setting under our noses scented ambrosia, so marvellously sweet that it abolished the animal stink. Thus the whole morning we endured hardily while the seals came out all together from the main and basked in ranks along the water's edge. At noon the Ancient of the Sea himself came forth and found his fat seals and went down the line of them to add up their number; counting us as the first four beasts, his heart not warning him of the fraud afoot. Then he laid himself down. We shouted our cry and leaped upon him grappling him with our hands: to find that the old one had in no wise forgotten the resources of his magic. His first change was into a hairy lion: then a dragon: then a leopard: then a mighty boar. He became a film of water, and afterwards a high-branched tree. We hardened our hearts and held firmly to him throughout.

'At long last the old wizard grew distressed and broke into words, questioning me: "Son of Atreus, which God conspired with you in this plan to ambush me and take me against my will? What is it that you must have?" So he said, and in reply I spoke as follows: "Ancient: you know. Why confuse our issue by questions? I am detained too long in this island and can find no token why: so that my heart grows faint. Therefore do you now, as one of the all-knowing Gods, tell me which of the Immortal Ones hobbles me here and delays my journey. How is my return to be contrived, over the sea and its thronging fish?"

'At once he answered me, "Why, of course your fault was in not paying to Zeus and to the other gods liberal sacrifice before your setting off. This would have ensured the quickest passage to your native land, by ship across the wine-dark sea. Now it is ordained that you shall not see your friends nor reach your well-appointed house in the country of your fathers until once again you have entered the river of Egypt (the divine river fed by heavenly rain) and offered their sacramental hecatombs to the eternal masters of the open skies. Thereafter the gods will give you the road of your desire."

'So he said, and my modest spirit quailed within me when I heard that I must once more cross the shadowy main that long and woeful way to Egypt. Nevertheless I found words to answer him. "I will carry out your bidding, Venerable One: yet I pray you give me also a clear word on this other matter. All those Achaeans whom Nestor and I left when we sailed from Troy – did they get home undamaged with their ships, or were some lost, either by harsh fate in shipwreck or in their comrades' arms, after their war had been well ended?"

'This was my question. And he replied, "Son of Atreus, why enquire too closely of me on this? To know or to learn what I know about it is not your need: I warn you that when you hear all the truth your tears will not be far behind. Of those others many went under; many came through. How many fell in battle your eyes saw: but two only of the chiefs of the bronze-corseletted Achaeans died on the way back. One other is still somehow alive, pent and languishing in the boundless sea. Aias was wrecked amongst his long-oared ships by act of Poseidon, who carried him to the huge cliffs of Gyrae, yet delivered him from the waves. Thus he would have escaped destruction despite the hatred which Athene nursed for him if he, infatuate in his frantic pride, had not cried out an overweening word – how in the teeth of the Gods he had escaped the sea's mighty void. Poseidon heard this high proclaiming and snatched at his trident: with labouring hands he let drive at the rock of Gyrae and hacked it through. The stump remained, but the jagged pinnacle on which Aias had first pitched, boasting and blaspheming, broke off and fell into the sea, carrying him down into the vasty seething depths: where he died, choked in its briny water.

"'As for Agamemnon, your brother, he somehow escaped his fates and got away in his shapely vessels. Our Lady Hera was his saviour, till he had almost attained to Maleia, that steep mountain. There a tempest fell upon him and snatched him from his course. It carried him, deeply groaning, across the fish-infested waves to that butt of land where Thyestes dwelt of old in his settlements: but now Aegisthus the son had succeeded him. Yet from here also prospect of a sure return appeared. The gods once again changed the wind to fair: homeward they came; and as the joyful leader touched upon his own land he bent down and kissed its soil with his lips, crying hot tears of gladness, for that at last he saw his native place.

"'Yet from above, from the look-out, the watchman had seen him – a sentry posted by guileful Aegisthus with promise of two gold talents for reward of vigilance. A whole year had he been on guard lest King Agamemnon get past without being spied and first signal his return by headlong attack upon the usurpers in his house. The watchman ran with his news to the house of Aegisthus, the shepherd of the people, who straightway put his cunning plot in train. A chosen twenty of the ablest-bodied local men he hid in ambush, while on the other side of the great hall he had a high feast spread. Then with welcoming horses and cars, but with iniquity in his hollow mind, he went forth to meet Agamemnon the king. Into his house Aegisthus ushered him (all unsuspicious of the death hidden there) and feasted him, and after cut him down – as a man might cut down an ox at its stall. Nor was there anyone left of the company of Atrides: nor even of Aegisthus' company. All of them fell there in the palace."

'Here Proteus ceased his tale: and again my kindly heart failed within me. Down I sank weeping on the sands nor did my spirit any more desire to live on and see the light of the sun. Yet later, when I had indulged to the full in tears, wallowing on the ground, the Venerable One of the Sea, the Infallible, further addressed me: "Persist no more, son of Atreus, in thus stubbornly weeping: we shall not thereby attain an end. Instead try your quickest to devise a return to your country: there you may happen on the criminal yet living: or Orestes may have just forestalled you and killed him: in which case you will be in time for the death ceremonies." So he said: and thereat my heart and stately spirit glowed once more in the breast of my sorrows: and I found winged words to answer him: "These men I have now heard of: but name me that third man who yet lives but lingers somewhere in the broad sea: or dead? I wish to know it, even though my grief be deepened."

'So I said, and he replied again: "The son of Laertes, the lord of Ithaca. I saw him in an island, letting fall great tears throughout the domain of the nymph Calypso who there holds him in constraint: and he may not get thence to his own land, for he has by him no oared ships or company to bear him across the sea's great swell. Hear lastly the fate decreed you, O Menelaus, cherished of Zeus. You are not to die in Argos of the fair horse-pastures, not there to encounter death: rather will the Deathless Ones carry you to the Elysian plain, the place beyond the world, where is fair-haired Rhadamanthus and where the lines of life run smoothest for mortal men. In that land there is no snowfall, nor much winter, nor any storm of rain: but from the river of earth the west wind ever sings soft and thrillingly to re-animate the souls of men. There you will have Helen for yourself and will be deemed of the household of Zeus."

'He spoke and plunged beneath the billows: but I went to the ships with my gallant following: and my heart as I went was shadowed by its cares. Yet we attained the ships and the sea-beaches and furnished ourselves a supper, while ambrosial night drew down, persuading us to stretch out in repose by the fringes of the tide. And with the early rosyfingered Dawn we first of all ran down our ships into the divine salt sea and placed masts and sails ready in their tight hulls. Then the men swarmed aboard, and sat down on their rowing-thwarts: and having duly arranged themselves they flailed the sea white with their oars. Back once again to the river of Egypt, the water of the gods, where I made fast the ships to make the ordered sacrifice of burnt offerings. When I had so slaked the resentment of the never-dying gods I heaped up a great mound in Agamemnon's name, that the glory of him might never be put out. All things were then accomplished. I turned back. They gave me a wind, did the Immortal Ones, which carried me swiftly to my beloved land.

'But see now, Telemachus. Remain with me in my palace until there dawns the eleventh or twelfth day from now: and then I shall dismiss you nobly, with conspicuous gifts – three horses shall you have and a two-seater chariot of the finest workmanship – yea, and a beautiful embossed cup, that each time you pour an offering from it to the deathless gods you may think of me, for all your days.'

To him said Telemachus, 'Atrides, I beg you, delay me not for all that time. It would be possible for me to sit still here in your presence and forget home or parents throughout a whole year, so wonderfully am I entranced to hear your words and tales. But my companions are already chafing in happy Pylos, and would you hold me yet many days in this place? As for the gift which it pleases you to give me, let it be an heirloom: for to Ithaca I cannot take horses. Better I leave them here to dignify your place. The plain of your lordship is wide, rich in clover and water-grass and wheat and grain and also strong-strawed white barley. In Ithaca we have no broad riding-grounds, no meadow land at all: of these our islands which rise rock-like from the sea, not one is fit for mounted work, or grass-rich: least of all my Ithaca. Yet are its goat-pastures more lovely in my sight than fields for grazing horses.'

So he replied: and Menelaus of the ringing battle-shout smiled and petted him with his hand, and naming him dearly said, 'My child, your gentle words disclose your breeding. Of course I will exchange my gifts. I have such choice. See, out of the store of treasures ranged in my house I give you the fairest and costliest: – Item, a wrought mixing-bowl of solid silver doubled with gold about the rim. Work of Hephaestus. Hero Phaedimus, King of Sidon, endowed me with it when I found shelter in his house on my way back here. I am happy to transfer it now to you.' As they so exchanged their phrases those whose turn it was to provide (and share) the entertainment that night in the palace of the god-like king came near, driving before them the needful sheep and carrying their generous wine. For them too their high-coiffed wives sent a store of wheaten bread.

∼

Here were these men, toiling orderly in the palace to make ready the feast for their night: while over in Ithaca the suitors before the great house of Odysseus were junketing with their established insolence, the whim now being to put the weight or hurl throwing-spears on the level fore-court. Antinous and imposing Eurymachus sat and looked on. These two were the lordliest suitors, pre-eminent in reputation. To them drew nigh Noemon, son of Phronius, who greeted Antinous and asked, 'Antinous, have we any idea in our heads (or none) of when Telemachus is due back from sandy Pylos? He went off with my ship, and now I am wanting her to take me across to Elis, in whose wide lands are twelve mares of mine at milk with stout mulefoals, yet unbroken. I have a design to drive off some one of these and break it in.'

His news amazed their minds. They had never imagined to themselves that the lad might have gone to Neleus' city, Pylos: rather that he was somewhere in the estate, with the flocks or perhaps keeping company with the swineherd. So Antinous son of Eupeithes turned to him and demanded: 'Let me have the whole truth of this. When did he go, and who were the young men who abetted him? Were they chosen Ithacans, or his serfs and house-thralls, of whom he might properly dispose at will? Also answer me this too, categorically, that I may be sure: – did he lift your black ship off you by force, against your will; or did you voluntarily lend her to him because he begged the favour formally?'

Phronius' son Noemon replied: 'I gave her to him freely. What could one do when such a man, having a heart-full of worry, asked a kindness? It would be churlish to refuse compliance. The youths who after us are the best men of the country-side formed his crew. The captain, when they went aboard, I recognized for Mentor, or some god his very image: the point has puzzled me, for I saw goodly Mentor here in the city at the dawning of yesterday, when already he had left in the ship for Pylos.'

He finished, and turned away towards his father's

house. The lordly wrath of his two hearers had been kindled. They made the suitors stop their playing and sit in conclave. Then Antinous son of Eupeithes rose to address them. He was deeply moved. His black-bound heart heaved with wild rage and his eyes were flashing fires.

'Heaven and hell!' he cried, 'here's a fine thing Telemachus has carried through in style to its very end – this journey of his. We used to swear it would come to nought: yet the young fellow has slipped clean away against all our wills like this – just launching out a ship and helping himself to the best company in the place. He threatens ever worse and worse for us: may Zeus cut the strength off from him before he reaches the height of manhood! I ask you to supply me a fast ship and a crew of twenty men, with which to watch and waylay him as he comes through the narrow gut between Ithaca and steep Samos: that this gadding about after his father may cost him dear at last.' He spoke: they cried applause and urged him to execution. Then they rose up and returned to Odysseus' house.

Not for very long did Penelope remain unaware of these plots which the suitors were hatching in the evil depths of their minds: for the poursuivant Medon told her what he had overheard of their council, he being just beyond the court-wall while they were thrashing out their schemes within. Medon hasted through the building to bring his news to Penelope who, as he crossed the threshold of her quarters, shrilled at him, 'Herald, why have the famous suitors sent you in here? Perhaps they now give orders even to the house-maidens of godlike Odysseus, and bid them lay aside their duties and prepare them a feast? May they be dining here to-day for their last and latest time, never again to meet, never to go on wooing! You! who ever swarm to spoil the great wealth, the livelihood of shrewd Telemachus. You! who never heard in days when you were children any word from your fathers of how Odysseus bore himself towards your parents, with never an arbitrary deed nor even an arbitrary word, in the city! Yet such are prerogatives of consecrated kings, who will hate this one and love that – all save Odysseus: for he wrought no iniquity upon any man whatsoever. Indeed your temper and ugly works come out plain in this: nor does any grace survive for past favours.'

Medon's enlightened mind advised him. He quietly replied, 'If only that, O Queen, were the worst of our troubles! The suitors discuss an evil deplorably greater; which may Zeus, son of Kronos, forfend: they are fully determined that their sharp swords shall slay Telemachus on his way home: he went to learn news of his father, you see, away to most holy Pylos and sacred Lacedaemon.'

At his speech her knees gave way, and her loving heart: and for long time stupor cut off her power of speech. Her eyes brimmed with tears and the copious fountain of her voice was stopped. After very long, words came to her for a reply: 'Herald, why has my son gone? He had no call, none whatever, to embark in any one of the swift-going ships which serve men as horses to ride the salt waves: nor to cross the great water. Was he determined that not even his name should survive among men?'

Well-advised again was the saying of Medon: 'I do not know if a god roused him out: or whether it was that his own great heart rushed him to Pylos upon enquiry as to his father's return or fate.' He spoke and turned back through the house of Odysseus: while upon her came down a heart-corroding agony: so that she could not even guide herself to one of the many stools which stood about the house. Instead she sank to the door-sill of her

richly-appointed room and wailed aloud in piteous fashion:
while round her came crooning all the women-servants of
the house, the young ones with the old ones: and across
the torrent of her grief Penelope sobbed to them: –

'Hear me, my people. Now the lord of Olympus has
given to me greater pain than has been the lot of all the
women born and brought up my mates. Of old had I lost
my mighty husband, the lion-hearted, most virtuously
endowed of all the Greeks; indeed a noble man whose fame
was bruited across Hellas and to the heart of Argos. But
now the whirlwinds have snatched my beloved son ignobly
from our halls without my hearing he had gone. O cruel
women whose hearts knew all, but did not think to call
me from my bed when the lad went down to his black
hollow ship. If I had known that he was intending the
journey, very surely he should have stayed, however eager:
or gone only by leaving my dead body behind him in the
halls. Hasten, some one of you, and call old Dolius, the
bondman my father gave me, even before I entered this
house, my gardener who keeps the orchard with its many
trees. He shall run to Laertes and sitting by his side shall
retail to him all these things. Perhaps Laertes may weave
some device in his heart for a public appeal to this people
who are coveting the final destruction of his seed and the
seed of god-like Odysseus.'

Privileged Eurycleia the nurse answered and said, 'My
lady, I must declare myself, whether you kill me therefor
with your pitiless blade or spare me to live on in your
service. I knew all his intent, and whatever he bade me I
gave him of food and sweet wine. He exacted of me a great
oath that I should not tell you before twelve days had
passed, unless you yourself missed him and heard that he
had left: for he would not that you should mar your lovely

flesh with tears. Do you therefore bathe yourself and choose clean clothing for your body: and afterward go to your upper room with your attendant maidens and supplicate Athene, daughter of aegis-bearing Zeus: if haply she may then save Telemachus from death. Increase not the affliction of old afflicted Laertes without cause: for I think the seed of Arceisius his ancestor is not so wholly hateful to the blessed gods that there will not be left some one of the house to enjoy its high-ceiled rooms and the fat lands which stretch hence ever so widely.'

Eurycleia's words lulled my lady's weeping, and freed her eyes of tears. She bathed, changed garments, and with her maidens gained the upper floor: and then she put the bruised barley of the heave-offering into its basket and prayed to Athene: –

'Hear me, unwearied Goddess, child of aegis-bearing Zeus: if ever experienced Odysseus burnt to you in these halls fat thighs of oxen or sheep, then be mindful of them now unto me and save my beloved son: deliver him from the suitors and the excesses of their evil will.' Her yearning broke in vibrant cry upon the goddess, who heard the supplication: while below stairs in the dusky halls the suitors were rioting, some rude youth now and again making boast, 'This much-courted queen goes on preparing her marriage with us, never guessing that death is decreed for her son.' The others took up and repeated the saying – they being the infatuates who did not guess how death had been decreed – till Antinous spoke out and said, 'Look here, my masters. Now will we cease uttering these words so pleased and proud, lest someone repeat them in the house. Instead let us rise up silently to carry out the scheme arranged which even now met all our fancies.' Thereupon he chose his twenty leading spirits, who rose up and went to the foreshore and the swift ships, where their first move was to drag down a ship into deep water. They stowed masts and sails into her blackness and refixed round the oars their raw-hide thole-loops, as was due and meet. They strained flat the white sails. The disdainful attendants carried war-harness to them. Then they took her well out to moorings in the road, and came ashore for supper and to wait for the fall of darkness.

All this while circumspect Penelope was lying in her upper room, without eating or even tasting any food or drink, agitated to know if her innocent son would escape death or be overcome by the hands of the intolerant suitors. Her distress was the distress of a lion beset and at bay in a throng of men, seeing with anxious eye how they spread round him in a crafty circle. With just such fears was she wrestling when the swoon of sleep came down on her. She lay back and slept: and all her frame relaxed.

Then the grey-eyed goddess, Athene, provided a fresh resource. She created a phantom, the bodily likeness of another daughter of stout Icarius, Iphthime, who had wedded Eumelus and lived at Pherae. This wraith she sent to the house of godlike Odysseus, to weeping, moaning Penelope, that she might lay aside her lamentation and loud tears. In it came to the wife's chamber, through the thong-hole of the latch, and took stand there behind her head and said its say to her as follows: 'Do you sleep, Penelope, with your loving heart so bruised? Not even the Gods resting at ease above our affairs can bear to let you so weep and suffer, forasmuch as there is a homecoming appointed for your son. He is no transgressor against the gods.'

Cautious Penelope murmured back as she slumbered very sweetly in the gate of dreams: 'Why come now, sister, seeing how rarely you get here from your so-distant home? You tell me to lay aside these many distressful griefs which torture my heart and mind. Why, a time ago I lost my lion-hearted hero husband, whose nobility was noised through Hellas and Argos: and now my beloved boy, a child untempered in affairs or words, has gone in a hollow ship. I sorrow more for him than for my man and tremble in fear of what he may suffer among the strangers he visits or in the wide sea. His many enemies invent snares for him, intending to kill him before he can reach home again.'

The dim wraith replied, 'Be brave: give not fear too large rule over your heart. There goes with him a guide of power such as all men would pray to have stand by them, even Pallas Athene. She takes mercy upon your grief and directly sends me that I may speak to you these comforts.'

Wise Penelope again said, 'If you are divine and have heard the voice of a god, enlighten me now upon my unfortunate husband, whether he yet lives and sees the light of day, or is now a dead man in the house of Hades.'

Said the dim shadow: 'Of that I will not tell you all, not even if he be alive or dead. It were ill to speak airily of that.' With which words the spectre vanished by the latch, and dissolved into the moving air: but Penelope the daughter of Icarius rose up from her sleep, her loving heart warmed by the vividness of the dream which had fallen on her in the gloaming.

The suitors set forth, harbouring sadden death for Telemachus in their hearts, and sailed the water-ways as far as a stony island in mid-sea, equidistant from Ithaca and craggy Samos, even the islet Asteris, no large place: which has a harbour with two approaches and in it a berth for ships. There they drew up to lie in wait for him.

BOOK 5

Dawn rose from her marriage-bed beside high-born Tithonus to bring her daylight to both gods and men. The immortals, with Zeus the high-thundering, their mightiest one, sat down in council: and to them Athene spoke thus, designing to remind them of the many misfortunes of Odysseus, whose long sojourn in the nymph's house lay heavy on her heart: –

'Father Zeus, and you happy ever-living Gods: henceforth let no sceptred king study to be kindly or gentle, or to ensue justice and equity. It profits more to be harsh and unseemly in act. Divine Odysseus was a clement and fatherly king; but no one of the men, his subjects, remembers it of him for good: while fate has abandoned him to languish sorely in Lady Calypso's island, kept there by her high hand, a prisoner in her house. Nor has he power to regain the land of his fathers, seeing that he lacks galleys and followers to speed him over the broad back of ocean. Moreover, there is now a plot afoot to murder his darling son as he returns from sacred Pylos or noble Lacedaemon, whither he went in hope to hear somewhat of his father.'

Zeus the cloud-marshal answered her and said, 'My

child, too fierce are the judgements of your mouth. Besides, I think this last move was of your scheming, for Odysseus to avenge himself on those men when he comes. You have the knowledge, the power and the skill to convey Telemachus again to his own place wholly unscathed. See that it is so: and that the suitors come back too in their ship, as they went.'

He turned to Hermes, the son he loved, and said, 'Hermes, hear your commission as our particular messenger. Inform this nymph of the love-locks of my fixed decision that long-suffering Odysseus shall return home as best he can, without furtherance from gods or mortal men. Therefore he is to lash together a raft as firm as may be, on which after twenty days of hazard and disaster he will make rich-glebed Scheria, the Phaeacian land. The Phaeacians, godlike in race and habit, will take him to their heart with all honour as divine: and send him forward to his native place in a ship laden with gifts of copper and gold and clothing of an abundance such as Odysseus would never have amassed for himself in the sack of Troy, even though he had come away intact, and with the full share of booty assigned him by lot. The decree is, that so furnished he shall once again behold his friends and enter his stately house in the country of his fathers.'

Such was the order: and the messenger, the Argus-slayer, made no delay in his obedience. Instantly he laced to his feet the fair sandals of imperishable gold by which he made equal way, swift as a breath of wind, over the ocean and over the waste places of the earth. He took the wand with which at will he could lure the eyes of men to slumber or wake them into activity, and with it in hand the Argus-slayer leaped out upon the air and flew strongly. Over mount Pierus he dived down from the firmament to sea level: and then along the waves he sped like a cormorant which down the dread troughs of the wild sea chases its fish and drenches its close plumage in the salt spume. Just so did Hermes skim the recurring wave-crests.

But when at last he attained that remote island, he quitted the purple sea and went inland as far as the great cave in which lived the nymph of the well-braided hair. He chanced to find her within where a great fire burned on its appointed hearth, perfuming the island far across with the fragrance of flaming cedar-wood logs and straight-grained incense trees. Inside the cavern the nymph's sweet voice could be heard singing as she went to and fro before her loom, weaving with a golden shuttle. All round the cave-mouth there flourished a luxuriant copse of alder trees and black poplars and richscented cypresses: therein roosted birds of long wing, owls and hawks and chattering hook-billed crows – birds of the sea whose livelihood was from the waters. A young strong vine loaded with bunches of grapes wreathed the opening of the cave. Four springs quite near together jetted out translucent water in separate rills ingeniously contrived, each to water its own garden-plot. The soft lawns were starred with parsley and violets. Even an immortal coming upon the nook would pause before its beauty and feel his heart made glad: the messenger, Argus' bane, halted in amazement.

When his heart had taken its fill of wondering, he entered the great cave: nor was his figure strange to Calypso, the very goddess, when she saw him come into her presence. (It is a gift to the gods, to know one another when they meet, however distant the home of one of them may chance to lie.) In the cavern he did not find great-hearted Odysseus, who sat weeping on the shore as was his wont, crying out his soul with groaning and griefs and letting flow his tears while he eyed the fruitless sea.

Calypso, the fair goddess, made Hermes seat himself on a splendid polished throne, and asked him, 'Hermes of the gold rod, ever honoured and welcome, from of old you have had no habit of visiting me: why do you come here to-day? Tell me your mind. My spirit is eager to second your desire if its fulfilment be in my gift and such a thing as may law-fully be fulfilled. Yet first enter further into the cave that I may put before you the meed of guests.' With such words did the goddess bring forward a table boun-teously set with ambrosia. She blended him ruddy nectar. Then did the messenger, Argus' bane, drink and eat: but when he had dined and made happy his spirit with the food, he opened his mouth and said: –

'As goddess to god you ask me, you order me, to tell why I have come. Hear the truth of it! Zeus commanded my journey: by no choice of my own did I fare to you across so unspeakable a waste of salt water. Who would willingly come where there is no near city of men to offer sacrifice to the gods and burn us tasty hundreds of oxen? Listen: – in no way can another god add or subtract any tittle from the will of Zeus, the aegis-bearer. He declares that you have with you the unhappiest man of men – less happy than all those who fought for nine years round the citadel of Priam and in the tenth year sacked the city and went homeward. Yet during their return they sinned against Athene, and she worked up against them an evil wind and tall waves by which this man's entire splendid company were cast away. As for himself, the wind blew him and the sea washed him to this spot. Wherefore now the Father commands that you send him hence with speed: for it is decreed that he is not to die far from his friends. On the contrary he is to behold these friends again and is to sit under his lofty roof in his own land.' So he said: and as he spoke Calypso the lovely goddess grew cold and shuddered. Then with barbed words did she reply: 'Cruel are you gods and immoderately jealous of all others; especially do you hate it when goddesses elect to lie openly with men, or fall in love and make a match of it with some mortal. Remember how it was when pink-fingered Dawn chose Orion. You gods at ease in your heaven grudged the union bitterly, even until chaste Artemis of the golden throne killed him in Ortygia by an infliction of her gentle darts. So again it befell when long-tressed Demeter unleashed her passion and coupled herself for love and venery with lasion in the thrice-broken fallows. Not for long was Zeus unaware: and then He slew him with a cast of his blinding thunderbolt.

'Just in that same way you gods are now envying me this man I live with. Yet it was I who saved him as he clung astride his vessel's keel, alone and adrift in the wine-dark ocean. Zeus had launched a white thunderbolt at his ship and shattered her: and in her wreck were all the worthy henchmen lost. Only it chanced that he himself drifted to my shore before the wind and waves: and I have loved him and cared for him and promised myself he should not die nor grow old all his days. Yet very justly do you say that no lesser god can overpass or make vain the purpose of aegis-bearing Zeus: accordingly, if the impulse and order are from Him, I must let my man go hence across the sterile sea. Yet shall the sending be in no wise mine. Here are neither oared ships nor crews to convoy him over ocean's broad back. Unreservedly however will I furnish him my very best advice as to how he may come safe to his native land.'

The messenger, the Slayer of Argus, answered: 'Of a surety send him away now, in utter obedience and regard for the wrath of Zeus: lest He, being angered against you, later bear malice.' And after this parting word the mighty

Argus Slayer went away: while the nymph set out to find great-hearted Odysseus, in accordance with the command which Zeus had sent. She found him sitting by the water's edge: his eyes as ever dewed with tears at this ebbing of his precious life in vain lamentations after deliverance – seeing that the nymph no longer pleased his fancy. True, that every night would he sleep with her: he had no choice while he lived in her vaulted cave. Yet was he not willing, and she willed too much: consequently day-long he haunted the rocks and pebble-beaches of the island's shore, retching up his heart with crying and sighs and misery, his gaze fixed upon the desolate main through a blur of tears.

The goddess approached him and said: 'Ill-fated man, grieve no longer in this place. Your life shall not so fade away: for see, my mind is most ready to send you hence. Up now and fell yourself tall tree-trunks and carpenter them with metal tools into a great raft, substantial enough to carry an upper deck clear of the water, on which you may journey over the misted sea. I will supply food to guard you against hunger, and water and red wine such as you enjoy: and I will put rich robes on you and ensure a mild wind in your wake that you may come without misadventure to your native place – if so the Gods will: for that company of the wide heavens are more potent than myself, alike in purpose and fulfilment.'

Her speech made steadfast Odysseus shiver. He loudly shot back at her, 'Surely, Goddess, something not at all to my advantage, something quite contrary, lies behind this your command – that on a raft I launch out over the great soundings of a sea which is so perilous and difficult that not invariably do the tall swift-running ships pass it in safety: not even when Zeus blesses them and makes them happy with his assisting winds. Understand therefore that

I shall not embark upon this raft-venture without your will: not unless you as a goddess consent to swear me a great oath that in this you do not plan further misfortunes for my account.'

His words made Calypso, the beautiful nymph, smile. As she soothed him with her hand, repeating his name, she spoke to him as follows: 'Sharp-witted rogue you are, to imagine and dare say such a thing to me. Bear witness now, Earth, and spacious Heaven overhead, and the river of Styx that slideth downward (which oath is the greatest and most terrible in the use of the blessed gods) how in this counsel I intend no sort of evil against you. Rather am I planning and advising you with the scrupulous care I should have for myself, if ever I stood in such case. Believe me that my understanding is ripe: and the heart in my breast is not made of iron, but very pitiful.'

Having ended, the goddess turned back abruptly. Odysseus followed the divine leader so that they re-entered the cave, immortal and mortal keeping company. There the man sat him down on the throne from which Hermes had lately risen, and the nymph served him a various refreshment of such meat and drink as men usually take. Afterward she took place opposite her great hero, while the maids plied her with nectar and ambrosia. Freely they partook of the cheer at hand till they had had their fill of eating and drinking. Then Calypso the lovely goddess opened her mouth and said: –

'Kinsman of Zeus and son of Laertes, many-counselled Odysseus: is it your true wish, even yet, to go back to your own country? God forgive you: may you be happy there! Ah, did but the mirror of your mind show you what misfortune must yet fill your cup before you attain the home you seek, verily you would dwell here with me always, keeping my house and your immortality; to the utter rejection of this day-long and every-day yearning which moves you to behold your wife. Think not however that I avow myself her less than rival, either in figure or in parts. It were out and out impious for a mere woman to vie in frame and face with immortals.'

In his worldly wisdom great Odysseus answered, 'O Queen and Divinity, hold this not against me. In my true self I do most surely know how far short of you discreet Penelope falls in stature and in comeliness. For she is human: and you are changeless, immortal, ever-young. Yet even so I choose – yea all my days are consumed in longing – to travel home and see the day of my arrival dawn. If a god must shatter me upon the wine-dark sea, so be it. I shall suffer with a high heart; for my courage has been tempered to endure all misery. Already have I known every mood of pain and travail, in storms and in the war. Let the coming woe be added to the count of those which have been.' The sun fell and twilight deepened as he spoke. They rose and went far into the smooth-walled cave – to its very end: and there by themselves they took their joy of one another in the way of love, all night.

When the child of the first light, rosy-fingered Dawn, appeared then Odysseus clothed himself in tunic and cloak, while Calypso flung about her a loose silver gown, filmy and flowing. She clipped a girdle of fine gold about her loins and covered the hair of her head with a snood. Then she turned to speed the going of high-hearted Odysseus.

First she gave him a great axe of cutting copper, well-suited to his reach. It was ground on both edges and into the socketed head was firmly wedged the well-rounded handle of olive-wood. Then she gave him a finished smoothing-adze and led the way to the end of the island where the trees grew tall, the alders and the poplars with heaven-scaling pines, withered long since and sapless and very dry, which would float high for him. She showed him where the loftiest trees had grown, did Calypso that fair goddess: then she returned to her cavern while he busily cut out his beams, working with despatch. Twenty trees in all he threw and axed into shape with the sharp copper, trimming them adeptly and trueing them against his straight-edge.

Then his lovely goddess brought to him augers with which he bored the logs for lashing together: firmly he fastened them with pegs and ties. As broad as a skilled shipwright would design and lay down the floor of a roomy merchantship, just so full in beam did Odysseus make his raft. To carry his upper deck he set up many ribs, closely kneed and fitted, and he united the heads of these with long rubbing-strakes, for gunwales. He put a mast into his craft, with a yard in proportion: also a stern sweep with which to steer her. To defend himself from breaching seas he fenced in the sides of the raft with wicker work, wattling it cunningly all of osiers like a basket and adding a lavish reinforcement of stanchions. Calypso came again with a bolt of cloth for sails, which he stitched strongly. Then he set up stays and sheets and halyards, and at last with levers he worked the raft down into the sacred sea.

By the fourth evening the work ended: and on the next, on the fifth day, beautiful Calypso sent him away from her island, having washed him and adorned him with sweetsmelling clothes. On his raft the goddess put provisions; one skin of dark wine, another (a very large one) of water; like-wise a leather sack of foodstuffs which included many dainties dear to his heart. She called forth a kindly warm wind in his favour. The delighted Odysseus spread wide his sail to this fair breeze and sat down by the stern oar, most skilfully steering. Nor did sleep once take possession of his eyelids, so continually he kept gazing on the Pleiades, or on Arcturus that goes down so late, or on the Great Bear (they call it also Wain) which revolves in constant narrow watch upon Orion and alone of stars will never enter the bath of ocean. Goddess Calypso had exhorted him to keep this star always on his left while he voyaged, as he did for seventeen days; and on the eighteenth day the loom of the nearest mountain top of the Phaeacian land rose up into his sight. Over the clouded face of the sea it appeared as it were a lifted shield.

Yet then the God, the Earth-Shaker, spied him from far off by the mountains of the Solymi, by which way he was returning from Aethiopia. The mind of Poseidon was mightily enraged when he saw who was sailing his sea. With a wagging of the head he began to mutter to himself, 'There now, while I have been away amongst the Aethiopians these gods have changed their mind about Odysseus. Alas, he nears the land of the Phaeacians where the decree runs that he shall escape the balance of the miseries he has encountered. However I think I can give him yet a long excursion into sorrow.'

With this he drove the clouds into a heap and, trident in hand, tossed together the desolate waters. He summoned all the violent gusts that were in all the winds and let them loose, blind-folding sea and land with storm-clouds. Night leaped into heaven. Mightily the surge rolled up, for east wind clashed upon south wind, the ill-blowing west with the north wind from the upper sky. Therefore the knees and warm heart of Odysseus shook and heavily did he commune with his own high courage.

'Ill-fated one, what is this latest misery in the path? I

fear the goddess spoke no more than truth when she said I should fill the cup of my disasters in the deep before I reached home. Surely this is the end at last. See with what storms Zeus has wreathed all his heaven and how the deep sea is moved. Squalls rush down from the four corners of the world: utter and inevitable is my doom. Thrice blessed, four times blessed were the Greeks who perished in the plain of Troy to oblige the sons of Atreus. Indeed I should have met my end and died there on that day when the throng of Trojans made me the anvil of their copper-bladed spears round the dead body of the fallen son of Peleus. So dying I should have won my funeral rites and the Achaeans would have bruited my glory: but now fate traps me in this ignoble death.'

Just as he ceased a huge rushing wave towered, toppled, and fell upon the raft, whirling it round. The winds came down confusedly in fierce turmoil and snapped the mast across in the middle. Yard and sail flew wide into the deep. Odysseus let the steering oar jerk from his hand and was himself thrown far from the raft into the body of the wave, whose weight of water long time buried him: nor did his struggles easily avail to get him out from under its wash, because of the hampering heavy clothes of honour in which divine Calypso had dressed him.

Yet at the last he did emerge, spewing bitter brine from his lips while other wet streams ran gurgling down his face. Yet not even in such dire distress did he forget his raft, but swam hard after it and caught it amongst the breaking waves and crouched down in its centre to escape, for the moment, the imminence of death.

His refuge was tossing hither and thither in the eddies of the waves, as when in autumn's stormy days the North wind pitches dried thistles along the fields, so that they lock spines into each other as they roll. Just in this way did the winds bowl the raft hither and thither across the face of the water. Sometimes the South wind flung it across to the North wind to carry, or the East wind would let the West wind chase it back.

But Ino of the slim ankles had seen him, – Ino the bright, a daughter of Cadmus. She had been born mortal in the beginning: just a simple-speaking girl: but she had attained honour amongst the gods and now was made free of wide ocean's salty depths. She pitied Odysseus so carried to and fro in anguish. Easily, like a sea gull, she rose from the level of the sea to light on the raft and say, 'Unhappy man, why is Poseidon so cruelly provoked against you as to plant these many harms in your path? Yet shall you not wholly perish, for all his eager hate. See: – if, as I think, you are understanding, this is what you must do. Strip off these clothes that are upon you and abandon the raft to go with the winds, while instead you try by swimming to gain the Phaeacian shore, your destined safety. Further, take this divine veil of mine and strain it round your chest. While you wear it you need not be harmed, or die: and afterwards, when you have solid land in your possession, unbind the veil from you and fling it far out from shore into the wine-dark sea, yourself turning away the while.'

The goddess spoke, gave him the scarf, and with bird-swiftness sprang back again into the breakers: and the blackness of the water closed over her. Then was staunch Odysseus sore perplexed, and he thus held debate in his brave heavy-laden heart: 'Travail upon travail for me. This may be some new snare set for me by a grudging goddess who would have me abandon my raft. I dare not obey her at the moment: for with my own eyes I saw how far off was the coast to which she would have me escape. Perhaps it will be my best course if, so long as the logs cling together in their setting, I remain here and put a bold face on my plight: but when the waves have battered the frame of the raft to pieces, then will I swim for it; for by that time the wit of man could not devise a better scheme.'

While his judgement and instinct pondered thus Poseidon the earth-shaker heaped up against him a wave of waves, a terror and tribulation, so high and combing it was. With this he smote him. It flung the long baulks of the raft apart as a powerful wind lays hold on a heap of dried chaff and whirls its straws everyway in confusion. Odysseus leaped astride a single beam, riding it as a man rides a plunging horse: while he tore off the clothes which had been fair Calypso's gift. Then he wrapped the veil about his breast and headlong leaped into the waves, striking out with his hands and urgently swimming. The proud Earth-shaker saw him, wagged his head and gloated to himself thus: 'Everywhere in trouble, all over the seas, wherever you go! In the end doubtless you are to slip in amongst those Zeus-favoured people and be happy: yet I trust you will never complain that your punishment has been inadequate.' He whipped up his glossy-coated horses and departed to Aegae, to his splendid place.

And now did Athene the daughter of Zeus take counter-measures. She bound fast the other winds in full career, ordering every one to be hushed and fall to sleeping: all but the impetuous North wind. Him she encouraged and by his power she laid the waves flat, that Odysseus, kinsman of Zeus, might indeed attain the sea-faring Phaeacians and escape death and the fates.

Nevertheless for two nights and two days he strayed across the waves and the currents, and many, many times did his heart presage to him of his death: but when at last

well-tressed Dawn fairly brought in the third daylight then
the gale died away and an ineffable quietness held air and
sea. Still the mighty rollers rolled: but when he was upon
the crest of one of these he happened to glance quickly up,
and behold! land was only just ahead. To Odysseus the
sight of those fields and those trees was welcome as is to
a man's children the dawning of life once again in the
father who has been outstretched on a sick bed, pining all
too long in severe agony beneath the onslaughts of some
angry power. As the children rejoice when the gods relax
their father's pain, so also did Odysseus gladly swim hard
forward to set his feet on the dry land. But when it was
no further distant than the carry of a good shout, he could
hear the heavy boom of surf against a broken shore and
see how the great billows thundered down upon the naked
coast in terrible clouds of spray which spattered all the sea
with salty foam: for here were no inlets to welcome ships,
nor roadsteads: but tall headlands, crags and cliffs. Then
did the knee-joints and courage of Odysseus fail him, and
sadly he questioned his own brave spirit: –

'Woe is me! Has Zeus let me behold this land only
to make me despair? See, I have won my way from the
depths of the tide, to find that here is no escape out of
the foaming waters. There face me walls of sheer cliff,
about which tumultuous seas clash loudly; and smooth
the rocks run up, steep-to, so that nowhere is there lodging
for my feet to bear me free from disaster. Should I try to
climb, the next wave would take me and fling me against
the broken rocks; and my effort have been in vain. As for
swimming further, on the chance of gaining some sheltered
beach or quiet inlet of the sea, then there is fear that a
fresh storm-blast may drive my groaning body again far
into the fish-haunted deep: or some god may rear up

against me leviathan from the sea: for illustrious Amphitrite breeds many such, and I have proof how the Earth-shaker, her lord, is wrought up against me.'

He was still weighing such things when a huge wave flung him upon the rugged shore. There would his flesh have been torn off him and his bones shattered had not the goddess Athene prompted him to seize the rock hastily in both hands. To it he held, sobbing, until the force of the wave had passed him by. So he evaded that danger; but afterwards the backwash enveloped him and cast him once more into deep water. Exactly as when a squid is dragged out from its bed the many pebbles come away in the suckers of its arms, so did the skin peel off Odysseus' strong hands against the stones. Then the billows closed over his head.

And there of a surety had woe-begone Odysseus died, contrary to fate's decree, had not grey-eyed Athene now given him a deeper wisdom, by light of which when he once more came to the surface he swam out beyond the breaking surf and along, closely eyeing the shore to see if he might achieve a sheltered landing by help of some spit or creek: and so swimming he encountered the mouth of a fair-running river which seemed to him the best spot, forasmuch as it was clear of reefs and sheltered from the wind. He felt then the outward-setting current of the river's flow and prayed to its god in his heart: –

'Hear me, whatever lord you be! I come to your worshipful presence, a fugitive from the threats of Poseidon – from the sea. Immune and respected even by the deathless gods, are wanderers like me, who now very weary come to your stream and knees. Have mercy upon me, Lord. I pray that my supplication be acceptable in your sight.'

Thus his petition: and the god forthwith allayed the current, smoothed out the eddies and made his way calm, safeguiding him within the river's mouths. Odysseus' knees gave way together, and his sinewy arms: for his reserve of manhood had been used up in the long fight with the salt sea. The flesh had puffed out over all his body and the sea water gushed in streams from his nostrils and mouth. Wherefore he fell helpless, not able to breathe or speak, and terrible was the weariness which possessed him.

But when at last he breathed again and some warmth rallied in his heart, then he loosed from his body the veil of the goddess and let it down into the river as it was running towards the sea. The fast current bore it back, down-stream, where lightly and gladly did Ino catch it in her hands. Then Odysseus struggled up from the river, to collapse in a bed of reeds: there he embraced the fruitful earth, the while he strove to rouse his great heart to action, saying, 'Alas, what next am I to do? What will become of me, after all? If I watch through the anxious night, here by the river, it may be that the joint severities of hoar-frost and heavy dew will be too much for my feebly-panting heart: surely the reek off the river valley will blow chill towards the dawn. Yet if I climb the slope to the dark wood and take cover there in some dense thicket, perhaps cold and its exhaustion may be spared me and a sweet sleep come on: but then I have to fear lest the wild beasts make me their prey and prize.' Yet, as he turned the choices over in his mind, this seemed the more profitable. He forced himself up into the wood which he found standing high and not far from the water. He got under a double bush, two trees with a single root: one wild olive, the other a graft of true olive. So closely did they grow together and supplement each other that through them no force of moist winds could pierce: nor could the shining of the sun cast in any ray: nor would any downpour of rain soak through.

Beneath them did Odysseus creep, and set to scraping together with his own hands a broad bed for himself: for inside there had drifted such pile of dry leaves as would have covered two or three men well enough for a winter-time, however hard the weather. When bold Odysseus saw the leaves he rejoiced and laid himself down in the midst of them and fell to pouring the litter by handfulls over his body, till he was covered: – even as a neighbourless man in a lonely steading, before he goes forth covers his charring log under black wood-cinders: and thus hoards all day against his return, a seed of flame, which otherwise he would have had to seek for himself from some other place. Just so did Odysseus lie while Athene shed down sleep upon his eyes, to shroud the dear eyelids and the sooner deliver him from the pains of his weakness.

BOOK 6

So at last long-suffering Odysseus yielded to his weariness and slept there; while Athene proceeded to the district and chief town of the Phaeacian people. These had formerly occupied broad lands in Hypereia near the Cyclopes, that race of rude bullies who, being brawnier than the Phaeacians, were wont to plunder them. Wherefore god-like Nausithous rose up and removed his people to Scheria beyond reach of the world's covetousness. There he threw a wall around the new town-site and built houses and erected temples to the gods and apportioned the plough-lands.

Nausithous in due time yielded to fate, and went down to Hades: so now Alcinous reigned; wisely, for the gods prompted him. Therefore it was to his house that the goddess, grey-eyed Athene, descended to plan the reception of great-hearted Odysseus: and of his house she chose to enter the precious room where slept Nausicaa, daughter of royal Alcinous, a girl beautiful as an immortal in nature and form. Beside her, on each side of the entry, slept two hand-maidens whom the Graces had blessed with the gift of loveliness: and the gleaming doors were shut. Yet through them Athene swept like a sharp wind to the girl's head.

For the sake of her message the goddess had assumed the likeness of a playmate of Nausicaa's own age and dear to her, the daughter of Dymas a famous sea captain. In this character then the grey-eyed Athene said: –

'O Nausicaa, how careless has your mother's daughter grown! These rich clothes all lie neglected, while your marriage season draws near: and that is the very time when you must clothe yourself rarely and have other things to give those who will take you in the bridal procession. By trifles like these is a good name won in the world, and fathers and mothers made proudly happy.

'Therefore let us go washing to-morrow at the break of day: for I will lend you my aid, as fellow-worker, that you may be the sooner decked ready for that near time when you shall cease to be a maid. Do not the best lads of the Phaeacians, your kith and kin throughout the country-side, already ask your hand? So remember now to beg your father, first thing in the morning, to give you the mules and a waggon big enough to hold the men's body-wrappers and your dresses and the glossy bed-covers. It will be better if you ride in it, too: for the washing pools are a very long foot-journey from the town.'

Having thus fulfilled her purpose Athene went away to Olympus where evermore they say the seat of the gods stays sure: for the winds shake it not, nor is it wetted by rain, nor approached by any snow. All around stretches the cloudless firmament, and a white glory of sunlight is diffused about its walls. There the blessed gods are happy all their days: and thither, accordingly, repaired the grey-eyed One after clearly imparting her message to the maiden.

High-throned Dawn came to rouse Nausicaa of the goodly robe. She, waking, wondered at her dream and went straight through the house to tell her dear father and mother.

She found them within. Her mother sat by the hearth with her serving women, twirling on the distaff yarn which had been dipped in sea-purple dye: while her father she crossed in the doorway as he went out to consult with the illustrious princes of the people – a council to which the noblest of the Phaeacians had summoned them. She went near to this father she loved, that she might softly say: –

'Dear Father, will you not let me have the deep easy-wheeled waggon, that I may take all the good soiled clothes that lie by me to the river for washing? It is only right that you, whenever you go to sit in council with the leaders, should have clean linen to wear next your skin: while of your five sons begotten in the house only two have taken wives: and the three merry bachelors are always wanting clothes newly washed when they go out to dances. Thinking about all these things is one of my mind's cares.'

So much she said, too shy to name to her dear father the near prospect of her marriage: but he saw everything and answered in a word: 'My child, I do not grudge you mules, or anything. Go: the bondsmen will get you the tall, light waggon with the high tilt.'

As he spoke he called his men, who obeyed. They brought the easy-running mule cart to the outside of the palace and led forth the mules and yoked them to it, while the girl was carrying down the gay clothes from her bed-chamber and heaping them into the smooth-sided cart. The mother packed tasty meats in a travelling-box; all sorts of good things to eat, including relishes: and filled a goat-skin with wine. Then as her daughter climbed into the cart she gave to her a golden phial of limpid olive oil, that she and the hand-maidens might anoint themselves after bathing. Nausicaa took up the whip and the polished reins. She struck the beasts to start them: there came a clitter-clatter from the mules who laid vigorously into the collar and bore off the linen and the girl – not alone, of course: her maids went too.

At journey's end they came to the flowing stream of the lovely river and found the washing-places, within which from beneath there bubbled up such abundance of clear water that its force was sufficient to clean the very dirtiest things. There they loosed the mules from the cart and drove them down to the rippling water, where was honey-sweet herbage for their cropping. Then they took the garments from the waggon in armfuls and laid them in the shadowed water of the washing pools: where they danced on them in emulation, each striving to out-knead the rest. Afterward, when all the dirt was worked right out, they stretched the linen wide and smooth upon the foreshore, even on the pure shingle where the sea had washed it clean.

The work being done they fell to bathing, and then anointed themselves to sleekness with their olive oil before carrying their provisions to a nook which overlooked the sea; where they ate and waited as the clothes lay out in the sunlight drying. The food having satisfied their appetites the hand-maids and their young mistress next threw off their scarves and turned to playing with a ball. The white forearms of Nausicaa, leading the chorus, beat time for this ball-dance. She moved with them, as arrow-loving Artemis goes down the mountain-steeps of supreme Taygetus or Erymanthus when she is pleased to chase wild boars or flying stags with all her rout of nymphs (those shy ones, daughters of our lord of the aegis, Zeus): and then the heart of her mother Leto delights in Artemis for that she bears her head so high, and her brows, and moves carelessly notable among them all where all are beautiful – even so did this chaste maiden outshine her maids.

When at last it was time for her to fare homeward they set to yoking-in the mules and folding the fair garments: then the grey-eyed goddess Athene took thought how to arouse Odysseus from sleep that he might see the fair maiden who should lead him to the city where the Phaeacians lived: – which was why, when the girl next flung the ball to one of her retinue, she threw wide of her and put the ball into a deep eddy. Whereat their shrieks echoed far: and awoke great Odysseus who sat up and brooded dully in his heart and head. 'Alack now, and in what land of men do I find myself? Will they be inhospitable and savagely unjust; or kind to strangers, of godfearing nature? How it plays round me, this shrilling of girls or of nymphs who hold the inaccessible heads of the mountains and the springs of rivers and water-meadows of rich grass. By the voices I do think them human. Let me go forward, and if I can see. . .

Thus muttering Odysseus crept out from his bushes, snapping off in his powerful hands from the thick tree one very leafy shoot with which to shield from sight the maleness of his body. So he sallied forth, like the mountain-bred lion exulting in his strength, who goes through rain and wind with burning eyes. After great or small cattle he prowls, or the wild deer. If his belly constrain him he will even attempt the sheep penned in solid manors.

So boldly did Odysseus, stark naked as he was, make to join the band of maidens: for necessity compelled him. None the less he seemed loathsome in their sight because of his defilement with the sea-wrack; and in panic they ran abroad over all the spits of the salt beaches. Only the daughter of Alcinous remained; for Athene had put courage into her heart and taken terror from her limbs so that she stood still, facing him, while Odysseus wondered whether he had better clasp her knees and entreat this handsome girl or stand away by himself and cajole her with such honeyed words as should bring her to clothe his necessity and introduce him within her city. Even as he weighed these courses, it seemed to him most likely to benefit him if he stood off and coaxed her: for by taking the girl's knees he might outrage her modesty. Wherefore he began in soft wheedling phrase—

'I would be suppliant at your knees, O Queen: yet am I in doubt whether you are divine or mortal. If a goddess from high heaven, then Artemis you must be, the daughter of great Zeus and your nearest peer in form, stature and parts. But if you are human, child of some dweller on this earth of ours, then thrice blessed your father and lady mother, thrice blessed your family! What happy joy in your regard must warm their hearts each time they see this slip of perfection joining in the dance: and blessed above all men in his own sight will be that most fortunate one who shall prevail in bridal gifts and lead you to his home! Never, anywhere, have I set eyes on such a one, not man nor woman. Your presence awes me. Yet perhaps once, in Delos, I did see the like – by the altar of Apollo where had sprung up just a slip of a palm-tree. For I have been at Delos, in my time, with many men to follow me on this quest which has ended for me so sorrily. However as I said, there by the altar of Apollo, when I saw this palm-sapling my heart stood still in amaze. It was the straightest spear of a tree that ever shot up from the ground. Likewise at you, Lady, do I wonder. With amazement and exceeding fear would I fain take your knees. I am in such misery. Only yesterday, after twenty days, did I escape from the wine-dark sea. That long the surges have been throwing me about, and the tearing storms, all the way from the island of Ogygia. And now some power has flung me on this shore where also it is likely I shall suffer hurt. I dare not yet look for relief. Before that comes the gods will have inflicted on me many another pain.

'Yet, O Queen, have pity. The sport of many evils I come to you, to you first of all, for of the many others who hold this town and land I know not a soul. Show me the city: give me a rag to fling about my body – the wrapper of your washing bundle would do, if you brought one here – and to you may the Gods requite all your heart's desire; husband, house, and especially ingenious accord within that house: for there is nothing so good and lovely as when man and wife in their home dwell together in unity of mind and disposition. A great vexation it is to their enemies and a feast of gladness to their friends: surest of all do they, within themselves, feel all the good it means.'

To him replied Nausicaa of the white arms: 'Stranger – for to me you seem no bad or thoughtless man – it is Zeus himself who assigns bliss to men, to the good and to the evil as he wills, to each his lot. Wherefore surely he gave you this unhappiness and you must bear it: but inasmuch as you have attained our place you shall not lack clothing nor the other things which are the due of a battered suppliant, when he has been received. I will show you the city and name those you see there. The town and the district belong to the Phaeacians whose strength and might are vested in Alcinous, their king: and I am his daughter.'

She spoke, and cried orders after her maidens with the braided hair. 'Rally to me, women. Why run because you see a man? You cannot think him an enemy. There lives not, nor shall there live, a man to come upon this Phaeacian land to ravage it. The gods love the Phaeacians too well. Also we are very remote in the dashing seas, the ultimate race of men: wherefore no other peoples have affairs with us. This man appeals as a luckless wanderer whom we must now kindly entertain. Homeless and broken men are all of them in the sight of Zeus, and it is a good deed to make them some small alms: wherefore, my maids, give our bedesman food and drink and cleanse him in the river at some spot shielded from the wind.' So she said. Slowly they stood firm, and each to the other repeated her order. Soon they had set Odysseus in the sheltered place according to the word of Nausicaa, daughter of large-minded Alcinous. They laid out clothes, a loose mantle with a tunic, and gave to him their pure oil in its golden phial and urged him to be washed in the waters of the river: but noble Odysseus up and spoke to the serving maids, saying, 'Handmaidens, stand you thus far off, in order that I may myself cleanse my body of the sea-stains and anoint it with oil. Too long has my skin been a stranger to ointment. Yet in your sight I will not bathe. I am shy of my nakedness among maidens so carefully tressed.' Thus he said: and they went to tell it to their young mistress.

Meanwhile great Odysseus in the river scrubbed the salt crust from the flesh of his back and broad shoulders and cleaned his hair of the frothy scum dried in it from the infertile sea. When he had so thoroughly washed and anointed himself smoothly and put on the clothes given him by the girl, then did Athene daughter of Zeus contrive to make him seem taller and stronger, and from his head she led down the curls of his hair in hyacinthine tendrils. As when some master craftsman (trained by Hephaestus and made wise by Pallas Athene in all the resources of his art) washes his silver work with molten gold and betters it into an achievement that is a joy for ever – just so did the goddess gild his head and shoulders with nobility. Then he went far apart and sat down by the margin of the sea, radiant with graciousness and glory, so that the girl in wonder said to her well-coiffed maidens:

'Hush now and listen, my white-armed attendants, while I speak. Not all the gods inhabiting Olympus have opposed the entering in of this man among the sanctified Phaeacians. At first he appeared to me not a seemly man: but now he is like the gods of spacious heaven. O that such a man might settle contentedly in our city, and agree to be called my husband! But come now, women, give the stranger food and drink.'

They most willingly obeyed. They placed refreshment before daring divine Odysseus who had been so long without tasting food that he fell upon it and ate and drank greedily: while Nausicaa of the white arms passed to her next concern. The folded clothes were duly restored to the splendid waggon and the strong-hoofed mules harnessed up. Then the maiden mounted and calling Odysseus spoke to this intent.

'Rouse yourself now, Stranger, to go as far as the city, where I shall show you the house of my wise-thinking father: in whose halls, as I assure you, acquaintance with all the best of the Phaeacians will be yours. Yet have a special care to do as follows if, as I think, you are a man of judgement. While we are passing people's fields and country-places do you march briskly forward with my maids after the mules and their cart. I will lead the way, so far: but at the entering in of the city – easy to know for its high towers – a good haven lies on either hand and the fairway between them is narrow, for it is lined by the swelling hulls of ships berthed or drawn up high and dry in the spaces allotted each ship-owner for his vessels. There is the assembly-ground round the temple of Poseidon, and it is fitted with stone slabs very solidly pitched into the earth.

Hereabout they manufacture tackle for the black ships, cables and canvas: also they shave down the blades of oars. For know that amongst us Phaeacians the bow and the quiver get no honour. All delight is in masts and ships' oars and trim vessels in which to cross the foaming sea.

'I shrink, stranger, from the rude scoffing of these seafarers: lest someone later chide me – there are too many ill-natured tongues amongst the crowd – lest some rascal accuse me, sneering, "Who is this grand tall stranger following Nausicaa? where did she pick him up? He will be the husband, doubtless, to her taste. Some wandering castaway of a foreigner rescued off a ship, perhaps: for we have no neighbours of that sort. Or he may be some god who after long entreaty has come down from heaven to answer her, and keep her for ever and ever. Good riddance, if she has dug out some mate for her own from somewhere: for she has never seen good in Phaeacians of her own sort, the many young excellencies who have courted her.' Thus will they speak, and these things become a reproach to me: indeed I too would blame another girl who did such things as consort with men before she had come to public marriage, against the will of her friends while her father and mother were still alive.

'Therefore, stranger, consider well these directions from me that you may secure from my father your earliest safe-conduct and carriage homeward. You will find a stately grove of Athene near the road: a grove of black poplars. Within it is an eye of water: and about it meadows. That is an estate of my father's and his abundant garden, no further from the town than a man's voice can carry. Sit in it and wait, while we pass into the city and attain my father's house. Then, when you judge me home, do you enter the city of the Phaeacians and ask for the palace of my father, Alcinous the Generous. It is easily to be distinguished, or the veriest child will guide you to it. In no way worthy to be compared therewith is the style of the citizens' houses: not like the palace of King Alcinous.

'But when the buildings and court have swallowed you up, then hurry your fastest through the great hall, till you find my mother. She will be sitting at the hearth in a glare of firelight spinning yarn tinctured with sea-purple, a marvel to the eye. Her chair will be backed against a pillar and her maidens all orderly behind her. My father's throne is propped beside hers, and on it he sits, drinking his wine and sitting like an immortal. Pass him by and throw your hands about my mother's knees, if you wish to ensure the dawning, fair and soon, of the day of your return. For no matter how distant your land, if only my mother favours your impression in her heart you may hope to see your friends and come to your stately home and fatherland.' She ceased and struck the mules with her shining whip. Quickly they left the valley of the river and neatly their feet plaited in and out as they paced onward, with Nausicaa reining them in and laying on the whip discreetly, so that her attendants and Odysseus could keep up with them on foot. The sun sank and they were at the famous grove dedicated to Athene, where Odysseus tarried and at once prayed a prayer to the daughter of great Zeus.

'Hear me, Unwearied One, child of Zeus who holds the Aegis. Especially I pray you now to hear me, forasmuch as you did not lately when I was broken – when there broke me the famous Earth-shaker. Give me to find love and pity among the Phaeacians.'

So he prayed. Pallas Athene heard him but would not yet show herself to him, face to face, out of respect for her father's brother, whose furious rage against Odysseus lasted till he regained his own shore.

BOOK 7

Wherefore proud Odysseus waited in his place and prayed, all the time that her two strong mules were drawing the girl into the city as far as the palace of her illustrious father. Before its door she halted: her brothers, men like gods, came out and clustered round her. They freed the mules from the wagon and carried the washed clothes into the house: but she went up to her room, where a fire had been lit for her by the old woman of Aperaea, her chambermaid, whose name was Eurymedusa and who had been captured from Aperaea during a raid over-sea. Afterwards she had been set aside as prize of honour for Alcinous, because he was supreme ruler among the Phaeacians, obeyed by the common people as if he were a god. She had tended the infancy of white-armed Nausicaa in the palace; and now was wont to kindle the fire and lay her supper in her bower.

At length Odysseus bestirred himself and moved towards the city: whereupon Athene for the love she bore him muffled his shape in a wreath of mist to prevent any swaggering Phaeacian from standing in his road and trying by jeers and questions to find out who he was. For further care there met him in the entrance of the gracious town

Athene herself, grey-eyed and goddess but now subdued to the likeness of a quite young girl bearing a water-jar. She hesitated, when she was very near him, and of her Odysseus begged, 'Child, will you not guide me to the dwelling of Alcinous, King over the people here? I am a stranger and have met and endured sore tribulation on my way from a distant land. Nor do I know this people, not one citizen or house-holder from among them all.' To him the Goddess answered: 'Very readily, father and stranger, will I show you the house you want, the more so because it stands next to my revered father's home. Yet I pray you to follow me in dead silence along the way I show, not staring at any men we meet, nor accosting them. The people here are short with strangers and do not use any love towards foreigners. Their trust is in the swiftness of their ships (a grace granted them by the Earth-shaker) in which they overpass the deepest seas with the speed of wings or of a thought.' Upon this exhortation Athene tripped forward hastily, Odysseus treading so closely in the divine footsteps that the Phaeacians, those famous seamen, were not aware of his passage through their midst. The goddess, remote and awful beneath her coronal of hair, forbade their knowing it; out of her heart's friendliness towards him she closed about him that supernatural mist.

Odysseus was astonished at the havens and ships he saw; as at the assembly-grounds of the heroes. Astonishment took him also at the long, lofty walls with palisades atop: a marvellous sight: but when they reached the famous palace of the king, Athene again broke into speech: –

'This is the house, venerable stranger, which you asked me to point out. Within it you shall find kings, god-children of Zeus, feasting in the hall. Thrust in fearlessly: however foreign a man may be, in every crisis it is the high face which will carry him through. Haply you may light first upon the Queen (Arete her name) whose lineage is the same as the King's, a line which began in Nausithous, son of Poseidon the Earth-shaker by Periboea, the fairest woman of her time. She was the youngest daughter of magnificent Eurymedon, anciently king of the too-proud giants, whom he served to destroy in their impiety; yet with their destruction was himself destroyed. Poseidon however lay with the daughter, who conceived this son, large-hearted Nausithous, afterwards king of the Phaeacians. Nausithous begat two sons, Rhexenor and Alcinous, of whom Rhexenor died soon after marriage, smitten by the silver archer, Apollo; and left no son, but one daughter Arete, an infant. Her, later, Alcinous made his consort, treating her as no woman on earth has been entreated, with consideration above the lot of all wives who keep house for their men. So she has been and is honoured amazingly in her dear children's eyes; as by Alcinous her lord and by all his people, who revere her as divine and acclaim her devoutly whenever she makes progress through the city. Nor is she less gifted in qualities of mind. She will resolve the disputes of those for whom she has countenance, even when the affair is an affair of men. If she can be brought to look kindly upon you, then may you entertain real hope of again seeing your friends, your lofty house and native land.'

With this saying Athene left him. She left lovely Scheria, and went over the sterile sea to Marathon and the broad ways of Athens, where she entered the massive house of Erectheus. Odysseus the while lingered before the gate of Alcinous' renowned dwelling. He stood there, not crossing its copper threshold, because of the host of thoughts thronging his heart. Indeed the brilliance within the high-ceiled rooms of noble Alcinous was like the sheen of sun or moon: for the inner walls were copper-plated in sections, from the entering in to the furthest recesses of the house; and the cornice which ran around them was glazed in blue. Gates of gold closed the great house: the door posts which stood up from the brazen threshold were of silver, and silver, too, was the lintel overhead: while the handle of the door was gold. Each side the porch stood figures of dogs ingeniously contrived by Hephaestus the craftsman out of gold and silver, to be ageless, undying watch-dogs for this house of great-hearted Alcinous. Here and there along the walls were thrones, spaced from the inmost part to the outer door. Light, well-woven draperies made by the women of the house were flung over these thrones, and on them the chiefs of the Phaeacians would sit to drink and eat: for the hospitality of the palace was unstinting. The feasters in the great hall after dark were lighted by the flaring torches which golden figures of youths, standing on well-made pedestals, held in their hands. Of the fifty women servants who maintain this house, some are ever sitting to grind the golden grain in querns, some weave at the looms, while others sit carding wool upon distaffs which flutter like the leaves of a tall poplar: and so close is the texture of their linen that even fine oil will not pass through it. For just as the seamen of Phaeacia are the skilfullest of human kind in driving a swift ship through the water, so are their women marvellous artists in weaving. Athene gave them this genius to make beautiful things.

From outside the court, by its entry, extends a great garden of four acres, fenced each way. In it flourish tall trees: pears or pomegranates, stone fruits gaudy with their ripening load, also sweet figs and heavy-bearing olives. The fruit of these trees never blights or fails to set, winter and summer, through all the years. A west wind blows there perpetually, maturing one crop and making another. Pear grows old upon pear and apple upon apple, with bunch after bunch of grapes and fig after fig. Here, too, a fertile vineyard has been planted for the King. A part of this lies open to the sun, whose rays bake its grapes to raisins, while men gather ripe grapes from the next part and in a third part tread out the perfected vintage in wine-presses. On one side are baby grapes whose petals yet fall; on another the clusters empurple towards full growth. Beyond the last row of trees, well laid garden plots have been arranged, blooming all the year with flowers. And there are two springs, one led throughout the orchard-ground, whilst the other dives beneath the sill of the great court to gush out beside the stately house: from it the citizens draw their water. Such were the noble gifts the gods had lavished upon the palace of Alcinous.

Great Odysseus stood there and gazed: but when he had studied all and seen it with his understanding, swiftly he passed the threshold and was swallowed up within the house. He found the chiefs and leaders of the Phaeacians emptying their beakers to the keen-eyed slayer of Argus: for it is their custom, when their minds turn towards bed, to pour a last cup of the night to Hermes. He strode across the hall, and the thick vapour which Athene had condensed about his form wrapped him round till he came to Arete and King Alcinous. Then Odysseus threw his arms about the knees of Arete. The god-given mist rolled back from him: throughout the house men's voices failed them when they saw the hero there. They gaped, dumb-founded; and Odysseus prayed: –

'O Arete, daughter of godlike Rhexenor, to your husband and to your knees I come, in my extremity. And to these guests too. May the gods give them happiness, while they live; and permit each to hand down his goods and houses to his children, together with such consideration as the world has rendered him. But for me, I pray you, hasten my despatch by the quickest way to my native place. Now for so long have I been sundered from my friends and in torment.' After speaking he crouched down on the hearth among the ashes of the fire: and for a time the hall was very still.

At last there sounded the voice of manful old Echeneus, an elder Phaeacian who excelled in speaking and knew the ancient wisdom. Heartily he addressed them, protesting as follows: 'Alcinous, it does not conduce to your credit, nor is it right that this stranger should sit upon the ground among the ashes of our hearth. Yet must every other voice hold back, awaiting your lead. Up then, and set the stranger on a silver-studded throne. Command the servers to mix wine ready for us, that we may pour offerings to Zeus the thunder-lover, patron of all self-respecting suppliants; and let your housekeeper give the stranger a supper of whatever she has at hand within.'

When Alcinous the consecrated king had heard this counsel, he took deep, devious Odysseus and raised him from the hearth to the seat nearest himself, a silver-studded throne from which he displaced Laodamas, his own well-grown son whom he dearly loved. The serving woman from her rich golden ewer poured the water for rinsing hands over its silver basin, and drew up a polished table on which the sober housekeeper displayed her bread and many dainties, freely offering all the cheer she had. Grave Odysseus drank and ate: and then the king's majesty commanded the herald: 'Pontonous, dilute us wine in the mixing bowl and hand round drink to all in the house, that we may pour general libation to Zeus the thunder-lover, who tends all deserving suppliants.'

He spoke. Pontonous mixed the honeyed wine and served afresh to each man's drinking cup. They poured forth and afterward drank their hearts' fill, when Alcinous again addressed them, beginning: 'Hear me, you leaders of the Phaeacians in peace and war, while I declare the prompting of my heart. We have feasted: and now it is fitting that you go home and woo your beds. In the morning let us summon a larger gathering of elders and fulfil for this stranger in our guest-hall the whole rite of hospitality, together with worthy sacrifice to the gods: and after these ceremonies let us deliberate upon his escort, to see how we may quit him of further travail and accident and ensure his blissful return home, instantly. This home may be very far away: none the less we must guard him from evils or penalties in mid-passage, and until he disembarks on his native land. Once there, our part is done. He must suffer whatever haps the grave Fates spun for him in his thread of life, when his mother bore him. Perhaps, though, he is one of the immortals come down from heaven? Yet, if so, have the gods utterly changed their grace towards us. Always in the past they have been wont to appear plainly, after we had consummated some outstanding sacrifice; and plainly would they feast with us, sitting in our midst in their true forms. Why, even when a simple traveller journeying alone has happened upon a god, it has been a manifest undisguised God: after all, are we not their near of kin, near as the Cyclopes or the lawless tribe of Giants?'

Then subtle Odysseus took up the word and answered him thus: 'Alcinous, think some other thought than this! I am not like the Immortals of spacious heaven, either in my body or in my nature, which are altogether mortal and bound to suffer death. Think, rather, of those men who in your experience have been most vexed with pains and griefs: for it is to them that I would liken myself in my miseries. Indeed I might drool on and on, telling the tale of all that I have suffered, of the manifold trials inflicted on me by the will of the Gods. But instead I will ask leave to obey my instincts and fall upon this supper, as I would do despite my burden of woe. See now, there is not anything so exigent as a man's ravening belly, which will not let him alone to feel even so sore a grief as this grief in my heart; but prefers to overwhelm his misery with its needs for meat and drink, forcibly and shamelessly compelling him to put its replenishment above his soul's agony. None the less will I beseech you to be stirring at the break of day, to scheme how you may put this unlucky, toil-worn self of mine ashore in the land of my fathers. Let life leave me then – so that my dying eyes behold my property, my men and my wide stately house.'

So he said. All men applauded the speech and cried that indeed the stranger must be sent on to his home, as he so justly claimed. By now had they offered and drunk to the fill of their bent, so away went the company homeward to sleep, leaving great Odysseus, with Arete and Alcinous sitting by him, in the hall where the serving women went to and fro clearing away the plenishings of the feast. Forthwith Arete began a questioning, for she had recognised the tunic and cloak upon Odysseus as part of the goodly raiment which she and her maidens were used to fashion. So she flung at him these searching words: 'Stranger, this have I to ask of you, from myself; first, What man are you, and where from? Who gave you those clothes? Your tale to us just now was of your coming here from adventure in the deep.'

Resourceful Odysseus answered: 'It is grievous for me, O Queen, to give you a connected history of my pains: the celestial gods have given me too many. Yet this I will say to meet your questioning. There is an island, Ogygia, lying afar in the ocean, and in it the daughter of Atlas, subtle fair-haired Calypso, dwells. She is divine, and strange: no one, either of gods or men, has traffic with her. However, it was a divine power which carried my hapless self into her house-hold – myself alone: for Zeus had let drive with a dazzling thunder-bolt at our good ship and riven it in the wine-dark unbounded sea. All my good comrades died then: only I clung with both arms about the keel of the curved ship and rode it for nine days. On the tenth, in black night, the gods brought me near to this island, Ogygia, where was Calypso. The awesome goddess took me in and loved me passionately and tended me, vowing that she would make me immortal and ageless for ever and ever. Withal she did not wholly beguile the heart in my breast. Nevertheless for seven years did I endure, years without end. Ever I would water with my tears the clothes (immortal clothes) in which Calypso did me honour. But when the eighth year had duly come, then suddenly she ordered and hastened my going. I know not if some message reached her from Zeus, or if her own inclination at last had changed.

'It was on a raft, most firmly put together, that she despatched me, loaded with gifts; food and sweet liquor and divine clothes to wear: also there was a warm mild wind to favour me, before which I sailed for seventeen days, and for the eighteenth until the hill-crests of your land loomed up through the haze. My heart exulted – too soon: for it was written that I should yet know the further dour griefs allotted me by Poseidon the Earth-shaker, who stirred up the winds to block my passage and raised such seas as not even the gods could tell of. The breakers raged so that they unseated my unhappy self from the raft I rode.

Yes, the squalls scattered its beams every way: while for me, I swam with my hands, swam right across the gulf, until between wind and water I approached your coast. There I was climbing out upon the beach when a wave violently took me and flung me against the huge reefs of this dreadful shore. Wherefore I had to give up that plan and swim back, till I found a river mouth which looked to me auspicious for a second attempt, seeing that it was free of rocks and covered from the wind. So it proved. I escaped out and began to collect my courage: then immortal night came down.

'I left behind me the heaven-watered river and struck into the underwood where I slept marvellously well under a pile of leaves. For the God poured down over me, the heart-sick and sorry, so profound a sleep that there I slept all that night among the leaves, and the next morning and half that day. As a fact, the sun was going down the west before that sweet sleep let me go – to discern the attendants of your daughter playing on the beach, with her in their midst, like any goddess. I supplicated her. She proved the mistress of a sounder judgement than is to be expected of the young: the coming generation is so commonly thought-less. However, she gave me a fill of bread and sparkling wine, and a wash in the river and these clothes you see. Now I have told you the truth, though it put me in disfavour.'

Alcinous replied, 'Stranger, where my daughter's thought fell short of your desert in this was that she did not bring you here to our place directly, in her train. It was her duty, as the one to whom you first appealed.' Odysseus at no loss answered: 'Hero, blame not the blameless maiden therein. She did tell me to follow with her attendants, but I shrank from it lest I be disgraced if your heart took offence

at the sight of me there. We sons of men are in our genera-
tion so exceeding suspicious.' To which Alcinous cried out:
'Stranger, this heart of mine is not so light in my breast as
to be moved for an idle cause. Yet I grant you that it is
better to observe a certain seemliness in all things. Ah me!
by Zeus the Father, and Athene and Apollo! Would there
might be found some man like you, my double in niceness
and sentiment, to accept my daughter and the name of my
son-in-law, and to live here for good. It would delight me
to provide house and property, if you would stay! Yet fear
not that any one of us Phaeacians will detain you here by
foul means. It would not be pleasing in the sight of Zeus.
On the contrary, that you may know for certain, I shall
here and now fix the actual day of your going. To-morrow,
let it be. To-morrow you shall lie down and slumber
soundly, while the oars of your crew smite the smooth sea,
bringing you all the way to your land and house, those
things you love. It matters not how far they be: let them
be further than Euboea, which some of our fellows maintain
is the last land of the world. Euboea they saw when they
took pale Rhadamanthus to meet Tityus, the son of Earth.
They reached it effortlessly, so attaining their goal in the
one day: and got right the way home here, too. Let your
heart understand from this the surpassing goodness of my
ships, and how my lads churn the salt sea with their
oar-blades.'

So he said: Odysseus became happy. He opened his
mouth and prayed a short prayer, invoking the God:
'All-father Zeus, grant it that Alcinous fulfils all things even
as he says: then may his glory never be dimmed on this
bountiful earth, and I come to my own.' In such wise they
talked among themselves, till white-armed Arete told her
maids to arrange bedsteads under the sun-porch, piling

them with fine purple blankets, over which were rugs, and thick mantles on top of all as upper covering. Away went the women from the hall, torch in hand. Diligently they smoothed the soft couch and then summoned Odysseus, standing by his chair and murmuring: 'Rise up now and come to sleep, Stranger. Your bed is prepared.' When he heard their saying he felt that sleep would be right welcome. So he slept there, did tried Odysseus, on his fretted and inlaid bedstead under the echoing porch: but Alcinous retired into the depths of the great house where in his place his lady wife had also laid out bed and bedding.

BOOK 8

At the first show of Dawn, great Alcinous left his couch, as did that ravager of cities, Odysseus, kinsman of Zeus. The anointed King led him to the formal meeting place of the Phaeacians, where it had been contrived amongst the shipping. There they sat them down side by side on benches of polished stone: while Pallas Athene in the guise of the King's herald went up and down the city furthering her scheme for getting brave Odysseus home. She accosted for a moment everyone she met, saying urgently: 'Go across now to the council, all you leaders of the Phaeacians, wise men and warriors; there to make up your minds upon this stranger who has just come in from wandering through the deep, and claims the hospitality of our wise Alcinous: he has an air with him, like the Deathless Ones.' By such words she sharpened the zeal and curiosity of everyone, so that in a trice the standing ground and seats were thronged with burgesses. To many of these the look of Laertes' cunning son was wonderful: for Athene had endued his head and shoulders with a benediction of glory, and made his figure tower up and bulk to fill the eye. The goddess would have him win the love of every Phaeacian, and their reverence and awe: and therefore had empowered him to perform miracles of strength when they put him to the test.

After all men were assembled in their places, Alcinous lifted up his voice and said: 'Hear me, leaders of the Phaeacians in war and peace, as I utter the bidding of my heart. This stranger (for I know him not) has wandered into my house with no one to vouch for him: not even to say if he is from the peoples of the dawn or of the sunset. He asks a passage, and presses that it be assured him: and I say that according to precedent we should hasten his going. Never, never shall any visitor to my house linger there in distress for want of setting forward. Wherefore let us pull a black ship down to the sacred sea, a new ship for the maiden voyage, and choose from among the people fifty-two young oarsmen of proven excellence; and these shall be their present orders: "Lash the sweeps firmly into place by the benches: then make haste ashore, every one of you, back to my house where by my care you shall find a banquet ready for your falling-to." Unto the rest, to the sceptred kings, I would say, "Repair now to my goodly house; there will we kindly entertain the stranger in the great hall." Let no one of you fail this tryst. Nay, further, let some one bid to the gathering our divine minstrel Demodocus, to whom the God has given such gift of music that he charms his hearers with every song to which his heart is moved.'

The King ceased and led on. The sceptred ones followed him and a herald sought the godlike musician, whilst the chosen youths, the fifty and two, went down to the brink of the waste of waters. When they were arrived at the sea and the ship they launched the black hull into the briny deep, stepped the mast, carried her sails aboard, and fixed the sweeps into their raw-hide loops, all proper.

They bent the white sails and moored her, high-riding on the swell. Afterward they took their way to the palace of profound Alcinous, whose courts and galleries and rooms were now all a press of men, citizens of every age having thronged in. To entertain them Alcinous devoted twelve sheep, eight boars with gleaming tusks, and two heavy-gaited oxen, which they flayed and prepared busily for a heart-warming feast.

The herald came to hand leading the beloved minstrel, whom the Muse did especially love: yet had her gifts to him been mixed, both good and evil. She had taken from him the sight of his eyes, and given him a power of harmony. Pontonous backed a silver-studded throne against a tall pillar in the midst of the feasters and set it for the musician and put him on it; then hung the resonant lyre on a peg above him and guided his hand to the place, so that later he might know to reach it down. Beside him he set a food basket and a goodly table and a wine-cup ready, that he might drink as his spirit prompted. The company plunged hands into the bounty provided, until they had satisfied their lust for drink and meat. Then the Muse pricked the musician on to sing of the great deeds of heroes, as they were recounted in verses whose fame had already filled the skies: telling of the feud between Odysseus and Achilles son of Peleus, and how once at a splendid feast of the gods they had accused each other with terrible words; whereat the king of men, Agamemnon, secretly was glad, gleeful that the best of the Achaeans thus fell out: because Phoebus Apollo had prophesied it to him that day Agamemnon crossed the precinct of naked rock at most holy Pytho to consult his oracle. Those were the beginnings of that tide of sorrow which was to whelm down Trojans and Danaans alike; as Zeus, the all-mighty, willed.

Of this was the song of the very famous minstrel: but Odysseus with two strong hands drew the broad purple cloak over his head to hide his goodly face. He was ashamed to let the tears well from his deep-set eyes publickly before the Phaeacians. Each time the divine singer broke off his song Odysseus dashed away the tears, freed his head from the cloak, and poured from his loving cup a libation to the God. But as soon as the song began again, at the bidding of the Phaeacian chiefs to whom the verses were unalloyed delight, then would Odysseus again hide his head and stifle his sobs. The other company failed to see how his tears ran down: only Alcinous remarked it, for he sat next him, and could not but notice and overhear his deep-drawn agony. Wherefore at an early chance he broke in upon the oar-loving Phaeacians: 'Pay heed, champions and councillors. We are glutted with feasting together and with the lyre which is the complement of splendid food. Instead let us sally out and divert ourselves with feats of strength, that when the stranger goes home he may tell his friends how we surpass others in boxing and wrestling and jumping and foot-racing.'

He spoke and went out. They followed. The herald hung the sounding lyre upon its peg, took Demodocus by the hand, and led him forth from the hall by the way which the other Phaeacian leaders had taken to witness the exercises. An immense company, a concourse of thousands, followed them to the appointed place: and many gallant youths stood up as contestants. Acroneus rose up and Ocyalus and Elatreus; Nauteus and Prymneus with Anchialus and Eretmeus; Ponteus, Proreus, Thoon and Anabesineus with Amphialus son of Polyneus son of Tekton: also Euryalus son of Naubolus (the match of deadly Ares) who in face and proportions excelled all the Phaeacians except noble Laodamas. Three sons of royal Alcinous stood up also, Laodamas, Halius and god-like Clytoneus.

Their first trial was of running: the course was laid out straight from its start, for speed. The field of them raced across the flat land in a storm of dust. However noble Clytoneus surpassed all in this. When he came back to the crowd his advantage in lead was as that of a yoke of mules in breaking unbroken ground: so distant were the others behind him. Then they wrestled their hardest: and Euryalus proved champion of champions. Amphialus carried off the jumping and Elatreus easily won the weight-throwing: while the boxing fell to Laodamas, Alcinous' doughty son.

When every spirit had been delighted with the sports, then said Laodamas the son of Alcinous, 'Come with me, friends, and let us question the stranger, to learn if he is skilled in games and can show us any feats. He is not in any sense ill-built: those thighs and calves, bull-neck and vigorous hands are tokens of enormous power. Nor has he lost his prime: it is only that he is broken by excess of hardships. I give you my oath that for wreaking havoc upon a strong man, even the very strongest, there is nothing so dire as the sea.' Euryalus answered him and said, 'Laodamas, you have spoken to the point: go up now, declare yourself and call him out.' Upon which the honest son of Alcinous moved through the crowd and addressed Odysseus: 'Will you not, father stranger, now attempt some feat, if you have the skill I credit you? For there is no surer fame, in a man's own life-time, than that which he wins with his feet and hands. Also at this juncture you may well purge your heart of care and prove yourself, for soon you will be on your journey. Is not your ship launched and your crew told off?'

Wily Odysseus replied: 'Laodamas, why do you thus invite me, in mockery? The fashion of my heart is more like grief than games. For long I have been a toiling and a suffering man: my very purpose here in your gathering is only as a suppliant before your king and people, to crave my passage homeward.' Euryalus took him up and sneered in his face: 'Truly, stranger, I do not reckon you a man good at games, like the generality of real men: but rather a master of peddling sailors, one who traffics up and down in a heavy merchantman, mindful always of cargo and husbanding freights, with a sharp eye on gain. You are not built like a champion.'

Deep Odysseus glared at him and thundered: 'You, whoever you are, do not speak well. You behave like a low fellow. So true is it that the Gods do not lavish graciousness entire, their whole endowment of beauty and wit and eloquence, upon all men alike. There will be one rather feebler than average in build, and yet the God will so crown what he says with a bloom of beauty that all who look on him are moved. When he holds forth in public it is with assurance, yet with so honey-sweet a modesty that it makes him shine out above the ruck of men who gaze at him whenever he walks their city as if he were a god. Another will be handsome as the Immortals, yet will lack that strand of charm twined into his words. Take yourself – a master-piece of body in which perhaps not even a god could see amendment : yet naught in mind. Your reviling made the heart beat faster in my breast. I am no ninny at sports, as you would have it. Indeed I think I was among the best, in my time, while I yet heard the prompting of my youth and hands. In my time – for here I subsist in pain and misery, having risked and endured much in the wars of men and the wearisome seas. Yet despite the ravages of these evil things I will essay your tests of strength: for that sneer galled me and your word has stung me to the quick.'

He spoke and sprang to his feet. All cloaked as he was he seized a throwing weight, a huge heavy stone far bigger than those with which the Phaeacians had been competing. He whirled it up and flung it from his mighty hand, and the stone sang through the air. Down they quailed to the earth, those Phaeacians of the long oars, those master mariners, beneath the hurtling of the stone which soared so freely from the hero's hand that it overpassed the marks of every other. Athene, in her human shape, appeared suddenly and marked the place where it touched earth. Loudly she cried to Odysseus: 'Stranger, even a blind man's dim groping hand would pick out the dint of your stone: because it does not lie confused among the crowd of marks, but is alone, far in front of all. Be confident, for this event at least. No Phaeacian will reach your throw, much less exceed it.' So the goddess cried, and great Odysseus was glad, at the pleasure of finding in the assembly one stout-hearted friend. Wherefore gaily he challenged the Phaeacians: –

'Now, my young athletes, match me this throw; and very soon after you do, I think I will send down another as long or longer. For the rest, let any man whose spirit or temper prompts him come out and take me on in boxing or wrestling or foot-racing, as you will. To such a pitch have you wrought me that I shall not flinch from anything, nor refuse any single Phaeacian, except only Laodamas, my host. For who but a shallow-pated fool would strive with his bene-factor? To challenge one's host, while being kindly entreated in a foreign land, would be to spite one's self. But for the others, I refuse none and shirk nothing. I shall look all in the face and prove them. In none of the sports which men use do I disgrace myself. I can well handle the polished bow. In the thick of each fight I would be ever the first to loose arrow and bring down my man, no matter how many followers of mine were there, shooting at the enemy. In the Trojan plain, where the Achaeans made such trial of shooting, only Philoctetes surpassed me with the bow. Wherefore I avouch myself more adept therein than any other man who now eats earthly food. With the men of old time I do not wish to rate myself; not with Herakles, nor with Eurytus of Oechalia, who would make a shooting match with the Immortal Gods: of which ambition great Eurytus early died, cut off young from his house: for Apollo slew him in rage at being challenged to a bout in archery. I will send my spear further than any man his arrow. I fear only that in swiftness of foot some of the Phaeacians may beat me; for I have been shamefully mauled by incessant waves on a ship destitute of comfort. Therefore are the joints of my knees enfeebled.'

So he protested, and they all waited in a hush: only Alcinous answered and said: 'See now. Stranger, we do not resent these words you have uttered because you, in anger at such a fellow's facing you in the ring and upbraiding you, have been pleased to make so plain to us your inbred prowess that no mortal man who knows what words are worth may question it. Yet listen now to what I say and remember our accomplishment and the skill Zeus has given us – from our fathers' times even until now – that you may tell the tale to some other hero when you sup in your own house with your wife and children: for my part I confess that we are not polished fighters with our fists, nor wrestlers: but we can run swiftly on our feet and are experts on shipboard: we love eating and harp-playing and dancing and changes of clothes: and hot baths and our beds. Wherefore, my people, bestir yourselves and cause the best dancers of the Phaeacians to dance before us, so that when the stranger is got home he may acquaint his friends with our surpassing goodness in seamanship and running and dancing and singing. Let someone go quickly to our house and fetch for Demodocus that sounding lyre which he will find hung up somewhere.'

At the word of Alcinous his herald ran to find the polished lyre in the palace. Other nine men stood up, the elect and appointed stewards of the crowd, whose duty was to set the stage. They levelled the dancing ground, making its ring neat and wide. The herald arrived with the minstrel's singing lyre. Demodocus advanced into the cleared space. About him grouped boys in their first blush of life and skilful at dancing, who footed it rhythmically on the prepared floor. Odysseus watched their flying, flashing feet and wondered.

Then the lyre-player broke into fluent song, telling of the loves of Ares and coiffed Aphrodite in the house of Hephaestus. How they first came together by stealth and of the many gifts that Ares gave her, until he was able to defile the bed and marriage of Hephaestus the King: and of the eventual coming of Helios, the Sun, to the King, with word of their loving intercourse as he had witnessed it. When Hephaestus had heard the dismal tale he hastened to his forge, elaborating evil for them in the depths of his breast. He set the great anvil in its stock and wrought chains which could be neither broken nor loosed, that the guilty pair might be gyved in them for ever and ever. Out of his bitter rage against Ares was born this device. He went then into his marriage chamber, where stood the bed he had cherished, and about its posts he interlaced his toils. Others, many of them, hung down from aloft, from the main roof-tree over the hearth; gossamer chains so fine that no man could see them, not even a blessed God, with such subtlety of craft had they been forged. When Hephaestus had meshed all the bed in his snare he pretended to set forth for Lemnos, that well-built city which in his eyes is much the dearest land of earth. Nor was it a loose watch that Ares of the golden reins was keeping upon Hephaestus. As soon as he saw the great craftsman leave he took his journey to the famous house, chafing for love of well-crowned Cytherea. She was but newly come from Zeus, her mighty father, and had just sat down when Ares was in the house, grasping her hand and saying: 'Come, darling, let us to bed and to our pleasure; for Hephaestus is now abroad, visiting in Lemnos among the barbarous-spoken Sintians.'

His word of their lying together gave her joy. They went to their bed and snuggled deep into it, whereupon the springes of artful Hephaestus closed about them and tightened till they were not able to lift a limb nor move it. At last they understood there was no escape. Then the great God of the mighty arms drew near again and re-entered: he had turned back short of Lemnos when Helios, the spying Sun, had given him word. As he made heavily toward his home grief rooted in his heart: but when he stood there in its entry savage passion gripped him so that he roared hideously and declaimed to all the Gods: –

'Father Zeus and every other Blessed Immortal, hither to me, and see a jest which is unpardonable. Because I am crippled. Aphrodite daughter of Zeus, does me dishonour, preferring Ares the destroyer. Ares being beautiful and straight of limb while I was born crooked. And whose fault is that, if not my parents'? Would they had not brought me into life! Look how these two are clipped together in love's embrace, here, in my very bed. To watch them cuts me to the heart. Yet I think they will not wish to lie thus, not even for a very little while longer, however mad their lust. Soon they will not wish to be together, yet shall my cunning bonds chain them as they are until her father has utterly repaid the marriage fee – every single thing I gave him for this bitch-eyed girl: though indeed his daughter is beautiful, despite her sin.'

His mouthing gathered the gods to the house of the brazen floor. Poseidon the Earth-girdler, beneficent Hermes and royal Apollo the far-darting, came: but the Lady Goddesses remained at home, all of them, quite out of countenance. In Hephaestus' forecourt collected the Givers of Weal: and unquenchable was the laughter that arose from the blessed Gods as they studied the tricky device of Hephaestus. One would catch his neighbour's eye and gibe: 'Bad deeds breed no merit. The slow outrun the speedy. See how poor crawling Hephaestus, despite that limp, has now overtaken Ares (much the most swift of all divine dwellers upon Olympus) and cleverly caught him. Ares will owe him the adulterer's fine.' Words like this one whispered to the other: but of Hermes did Zeus' royal son Apollo loudly ask: 'Hermes, son of Zeus, messenger and giver of good things: would you not choose even the bondage of these tough chains, if so you might sleep in the one bed by golden Aphrodite?' And to him the God's messenger, Argus-bane, replied: 'If only this might be, kingly, far-darting Apollo! If there were chains without end, thrice as many as are here, and all you Gods with all the Goddesses to look on, yet would I be happy beside the Golden One.'

At his saying more laughter rose among the Immortals: only Poseidon laughed not but was still entreating lame Hephaestus the craftsman to let Ares go. Now he spoke out, with winged words: 'Loose him: and for him I promise whatever you require; as that he shall discharge the penalty he has incurred before the undying Gods.' The famous strong-thewed God answered him: 'Do not thus constrain me, Poseidon, Earth-girdler. The bonds of a worthless man are worthless bonds. How could I hold you liable before the Immortals, if Ares gets away free of his debt and this snare?' And to him replied the Earth-shaker: 'Hephaestus, even if Ares absconds, leaving his debt unpaid, I myself will discharge it to you, wholly.' And the lame master said, 'I cannot refuse: nor would it be seemly to refuse such surety.' So saying great Hephaestus loosed the chain and the couple when they were freed of the trap and its restraint swiftly fled away – he to Thrace and smiling Aphrodite to Cyprus, to Paphos, her sanctuary with its incense-burning altar. There the Graces bathed her and anointed her with ambrosial oil, such as is set aside for the ever-living Gods. There they put upon her glorious clothing, till she was an enchantment to the eye.

Such was the song of the famous minstrel. Like the Phaeacians, the long-oared notable mariners, Odysseus had rejoiced in heart as he listened. Then Alcinous ordered Halius and Laodamas to dance, by themselves, for never did any one dare join himself with them. They took in their hands the fine ball, purple-dyed, which knowing Polybus had made them, and played. The first, bending his body right back, would hurl the ball towards the shadowy clouds: while the other in his turn would spring high into the air and catch it gracefully before his feet again touched ground. Then, after they had made full trial of tossing the ball high, they began passing it back and forth between them, all the while they danced upon the fruitful earth. The other young men stood by the dancing ring and beat time. Loudly their din went up: and great Odysseus turned to Alcinous, saying, 'O my lord Alcinous, ruler of rulers, you did assure us that your dancers were the best: and now it is proved true: this sight is marvellous.' Thereat Alcinous the sacred King rejoiced and quickly said to the Phaeacians: 'Hear me, war-lords and statesmen of the Phaeacians: this stranger seems a man of singular understanding. Let us bestow on him the stranger's meed, in due form. Here are twelve noble kings who rule among the people, with myself the thirteenth. Let each generously contribute a fresh robe and a tunic and a talent of precious gold. If all these gifts are brought promptly the stranger will have them in hand before supper and will go to it gallantly. As for Euryalus, let him atone for his ill manners by words of satisfaction and a gift.'

All accepted his counsel and enjoined it. The pursuivants went forth to collect and bring the gifts, while Euryalus said: 'My lord Alcinous, leader of our rank, right truly will I make amends to the stranger, as you bid. See this short sword of the true metal: that I give to him with its silver hilt and the scabbard of new-sawn ivory which contains it. It shall be worth much to him.' At the word he put the silver-mounted weapon into the hands of Odysseus and spoke wingedly therewith: 'Hail, father stranger: and if some too-harsh word has slipped out, may the storm winds take it and cast it afar. For yourself, the Gods grant that you reach your land and see your wife: all too long have you been afflicted and far from the solace of your friends.' Readily Odysseus answered him, saying, 'To you too, my friend, a warm greeting: may the Gods give you happiness: and may you never feel the lack of this sword which you to-day give me, with the balm of healing words.' He slung the silver-mounted weapon about his shoulder. The sun went down and the presentation of the costly gifts began. In state the heralds bore them to the palace, where the great king's sons received them for Odysseus and bestowed them for safe keeping with their revered mother, while the king himself led in the guests to take places on the lofty thrones.

Then did Alcinous call to Arete his wife: 'Woman, bring hither a very rich chest, your noblest. Put in it a newly-washed robe and tunic. Then warm a copper for the guest by the fire and heat water, that he may bathe himself before he views this show of gifts which the Phaeacian leaders have presented to him: and afterward he will be able to enjoy the feast and our minstrel's music. Stay: to his treasure I will also add this my very beautiful wrought cup of gold, that he may call me to mind always when in his house he pours drink-offerings to Zeus and the other Gods.' So he said, and Arete told her maids to set, as soon as might be, a great three-legged pot by the fire. They placed over the roaring flames the cauldron which served for the bath, and poured water into it and piled kindling wood beneath. The fire licked round the pot's belly and the water warmed, while Arete brought out of the bed-chamber a fair coffer for the visitor and put into it the splendid gifts, the clothing and the gold, which the Phaeacians had given. From her own store she added a fine tunic and outer garment and then addressed him succinctly, as follows: 'See to the lid now, yourself: and quickly contrive a sure fastening about it lest anyone rob you on your way as you are enjoying the sweetness of sleep while your black ship glides on.' Odysseus at once fixed the cover to her asking, and secured it with that intricate knot which Dame Circe had taught him. Then straightway the housewife bade him go to the bath place and wash. It gladdened him to see the steaming water, for it had not been his good fortune to meet such comfort since he left the dwelling of bright-haired Calypso, with whom he had had the entertainment of a god, continually.

When the maids had washed and anointed him they draped him in a rich robe and tunic; and he went out from the bath-house to join the men at their wine-drinking. On the way, by the pillar of the massy roof, stood Nausicaa in her god-given beauty, admiring Odysseus with all her eyes: until words came and she addressed him directly: – 'Farewell, Stranger; and when in your native land think of me, sometimes: for it is chiefly to me that you owe the gage of your life.' Odysseus answered her, saying, 'Nausicaa, daughter of high-souled Alcinous: if Zeus, Hera's Lord, the Thunderer, wills that I reach home and see the day of my return, there and then will I pay vows to you, as to a Divine One; and for ever and ever throughout all my days. For you gave me life, Maiden.'

He ended and passed to his throne beside King Alcinous. The servers were mixing wine and distributing meats. The herald drew near, leading Demodocus the sweet singer whom the people honoured into the midst of the feasters; he set him there with his back to a tall column: and to the herald wily Odysseus called, having cut off from the chine of a white-toothed boar (there was abundance and to spare) a piece rich all round with fat. 'Herald,' said he, 'take and offer this portion of flesh to Demodocus that he may eat it with a greeting from me that not even the depth of my misfortunes can call; for it is right that bards should receive honour and reverence from every man alive, inasmuch as the Muse cherishes the whole guild of singers and teaches to each one his rules of song.'

When the hero had made an end of speaking, the herald bore his meat in hand to Demodocus who received it and rejoiced. All stretched out and helped themselves to the ready cheer; and when they were filled with drink and food then Odysseus addressed Demodocus. 'Demodocus, I laud you above all mortal men: I know not if it was the Muse, daughter of Zeus, that taught you, or Apollo himself. Anyhow you have sung the real history of the mishaps of the Achaeans, their deeds, their sufferings, their griefs, as if you had been there or had heard it from eye witnesses. But now change your theme and sing of how Epeius with the help of Athene carpentered together that great timber horse, the crafty device, which wise Odysseus got taken into the citadel after packing it with the men who were to lay Troy waste. Tell me all this in order, and then I will maintain everywhere that the God's grace has conferred the bounty of inspiration on your singing.'

So he said; and the minstrel, fired by the God, gave proof of his mastery. He took up his tale where the main body of the Argives embarked on their well-decked ships after setting fire to their hutments, and sailed away; leaving the remnant, the companions of famous Odysseus, enclosed in the heart of Troy-town, in the meeting-place, hidden within the horse which the Trojans themselves had dragged up to their citadel. There the horse stood while the people hung about it arguing this way and that, uncertainly. They were of three minds: – either to prize open its wooden womb with their pitiless blades; or to drag it to the cliff's edge and roll it down among the rocks; or to leave it there dedicated as a mighty peace offering to the Gods. In the end this last counsel had it, for it was fated that they should perish when their city gave lodgement to the monstrous beast in which crouched all the flower of the Argives with their seeds of death and doom for Troy. He sang how the sons of the Argives quitted their hollow den, and poured out from the horse, and made an end of Troy. He sang the share of each warrior in the wasting of the stately town, and how Odysseus, Ares-like, attacked the house of Deiphobus with great Menelaus. There, he said, Odysseus braved terrible odds but conquered in the end, by help of resolute Athene.

Thus ran the famous singer's song: but Odysseus melted and tears from his eyelids bedewed his cheeks. So it is when a loving wife flings herself, wailing, about the body of her man who has fallen before his township and fellow-citizens, defending the town and his children from their cruel day of sack and rapine. The sight of him labouring his last breath and dying makes her wail aloud and wind herself about him. Yet do the enemy from behind beat her with their spear-shafts across her bowed shoulders and lead her into servitude, to her fate of toil and grief. Just as that woman's cheeks are ravaged with despair, just so piteously did the tears fall from Odysseus' brows. Yet this time, too, his falling tears were missed by all the company, save only Alcinous who sat by him and marked his grief, unable not to hear the moaning deep within his breast. Alcinous at once spoke to the oar-loving Phaeacians: –

'Lend me your ears, captains and councillors. It is for Demodocus now to let be his echoing lyre: his song does not delight us all. From supper-time when the divine singer began, the Stranger has not ceased from bitter grieving. Some sore pain besets his heart. Wherefore cease, that we may all, hosts and guest, make merry as we fairly ought: for have we not contrived in our guest's honour just what he required of us – an escort – and further added to him love-tokens in proof of our regard? Any sufficient man who has the wit to pierce a little beneath the surface will entertain a stranger or a suppliant as his brother. Wherefore, Stranger, do not in crafty purpose conceal the news I seek:

but make a virtue of frankness. Tell us by what name they call you there at home – your mother and father and the others in your city and district. For all parents fit names to their children as soon as these are born, so that there is no one so poor or so gentle that he is nameless. Tell me your land and district and city, that our sentient ships may get their bearing for your journey. Understand that the Phaeacians do not carry steersmen or steering oars, like ordinary ships. Their vessels know what men think and purpose. They know the cities and rich lands of every people and swiftly cross the ocean-gulfs, through the thickest veils of rain-cloud or mist. Nor are they troubled by panic or disaster, ever. Yet did I hear my father Nausithous once say that Poseidon was vexed with us for giving safe-conduct impartially to all mankind: and would one day shatter a trim Phaeacian ship homeward bound across the misty sea from such a sending, and would shroud our city under a high mountain on every side. So the old man said. The God may do it, or may forbear. It shall be as He wills.

'But open your heart now, and inform me plainly whither you wandered and what coasts of men you have visited. What were the peopled cities like, and what the peoples? Whether harsh, savage and unjust; or humane men, hospitable and god-fearing. Tell us why you wept so bitterly and secretly when you heard of the Argive Danaans and the fall of Ilion. That was wrought by the Gods, who measured their life's thread for those men, that their fate might become a poem sung to generations yet to be. Did some kinsman of your wife's die before Ilion, some one of those worthy relatives by marriage who become nearest to us after our own flesh and blood? Or perhaps it was a friend, some man loving and true? Friends with understanding hearts become no less dear to us than brothers.'

BOOK 9

Many-sided Odysseus then began: 'Lord Alcinous, most eminent, we are in very deed privileged to have within our hearing a singer whose voice is so divinely pure. I tell you, to my mind the acme of intelligent delight is reached when a company sits feasting in some hall, by tables garnished with bread and meat, the while a musician charms their ears and a cup-bearer draws them wine and carries it round served ready for their drinking. Surely this, as I say, is the best thing in the world.

'Yet, lo, at such a moment your heart prompts you to seek the tale of my dismal fortunes: whose telling will wring from me yet deeper tears. How shall I rank my sorrows, to put this first, that afterwards? The Gods of heaven have given me such excess of woe. I will begin with my name to make you sure of me, that when this cruel spell is past I may become your host in my house – my very distant house, alas! I am Odysseus, son of Laertes: a name which among men spells every resource and subtlety of mind: and my fame reaches heaven. I live in pellucid Ithaca, the island of Mount Neriton, whose upstanding slopes are all a-quiver with the wind-blown leaves. About it lie many other islands very near to one another, Dulichium and Same and wooded Zacynthus. My island stands deep in the sea and nearer the west than its neighbours which rather face the dawning and the sun. It is a harsh land, yet it breeds good youths: but perhaps in every man's sight there is nothing better than his native land. Take my case: Calypso the fair goddess sought to keep me in her hollow cave and would have used me as her husband: and likewise Circe, the wily lady of Æaea, tried to detain me in her house, she too wanting me for a husband: but neither the one nor the other could pervert the heart in my manly breast. Wherefore I say that no matter how rich a man's circumstances may be abroad, among foreign parts, there is no sweet in life to compare with home and parents. However, let me hark back to the tale of the calamitous homeward journey with which Zeus had afflicted my return from Troy.

'From Ilion the wind served me to near Ismarus of the Cicones. I sacked the city and slew them. Their wives and wealth we took and divided precisely, so that no one of us, through me, should go short of his just share. I suggested then that we all flee, hot-foot: but my utter fools of men would not obey. There was much wine for the drinking, yet; and mutton or beef from the great droves of sheep and heavy screw-horned kine that they had butchered by the shore. Whilst they so dallied, our Cicones cried for help to the inland Cicones, their neighbours, but more numerous and better men of their hands; men who could fight mounted, but also (when need was) on foot with footmen. They were upon us, thick as the leaves and buds of spring-tide, at the first show of morning; while over us there hung a foreboding of disaster, by doom of Zeus who had further pains in store for our ill-fated heads. The troops set themselves to battle by the swift ships and rained thickly at one another their copper-bladed spears. So long as the dawn lasted and while the blessed day increased, just for so long we stood firm and repulsed their swarms; but when the sun had crossed his stage and brought near the hour for loosing plough-oxen homeward in the evening, then finally the Cicones caused the Achaean lines to waver and give way. Six warriors perished out of each ship's complement. We others who for that time fled our death and doom sailed from the spot with mixed feelings; rejoicing to have avoided fate, yet mourning our comrades for whose sake not one of those full-bellied ships of mine stirred thence till we had thrice invoked the name of each unhappy victim of the Cicones' violent hands, on the flats there by the shore.

'Next Zeus, the cloud-marshal, incited against our fleet a North wind, with screaming squalls. He blinded land and sea alike with clouds. Night plunged down from heaven. The ships were swept aside before the blast and their sails shredded into tatters by the gale. We had to strike them in instant fear of death, and take to the oars. Vehemently we tugged our ships shoreward. For two days and two nights we lay there, making no way and eating our hearts out with despair and the unceasing labour: but on the third morning bright-haired Dawn achieved clear daylight; wherefore up went our masts and white shining sails, enabling us to sit there at our ease watching how the winds and the steersmen held us to our course. Indeed, that time I nearly came unscathed to my fatherland; only for the swell and the seacurrents and a north wind which united against me as I beat round Cape Maleia and deflected me wide of Cythera. Thereafter for nine days I was driven by ravening winds across the sea. On the tenth day we made the land of the Lotos-eaters, men who browse on a food of flowers. We landed there to fill our water-butts, while my crews snatched a meal on the shore, beside their likely vessels. As soon as the first hunger for food and drink had passed, I chose out two fellows and added to them a third, as runner, that they might go inland to spy out and enquire what were the human beings there existing. Off they went at once and met a party of these Lotos-eaters, who had no notion of slaying my emissaries: instead they gave them a dish of their Lotos-flower. And so it was that as each tasted of this honey-sweet plant, the wish to bring news or return grew faint in him: rather he preferred to dwell for ever with the Lotos-eating men, feeding upon Lotos and letting fade from his mind all memory of home. I had to seek them and drag them back on board. They wept: yet into the ships we brought them perforce and chained them beneath the thwarts, deep in the well, while I constrained the rest of my adherents to hurry aboard, lest perhaps more of them might eat Lotos and lose their longing for home. They embarked promptly and sat to the rowing benches; then in their proper ranks, all together, they swung their oars and beat the sea hoary-white.

'We left in low spirits and later came to the land of the arrogant iniquitous Cyclopes who so leave all things to the Gods that they neither plant nor till: yet does plenty spring up unsown and unploughed, of corn and barley and even vines with heavy clusters: which the rains of Zeus fatten for them. They have no government nor councils nor courts of justice: but live in caves on mountain tops, each ruling his wives and children and a law unto himself, regardless. Across the bight of the Cyclopes' country extends a fertile island, a wooded island; not very far, yet not close. In it there harbour uncounted wild goats. No trace of man scares these, nor do hunters with dogs track them out, fighting their way through the bush to explore the summits of the hills. The herbage is not grazed down by flocks of sheep nor broken by any plough. Rather the spot continues in solitude, wholly uncultivated, a paradise for the bleating she-goats, by reason that the Cyclopes have no ruddle-cheeked ships, nor ship-wrights to make them such seaworthy vessels for pleasuring among the cities of mankind, like those ordinary men who tempt the seas to know others and to be known. Otherwise they might have made this island theirs, it being not at all bad land. Anything would grow well there in season, in the soft moist meadows behind the dykes of the silvery sea: and its vine-stocks would bear for ever. The crop to be harvested at the due time from such smooth plough-loam would be heavy, seeing that the undersoil is fat. Its haven is a natural port requiring no such gear as anchors or warps. Ships can be beached directly, to lie there in peace while the sailors screw up their hearts to venture farther or until the winds blow kind. And at the head of this inlet is pure running water from a spring rising in a cave. Black poplars shadow it.

'Thither we sailed, some God assuredly guiding us, for the night was utterly dark, without glimmer. The ground-fog shrouded our boats nor could any moon-beam from the sky pierce the low-lying clouds. Wherefore no one of us saw anything of the island, or of the long slow waves rolling unbroken upon its shelving beach. All we knew was that our good ships gently grounded. As they touched we struck sail and climbed out: and there, just beyond the water's edge, sunken in a depth of sleep, we waited the goddess of Dawn. When She came, rosy-fingered, we began in amazement to compass the island, exploring it: and the nymph-daughters of Zeus himself flushed for us the wild goats of the hills, to give my men whereon to dine. We ran to seek our carved bows and long-tanged throwing spears from the ships and began shooting, after forming ourselves into three bands. Very quickly did the God provide us game to our hearts' content: so great was the bag that nine goats could be shared out to each of the twelve ships that made up my command. For my own ship, as a special allowance, ten were allotted. Afterwards throughout the live-long day and until the sun went down we sat about feasting; for the meat was unlimited and the drink good, the red wine being not yet altogether exhausted within our ships, since we had carried off a great store in jars from the hallowed little capital of the Cicones when we sacked it. While we ate we stared across at the land of the Cyclopes, so near that we could see its smoke going up and hear the sounds of its men and the bleating of their sheep and goats; until at last the sun sank and dusk drew down, causing us to stretch out in slumber where we were, on the margin of the sea.

'At dawn I met my men in council and delivered myself as follows: "You, my trusty ones, will remain here while I with my ship and crew run over to try those men and find out if they are brutal savages or kindly to guests, reverent and just." After giving these orders I went up into my ship and told her crew to get aboard when they had let go the hawsers. They obeyed at once and manned the rowing benches smartly. The sea turned pale beneath the flailing of their oars. As we came to the nearest point of land we could see a cave at its seaward extremity – a lofty cave, embowered in laurels. There were signs that large flocks of sheep and goats were wont to be penned within it for the night. Round the cave-mouth a strong-walled yard had been contrived of rocks deeply embedded, with a fence of logs from tall pines and spreading oaks. Actually it was the lair of a giant, a monstrous creature who pastured his flocks widely from that centre and avoided traffic with any man. He was a solitary infidel thing, this ogre, and fearfully made; not in the fashion of a bread-eating man but altogether singular and out-standing like a tree-grown crag of the high mountains.

'I ordered my faithful crew to stand by the ship and guard the ship, while I picked the twelve men I judged best and set off with them. I took, as an afterthought, a goat-skin of potent wine, very mellow, which I had been given by Maron son of Euanthes, the priest of Apollo tutelary God of Ismarus. Maron lived in his dense grove (sacred to Phoebus Apollo) and when we sacked the town we had piously spared him and his wife and child. In reward he paid me valuable gifts – seven talents of refined gold and a mixing bowl of pure silver, over and above this great wine which he drew off neat for us into twelve wine-jars. Liquor for gods, it was. Only himself and his wife and the housekeeper knew of its existence; he had told none of his women slaves or housemaidens: and when he broached it he would draw off just the one cup of deep delight and pour it into twenty measures of water: whereupon there would waft abroad from the bowl a smell so sweet that it was heavenly: and to hold back from drinking, then, would indeed have been no joy. A great skin I filled with this drink and took with me; also corn in a leathern wallet; for at this very moment some masterful instinct warned me that we might have to do with a strange fierce being of vast strength, knowing neither right nor wrong, and ungovernable.

'Soon we were within the cave, to find its owner absent, grazing his goodly flocks in their pastures. So we explored the cave, staring round-eyed at cheese racks loaded with cheeses, and crowded pens of lambs and kids, each sort properly apart, the spring-younglings in this, mid-yearlings there, and the last born to one side. There were pails, buckets and tubs all brimming with whey: well-made vessels too, these milk-vessels of his. My men's first petition was that they might lay hold of the cheeses and make off with them, to return at a run and drive kids and lambs from the pens to the ship, in which we should then put hastily to sea. This advice, in the issue, would have profited us: but now I would not heed it, so set was I on seeing the master and getting (if he would give it) the guest's-present from him. Yet was his coming to prove disastrous to my party.

'We built up a fire, made a burnt offering, helped ourselves to cheese and ate as we sat there inside the cavern waiting for our man to come home from the pastures. He brought with him an immense burden of dried wood, kindling for his supper fire, and flung it upon the cave's floor with a crash that sent us scurrying in terror to its far corners. Then he drove under the arch his splendid flock, or rather those of them that were in milk. The rest, rams and he-goats, he left in the broad yard before the entry. Next he lifted into place and fixed in the cave's mouth a huge tall slab of stone, gigantic like himself. Two and twenty stout four-wheeled waggons would not have shifted it along the ground, so huge was it, this rock he used to block his door. Then he sat down to milk his ewes and bleating goats, all orderly, later putting her young lamb or kid beneath each mother-animal. One half of this white milk he curdled and put to press in the wicker cheese-baskets. The other half he left standing in the buckets as provision against his supper-time when he would drink it and satisfy himself.

'So far he had been wholly engaged in work, but now he rebuilt the fire and looked around and saw us. "Why, strangers," said he, "who are you and where have you come from across the water? Are you traders? or pirates, those venturers who sea-prowl at hazard, robbing all comers for a livelihood?" So he asked, and our confidence cracked at the giant's dread booming voice and his hugeness. Yet I made shift to speak out firmly, saying, "We are waifs of the Achaeans from Troy, intending homeward, but driven off our course haphazard across the boundless ocean gulfs by adverse winds from heaven: it may be by the will and decree of Zeus. We can vaunt ourselves companions of Atrides, Agamemnon's men, whose is now the widest fame under heaven for having sacked earth's greatest city and brought such multitudes to death. Here therefore we find ourselves suppliant at your knees, in hope of the guesting-fee or other rich gift such as is the meed of strangers. Have regard for the Gods, Magnificent! We are your suppliants: and Zeus who fares with deserving strangers along their road is the champion of suppliants, their protector and patron-God."

'Thus far I got: but the reply came from his pitiless heart. "Sir Stranger, you are either simple or very outlandish if you bid me fear the Gods and avoid crossing them. We are the Cyclopes and being so much the bigger we listen not at all to aegis-bearing Zeus or any blessed God: so if I should spare your life and your friends' it would not be to shun the wrath of Zeus, but because my heart counselled me mercy. Now tell me where you moored the stout ship when you came. On the far shore was it, or the near? I want to know." With these words he laid a crafty snare for me, but to my subtlety all his deceits were plain. So I spoke back, meeting fraud with fraud: "My ship was broken by Poseidon the Earth-shaker, who swept her towards the cape at the very end of your land, and cast her against the reefs: the wind drifted us in from the high sea. Only myself with these few escaped." So I said.

'His savagery disdained me one word in reply. He leapt

to his feet, lunged with his hands among my fellows, snatched up two of them like whelps and rapped their heads against the ground. The brains burst out from their skulls and were spattered over the cave's floor, while he broke them up, limb from limb, and supped off them to the last shred, eating ravenously like a mountain lion, everything – bowels and flesh and bones, even to the marrow in the bones. We wept and raised our hands to Zeus in horror at this crime committed before our eyes: yet there was nothing we could do. Wherefore the Cyclops, unhindered, filled his great gut with the human flesh, and washed it down with raw milk. Afterwards he stretched himself out across the cavern, among the flocks, and slept.

'I was wondering in my bold heart whether I should now steal in, snatch the keen sword hanging on my hip, and stab him in the body; after making sure with my fingers where was that vital place in the midriff, below the heart and above the liver. Yet my second thoughts put me off this stroke, for by it I should finally seal our own doom: not enough strength lay in our hands to roll back the huge block with which he had closed the cave. So we sighed there night-long with misery, awaiting Dawn: upon whose shining the giant awoke, relit his fire, milked his flock in due order and put each youngling under its dam. After his busy work was done, he seized two more of us, who furnished his day-meal. Then he drove his sleek beasts out of the cave, easily pulling aside the great door-block and putting it back, as one of us might snap its lid upon a quiver. With loud halloos to the flock the Cyclops led them into the hills, leaving me imprisoned there to plot evil against him in the depths of my mind, wherein I sought means to pay him back, would but Athene grant me the opportunity for which I prayed.

'Of what came to me this seemed best. There lay in the sheep-pens a great cudgel belonging to Cyclops, or rather a limb of green olive wood from which he meant to make himself a staff when it had seasoned. In our estimation we likened it to the mast of a twenty-oared black ship, some broad-beamed merchantman of the high seas – it looked so long and thick. I straddled it and cut off about a fathom's length which I took to my fellows, bidding them taper it down. They made it quite even while I lent a hand to sharpen its tip. Then I took it and revolved it in the blazing flame till the point was charred to hardness. Thereafter we hid it under the sheep-droppings which were largely heaped up throughout the cave. Lastly I made the others draw lots, to see who would have the desperate task of helping me lift up our spike and grind it into his eye when heavy sleep had downed him. The luck of the draw gave me just the four men I would have chosen with my eyes open. I appointed myself the fifth of the party.

'Cyclops came back at evening shepherding his fleecy flocks and straightway drove them into the wide-vaulted cave, the whole fat mass of them, leaving no single one in the outer yard. Something on his mind, was it, or did some God move him? Then he lifted up the great door-stone and propped it into place before he sat down to his milking, dealing in turn with every ewe and noisy milch-goat and later setting their young beneath them. Briskly he attacked his household work; only after it to snatch up two more of us and dine off them. Then I went up to the Giant with an ivycup of my dark wine in hand and invited him, saying, "Cyclops, come now and on top of your meal of man's flesh try this wine, to see how tasty a drink was hidden in our ship. I brought it for you, hoping you would have compassion on me and help me homeward: but your unwisdom is far beyond all comprehending. O sinful one, how dare you expect any other man from the great world to visit you, after you have behaved towards us so unconscionably?" I spoke: he took and drank. A savage gladness woke in him at the sweetness of the liquor and he demanded a second cup, saying, "Give me another hearty helping and then quickly tell me your name, for me to confer on you a guest-gift that will warm your heart. It is true our rich soil grows good vines for us Cyclopes, and the moisture of heaven multiplies their yield: but this vintage is a drop of the real nectar and ambrosia." Thus he declared and at once I poured him a second cup of the glowing wine: and then one more, for in his folly he tossed off three bowls of it. The fumes were going to his Cyclopean wits as I began to play with him in honeyed phrase: – "Cyclops, you ask me for my public name: I will confess it to you aloud, and do you then give me my guest-gift, as you have promised. My name is No-man: so they have always called me, my mother and father and all my friends."

'I spoke, and he answered from his cruel heart, "I will eat No-man finally, after all his friends. The others first – that shall be your benefit." He sprawled full-length, belly up, on the ground, lolling his fat neck aside; and sleep that conquers all men conquered him. Heavily he vomited out all his load of drink, and gobbets of human flesh swimming in wine spurted gurgling from his throat. Forthwith I thrust our spike into the deep embers of the fire to get it burning hot: and cheered my fellows with brave words lest any of them hang back through fear. Soon the stake of olive wood despite its greenness was almost trembling into flame with a terrible glowing incandescence. I snatched it from the fire, my men helping. Some power from on high breathed into us all a mad courage, by whose strength they charged with the great spear and stabbed its sharp point right into his eye. I flung my weight upon it from above so that it bored home. As a ship-builder's bit drills its timbers, steadily twirling by reason of the drag from the hide thong which his mates underneath pull to and fro alternately, so we held the burning pointed stake in his eye and spun it, till the boiling blood bubbled about its pillar of fire. Eyebrows, with eyelids shrivelled and stank in the blast of his consuming eyeball: yea, the very roots of the eye crackled into flame.

'Just as a smith plunges into cold water some great axe-head or adze and it hisses angrily – for that is the treatment, and the strength of iron lies in its temper – just so his eye sizzled about the olive-spike. He let out a wild howl which rang round the cavern's walls and drove us hither and thither in terror. He wrenched the spike of wood from his eye and it came out clotted and thick with blood. The maddening pain made him fling it from his hands, and then he began to bellow to the other Cyclopes living about him in their dens among the windy hills. They had heard his screaming and now drew towards the closed cave, calling to know his trouble: "What so ails you, Polyphemus, that you roar across the heavenly night and keep us from sleep? Do not pretend that any mortal is driving your flocks from you by force, or is killing you by sheer might or trickery." Big Polyphemus yelled back to them from within his cave, "My friends, No-man is killing me by sleight. There is no force about it." Wherefore they retorted cuttingly, "If you are alone and no one assaults you, but your pain is some unavoidable malady from Zeus, why then, make appeal to your father King Poseidon."

'They turned away and my dear heart laughed because the excellent cunning trick of that false name had completely taken them in. Cyclops was groaning in his extremity of torment. He groped with his hands until he had found and taken the stone from the entrance. Then he sat himself in the cave's mouth with his fingers extended across it, to catch anyone who tried to steal through with the sheep. In his heart he judged me such a fool as that: while I was thinking my very hardest to contrive a way out for myself and my fellows from destruction, we being truly in the jaws of death. Many notions and devices I conceived thus for dear life, and the best of them seemed finally as follows. Some rams there were of big stock, fleecy great splendid beasts with wool almost purple in its depth of colour. I took them by threes silently and bound them abreast with the pliant bark-strips from which the wicked monster's bed was plaited. The middle beast could then take a man and the one on either side protect him from discovery. That meant three rams for each shipmate: while for myself there remained the prize ram of all the flock. I took hold of him, tucked myself under his shaggy belly and hung there so, with steadfast courage: clinging face upwards with my hands twisted into his enormous fleece. Thus we waited in great trepidation for the dawn.

'At its first redness the rams rushed out towards their pasture: but the ewes hung about their pens unmilked, bleating distressfully with bursting udders. The lord, distraught with his terrible pains, felt the back of each sheep as it stood up to march straight past him. The dullard suspected not that there were men bound beneath their fleecy ribs. Last of all the prime ram came to go out, walking stiffly with the weight of his wool and me the deep plotter. Strong Polyphemus stroked him and said, "Beloved ram, why are you the last of all my flock to quit the cave? Never before have you let yourself lag behind the others; but have been always the first to stride freely across the sward nibbling its smooth buds, and first into the hill-streams to drink: while at evening, which was homing time, you would be ever the first that wanted to turn back. And now you come last! Are you feeling the loss of your lord's sight, blinded by that villain with his knavish crew after he had made me helpless with wine? That No-man, who I swear has not yet got away from death. If only you could feel like me and had the gift of speech to tell where he skulks from my wrath. How I would dash his brains out against the ground and spill them over the cave, to lighten my heart of the pains which this worthless No-man has inflicted!"

'He pushed the ram gently from him through the doorway. When we were a little space from the cave and its surrounding yard I loosed myself and then set free my men. Often turning head to look back we drove the leggy flock, the fat ripe beasts, down to the ship where the sight of us gladdened the others at thought of the death we had escaped. They would have stayed to lament the fallen: but I would not have it. Sternly I bent my brows and checked each man's weeping: and set them instead by sharp gestures to tumbling the glossy-fleeced animals into the ship and launching out for the open sea. At once they were aboard and on their benches. Smartly they sat and gave way, so that the sea paled beneath their oar-strokes: but when we were just as far from the land as a man's shout might carry, then I hailed the Cyclops in malignant derision. "So, Cyclops, you were unlucky and did not quite have the strength to eat all the followers of this puny man within your cave? Instead the luck returned your wickedness upon yourself in fit punishment for the impiety that had dared eat the guests in your house. Zeus has repaid you, the other Gods agreeing."

'My cry stung his heart more terribly yet. He tore the crest from a great mountain and flung it at the black-prowed ship, but overcast by a hair's breadth. The rock nearly scraped the end of the tiller. The sea heaped up above its plunging, and the back-thrust, like a tidal wave from the deep, washed us landward again very swiftly, almost to shore. I snatched a long pole and used it as a quant, while I signed with my head to the crew how they must lay to it over the oar-looms if we were to avoid disaster. They put their backs into it and rowed till we were twice our former distance from the coast. Then I would have taunted Cyclops once more, but my followers each in his vein sought with gentle words to restrain me, protesting, "Hothead, why further provoke this savage creature who with his last deadly shot so nearly brought our ship to shore that we did already judge ourselves dead? Had he caught but a whisper or sound from us just now, he would have crushed our heads and our ship's timbers flat beneath some jagged stone, the marvellous thrower that he is." Thus ran their plea, but my pride was not to be dissuaded. Wherefore once again I spilled my heart's malice over him: "Cyclops, if any human being asks of you how your eye was so hideously put out, say that Odysseus, despoiler of cities, did it; even the son of Laertes whose home is in Ithaca."

'Thus I shouted, and his answer came back in a pitiful voice: "O miserable day, which sees the ancient oracle come true! We had a good and a great prophet living with us, Telemus, the son of Eurymus best of soothsayers, who passed all his life amongst us Cyclopes, practising that art. He told me it should so come to pass after many days, and I lose my sight by the hand of one Odysseus. Wherefore ever I watched for some tall man, bristling with might, to move impressively upon me: and instead there comes this mean poor pigmy and steals my eye after fuddling my wits with his drink. See here, my Odysseus, come back to me and take my guest-bounty together with a god-speed I will win you from the great Earth-shaker: for Poseidon avows himself my father, and so I dare call myself his son. He, if he be kind, will heal my hurt, which no other of the blessed Gods nor any man can do." "Heal your sight," I cried back at him, "never: not even the Earth-shaker will do it. Would God I had power to strip you of life and soul and send you down to Hades, so surely as I know that!"

'So far – but he lifted up his hands to the starry firmament and prayed to his Lord, Poseidon. "Hear me, dark-haired Girdler of the earth, if indeed I am yours and you my sire. Grant that there be no homecoming for this Odysseus, son of Laertes of Ithaca. Yet if it is fated that he must see his friends once more in his stately house and fatherland, let it be late and miserably, in a strange ship, after losing all his crews. And let him find trouble there in the house." So he made his petition and the dark God heard him. Then the giant bent to another stone (much larger than before) whirled it with immeasurable force and let fly. It too fell very near but this time a little short of the ship, just failing to shatter the rudder. The sea swelled over the bulk of the falling stone and a wave boiled up and swept us right across to the far side; to the island where were all my other well-decked ships, with their crews sorrowing near-by for that we had failed them so long. We ran our keel hard up on the sand and came ashore driving the sheep of the Cyclops. These we shared out, I being very exact to see that no one lacked his part in the division. My warrior company decreed the prize ram to me, as gage of honour, and I devoted him to cloud-wrapped Zeus, son of Cronos and Universal King, to whom I consumed the choice parts of the thighs with fire. Yet did Zeus not care for my offering, but was inventing ways to destroy all my trim ships and staunch company.

'However, the sun went down upon us while we sat there, filling ourselves with flesh in incredible abundance and with sweet wine. After the sun had gone and the shadow fallen we lay down by the water's brink till dawn's rosy showing: when I roused the force and bade them embark and cast off. Soon they were aboard and ready on their thwarts, sitting to the oars and frothing the sea with their well-timed strokes: our voyage being sad, insomuch as we had lost a part of our fellowship; and glad, that we had delivered our own souls from death.'

BOOK 10

So we came to the Aeolian island. In that sea-cradled fast-
ness, within a bulwark of invincible bronze from which
the cliff falls sheer, lived Aeolus son of Hippotas, a friend
of the eternal Gods, with his twelve children, six daughters
and six stalwart sons. Aeolus had so ordered it that the
daughters served his sons for wives. They all eat at the one
board with their father and revered mother and before
them a myriad dainty dishes are heaped up. Day-long the
steaming house echoes festively even to its court: but by
night they sleep, each man and his bashful wife between
soft rugs on ornate bed-steads.

'To this splendid palace and home we came, to find
entertainment for a month on end while Aeolus plied me
with questions upon Troy and the Argive ships and the
varied accidents of their journey home: all which things I
recounted as they had happened. Afterwards I broached
my own hope of returning and made appeal for his favour
thereto. He showed no disposition to refuse me, nor failed
to furnish his parting-gift, the hide of a nine-year-old bull,
flayed expressly, in which he confined for my sake the
complete range of every bursting wind that blew – Zeus

having made him keeper of the winds to still them or excite them as he pleased. This leathern sack he fastened with a shiny silver cord into my hull so tightly that not even the very littlest puff of wind might leak out. Besides, he gave a firm and fair West wind to blow my ships and ourselves along, though not to the easy issue he had meant. Our own heedless folly betrayed us to disaster.

'Nine whole days, nine nights and days, we happily sailed. On the tenth we raised our land's green slopes and came so near that we could see the figures tending its fires. Then at last I surrendered myself gladly to overwhelming sleep, for my strength was utterly gone with having myself managed the sheets throughout this voyage: not letting any man of my ship's company spell me, so keen was I to crack on to our native land. Whilst I slept my crew began to mutter of the gold and silver gifts I was bringing home from generous Aeolus. Said each to his mate, regardfully, "Strange how the world loves this man and runs to do him honour as soon as he arrives in any part or place. Think of the stored treasure he carries with him from the sack of Troy, while we, his partners in every last tribulation and danger of the way, return with empty hands. To crown it here is Aeolus loading more and more upon him in token of regard. Let us have a quick peep to see what wealth of gold and silver is hidden in this ox-hide" – thus their jealous words. The counsel of envy mastered my crew. They untied the skin and out rushed the winds in a heap, to smite them all at once. Away the storms swept us into the wide sea, away from the fatherland, while the crew burst into loud crying. I awoke to this scene and for a moment pondered in my heart whether to slip overboard and drown were not easier than prolonged life among the living with so great a burden of ill-luck to bear in silence. However I settled to endure and to survive; but for the present lay down in the ship and covered my head. All about me my men made lament continually while the fierce squalls carried the ships right back, even to the island of Aeolus. There we landed and watered; the crews prepared a quick meal where we beached.

'When hunger and thirst were satisfied I took one seaman and one attendant and climbed again to the famous house of Aeolus, reaching it as he sat at meat with his wife and the children. We pushed in as far as the pillars of the hall-entry and there sat down. They wondered to see me again and asked, "How now, Odysseus? Is this return some new freak of ill-fortune? Surely we despatched you heartily enough, equipped to attain your country or anywhere you wished?" I confessed sorrowfully: "My evil companions let me down – they and an untimely sleep which overcame me. Yet repair it, friends, of your ability." I had tried to make this plea persuasive, using my humblest tone. They stared at me in silence: only the father found words, and he hurled out: "Get off the island instantly, you vilest thing alive! Am I to make a habit of maintaining and fitting out one whom the Gods hate? Your being returned proves that you have incurred the abhorrence of those Deathless Ones. Out! out!" His words drove me from the house in grief. Our sailing was gloomy; and now we had no helping wind, wherefore we must labour continually at the oars, by which futile pain my men's fortitude was sapped.

'Six days and six nights was this voyage. On the seventh day we made the fortress of Lamos, which is nick-named Tall-tower by its people, the Laestrygons. In their region the extremes of day and night so nearly meet that the shepherd coming back with his full ewes exchanges greetings with the shepherd going out to pasture.

A sleepless man could there earn double wage, by doing neat-herd one half his time and shepherding small cattle for the remaining hours. Its harbour is good, for an unbroken wall of rock shelters it from side to side; while parallel headlands jut forth to mask the entrance which is rather narrow. Upon our arrival my other shipmasters steered straight into the cove and there moored their ships, each tightly to the next, together: not that it mattered, for inside the haven there was never any swell, small or big, but a white calm constantly prevailed. I however kept my own ship outside, yet near; making fast our lines to a rock at the extreme end of the point. I climbed its craggy slope to look out from the crest, but could see no trace of man's work or beasts': only there was smoke rising from behind a fold of land.

'I told my fellows they must discover what the breadeaters of this part were like and chose two of them to go, with a third for messenger. They went ashore and along a beaten waggon road, used for lading wood from the uplands to the town. A little short of the settlement proper they chanced upon a girl drawing water. The well-grown daughter of Antiphates the Laestrygonian had come down to this fountain of Artacia because it was the fashion of the town to water from its clear-running stream. They saluted her, asking after the king of the island and his subjects: she quickly pointed the way to the tall roofs of her father's hall: but when they came to that great house they found his wife inside, a mountainous woman whose ill-aspect struck them with horror. She summoned Antiphates, her powerful husband, from the assembly. His notion was to murder my men in cold blood. He seized hold of the first and proceeded to eat him for his dinner out of hand. The other two sprang away in headlong flight and regained the ships, while the master of the house was sounding an alarm through the city. This brought the stout Laestrygons in their thousands pell-mell together – not human-looking creatures, these, but giants. They gathered missile stones each a man's weight and cast them down on us off the cliffs. There went up from the fleet the ghastly sounds of splintering hulls and dying men, while the natives were busy spearing my people like fish and collecting them to make their loathsome meal.

'As they were so engaged in killing all within the close harbour I drew the sharp hanger from my side and cut the hawsers of my dark-prowed ship, shouting orders the while to her honest crew how they must be urgent upon their oars if we were to escape a terrible fate. Like one man they spumed up the water in dread of death, and my ship darted out from the over-shadowing cliffs into the welcome main. All the other vessels which had gone inside went down together: so it was in very disheartened mood that we rowed on, having lost every one of our dear comrades (yet with the consolation that we were still alive), till we came to the island of Æaea, where lived a formidable Goddess – though she spoke our speech – Circe of the luxuriant tresses, own sister of the warlock Æetes. Both were children of Helios, the Sun that lights mankind, and their mother was Perse, daughter of Oceanus.

'We floated into its land-locked harbour silently by divine guidance, right up on the beach: and disembarked to lie where we had landed for two days and two nights, our hearts devoured by fatigue and pain. But when Dawn with shining hair had made the third day bright then I took my thrusting spear and sharp sword and walked briskly from the ship to the nearest commanding height, hoping to catch sight of human-kind or to hear human voices. My look-out rock showed me smoke rising from the ample landscape, out of an oak-thicket in the forest where lay Circe's house. My heart and mind debated if I should go at once to explore this place where I had seen the flame-shot smoke, or not. It seemed wisest to go first to the shore and ship, issue rations, and after choose some of my men for a search-party. I was going down and already near the ship when surely some God took compassion on my forlorn state by sending a great stag with branching horns across my very path. The sun's heat had driven the beast from the grove where he had been feeding, down to the stream to drink. He was coming up from the water when I hit him in the spine, half-way along the back. My copper weapon went clean through, and with no more than a sob he fell in the dust and died. I put one foot on the carcase and drew my point from the wound. Then I laid the shaft on the ground near-by while I broke off and twined twigs and withies into a rope some six feet long, well-laid throughout. With this I bound together the four feet of my noble kill, passed my head through, and went staggering under the load and staying myself on the shaft of my spear, down to the ship. The burden was far too great for me to heave it to my shoulder and balance it there with the disengaged hand as usual, the beast being hugely grown.

'I dropped it on the shore before my vessel and summoned each individual man with honeyed words. "Friends, by no excess of grief can we get down to the House of Hades one day before our time. Therefore so long as there is meat and drink in the ship let us remember our stomachs and preserve ourselves from wasting away with hunger." They quickly accepted my counsel. All heads came out from the cloaks; upon the edge of the sea they stood to admire the stag, my wonderful great trophy. After they had looked their fill they cleansed their hands and prepared a glorious feast over which we sat till sundown eating the abundant venison and drinking wine. When the sun set and darkness came we slept by the sea: but with the Dawn I called a council of all hands to say: –

'"Hear my words, fellows; we are in desperate case. My friends, now we cannot find out which is East and which is West, or distinguish the dawn lands from the shadowed: nor where the Sun, our light, sinks beneath the earth and rises from it. Wherefore if anyone have counsel let him quickly give tongue. I confess I have no plan and think that none exists. Understand that lately I climbed the hill to look out, and saw that this is an island which the limitless sea encircles like a wreath. The island itself is flat and my eyes perceived how in its heart smoke rose from the midst of a dense wood." By my news their soft natures were distressed, for they recalled the outrage of Laestrygonian Antiphates and the over-weening cannibal cruelty of the Cyclops. They lamented shrilly, pouring out big tears: yet there was no use in this lamentation. So I numbered off my mail-clad followers and divided them into two sections, each with its leader. One would be mine and godlike Eurylochus took the other. The two of us tossed at once in a copper head-piece to see which should go. His counter jumped out, so tall Eurylochus marched off his two and twenty men, all of them weeping aloud. The twenty and two who stayed with me cried in sympathy.

'The party threaded the woodland glades till they found the hewn walls of Circe's house on a site which overlooked the country-side. Wolves from the hills and lions, victims of her witch's potions, roamed about it. These made no onslaught against my men but wagged their long tails and pawed them fondly, as dogs fawn at the feet of

masters who bring them from feasts some toothsome pick-
ings in the hand: with such delight did these lions and
strong-clawed wolves leap round my men, who were timid
amongst the strange formidable pets. From outside the
house-gates they heard Circe, the Goddess with the comely
braided hair, singing tunefully within by the great loom as
she went to and fro, weaving with her shuttle such close
imperishable fabric as is the wont of goddesses, some lively
lustrous thing. Polites, a file-leader very near and dear to
me, then said to the others: "Shipmates, this voice at the
loom, singing so heartily that the floor resounds again, is
a female voice – either of a woman or a goddess. Let us
give her a hail back." They agreed and shouted loudly. She
came at once, opening her doors to bid them in. In their
simplicity all went in to her: all except Eurylochus who
suspected some trick and stayed behind. She showed them
to thrones and seats and confected for them a mess of
cheese with barley-meal and clear honey, mulched in
Pramnian wine. With this she mixed drugs so sadly
powerful as to steal from them all memory of their native
land. After they had drunk from the cup she struck them
with her wand; and straightway hustled them to her sties,
for they grew the heads and shapes and bristles of swine,
with swine-voices too. Only their reason remained stead-
fastly as before; so they grieved, squealingly, at finding
themselves penned in sties. Presently Circe cast before
them such provender of acorns, chestnuts and cornel-fruit,
as rooting swine commonly devour.

'Eurylochus slowly turned back to the ship to report
his fellows' unsavoury end. Again and again he tried to tell
us while we grouped round him, but his heart was too
broken with grief: his eyes brimmed with tears: all his spirit
went out in great longing to lament. At last he was able to

meet our shower of questions and relate the disaster. "We went through the woods as you ordered, Odysseus, Sir: and in the glades we found a noble house of dressed stone, standing high. From a loom inside rose a singing voice, of goddess or woman. We shouted. She opened the door and invited us to enter. All crowded in, unthinking, except myself who imagined guile: and from that moment they vanished completely. Not one came back though I sat there long enough." At his news I belted my long silver-mounted sword with its heavy blade of copper over my shoulder: and then my bow: telling him to lead on, the way he had taken. He caught my hands and knelt to embrace my knees, imploring me with tears and flying words: "Zeus-born, do not force me back again. Let me stay here: or rather let us (such as are yet alive) flee at once and even now escape the evil day. Surely if you go you will not return – much less bring back the rest." I replied loudly: "Stay here if it pleases you, Eurylochus, in the ship, eating and drinking: but I am going. I must."

'I left ship and shore and plunged into the solemn wood, till near the great house of drug-wise Circe; when there came from it to meet me Hermes of the gold rod, seeming to be a quite young man, of that age when youth looks its loveliest with the down just mantling his cheeks. He called my name and took my hand, saying: "O unhappy one, do you again hazard the wild-wood alone? Your followers, no other than hogs to all appearance, are penned in the deep sties of Circe's house. Do you come to set them free? I tell you, yourself shall not get away but will join the others and be pent with them. But listen: I can save you and deliver you from this evil by a potent drug in whose virtue you can enter Circe's house and yet be immune. Hear the manner of Circe's deadly arts. She will prepare you refreshment, and hide a poison in it: but against you her spells will not avail, forbidden by this saving charm I give you. Let me explain your course of action. When Circe strikes you with her long thin wand draw the sharp sword that is on your hip and make for her as if you had a mind to run her through. She will cower, and implore you to be her bed-mate instead: and your best suit is not to spurn this divine paramour but to make the lying with her a lever to free your followers and win kindly treatment for yourself. Be sure though that she swears the Gods' great oath not to attempt more evil against you, lest she take advantage of your nakedness to unman you shamefully."

'Upon such explanation the Slayer of Argus plucked from the ground the herb he promised me. The Gods call it Moly, and he showed me its nature, to be black at the root with a flower like milk. It would be difficult for men and mortals to dig up Moly; but the Gods can do anything. Thereupon Hermes quitted the wooded island for high Olympus; and I went on, unquiet in mind, to the house of Circe. I halted at her gate and called. The Goddess heard, opened and bade me in. Reluctantly I entered. She set for me a silver-embossed throne, with foot-rest, of fair and cunning workmanship. She prepared me a drink in a golden cup, dropped into it a draught for my destruction and gave it to me. I took and drank it, scatheless; but she rose and struck me with her wand, crying: "Get you to your stye, wallow there with your friends!" Instead I drew sword sharply and leapt up, feigning to make an end of her. She gave a shrill scream, ran in under my stroke and clasped my knees in a flood of tears, while she wailed piercingly, "What kind of a man are you; from what city or family? It is a miracle how you have drunk my potion and not been bewitched. Never before, never, has any man resisted this drug, once it passed his lips and crossed the barrier of his jaws. How firmly seated must be your indomitable mind! Surely you are Odysseus the resourceful, who will come here (as Argusbane of the gold rod often tells me) on his way from Troy in his ship. I pray you sheath that sword and let us two go lie together, that we may mingle our bodies and learn to trust one another by proofs of love and intercourse."

'But to her appeal, I made answer: "How dare you request my favour when you have changed my retainers in your house to hogs, and when you invite me to your bed only in subtile contrivance to have me by you naked, to be mutilated and robbed of my manhood. Wherefore I shall not enter that bed of yours except you deign, Goddess, to swear a great oath that you harbour no further mischief against me." So I declared, and she instantly swore the oath I needed. As soon as she had taken it I went up to the splendid bed of Circe.

'Meanwhile the four maidens who keep her house were at their duties in the hall. They are children of the running springs and the coppices and the sacred rivers that run down to the salty sea. The first was draping the seats in noble purple palls, over a thin under-housing. The second was putting silver tables ready to these seats and laying them with baskets of gold. The third was mixing honey-hearted wine in a silver cistern and setting out golden goblets. The fourth had brought water and kindled fire under a huge copper till the water warmed. At last it seethed with heat in the polished cauldron. Then she put me in a tub and washed me with water from the great tripod, diluted to a pleasant warmth; sluicing my head and shoulders till the life-destroying weariness had melted from my limbs. When she had washed and anointed me with pure olive oil she wrapped me in a tunic and cloak and set me again on the silver-bossed intricate throne, with the footstool under my feet. The damsel of the ewer caught the water from her golden vessel in its silver basin as I rinsed my hands. She drew a shining table to my side: while a matronly woman offered me wheaten bread and a choice of her good things, cheerfully. She pressed me to eat, but eating was no pleasure to my heart whose thoughts were otherwise engaged. So I sat there, brooding unhappily.

'Circe saw me sitting still without helping myself to food because of the distress that lay upon me. She came near and asked, urgently, "Why, O why, Odysseus, do you sit there like a dumb man, gnawing your heart away but not touching my food and drink? Do you still suspect me of guile? Fear not: indeed the oath I have sworn to you is binding." I answered, "Circe, how could any decent man bear to eat or drink till he had freed his company and restored them to his sight? If truly you wish me to feast then deliver them and let these men I love come before my eyes." At the word Circe went out from the house wand in hand, opened the doors of the piggery and let out what seemed a drove of nine-year-old fat hogs. When they were all before her she went down amongst them and smeared each with a particular unguent. Then from their parts dropped away the coarse hairs which had sprouted in the might of the poison given them by the Goddess. They turned to men again as they had been before, but younger now, fresher, and much taller to the eye. They knew me, too: each and every one came up to put himself between my hands. A sorrow that was love's yearning so thrilled through them all, that the great house echoed with their sobbing. Even the Goddess was touched.

'Later she came to me and said, "Son of Laertes, go

now to your ship by the beach and drag her out on dry land, first: then store her fittings and cargo in my caves. Do it quickly and return with all your comrades." My high judgment marched with hers: so I went to the sea-side where my men were in sore grief and shedding great tears. Upon my arrival they ran to me, as the stalled calves of the country to the cows when the herd, glutted with hay, comes back to the muck-yard from grazing. At the sight of their mothers the calves skip so wildly that their pens can no longer hold them: they break loose, lowing all the while and gambolling. Just so my fellows cried and crowded round me when they saw me plain. To their hearts my coming was for one moment almost as though they had reached homely Ithaca, the city and place of their birth and upbringing. Their sorrow burst out in touching phrase: "Over your return, Heaven-born, we rejoice as if we saw again Ithaca our fatherland. Yet now tell us of those others, our friends, how they died."

'I sought to give them comfort in replying: "Nay: instead we will first draw our ship up the beach and store her gear and tackle in the caves. Then shall you follow me, one and all, to see those others feasting and pledging each other in the sacred house of Circe. They are in luxury." This was my word and presently all gave me credence but Eurylochus, who stood out and would have stayed the rest. He chided them sharply: "Poor fools, what next? Do you so love suffering that you would go again to Circe and all be turned into pigs or wolves or lions, forced to keep watch over her great house? It was so that Cyclops got his chance when some of us went into his private cave with insensate Odysseus: by that man's rashness they were cast away." His words so angered me that I had it in mind to whip the long sword from my huge thigh and smite him, to send his head rolling in the dust, though he was my near kinsman, the husband of my sister: but the others parted us and soothed me, promising, "Zeus-born, we await your guidance to Circe's sacred dwelling. As for this man, if you think fit, we can leave him here as ship-keeper by the ship." They spoke and set off from the sea. Yet was Eurylochus not left behind by the hulk. He came along too, trembling from my savage abuse of him.

'Meanwhile Circe had commanded baths for the others of my company in her house, with olive oil and fleecy tunics and outer garments for each one. So we found them attired at all points and feasting in the hall. When each saw the others and recognized them face by face, the tears ran afresh and they cried so shrilly that the rooms re-echoed through and through. The Goddess approached me with: "Son of Laertes, do not permit longer indulgence in such grief. Of course I know how sorely you were afflicted in the fish-haunted seas, and the outrages wreaked upon you by violent men along the coasts. But let that be. Eat my cheer and drink my wine till your courage returns to your breasts, as in rugged Ithaca long ago when you first quitted your ancestral homes. See how haggard and heart-sick you are with ever brooding on the evil of your wanderings! So long and terrible have been your pains that your hearts have become strangers to feasting and gladness." Our pride accepted her advice and we tarried day by day till an entire year had lapsed, sitting to table and delighting in her untold wealth of flesh and mellow wine. Slowly the year fulfilled itself, as the seasons turned about and the months died, bringing down the long days once more. Then my men took me aside, saying: –

'"Master, it is time you called to memory your native land, if fate will ever let you come alive to your well-built house and ancient estate." So they said, and my nobility assented to them. For that last day we sat and feasted on the abundant meat and wine till the sun went down. But when night had fallen and the men had stretched out in the darkling halls, I climbed to the lovely bed of Circe and prayed her by her knees, in supplication. The Goddess heeded me and the winged words I used: "O Circe, now grant me fulfilment of the promise you so largely made, to aid me towards my home. My heart pants with the thought, and my men's hearts too. When you are absent they come round me and shatter my contentment with their longing to be gone." Thus I made prayer. The beautiful Goddess of Goddesses answered me: "Zeus-kin, son of Laertes, ingenious Odysseus: against your will you must not be kept in my house. Yet learn that your next journey will be to a strange destination, even so far as the House of Hades and dread Persephone, to seek counsel of the spirit of Teiresias of Thebes, that sightless prophet whose integrity of judgment has survived death. For him Persephone has ruled that he alone, though dead, should know: all others of the dead are shadows that drift ineffectually."

'She ceased: and again my loving heart gave way. I wept as I sat there on her bed, nor did my soul any longer desire to feel or see the shining of the sun: till I had wept and wallowed myself impotent. Then I ventured again, asking: "But who, O Circe, can guide us by this way? No human being ever reached Hades in one of our black ships." Whereupon the Goddess of Goddesses replied, "Let not the need of a pilot for the ship concern you at all. Set mast, hoist sail, and then sit quietly. The northern airs will bring you thither. When you have cut across the river of Ocean you will find Persephone's shore and her grove of tall poplars and seed-blighted willows. Beach your ship there by the deep eddying Ocean stream and make your own way down to the dank house of Hades. There Pyriphlegethon (with Cocytus a tributary of the water of Styx) runs into Acheron; by a rock the two roaring rivers meet. When there, hero, step very near the face of the stream and dig a pit – like this – about a cubit each way, and pour a drink-offering around it to all the dead, of milk-in-honey first and then sweet wine and lastly water. Over it all sprinkle white pearl-barley. Then cry earnestly upon the wan muster of the piteous dead, promising that when in Ithaca again you will devote to them in your house a clean heifer, your best, on a pyre made rich with votive offerings: while for Teiresias particularly you will further sacrifice an all-black ram, the worthiest among your flocks. When thus with prayers you have entreated the grave's worshipful populations, slay for them a ram and a black sheep, pointing them towards Erebus while you yourself turn to face the stream of the river. Then many wraiths will repair to you of the dead who have died. At once straitly enjoin your fellows to flay the two sheep which lie there, butchered by your pitiless sword, and burn them: while they pray all the time to the Gods and to great Hades and to dreadful Persephone. Draw the sharp sword from your hip and sit with it ready, sternly preventing any one of the shambling dead from coming near the blood till you have had your word with Teiresias. Nor will the prophet be long in coming to you, O leader of the people; and he will explain to you your road and its stages and how, in returning, you may get across the teeming deep."

'She ceased, and then came gold-throned Dawn. The nymph put on a flowing silvery gown of light and lissom stuff, clasped her middle with a splendid golden girdle and hid her hair in a veil. She clad me in my under-garment and cloak and I went through the house, finding each of my men and rousing them with soft-spoken words: "No longer lie and dream in quiet sleep. Let us go. See, Lady Circe has told me the way." Their courage rose to my summons. Yet was I not to get every last one of them safely off. There was Elpenor the youngest (no great fighter, and loose-minded) in whom over-much drink had put a longing for cool air. So he had left his fellows and lain down on the roof of Circe's house. Hearing the bustle when the others rose and the trampling of their feet he leaped up all of a sudden with his wits too astray to think of coming down again by the long ladder. Instead he tumbled from the roof and broke his neck-bone, just where it joins the spine. His soul flew to Hades.

'As we went out together I said to my men, "You think that we are now heading for our loved country. But Circe has detailed us a quite different course, which will take us down to the House of Hades and to dread Persephone in search of the spirit of Teiresias the Theban." The news broke their hearts. They sat down where they were and tore the ringlets of hair by the roots from their heads, lamenting. Not that it was any good, the moan they made.

'So sorrowfully we proceeded towards the sea, shedding floods of tears. Yet meanwhile had Circe lightly outstripped us, gone down to the ship and tethered by it a ram and a black ewe. What mortal eye can see a God going up and down if He wills not to be seen?'

BOOK 11

At length we were at the shore where lay the ship. Promptly we launched her into the divine sea, stepped the mast, made sail and went: not forgetting the sheep, though our hearts were very low and big tears rained down from our eyes. Behind the dark-prowed vessel came a favourable wind, our welcomed way-fellow, whom we owed to Circe, the kind-spoken yet awesome Goddess: so when each man had done his duty by the ship we could sit and watch the wind and the helmsman lead us forward, day-long going steadily across the deep, our sails cracking full, till sundown and its darkness covered the sea's illimitable ways. We had attained Earth's verge and its girdling river of Ocean, where are the cloud-wrapped and misty confines of the Cimmerian men. For them no flashing Sun-God shines down a living light, not in the morning when he climbs through the starry sky, nor yet at day's end when he rolls down from heaven behind the land. Instead an endless deathful night is spread over its melancholy people.

'We beached the ship on that shore and put off our sheep. With them we made our way up the strand of Ocean till we came to the spot which Circe had described. There

Perimedes and Eurylochus held the victims while I drew the keen blade from my hip, to hollow that trench of a cubit square and a cubit deep. About it I poured the drink-offerings to the congregation of the dead, a honey-and-milk draught first, sweet wine next, with water last of all: and I made a heave-offering of our glistening barley; invoking the tenuous dead, in general, for my intention of a heifer-not-in-calf, the best to be found in my manors when I got back to Ithaca; which should be slain to them and burnt there on a pyre fed high with treasure: while for Teiresias apart I vowed an all-black ram, the choicest male out of our flocks.

'After I had been thus instant in prayer to the populations of the grave I took the two sheep and beheaded them across my pit in such manner that the livid blood drained into it. Then from out of Erebus they flocked to me, the dead spirits of those who had died. Brides came and lads; old men and men of sad experience; tender girls aching from their first agony; and many fighting men showing the stabbed wounds of brazen spears – war-victims, still in their blooded arms. All thronged to the trench and ranged restlessly this side of it and that with an eerie wailing. Pale fear gripped me. Hastily I called the others and bade them flay and burn with fire the sheep's bodies which lay there, slaughtered by my pitiless sword. They obeyed, conjuring without cease the Gods, great Hades and terrible Persephone, while I sat over the pit holding out my sharp weapon to forbid and prevent this shambling legion of the dead from approaching the blood till I had had my answer from Teiresias.

'The first I knew was the spirit of my fellow, Elpenor, whose body was not yet interred under the ample ground. We had left him unwept and unburied in the halls of Circe, for that these other labours came upon us urgently. When I saw him I had compassion and sharply cried across to him: 'Elpenor, how come you here into the gloomy shades? Your feet have been quicker than my ship.' He in a thin wail answered me: 'Son of Laertes, ready Odysseus, the harsh verdict of some God sealed my doom, together with my own unspeakable excess in wine. I had lain down on Circe's house-top to sleep off this drunkenness, but awoke still too confused to descend from the roof by the long ladder. Instead I plunged headlong over the parapet and broke my neck-bone in its socket: hence my spirit has come down here to Hades. Yet I implore you, my Lord, to remember me as you go past homeward; for of my sure knowledge your returning must be by Æaea. My Lord, I adjure you by those left behind, those not among us – by your wife and by the father who cared for you when you were a little child, as by Telemachus, the babe you had to leave in your house alone – do not abandon me unwept and unburied, lest I be the pawn to bring upon you God's wrath: but consume my body in fire, with those arms and armour which remain mine, and heap over the ashes a mound at the edge of the sea where the surf breaks white, for a token telling of an unhappy man to aftertime; and when the rites are completed fix above my mound the oar that in life I pulled among my fellows.'

'Thus he said and I promised him: "Luckless one, all these things will I see done, exactly." So we two sat there, exchanging regrets, I with my sword held out stiffly across the blood-pool and the wraith of my follower beyond it, telling his tale. Then advanced the spirit of my mother who had died, even Anticleia, daughter of kindly Autolycus. I had left her alive when I started for the sacred city of Ilios, so now the sight of her melted my heart and made me weep with quick pain. Nevertheless I would not let her near to touch the blood, for I awaited Teiresias to speak with me. And at last he came, the spirit of Theban Teiresias, gold sceptre in hand. He knew me and said, "Heaven-born Odysseus, what now? O son of misfortune, why leave the lambent sunshine for this joyless place where only the dead are to be seen? Stand off from the pit and put up your threatening sword that I may drink blood and declare to you words of truth." So he said and I stepped back, thrusting my silver-hilted sword home into its scabbard: while he drank of the blackening blood. Then did the blameless seer begin to say: –

"'You come here, renowned Odysseus, in quest of a comfortable way home. I tell you the God will make your way hard. I tell you that your movements will not remain secret from the Earth-shaker, whose heart is bitter against you for the hurt you did him in blinding the Cyclops, his loved son. Yet have you a chance of surviving to reach Ithaca, despite all obstacles, if you and your followers can master your greed in the island of Thrinacia, when your ship first puts in there for refuge from the lowering sea. For in that island you will find at pasture the oxen and wonderful sheep of Helios our Sun, who oversees and overhears all things. If you are so preoccupied about returning as to leave these beasts unhurt, then you may get back to Ithaca, very toil-worn, after all: but if you meddle with them, then I certify the doom of your men and your ship; and though yourself may escape alive, it will not be till after many days, in a ship of strangers, alone and in sorry plight, that you win back, having suffered the loss of all your company: while in your house you shall find trouble awaiting you, even overbearing men who devour your substance on pretext of courting your worshipful wife and chaffering about her marriage dues. Yet at your coming shall you visit their violence upon them, fatally. After you have killed these suitors, either by cunning within the house or publicly with the stark sword, then go forth under your shapely oar till you come to a people who know not the sea and eat their victuals unsavoured with its salt: a people ignorant of purple-prowed ships and of the smoothed and shaven oars which are the wings of a ship's flying. I give you this token of them, a sign so plain that you cannot miss it: you have arrived when another wayfarer shall cross you and say that on your doughty shoulder you bear the scatterer of haulms, a winnowing-fan. Then pitch in the earth your polished oar and sacrifice goodly beasts to King Poseidon, a ram and a bull and a ramping boar. Afterward turn back; and at home offer hecatombs to the Immortal Gods who possess the broad planes of heaven: to all of them in order, as is most seemly. At the last, amidst a happy folk, shall your own death come to you, softly, far from the salt sea, and make an end of one utterly weary of slipping downward into old age. All these things that I relate are true."

'So he prophesied and I, answering, said: "O Teiresias, surely these things are threads of destiny woven in the Gods' design. Yet tell to me one other thing. Before me is the ghost of my mother, dead. Lo there, how she crouches by the blood and will not look upon me nor address me one word. Tell me, King, how shall she know that I am her son?" So I said and he replied, "A simple thing for my saying and your learning. Any of these ghosts of the dead, if you permit them to come near the blood, will tell you truth: and to whomsoever you begrudge it, he shall go back, away." The spirit of King Teiresias ended his soothsaying and departed to the House of Hades, but I remained firmly there, while my mother came up and drank of the storm-dark blood. Then at once she knew me and wailed aloud, crying to me winged words: "My child, what brings you to visit here, a quick man in this darkness of the shadow? It is sore travail for the living to see such things, because of the wide rivers and fearful waters that run between: especially Ocean's flood, that mortals cannot cross on foot but only by ship, in a well-found ship. Are you still errant, you and your men, from Troy? The time has been long if you have not yet reached Ithaca nor seen your wife in the house."

'So she said and I returned: "My mother, I had no choice but to come down to Ḥades. I must needs consult the spirit of Theban Teiresias, inasmuch as I have not yet drawn nigh Achaea, not yet set foot upon my own land, but have strayed ever painfully from that day I followed great Agamemnon to fight the Trojans at Ilios of the fine horses. But tell me now plainly – by what fateful agency did Death strike you down? Was it a slow disease, or did arrow-loving Artemis slay you with a stroke of her gentle darts? Inform me of the father and son I left. Is my position still safe in their keeping, or has a stranger assumed it on the rumour that I shall not return? Also of my wife – what is her mood and conduct? Does she abide by the child and guard all things as they were, or has she married some noble Achaean?" My lady mother exclaimed: "Why, she is ever in your house, most patiently. The nights drag through for her heavily and her days are wet with tears. Your fair position has not fallen to another. Telemachus holds the estate unchallenged, feasting amongst his peers at all such entertainments as magistrates may properly attend. He is invited everywhere. For your father – he now-a-days dwells wholly in the country and does not come to town. Old age grows crankily upon him. He will not suffer for his own use any bed or couch, quilts or glossy blankets: nor aught but rags upon his body. In winter-time he sleeps at home as bondmen sleep, by the hearth in the ashes of the fire: but when the summer brings its rush of harvest-tide and all through his rich vineterraces the dead leaves are strewn for him in ground-carpets, upon them will he lie distressfully, sighing for your return with a sorrow that ever waxes in his heart. Also my death and doom were of that sort. No archer-goddess with piercing sight came upon me in the house and felled me with gentle arrows: nor any set disease, with a sorry wasting to drain the life from my limbs. Rather it was my longing for you – your cunning ways, O my wonderful Odysseus, and your tenderness – which robbed me of the life that had been sweet."

'She ceased her say. While my heart pondered the word a longing rose in me to take in my arms this spirit of my mother, though she were dead. Thrice I stepped toward her for an embrace, and thrice she slipped through my grasp like a shadow or a dream. The pain conceived in my heart grew very bitter and I cried to her in piercing words: "Mother mine, can you not abide the loving arms of one who yearns so sorely after you, that here, even here in Hades, we may tearfully sate ourselves with icy shuddering grief? Or are you only some phantasm which great Persephone has sent to increase the misery of my pain?" So I said; but my mother lamented: "Alas my hapless child! Here is no mockery from Persephone, daughter of Zeus: it is the common judgement upon all mortals when they die. Then the nerves will no more bind flesh and frame into one body, for the terrible intensity of searing fire subdues them till they vanish, as the quickening spirit vanishes from the white bones and the soul flies out, to hover like a dream. Therefore make your best speed back into daylight, noting all things as you go, for rehearsal hereafter to your wife."

'As we two asked and answered, the women arrived

in multitude, famous Persephone having sent up all those who had been wives or daughters of great men. They eddied and thronged about the dark blood while I was wondering how to get word with each. The best plan seemed to draw the sharp-edged sword once again from my strong thigh and with it prevent their drinking the blood in one rush: by my so doing they came up singly, each declaring her origin, and I questioned them, one and all.

'The first was nobly-born Tyro who avouched herself daughter of pure Salmoneus and former wife of Cretheus, Aeolus' son. She loved a river, the divine Enipeus, much the fairest of earth's streams. Wherefore she would haunt its reaches continually, till the God who shakes and girdles the earth put on the shape of Enipeus and lay with her in the out-pouring of the swift-eddying river. Round them a dark-blue wave arched itself hugely and bowed like a mountain wall to hide the God and his mortal woman. Then he unclasped the girdle of her maidenhead and put her into a sleep. When he had achieved love's labour he took her by the hand, calling her by name and saying, "Rejoice, O woman, in my love: and forasmuch as the couching of the Deathless Ones is never barren you will bear splendid children when the year has turned. Your task must be to care tenderly for these yourself. Till when, go home and set a watch upon your lips, not uttering my name. Yet know that I am Poseidon, Shaker of the Earth." He plunged beneath the frothing sea and in due time she conceived and bore Pelias and Neleus. When they grew up they both served Zeus heart and soul. Pelias, a sheep-master, lived in the plains of Iolcos: the other in sandy Pylos. The queenly woman also bore sons to Cretheus – Aeson and Pheres and Amythaon the chariot-knight.

'After her I saw Antiope daughter of Aesopus. She

boasted that she had spent one night clasped in Zeus' own encircling arms: and had two children by him, Amphion and Zethus, first founders of Thebes-with-the-Seven-Gates: its fortifiers, too, for not even men of their might could dwell in that open domain except it were walled and towered. After her came Alcmene, wife of Amphitryon, who from the embraces of great Zeus gave birth to lion-hearted Heracles, the bravely-patient; and Megara came, the daughter of proud Creon, whom that strong and hardy son of Amphitryon took in wedlock.

'I saw Epicaste, the mother of Oedipodes. She in ignorance sinned greatly when she let herself be married to her own son; the son who murdered his father, he it was that wedded her. Presently the Gods made their state notorious to all men. By their dooming he must linger in distress as king of the Cadmaeans in lovely Thebes: whereas she went down to Hades, that strong keeper of the gate of Hell. She tied a running noose to the high beam across her hall and perished, mad with remorse: leaving her son alone to face all the pains and obloquy which the avengers of a mother can impose.

Then came shining Chloris whose amazing beauty made Neleus pay fabulous marriage gifts for her and wed her. She was the last daughter of Amphion son of Iasus, once a great king in Minyan Orchomenus. Chloris became queen of Pylos and amongst her famous issue were Nestor and Chromius and lordly Periclymenus; besides a daughter, Pero the magnificent, a wonder of the world, whom all the neighbours wooed: but Neleus announced he would not part with her except to one who could recover from Phylace the cattle that great Iphiclus had taken. A hard task to win back these lurching broad-fronted beasts; so hard and dangerous that no one was found to try, but the ingenuous

Prophet himself; and he got no joy of it, for the Gods visited his attempt upon him by gyving him cruelly under guard of the boorish cowkeepers. Yet after lapse of time, as days and months were accomplished and the year revolved to perfect the destined hour, eventually did strong Iphiclus let him go, when he had uttered all his soothsaying: that the purpose of Zeus might be fulfilled.

'I saw Leda, the consort of Tyndareus: she bore him two strong – willed sons, Castor the breaker of horses, and Polydeuces who was good with his fists. This pair are now under the fertile earth; yet in a sense alive, by the great dispensation of Zeus who has endowed them with alternating life and death, to live one day and to die the next. Honours are paid to them even as to the Gods. After Leda came the wife of Aloeus, Iphimedia, to say that she had slept with Poseidon and got by him two sons; short-lived, alas, but the tallest children that our quickening earth ever nourished on its bread, and the handsomest after peerless Orion. These were godlike Otus and far-famed Ephialtes. At nine years old they were nine fathoms high and nine cubits across. They vowed to carry the din and shock of battle into Olympus, to spite the Immortal Gods. They strained to put Ossa on top of Mount Olympus, and Pelion with its shivering forest trees upon Ossa again, to be their stepping-stones to heaven: and would have done it, too, had they but come to man's estate. As it was, Zeus' son by fair-haired Leto slew them both, their cheeks yet innocent of hair, their chins not shaded with the bloom of down. I saw Phaedra and Procris: also fair Ariadne, daughter of vicious Minos. Theseus was carrying her from Crete towards the fair hill of holy Athens: yet did not reap his enjoyment of her, because Artemis killed her first in sea-cradled Dia on the evidence of Dionysus. I saw Maera and Clymene:

horrible Eriphyle too, she that took gold to sell her lawful husband.

'But how can I even name to you, much less describe, all those I saw? There were so many wives of heroes, so many daughters. Before I ended my tale the divine night itself would have worn through. Indeed, already it is time for sleep, though I know not if I should lie in the ship with the crew you have appointed me, or stay in the house. The hour of my starting rests in the hands of the Gods and in your guardian hands.'

Here Odysseus broke off his history: but the Phaeacians none the less stayed silent, spell-bound as it were, amidst the dim-lit hall: till Arete the white-armed suddenly broke out: 'Now, Phaeacians, what think you of this man, the cut and scale of him and his heart's poise? My stranger, look you, and my guest: though in the privilege of entertaining him all of you may share. Be in no haste to forward him hence, nor stint your gifts to so needy a man. Remember how the signal favour of the Gods has filled your homes with treasure.' After her rose the old hero Echeneus, whose age made him august among the Phaeacians. 'My friends, not far off the point nor unbecoming are these words from the mouth of our prudent Queen. Consider them favourably: yet with us must act and authority alike vest in Alcinous.'

The King cried back: 'So long as I am to have lordship and life amongst you, sea-faring Phaeacians, be it understood that the word of the Queen holds good. Wherefore, however he may crave to get home, let the stranger possess himself fairly till the morrow. Tomorrow I will round off the gifts he has received and complete his fortune. For his escort back, doubtless it is everybody's business: but mine especially, I being sovereign in this land.' Odysseus answered him with judgement and said: 'Alcinous, famous

Lord, had you directed me to tarry a whole year more while you increased my gifts – with assurance of eventual passage – why I should placidly choose that course as the profitable course. The more nearly full my hands on landing (if I do attain my beloved country) the better held and esteemed I shall be of all who meet me in Ithaca.'

Alcinous loudly replied: 'O my Odysseus, we who have you before our eyes will not be persuaded that you are a pretender or thief, like those many vagrant liars our dark earth breeds to flourish and strut behind so thick a mask of falsehood that none can pierce it to read their worth. In your words is a formal beauty to match the graceful order of your ideas: you frame and bedeck this tale of the Argives' hardship and your toils as knowingly as any bard. Yet tell me one thing more and let us have the truth of it – did you see your comrades in the under-world, any of those god-like ones who served with you before Ilion and there found death awaiting them? The night is still long, immeasurably long. No need yet to clear the hall for sleep: wherefore continue these marvellous histories. I would listen till the full dawn, here in the house, had you voice to set forth to me the tale of all your woes.' Odysseus answered saying, 'Most famous Lord: surely there is a time for long speaking and a time for sleep. But if you still ardently desire to hear me I shall not spare you the recital of sadder things than any I have told, a history of the ultimate agony of ill-starred men who survived the Trojan battle and its death-dealing clamour only to perish at their journey's end by an evil woman's resolve.

'To my tale. From the herd of women-ghosts chaste Persephone at last delivered me, driving them off helter-skelter; and in came, despondent, the spirit of Agamemnon son of Atreus. Round him were grouped the wraiths of those others who had fallen upon their fate and died with him in the house of Aegisthus. The chief knew me instantly, after he had drunk of the black blood: and greatly he sobbed, with tears running down his face. He stretched out his hands to me in longing to fold me to his breast: vainly, for no longer had he substance to stand firm or the vigourously free movements, such as once had filled his supple limbs. When I saw this the pity in my heart moved me also to tears and I lamented. 'Most famous Atrides, my King of Men, say now by what throw Death the champion flung you at the last? Did Poseidon overwhelm you in your ship by rousing against you terrible gale upon terrible gale: or did foemen beat you down on the shore, while you were cutting out their oxen and their goodly flocks of sheep or disputing with them some walled city and its women?'

'So I asked, but he replied: "Odysseus, Poseidon excited against me no too-great gale to destroy me in my ships nor did savages slay me on any coast. Aegisthus achieved my death and doom with the connivance and aid of my accursed wife, after inviting me to his house and setting me at table. Yes, I was killed feasting – struck down as one butchers an ox at stall. Inglorious, pitiful death! They slaughtered my men around me one by one and laid them out like whitetusked boars brittled for some banquet, or feast of peers, or wedding in a rich lord's house. You have stood by many killings, in single combats or in mellays; but never have you seen one gruesome as ours between the plenished tables, round the mixing bowl of wine, in a hall whose floor swam with blood. My bitterest pass was to hear the death-shriek of Cassandra, Priam's daughter, whom traitorous Clytemnaestra slew just over me. Verily I tried to raise my hands for her, but they fell back to earth again. I was dying then – dying upon the sword. The brutish woman turned her back nor would spend so much pity (though I was fast on my way to Hades) as to draw down my eyelids with her hands, or bind up my jaw. I tell you, there is nought more awful and inhuman than a woman who can fondle in her heart crimes so foul as this conception of my wife's to murder the husband of her youth. I was coming home, promising myself the joyous greeting of my children and my household: and then she, by her depth of villainy, smirches the whole breed of womanhood for ever and ever, even those yet unborn and virtuous."

'He ended and I rejoined: "Alas and woe is me! From the beginning has wide-seeing Zeus dreadfully visited the seed of Atreus through women's arts. What an army of us died for Helen; and now Clytemnaestra spins this web of death for you, while you are far away." So I said and he once again urged me, saying: "Never be very gentle, henceforward, with your wife, Odysseus. Tell her only a part of anything you know, and hide the rest. Yet need you not look for a bloody death from your wife: Penelope is so careful, knowing, and of such excellent discretion; the dear daughter of Icarius. Let me see, a young wife was she not, when we left her for the war? The infant then feeding at her breast may now be sitting with the men, one of them: a happy son to see his father's return and dutifully fold him in his arms. Upon my son Clytemnaestra gave me no time to feed my eyes. Before he came she slew me; slew her lawful husband. Now I will tell you something else to lay up in your heart. You must bring your ship to shore secretly and covertly, in your beloved land. There is no putting faith in women. In return, do you tell me something, bluntly. Have you heard of my son's activity either at Orchomenus or in sandy Pylos or guesting with Menelaus in Sparta? Noble Orestes has not yet died upon earth."

'To his question I returned, "Atrides, why trouble me

for news? I know not even if he is alive or dead: and touching life and death I will not vainly invent." As we two stood thus in sorrowful talk, weeping freely, up came the ghost of Achilles, son of Peleus, with Patroclus and gallant Antilochus. Also Aias, the handsomest man and goodliest figure of the Danaans – except for Achilles himself, that swift-footed descendant of Aeacus, whose spirit recognized me and gloomily flung out: "Ingenious son of Laertes, Odysseus of the seed of Zeus, daring unhappy soul! How will you find some madder adventure to cap this coming down alive to Hades among the silly dead, the worn-out mockeries of men?" So he questioned, bitterly, and I replied, "O Achilles, son of Peleus, mightiest man of valour among the Achaeans! Of dire necessity I came, to hear from Teiresias how best to arrive back in rocky Ithaca. In all this time I have not neared Achaea nor seen my country. Ill luck dogs me everywhere. How I envy your lot, Achilles, happiest of men who have been or will be! In your day all we Argives adored you with a God's honours: and now down here I find you a Prince among the dead. To you, Achilles, death can be no grief at all." He took me up and said, "Do not make light of Death before me, O shining Odysseus. Would that I were on earth a menial, bound to some insubstantial man who must pinch and scrape to keep alive! Life so were better than King of Kings among these dead men who have had their day and died. Enough – give me news of my admirable son! Did he get to the war and prove himself a leader; or not yet? Also of noble Peleus, if you have heard – do the Myrmidons still honour him or is he despitefully seen from Hellas to Phthia, because old age has crippled his hands and feet? No longer can I stand up in the eye of day his champion, the prodigy who succoured the Argives in the plains of Troy and brought death upon the stoutest Trojans. O if I could be, just for the briefest moment, in my father's house! How I would make my great strength and invincible hands a reproach and horror to all those who forcibly let him from his glory!"

'I replied, "Of illustrious Peleus I have not heard; but of your dear son Neoptolemus I can tell you the whole truth, just as you wish. It was with me, in my capacious ship, that he came up from Skyros to join the panoplied Achaeans. So often as we bandied counsel by the town of Troy he would be quickest to speak, and spoke ever to the point. God-like Nestor and myself were the only two to talk him down. And when we Achaeans joined battle in the plain of Troy he would never rest in the rank or ruck of men, but dashed ahead allowing no valour to outstrip his. He slew many men in mortal fight. I cannot remember even the names of all the chiefs who fell by his hand while he was aiding the Argive cause: but with what a sword-stroke did he cut down Eurypylus, heroic son of Telephus, about whom died many of his Ceteian company, victims of a woman's bribe! Royal Memnon apart, I saw no better man among them. Further, when the time came for us Argive leaders to mount into the horse that Epeius built, they charged me with the responsibility of closing or opening the trap-door of our crowded lair. The other chiefs and champions were wiping away tears and trembling in every limb: but though I gazed at him with my whole eyes never once did his comely skin turn white or a tear need dashing from his cheek. Repeatedly he begged me to let him sally forth from the horse: and he kept fondling his sword-hilt and heavy spear-blade, in deadly rage against the men of Troy. After we had sacked the hill-built city of Priam he departed in his ship with his full share of loot, escaping without a wound, for the flying shafts all missed him and the sword-play left him unhurt. The luck of war, that was: Ares often fights too haphazardly to give each one his due." So I said, and the wraith of swift-footed Achilles strode with large strides across the field of asphodel, exultant because I had told him that his son was famous.

'There hung about me others of the departed, each sadly asking news of his loved ones. Only the spirit of Aias the son of Telamon kept aloof, he being yet vexed with me for that I had been preferred before him when by the ships we disputed the harness of Achilles, the arms which his Goddess-mother had set as prize, and which the sons of the Trojans and Pallas Athene adjudged. Would I had not won that victory, since by it earth closed above so excellent a head. Verily, in sheer beauty of form and for prowess, great Aias stood out above every Danaan, the noble son of Peleus excepted. So to him I spoke very gently, thus: "Lord Aias, son of great Telamon, can you not even in death forget your anger against me over those cursed arms? Surely the Gods meant them as a plague upon the Argives. What a tower fell in your fall! For you we Argives mourn as for our lost crown, Achilles; because you died. Prime cause of it was Zeus, who in his terrible hatred of the Danaan chivalry laid upon you their guilty desert. I pray you, King, draw near to hear the things we say. Vail your fierce pride of heart." So I appealed, but he answered not a word: only went away towards Erebus with other spirits of the departed dead. Yet likely he would have spoken despite his wrath – or I to him again – only my heart was wishful to see other souls of the many dead.

'Thus I saw Minos, Zeus' illustrious son, with his golden sceptre, enthroned in the broad gate of the house of Hades to judge the dead, who sat or stood before his seat enquiring of the King upon their sentences. I picked out, too, gigantic Orion where he chased wild beasts across the meadows of asphodel: ghosts of the same beasts he used to slay among earth's lonely hills. His fist brandished a club of solid copper, unbroken and unbreakable. I saw Tityus, son of Gaia the famous Earth, lying outstretched over a flat ground. He covered nine roods. A vulture sat each side of him and tore at his liver, piercing deeply even to the bowels. With his hands he might not drive them off. This was because he had maltreated Leto, the stately mistress of Zeus, as she went through park-like Panopeus toward Pytho.

'There too was Tantalus in sorry plight, put to stand chin-deep in a pool. He gaped with thirst: but could not reach the water to drink it. As often as the old man bent towards it in his frenzy, so the water disappeared, swallowed into the ground which showed blackly below his feet. A God made it dry. Over the pool high-foliaged trees hung down their fruit, down to his head. Pears there were, and pomegranates, rosy apples, sweet figs and leafy olives. Yet every time the old man eagerly stretched out his hand to grasp, the wind would toss them cloud-high away. Another whom I saw in torment was Sisyphus, wrestling double-handed with a giant stone. He would thrust with hands and feet, working it towards the crest of his ridge: but when he was almost at the top, it would twist back irresistibly and roll itself down again to the level, the shameless stone. Once more he would go push and heave at it, with sweat pouring down his limbs, and a dust cloud mantling higher than his head.

'Also I distinguished great Heracles – I mean his ghost. Himself is happy with the Immortal Gods at their festivals, with his wife Hebe of the slim ankles, the daughter of all-mighty Zeus and golden-shod Hera. About this ghost eddied the dead, clangorously whirling like wild birds this way and that in bewildered fear. He stood, dark as night, naked bow in hand and arrow ready on the string, glaring fiercely like one about to shoot. His breasts were bound with a baldric, a striking work of solid gold, marvellously wrought with images: of bears, wild boars and bright-eyed lions; of fights and wars, slaughter and murderings of men. Its craftsman had surpassed himself by putting into the design all his mastery. Never might he produce its peer. As soon as I came within range Heracles knew me and greeted me compassionately: "So you too, deep-witted Odysseus, are in the toils of ill-luck and lead a life as cruel as mine was while I subsisted in the eye of the Sun. I might be a child of Zeus: yet was my lot a misery beyond belief, for I was subjected to a man meaner than myself who shamefully misused me upon inordinate labours. Why, he sent me down here to fetch their hound away! It was, he thought, the worst task he could devise. Yet I did it and carried the beast up from Hades to him: with Hermes to give me a start and grey-eyed Athene's help." Heracles spoke and went back into the house of Hades; while I lingered yet, to see some of the long-dead antique heroes: for I was very desirous of such dim and distant ones as Theseus or Pirithous, legendary children of the Gods. But before they could come, there beset me ten thousand seely ghosts, crying inhumanly. I went pale with fear, lest awful Persephone send me from Hades the Gorgon's head, that fabulous horror. So I turned to my ship and told the companions to get in and let go the cables. They were quickly embarked and on their thwarts: when the current of the flood bore us down to the river of Ocean, along which at first we rowed, but later found a helpful breeze.'

BOOK 12

From Ocean's pouring stream our ship measured the open rolling seas even to Æaea, the isle of sunrise where Dawn the fore-runner has her house and dancing-floor: there we grounded the ship among the sand-banks and went out upon the beach, to sleep and wait for day. When the light came I sent a party up to Circe's house to bring down dead Elpenor's body. We hewed logs and built his pyre upon the tallest headland where it runs out above the sea: duly we made his funeral, bewailing him with bitter tears. After body and armour were quite burned away we piled a mound over them, and to crown it dragged up a monolith, on top of which we fixed his goodly oar. The busy work was scarcely done when Circe came, decked to receive us: our departure from Hades had not been hidden from her. Attending her were maids laden with bread and meat in plenty and red wine with a fiery sparkle to it. She stood in our midst, saying: –

"'A hardy adventure, men, this going down to Hades alive. Now you will twice encounter death, whereas others do die but once. So I pray you rest here in the island all to-day, eating my food and drinking this wine.

If you sail to-morrow at the daybreak I shall have time to plot you a course and detail its leading-marks: that you may be saved the hurt and pain of untoward, unforeseen accidents by sea or land." Her counsel convinced our prides. We sat and feasted all day till the sun went down, the flesh being plenteous and the wine excellent. When sunset had darkened into the shadows of night, the others stretched themselves to sleep among the mooring ropes: but the lady Circe took me by the hand apart from my friends, made me sit, and set herself by my side asking me to tell her our story as it had happened. After which she said: –

'"So much has been well done. Now heed what I say and the God himself will quicken it in your memory. Your next land-fall will be upon the Sirens: and these craze the wits of every mortal who gets so far. If a man come on them unwittingly and lend ear to their Siren-voices, he will never again behold wife and little ones rising to greet him with bright faces when he comes home from sea. The thrilling song of the Sirens will steal his life away, as they sit singing in their plashet between high banks of mouldering skeletons which flutter with the rags of skin rotting upon the bones. Wherefore sail right past them: and to achieve this successfully you must work bees-wax till it is plastic and therewith stop the ears of your companions so that they do not hear a sound. For your own part, perhaps you wish to hear their singing? Then have yourself lashed hand and foot into your ship against the housing of the mast, with other bights of rope secured to the mast itself. Ensure also that if you order or implore your men to cast you loose, their sole response shall be to bind you tighter with cord upon cord. That way you may safely enjoy the Sirens' music. And after your crew have rowed you past these sisters, there will come a stretch upon which I do not advise you in so many words how you should steer. The decision must be yours, on the spot. Hear the alternatives: –

'"On this side tower up precipitous cliffs, against which the giant swell of dark-eyed Amphitrite breaks with a shattering roar. The blessed Gods call these rocks the Skurries. Between them not even a bird may slip unhurt; no, not All-Father Zeus's own shy ring-doves carrying his ambrosia. From each flight of them the sheer rocks rob some bird or other and the Father has to add one more to maintain the tale. Suppose a ship of men drives in thither. It is lost. Scattered planks and the corpses of its crew will be descried tossing in the bitter waves amid the lightnings which flash from out the whirlwinds there. Only one ship of all the ships on the sea has threaded this passage: it was Argo the world-famed, on her voyage from Æetes; and she, like the rest, would have been quickly dashed to death against those mighty reefs, had not Hera passed her through because Jason was her love.

'"On the other side stand two huge crags, one of which thrusts into heaven its sharp peak, which yet is covered always by a sombre cloud-cap that never melts away. So there is never any clear light to sparkle round its crest, not even in summer or in autumn's heat. No mortal man could scale that height or ever keep his footing there – not with twenty hands and feet – for its sides are smooth, like well-polished rock. Half way up the cliff on the western side, facing Erebus the land of death, opens a murky cave. By it, noble Odysseus, you can take a bearing to check your course. Yet no archer born is mighty enough to flight an arrow from a ship into that deep cave, within which lurks dread yelping Scylla – yelping, for she squeals like a new-born puppy, being in truth no puppy but a repulsive monster on which not even a God could look without dismay, should his path cross hers. She has twelve splay feet and six lank scrawny necks. Each neck bears an obscene head, toothy with three rows of thick-set crowded fangs blackly charged with death. She keeps herself bedded waist-deep in the bowels of her cave but sways her heads out across the dizzy void, and angles with them, sweeping the reefs ever and again keenly for dolphins or dog-fish or some greater quarry from among the countless droves which breed in loud Amphitrite's thundering waves. Particularly she battens on humankind, never failing to snatch up a man with each one of her heads from every dark-prowed ship that comes. No sailors yet can boast to have slipped past her in their craft, scot-free.

'"The second, lower crag you will observe, Odysseus, near this one. Quite near, only a bow-shot off. Mark its wild fig tree, florid with leaves, for beneath that is the spot where enormous Charybdis blackly sucks down the sea. Three times a day she sucks it down and three times she spews it out: an awful sight. May you not be there while she sucks in! No power, not the Earthshaker's own, could then deliver you from ruin. Better bear sharply across towards Scylla's rock, hug it, and coast by at speed. It is less grievous to mourn six men gone from a crowd than for all to be lost together." She paused and I broke in, "Goddess, I must ask you a plain question about all this. Is there no way for me, while avoiding deadly Charybdis, to fight off that other as she tries to harry my men?" So I asked. "Presumptuous wretch!" cried the Goddess, "how your nature leaps at once to thoughts of action and of bloodshed. Will you not give even the Gods best? I tell you, Scylla is not mortal, to be fought off, but an immortal blain: unpitying, fierce, fiendish, invincible. Resign yourself: to flee from her is the better part of valour. Should you linger below her rock to array yourself against her I fear lest she let fly her heads a second time at you and again pick off one man in each. Your best course is to push hard past her, invoking Crataiis, Scylla's dam, who whelped this curse of humanity. Crataiis, if called upon, will keep Scylla from a second plunge.

'"Afterwards you will make the island of Thrinacia, a grazing ground of the many cattle of the Sun and of his noble sheep. The cattle are seven herds and there are as many flocks of sheep, with fifty head in each. Upon these neither birth nor death can pass. Two divine creatures tend them, Phaethusa and Lampetie, fair-tressed nymph-daughters of Neaera and exalted Helios. Their mother, the Goddess, after they had been weaned, sent them to live apart in this Thrinacian island, where they keep their father's flocks and his rolling-gaited kine. Should you be so bound up in the thought of returning home that you leave these beasts unharmed, then through much tribulation you may indeed attain Ithaca at the end of all: but if you hurt them I solemnly predict the certain doom of your ship and men. You may yourself escape, but your return will be at the least tardy and miserable, effected only with the loss of your whole company."

'As Circe spoke Dawn assumed her golden throne. Back into the island went the Goddess, while I rejoined the ship and summoned my men aboard to loosing the hawsers. Soon they embarked, sat to their tholes and dipped the oars in unison, whitening the sea to spray. After the ship Circe sent us a kindly way-fellow, a fair wind which filled our sails. Each man performed his duty in the ship and afterward we sat at ease, while wind and helmsman took us along.

'After a while to my crowd I spoke gravely: "Friends, I do not mean to keep to myself, or among just one or two, the disclosures now made me by Circe, Goddess of Goddesses: but I will publish them freely in order that we may die – if we die – informed: or else trick death and fate to get clean away. Her first warnings concern the marvellous Sirens and their flowery meadow. Our prime duty will be to turn a deaf ear to their singing. Only myself may listen, after you have so fastened me with tight-drawn cords that I stand immovably secured against the tabernacle of the mast, with further short lashings dependent from the mast itself: and if I beg you or bid you let me loose, then must you redoubly firm me into place with yet more bonds." I repeated this till all had heard it well, while our trim ship was borne swiftly towards the island of these Siren-sisters by the breath of our fair breeze. But suddenly this flagged. A breathless calm supervened, some higher power lulling all the waves. My crew rose to take in the canvas, which they stowed in the capacious well: then sat down again to row, frothing the water with their blades of polished pine. I took a great round of wax, chopped it small with my sword-edge and worked it with all the power of my hands. Soon the wax grew warm by this dint of kneading in the glare of the lordly Sun: when it was soft I filled with it the ears of all my party. Then they tied me stiffly upright to the tabernacle, with extra ends of rope made fast to the mast above. Once more they sat and their oar-beats whitened the sea.

'Speeding thus lightly we arrived within earshot of the place. The Sirens became aware of the sea-swift vessel running by them: wherefore they clearly sang to us their song – "Hither, come hither, O much-praised Odysseus: come to us, O Glory of Achaea. Bring your ship to land that you may listen to our twin voices. Never yet has any man in a dark ship passed us by without lending ear to the honeysweet music of our lips – to go away spirit-gladdened and riper in knowledge. For we know all the toils wherewith the Gods did afflict Argives and Trojans in the broad Troad: and we know all things which shall be hereafter upon the fecund earth." Such words they sang in lovely cadences. My heart ached to hear them out. To make the fellows loose me I frowned upon them with my brows. They bent to it ever the more stoutly while Perimedes and Eurylochus rose to tighten my former bonds and wreathed me about and about with new ones: and so it was till we were wholly past them and could no more hear the Sirens' words nor their tune: then the faithful fellows took out the wax with which I had filled their ears, and delivered me from bondage.

'We had left that island behind when I began to see smoke and broken water: the thundering of breakers came to my ears. My crew took fright: the oars slipped from their grasp to swing with an idle clatter in the ship's wash. We lost way, as the moulded blades ceased their even stroke. I went about the ship, appealing to man after man and bracing them with these hearty words, "Fellows, surely we are not quite novices at danger? This evil which faces us is no blacker than our pass in Cyclops' cave, when he held us there in his mighty toils. We escaped him, thanks to my intrepid resourcefulness and energy of mind. I fancy some day we may look back upon to-day's adventure like that. To which end let each one do exactly as I bid. You others, sit well into your benches and grip the sea's swelling fullness with your oars. We shall see if Zeus will not accord us rescue and deliverance from this extremity. For you, quartermaster, I have a special charge. Impress it on your heart, because you hold the tiller of the ship that holds us all. Keep her away from this smoke and broken water, and skirt the rock lest the ship surprise you by yawing suddenly to that other side. So should you cast us into the danger." These were my orders. All heeded them. Scylla I did not mention: for had I added her hopeless horror to my men's burden, they might have deserted their oars in panic and run below decks to hide themselves away. Also I did not honour Circe's hard saying that I must not arm myself. I dressed all in my famous armour, took two long pikes in hand and mounted to the fore-sheets of the ship, thinking it the best place to watch for cliff-dwelling Scylla's raid upon my crew. However, I could see nothing, though I stared my eyes bleary with trying to pierce the shadows of the gloomy cliffs.

'We went on up the narrow strait, thus anxiously. On this side lay Scylla, while on that Charybdis in her terrible whirlpool was sucking down the sea: and vomiting it out again like a vat on a hot fire. The briny water did gush from her abysses in such a seethe that the froth of it bespattered the tops of both rocky walls. Whenever she swallowed-in the yeasty ocean one could see right down the whorl of her maw. At its very bottom the sea's floor showed muddy and dark with sand. The cliffs about thundered appallingly. My crew turned sallow with fright, staring into this abyss from which we expected our immediate death. Scylla chose the moment to rape from the midst of the ship six of our party – the six stoutest and best. I happened to cast my eye back along the thwarts, over the crew, and thus marked their dangling hands and feet as they were wrenched aloft, screeching my name for the last time in voices made thin and high by agony. So may a longshoreman be seen, on some cape of rock which he has ground-baited for the lesser fish, darting down into the sea his very long shaft with its rustic cow-horn tip. As he hurls shoreward each wriggling prize to gasp for life, so did they swing writing upward to the cliffs; where in her cave-mouth she chewed and swallowed them, despite their screaming and stretching of hands in final appeal to me for help in their death agony. This was the most pitiful thing of all the sorrows that ever my eyes did see while I explored the by-ways of the deep.

'Now we were through the danger of the Skurries and of Scylla and Charybdis. We neared the God's good island, where Helios Hyperion kept his broad-browed splendid cattle and many flocks of fat sheep. Even from our decks out at sea I could hear the lowing of cattle driven to stall, and the bleating of sheep. The sound revived in my memory the words of the blind prophet Teiresias of Thebes, and of Æaean Circe. Both had rigidly adjured me to be wary of this island of the Sun-God who gladdens with light the hearts of men. So I spoke earnestly to my followers: –

'"Hear me, long-tried and suffering ones, while I tell you a thing. In their warnings Teiresias and Circe were very stringent with me to beware this island of Helios, Delighter of Mankind. She foretold that here might be our last and deadliest peril. Wherefore let us drive right past the place and avoid it." So I said, but their hearts were too broken with hardship. Eurylochus mutinously voiced to me their discontent. "You are enduring, Odysseus, and uncommonly strong, nor do your joints grow tired: but if you can prevent us your crew from setting foot on this shore in whose sea-bound security we might sup at ease and heal our weariness in sleep – why then must you indeed be wholly a man of iron. Would you have us plunge into the oncoming night and abandon this island, to wander, all broken as we are, through the dark misty deep? Of Night are born the fierce ship-wrecking winds. How shall any of us be saved from utter destruction, if some sharp gust unlicensed by the Gods our masters come suddenly out of the South or from the windy West, those two quarters most rife in fatal gales? Wherefore let us bow before the power of darkness, sup well, and rest peacefully near the ship till daylight lets us sail across a clear sea."

'Thus Eurylochus, and the others sided with him. I felt that here was some Power intending evil, and cried out to them very greatly with barbed words: "Eurylochus, I am one and you are many, and you will have me yield. But at least let each man swear before me a binding oath that should we find on shore some herd of cattle or great flock of sheep, no one of you will be mad enough or bad enough to slaughter any single beast: but will in all quietude rest contented with the victuals that immortal Circe gave." So I urged and presently they took the oath. After all had been duly sworn we brought our staunch ship to rest in the sheltered haven by a spring of fresh water. The company landed and skilfully made our supper. But when they had discharged the needs of drink and food then they minded and bewailed their loved companions whom Scylla had plucked from the ship and eaten alive. Sleep the consoler came on them while they wept.

'We were at the third watch of the night and the stars were going down when cloud-marshalling Zeus brought on a gusty wind so full of the wildest squalls that storm-clouds mantled earth and sea, and night reigned in heaven. Wherefore at the earliest daylight we dragged our ship up the beach and secured it in a hollow cave beneath whose shelter stretched fair dancing-places for the nymphs, with cunning seats about them. Thither I called my men to council and exhorted them saying, "Friends, we have food and drink stored in our hull: accordingly to avoid trouble let us abstain from the cattle of this island. They and its goodly sheep belong to a jealous God, Helios the Overseer and Over-hearer of all." Their high hearts bowed to my word: but for a whole month the wind blew always from the South without abatement and steadily, veering only some points towards East and back again. So long as the corn held out and the red wine, so long my crew, in the wish to survive, kept their hands from the cattle: but there dawned the day when the ship's supplies all failed. Hunger came to rack their bellies. Under the spur of necessity they scattered abroad in search of provender, to try for fish with barbed hooks, or for birds – avid of anything that might fall within their dear hands. As for me, I went up into the island to pray to the Gods on the chance that one of them might disclose a way out. After going far enough to throw off the rest I washed my hands in a calm spot and supplicated the chapter of the Olympian Gods: who sent down a sweet sleep upon my eyelids.

'Meanwhile Eurylochus was preaching treason to his fellows: "Hear me, afflicted and unfortunate ship-mates. No variety of death is pleasing to us poor mortals: but commend me to hunger and its slow perishing as the meanest fate of all. Up therefore; let us take our pick of the Sun's cattle and dedicate them in death to all the Gods of heaven. If ever we do reach Ithaca, our own, there can we quickly erect some splendid fane for Helios Hyperion and fill it with every precious gift. But if he is angered enough by the loss of his high-horned cattle to want the ruin of our ship, and if the other Gods cry yea to him – why then, I choose to quit life with one gulp in the sea rather than waste to death here by inches in this desert island." So said Eurylochus and the rest agreed. The cattle of the Sun were there to hand, gorgeous lurching-gaited broad-horned beasts, browsing quite near the ship. Forthwith the fellows drove aside the choicest and stood round them in a ring praying to the Gods. For heave-offering they plucked and strewed fresh leaves from a branching oak, in place of the white barley no more to be found in the ship. They prayed and cut the beasts' throats: then flayed them, jointed the legs, wrapped the thigh-bones above and below with fat and set bars of flesh on them to grill. They had now no wine left to pour over the flaming sacrifice; instead they kept on sprinkling water for libation. The entrails they roasted whole. When the thighs had burned right down and they had touched the offal with their lips, they sliced the other flesh small and spitted it for cooking. It was then that the burden of sleep was lifted from my eyelids and I rose to regain the ship and the beach. While I went, when I was near the curved ship, there came all about me the savoury smell of roasted fat. Wherefore I groaned and protested to the deathless Gods: "Father Zeus and all Blessed Ones that are from everlasting to everlasting! By this cruel sleep you have cozened me to doom. My crew, left to themselves, have imagined and done the awful thing."

'Swiftly to Helios with the news ran Lampetie of the trailing robes. She told him how we had slain his cattle: wherefore in a fury he declaimed to the Immortals: "Father Zeus and you other blessed Gods: I cry for your vengeance upon the followers of Odysseus, son of Laertes, because they have insolently dared to kill my cattle, the sight of which was my chief joy whenever I mounted the starry sky or swung back from the height of heaven, earthward. If they do not pay me a full retribution, I shall quit you for Hades and shine my light there upon the dead." Zeus answered him and said: "Nay, Helios: do you go on shining amongst the Gods and for the mortals who go their ways about the fertile earth. Upon me be it to smite their ship with one cast of my white thunderbolt and shiver it amid the wine-dark sea." [These sayings were reported me later by Calypso, who heard them from Hermes the Guide.]

'When I reached the ship in its bay, I upbraided each man for the guilty deed, but there was no amending it. The cattle were dead, and for another six days my comrades fed off the finest of these beasts of Helios which they had driven off. Yet the Gods were not slow to manifest portents. The hides of the slain beasts crawled slowly along, and the meat (alike the raw and the cooking) bellowed with a lowing like the lowing of a herd. When Zeus had brought the seventh day, then the wind ceased its unreasonable blowing. We leaped aboard and made for the open sea, stepping our mast and hoisting sail. We lost the isle and after it saw no more land, only sky and seas: but then the son of Cronos caused a lowering cloud to gather and stand over our hollow ship. Beneath it the deep turned thunder-dark. Nor did we scud much longer on our course: for suddenly a hurricane shrieked upon us from the West, ravening with mad gusts of wind, whose tearing violence carried away both our forestays. The mast toppled aft and all its gear ruined down into the waist; while the mast itself stretched backward across the poop and struck the helmsman over the head, smashing his skull to pulp. He dropped from his high plat-form in one headlong dive, and the brave spirit left his bones. Then Zeus thundered and at the same moment hurled a bolt of lightning upon the ship. Her timbers all shivered at the shock of the levin of Zeus. She filled with choking sulphur and brimstone smoke: her crew pitched out of her. For one instant they rode black upon the water, upborne like seafowl on the heaving waves past the black ship. Then the God ended their journey home.

'I reeled up and down the hulk for yet a little, while

the smashing seas stripped the plankings from the keel till it floated off bare by itself. The heel of the mast had torn out from the keelson – to which, however, the backstay (a thong of raw bull's-hide) had been made fast. It still held; so that I could draw mast and keel together and lash them into one. Athwart them I drifted through the raging storm.

'At last the West wind ceased its frantic blowing: only to be succeeded by a South wind whose strengthening brought more pain to my heart; for it meant my measuring back each wave towards fatal Charybdis. All night I was sea-borne, and sunrise found me opposite Scylla's cliff facing dire Charybdis as she gulped down the ocean. Her eddy whirled me upward to the tall fig-tree. I caught and clung there like any bat: not able, though, to find a foothold or any standing-place thereon: so far beneath were the roots and far above me the boughs. Long and vast these boughs were, shading all Charybdis. I held on grimly waiting for her to disgorge my mast and keel. Very late it was before my hopes were answered and they came: as late as the supper-rising of a justice from the courts, who has stayed to settle the many suits of his hot-blooded litigants: so late it was before the spars reappeared. I let go and dropped with sprawling hands and feet, to splash heavily into the water on the lee side of these great beams. Across them I sat and paddled hard with my hands. The Father of Gods and men spared me further sight of Scylla, else should I inevitably have died.

'So I drifted for nine days. In the tenth darkness the Gods cast me ashore on Ogygia, where lives Calypso, the high but humane-spoken Goddess who greeted me kindly and tended me. Yet why rehearse all that? Only yesterday I told it within to you, O King, and to your famous wife. It goes against my grain to repeat a tale already plainly told.'

BOOK 13

He ceased, but his audience were so entranced by the tale that no one moved in the hushed twilit hall. At last the voice of Alcinous replied to him across the silence: 'Lord Odysseus, however great your misfortunes hitherto, now that you have eventually attained my bronze-floored house, my stately house, I think you will not suffer further deflection from your way home: touching which I have a charge for all you frequenters of my palace, who come to hear our minstrel and drink our ruddy aldermanic wine. Already a polished coffer has been packed with the clothes and gold ornaments and other gifts brought in for the stranger by the Phaeacian councillors. Let all of us here, as from ourselves, now present him with a great tripod complete with cauldron. Later we can strike a levy from the common herd and recoup our costs, for it would be a sore business if such liberality fell unrelieved on any single party.' So said Alcinous and he was warmly approved. The gathering dispersed sleepily homeward; but in the dawn light they were hastening toward the ship with their copper treasures. To ensure everything being shipshapely stowed His Majesty himself came down to the ship and saw them packed beneath the thwarts, where they would not foul the crew tugging at their oars. Thence the crowd rallied to Alcinous' house and prepared a banquet. Publicly for them the King sacrificed an ox to the cloud-mantled son of Cronos, Zeus the lord of all. After the thighs had been duly burnt they fell to feasting joyously, while in their admiring midst Demodocus plied his rich minstrelsy.

Yet was Odysseus ever turning his head toward the all-glorious sun, as though to urge it earthward by the fervency of his longing for home. A husbandman yearns in this fashion toward supper, if he has been all day attendant upon his two dun oxen breaking a fallow land with the curved plough they drag. Because it dismisses him in quest of supper the sunset gladdens such a man, for all that his knees are sagging beneath him as he goes. So Odysseus felt relief as the light of the sun faded and died. Abruptly he broke out among the sailor Phaeacians, addressing himself primarily to Alcinous: 'Admirable King, perfect your offering! Then send me duly forth and God give you joy of it. Now is fulfilled my heart's desire – escort with endowment. May the heavenly Gods turn it to my good, and grant me to find my noble wife safe at home amid the unbroken circle of my friends: while you dwell here to fill the pleasant cup of your faithful wives and your children. The Gods shower down their grace upon this people, so that no evil harbour among them for ever and ever.' All clamoured applause and judged that the stranger must be given the god-speed he rightly claimed. Royal Alcinous commanded his herald: 'Pontonous, stir the mixing bowl and carry drink to the entire hall, that our despatching the stranger to his land may be with prayer to Zeus the Father.' At his bidding Pontonous mixed the honey-natured wine and served the company. From their seats, as they were, all offered libation to the blessed host of heaven. Only Odysseus the Great rose to his feet and reached his loving cup into Arete's hand while his voice rang out: 'May your happiness endure, O Queen, until the coming of Age and Death, those twin presences which wait for all mankind. Now will I be going. Gladness attend you in this house, with your children and people and Alcinous the King.'

Odysseus ended. His stride cleared the threshold of the door; but as far as the beach, where his vessel waited, Alcinous had a herald conduct him; while Arete sent one of her serving women to carry his laundered vest and robe, another in charge of the stout casket, and yet a third with victuals and ruddy wine. So he came to the sea; where the proper men, his escort, quickly took the baggage, the food and the drink, and stowed all within their ship. They spread for Odysseus a tappet and smooth sheet on the poop deck right aft where he might sleep undisturbed. Then did he also embark and lie down, saying never a word. The crew took station along their thwarts. They cast off the cable from its ring-stone and bent to their work, spuming the sea high with their oar blades: while a sleep that was flawless closed down upon the eyes of Odysseus – a most sweet sleep, profound, and in semblance very near to death. As he slept the stern of the ship towered, shuddered, and sank again towards the huge dark waves of the clamorous sea ever rushing in behind. So a team of four stallions yoked abreast will rear and plunge mightily beneath the lashing of the whip, as they strain forward to run their level course in the twinkling of an eye. Like them the ship heaved, and unfalteringly sped forward in her race, lighter than the circling hawk, though that is swiftest of the things that fly. So she went, cleaving the ocean surges and bearing within her a man deep-witted as the Gods, one who had in the past suffered heart-break as the common sport of men's wars and the troublous waves, but who now slept in tranquil forgetfulness of all he had endured.

Upon the rising of that most brilliant star which is the especial harbinger of early dawn, the ship in her rapid seafaring drew toward the island, toward Ithaca. On its coast is an inlet sacred to Phorkys, the ancient of the sea, where two detached headlands of sheer cliff stand forth and screen a harbour between their steeps against the great breakers which rage without whenever the harsh winds blow. Once they are berthed inside this port even decked ships can lie unmoored. By the creek's head is a long-leaved olive tree and very near it a cave set apart for those nymphs they call Naiads; a charming shadowy place containing store-bowls and jars of stone in which the honey-bees hive and lay up their sweetness. There on great long looms of rock the nymphs weave sea-purple robes, marvellously beautiful; and its springs of water never fail. The cave's entries are two: one with doors opening northward, by which men come in; while the other entry faces the south and is holy indeed. No human foot trespasses there; it is the pathway of the Deathless Ones.

The mariners knew this bay of old: they drove in with such way on their ship that she took the ground for full half her length: judge by this the stroke they pulled. They filed down off her benches, raised Odysseus from the hollow hull and bore him to land just as he was, on his sheet and gay carpet. He was yet lost in sleep as they bedded him gently on the sand. Then they passed ashore his belongings, the treasures with which by Athene's contriving the Phaeacian nobles had speeded his parting. These they piled in a little heap against the olive-trunk, aside from the road for fear some wayfarer might pass while Odysseus still slept; and plunder him. Then they pushed off for home.

The Earth-shaker had not yet forgotten his fateful word against great Odysseus long ago. Wherefore he began to sound the mind of Zeus, saying, 'Father Zeus, now the Eternal Gods will regard me no more, seeing that I can be slighted by mortals, even by the Phaeacians, that race of men so lately issued from my loins. I did announce that Odysseus should not get home before he had exhausted the sum of miseries. That I allowed him a return at all was for your sake, because when it was first broached you had acceded to it and signified assent. But now while he sleeps at ease these fellows ferry him swiftly across the ocean and set him down in Ithaca, after enriching him beyond my telling with gifts of bronze and gold and woven garments in great store, more wealth than ever he could have amassed for himself had he got away from Troy in good order with all his loot.'

The Cloud-compeller rejoined: 'This complaint of yours is too great and grievous, potent Earth-shaker. In no sense dare the Gods cease from honouring you. How could they? It would go sorely against them to diminish the prestige of their gravest senior. As for men, if any so purblindly follow the dictates of their passion and self-will as to scamp your due reverence – the remedy is yours and ultimate revenge awaits your bidding. Unleash yourself: do what your heart inclines.' To him Poseidon: 'That, Cloud-shadowed One, is exactly what I should have done of my own accord, only I ever weigh and respect your feelings. My present impulse is to destroy this splendid Phaeacian ship as she sails back from her mission across the hazy sea. So shall I teach them modesty, and to leave off escorting every sort of man. Also I would mew their city up behind a wall of mountain.'

To him Zeus answered: 'Why, friend, if you hear my counsel you will smite this good ship into a rock of her own size and shape quite near the shore, while the whole populace gaze from the quays upon her arrival. So will every man be wonder-struck. Then close your hill about the city.' Poseidon embraced the advice and betook himself to Scheria, the Phaeacian home-town, where he waited till the trim vessel in its light coursing had almost made the land. Then he leant over to her and with a single sweep of the flat hand turned her into a rock firmly rooted upon the bottom of the sea. After that he went away. The Phaeacians, famous masters of great-oared galleys, gazed into one another's faces. Knots of them stammered such quick words as these: 'Tell me, who arrested our swift ship like that amidst the waves at the very entrance of the home port? Only now we saw every detail of her plain.' They might well ask. It remained a mystery till Alcinous proclaimed aloud: 'Alas, my people, now are fulfilled the antique prophecies my father used to tell me, how Poseidon was so contraried by our granting free passage to all and sundry that upon a time he would destroy one of our best ships as she came in through the ocean-haze to land: and then would obscure our city within a wall of hills. So the old man would say, and here it comes true. Yet pay heed, everyone; let all of us obey the word. From now, give up this passing onward any stranger who happens to enter our city. Also we will sacrifice twelve picked bulls to Poseidon on the chance that he may repent from hiding our place under the shadow of some huge peak.'

They heard him and feared greatly: forthwith they prepared the bulls. So it was that all the chief men and warriors of the Phaeacians were standing in supplication about royal Poseidon's altar as Odysseus stirred and woke from sleep in the land of his fathers. Not that he knew his whereabouts. Partly he had been absent for so long; but in part it was because Pallas Athene had thickened the air about him to keep him unknown while she made him wise to things. She would not have his wife know him, nor his townsmen, nor his friends, till the suitors had discharged their frowardness.

So to its King Ithaca showed an unaccustomed face, the pathways stretching far into the distance, the quiet bays, the crags and precipices, the leafy trees. He rose to his feet and stood staring at what was his own land, then sighed and clapped his two palms downward upon his thighs, crying mournfully, 'Alas! and now where on earth am I? Shall I be spurned and savaged by the people of this place, or find them pious, hospitable creatures? Why do I lade all this wealth about? Come to that, what do I here myself? Would the stuff had stayed with its Phaeacians, if only I might have reached some lord strong enough to befriend me and pass me to my home. Now I have no place to store it, yet cannot leave it a prey for others. I fear that both right instinct and honesty of judgment must have been to seek among the Phaeacian chiefs and councillors, for them to abandon me in this strange country. They swore to land me on prominent Ithaca, and are forsworn. May Zeus the surveyor of mankind and scourge of sinners visit it upon them in his quality as champion of suppliants: and now, to make a start, let me check my belongings and see if the crew took off anything in their boat when they vanished.'

Whereupon he totted up his tripods and their splendid cauldrons, the gold and the goodly woven robes. Not a thing was gone. So his lament must be entirely for his native land as he paced back and forth in bitter grieving beside the tumultuous deep-voiced waves, till Athene in male disguise manifested herself and drew nigh, seeming a young man, some shepherd lad, but dainty and gentle like the sons of kings when they tend sheep. She had gathered her fine mantle scarf-like round her shoulders and carried a throwing spear; on her lovely feet were sandals. Odysseus, glad to see anyone, went forward with a swift greeting: 'My friend – for in you I hail the first soul to meet me in this place – all hail! and may your coming be with good will: for I would have you save these things of mine and save myself, entreating you as a God and making my petition at your beneficent knees. I pray you teach me for sure what land, what government, what people we have here. Is it some distinct island, or a thrusting spur from the mainland which leans out its fertile acres into the deep?'

Said the Goddess in answer: 'Stranger, you must be untutored or very strange if you ask me of this spot, which is not obscurely nameless but a familiar word across the populous lands of the dawning east, and towards the twilight and its peoples of the declining sun. Rugged it may be and unfit for wheels, but no sorry place, for all that it is straitened. The corn-yield here has no limit and wine is made. The rains never fall short nor the refreshment of dews. Goats find plenteous grazing and cattle pasture. The isle has every sort of timber-tree and perennial springs. Because of all these things, stranger, the name of ITHACA is rumoured abroad, even to Troy which is said to be so far from our Achaean coasts.'

Her word made great Odysseus' heart leap for happiness in this his native land, now divine Athene made him aware of it. To her he again uttered winged words; yet not true words, for he swallowed back what had been on his lips to make play with the very cunning nature instinctive in him. 'Of Ithaca I had heard, indeed, even from far Crete's wide land behind the seas: and have I now reached it myself? I, and this portion of my wealth, though as much again rests with the children in my house, whence I have fled for killing Idomeneus' dear son, Orsilochus the runner, who was fleeter-footed than any of the gainful men in ample Crete. I killed him because he wished to rob me of all the loot I brought from Troy at great pains to myself, loot which I had won by fraying me a path through the wars of men and the difficult seas. My offence lay in having failed to oblige his father, who would have had me serve in his retinue for the Trojan war. Instead I went at the head of my own men-at-arms. Wherefore with just one follower I lay in wait by the roadside and caught him with my bronze spear-head while he came down from the country. At the very dead of night it was, a black night which held all heaven in fee. Wherefore no human eye saw us as I privily took away his life. Immediately after the deed I made for a Phoenician ship and laid suit to its grave masters, paying them liberally from my warspoil to receive me aboard and set me down either at Pylos or in Elis the Epean headquarters. However the force of the wind forbade them this goal, though they tried for it their hardest without a thought of cheating me. Instead we beat up and down, till after dark last night we made this place, getting into the harbour by dint of rowing. After having beached we came straight ashore and lay down as we were, regardless of supper despite our great need of food. I was so tired that sleep came heavily upon me where I lay out on the sand; and I slept while the seamen were discharging my stuff from the ship's hold and heaping it by my side. Then they pushed off for Sidon, that nobly-sited port. But I am left in some distress of mind.'

As he was running on the Goddess broke into a smile and petted him with her hand. She waxed tall: she turned womanly: she was beauty's mistress, dowered with every accomplishment of taste. Then she spoke to him in words which thrilled: 'Any man, or even any God, who would keep pace with your all-round craftiness must needs be a canny dealer and sharp-practised. O plausible, various, cozening wretch, can you not even in your native place let be these crooked and shifty words which so delight the recesses of your mind? Enough of such speaking in character between us two past-masters of these tricks of trade – you, the cunningest mortal to wheedle or blandish, and me, famed above other Gods for knavish wiles. And yet you failed to recognize in me the daughter of Zeus, Pallas Athene, your stand-by and protection throughout your toils! It was thanks to me that you were welcomed by the entire society of the Phaeacians, and now I join you to invent further stratagems and help hide these treasures wherewith by my motion and desire the great men of Phaeacia enriched your homeward voyage. Further, I have to warn you plainly of the grave vexations you are fated to shoulder here in your well-appointed house. So temper yourself to bear the inevitable and avoid blurting out to anyone, male or female, that it is you, returned from wandering. Subdue your pride to plentiful ill-treatment and study to suffer in silence the violences of men.'

Fluently Odysseus answered: 'Your powers let you assume all forms, Goddess, and so hardly may the knowingest man identify you. Yet well I know of your partiality towards me, from the day that we sons of the Achaeans went to war against Troy until we plundered Priam's towering city. But after we had embarked thence and the might of the God scattered the Achaeans – since that day I have not set eyes on you, O daughter of Zeus, nor been aware of you within my ship to deliver me from evil. So it became my lot to wander broken-heartedly waiting for the Gods to end my pain: until at long last you did appear in the Phaeacians' rich capital and heartened me by your bold words to venture in. Accordingly I now conjure you for your father's sake . . . surely I am not in clear-shining Ithaca? I think I have lighted on some foreign land, and you are telling me it is Ithaca only in mockery, to cheat my soul. If in very deed this is my native land, assure me of it.'

Said Athene: 'Your mind harps on that, and I cannot leave on tenterhooks one so civil, witty and shrewd. Any other returned wanderer would have dashed home to see his children and his wife. Only you choose to be sceptical and to reject the evidence till you have further proved the wife who as from the beginning sits awaiting you in the house, miserable through the long nights and tearful all her days. I was never one of those who despaired for you, because I knew for certain you would return, though not till after losing all your party. Wherefore I refrained from open warfare with Poseidon, my uncle, who always wished you ill because of his rage at your blinding his dear son. But now let me show you the substantial Ithaca, to convince you. This is Phorkys' bay, haunted by that ancient of the sea: there at its head stands the spreading olive tree, near which is the mouth of that cool and dusky cave consecrate to the nymphs that are called Naiads. How often under its broad vault have you sacrificed full hecatombs of choice victims to the Nymphs! And lo, where Mount Neriton rears its tree-clad flanks.' As she spoke the Goddess thinned away her mist and the landscape plainly appeared. The joy of seeing his own place so wrought upon Odysseus that he fell to kissing its bounteous soil, before invoking the Nymphs with up-stretched hands. 'O Naiad-nymphs, daughters of Zeus, I had told my heart that I had set eyes on you for the last time: wherefore I now greet you most dearly in this prayer. Verily will we lavish gifts upon you even as of old, if the providence of Zeus' daughter, the Reiver, allows me life and adds to me my beloved son grown to manhood.'

The grey-eyed Goddess exhorted him: 'Be bold and dismiss these concerns from your mind, while we turn to laying up your goods in the hinder end of this cave of marvels, where they will be safe for you. Then must we ponder and advise ourselves the best course of action.' Athene spoke and plunged into the gloom of the cavern to search it for hiding-holes, while Odysseus carried in the Phaeacian gold, the tempered bronze, the goodly raiment. After everything had been carefully laid by, Pallas sealed the passage with a rock. Then they sat together by the bole of the sacred olive to plot the doom of the extravagant wooers, Athene opening thus: 'Son of Laertes, next you must settle how to get these shameless suitors into your hands, for it is now three years that they have been lording it in your palace, plaguing your glorious wife with their suits and proffering marriage settlements; while she, despite heart-racking anxieties over your return, still keeps them all in play by giving each one hope and separate promises and privy messages, with her mind set constantly elsewhere.'

Wily Odysseus replied: 'My hard fate on reaching home, Goddess, would have been such another pitiful death as Agamemnon's, but for your timely acquainting me with the true situation. Wherefore extend your bounty and disclose how I may avenge myself upon these suitors. Stand by me, Mistress, fanning my valorous rage as on the day we despoiled shining Troy of its pride of towers. With your countenance, august One, I would fight three hundred men together: only buoy me up with your judicious aid, O wise-eyed Goddess.' Athene answered him: 'Surely I shall be by your side always taking thought for you, so soon as we undertake this deed. As for these wooers of your wife and wasters of your substance, I feel that some are about to be-spatter the great earth with their blood and brains. But now I must so work on you that no human being will know you; by parching the fair flesh of your agile limbs and laying waste the yellow locks on your head. I shall even make dim your eyes which are so lovely, and afterward clothe you in tatters to affront every eye. Then your guise will repel the united suitors, as also the wife and son you left in the house. You will begin by joining company with the swine-herd who keeps your swine: a man of single heart toward yourself and devoted to your son and judicious Penelope. You will find him watching his beasts grubbing round the Raven's Crag and Arethusa's fountain. Thereby they grow into fat and healthy pigs, by virtue of the acorns they love and the still waters of the spring they drink. Sit with him and wait, learning all his news till I have been to Sparta, the land of fair women, and recalled your dear son Telemachus who went to the house of Menelaus, there in wide Lacedaemon, trying to find out if you are still alive.'

He said to the Goddess: 'Why did you not tell him so much, out of your all-knowing heart? Must he, too, pain-fully roam the barren seas while others devour his living?' The grey-eyed one replied: 'Take it not so much to heart. I was his guide, even I who stirred him up to win favour by this activity. He suffers no hardship, but rests tranquilly in Atrides' palace, lapped in abundance. Admitted, the cadets of the suitors lie in ambush with their black ship, hot to kill him before he can regain his fatherland. Yet I think this will not be: instead, the earth will cover certain suitors who devour your estate.'

Athene touched him with her rod, withering the firm flesh of his active limbs, robbing his head of its fair hair and making the skin over all his body old, like an aged man's. She quenched the sparkle of his handsome eye and flung round him for covering foul and sorry rags, all crusted with a sooty reek. Over these she draped a great deerskin from which the hair was quite worn off. She gave him a stick and a shameful leather pouch, of stiff, cracked leather, slung from a common cord. Then, having reached agreement upon their plans, they separated; her intention being for Lacedaemon, to summon home the son of Odysseus.

BOOK 14

Meanwhile Odysseus strode up the hill-path that climbed straight from the timbered plains into the highlands, the way Athene had pointed him to that devoted swineherd who cared more for his lord's substance than any other of the serfs Odysseus owned.

He found him sitting in the lodge of his high-walled steading which was a landmark because it stood by itself and was well built and large. Without telling his lady or grandfather Laertes, the swineherd had made it himself for his absent master's pigs by lining up boulders from round about and topping them with a dense hedge of prickly pear. For outer fence he had run round it a stiff, very close-set paling of heart-of-oak, the tree's dark core. All in a row inside the pound he had contrived twelve sties to lodge his beasts. Fifty each sty held, of the brood sows be it understood, supine on beds of litter in their pens: as for the boars, they were kept in the yard outside and were far fewer because of the drain of the suitors' appetites which forced the swineherd to keep them daily supplied with a prime fatted hog. So these now came to just three hundred and sixty. They were always watched by four wild-looking dogs of the accomplished swine-herd's own breeding.

The man himself was shaping to his feet a pair of sandals, cutting them from the hide of what had been a stout ox. Of his men, three happened to be out somewhere or other with their herds of swine, while the fourth the swineherd had sent perforce to the city with a boar whose sacrifice might appease the proud suitors' lust for flesh.

When the noisy dogs saw Odysseus they plunged suddenly towards him, baying: but he cunningly let fall his staff and sank to the ground. Yet even so he risked a savage onslaught there in his own estate, but was saved by the ready swineherd who flung aside the slab of leather and rushed towards him through the gate on flying feet, shouting and raining stones at the dogs to drive them off. Then said he to the prince: 'One moment more, father, and the dogs would have killed you. Quickly too: and thereby you would have added disgrace to me whom the Gods have already afflicted with a variety of griefs and pains. Here I languish, mourning a god-like master and tending his fat pigs for others to eat, while he maybe starves for food, adrift in some land or place of strangers – if, that is, he yet lives under the sun. However follow me inside to our quarters, old man, where our food and wine will nerve you to tell us of yourself and the hardships you have survived.' With no more ado the honest swineherd led him to the inner room and there shook down for him a couch of springy twigs, which he covered with the great thick hairy goat-skin that was his own sleepingmat. Odysseus rejoiced at being thus received and thanked him saying: 'Host, may Zeus and the other immortal Gods concede your dearest wish in return for this ready welcome you proffer.'

And what was it, O Eumaeus the swineherd, that you

answered? 'My guest, I should sin if I failed in attention to any stranger, even one poorer than yourself. The needy and the strangers are all from Zeus; and with the likes of us a quite slender gift can convey good-will, for alas the state of bondmen is never wholly free from fear when their lords and masters are young. My proper lord has, I think, been denied his return home by the Gods. Surely he would have favoured me with the endowment a good master gives his house-men (things like a cottage with its scrap of garden, and a prudent woman) in reward for faithful labour whose fruits God has multiplied and blessed, as He has blessed and multiplied my unremitting toil. Indeed my lord would have largely benefited me as years came upon him in the house; but he has perished – and I would that every one of Helen's kind might be beaten to the knee and broken, in revenge for all the manhood she has undone. See you, my master was one of those who went to Ilium of the goodly horses to fight the Trojans for Agamemnon's fair name.'

As he was speaking he hitched the slack of his smock quickly into his loin-cord and betook himself to the sties that held the piglet clans. From their mass he chose two young ones for butchery, singeing and chopping them up before spitting them to roast. When they were done he carried them to Odysseus and set them in front of him, still on the spits and piping hot. He dusted them over with barley meal and in an ivy-bowl diluted wine till it was sweet for drinking. Then he sat down face to face with Odysseus and invited him, saying: "Eat now, my guest, of our bondman's ration, this young pork. All fatted hogs go to feed those suitors devoid of ruth or any sense of shame. Yet lawlessness does not commend itself to the blessed Gods, who lean towards justice and human integrity. Why even foemen-freebooters feel a foreboding of vengeance and retribution stealing into their hearts' core when ever Zeus has let them raid a strange coast and collect plunder enough to bring their ships heavy-laden home. Therefore surely some whisper from a God must have given these men a certainty of my lord's sad fate, for them to have no care either of wooing with decency, or of ceasing to woo and going home. Instead they devour and devour all that we produce, with a calm insolence that has no bounds. During each Zeus-given night or day they will have their victims, not limiting themselves to just one or two, either. As for our wine, they spill it and lavish it wantonly. The master's wealth was beyond computation. No hero from Ithaca proper or from the dark mainland possessed so much – why, not twenty of them conjoined could match his fortune! Let me recite it you. On the mainland twelve droves of cattle, twelve flocks of sheep, twelve herds of swine, twelve large troops of goats: hired men and his herding-thralls keep all these at pasture. In the extremity of our island are other great troops of goats, eleven in all, each in hand of trusty watchmen: and daily a herdsman will drive the ripest beast of all these to the roisterers in the house. But my plan with the swine is to pen them here out of the way under guard, only sending in, out of the herd, what beast I judge suitable." So he explained to Odysseus who ate his meat and drank his wine in a burning silence, while his longing to injure the suitors grew mightily within him.

But after he had dined and was heartened with the food, then did the swineherd fill to the brim and pass the cup, his own cup he always used. Odysseus took it with an inward thankfulness, while aloud he questioned him shrewdly, saying: 'Now, friend, who was this wealthy man who bought you, this master whose power and riches you so laud? You say he died vindicating Agamemnon's honour. As one of those, maybe I met him. Pray you, his name: for so widely have I roamed that only Zeus and his fellow immortals can say for sure if I have news of seeing him, or no.' Said the swine-herd, that prince of servants, 'Old man, no vagrant body's tale of seeing him will get past me to win credence of his widow and son. It is too much the yarn any conscienceless waif might spin to earn him board and lodging. Wanderers land in Ithaca and go to my mistress with their moonshine. She welcomes them ever so kindly and enquires of this and that, while the tears a woman should shed for her husband fallen in a far country rain grievously downward from her eyes. You too, my ancient, would soon pitch some story, if it was to be paid in kind with a cloak and tunic. Whereas in very deed his spirit fled long since, abandoning his bones either to the dogs and birds of prey to pick clean or to lie shrouded in deep sand upon some shore after the fishes of the sea have fed upon him. And this death of his has brought down upon me directly, as upon all who loved him, a load of care: for go where I may, never shall I light upon so gentle a lord, not though I was to regain the home of my birth and the father and mother who reared me. Yea, deeply as I yearn to set eyes on them and on my own place, to-day my deeper grief is for my lost Odysseus. See, stranger, how I blush only to pronounce his name, though he is far away. Truly he cared for me beyond measure and cherished me in his heart, wherefore despite his extreme absence I title him with all respect.'

Odysseus replied: 'My friend, with your unbelieving heart so certain sure that he will never come again I shall not merely assert the returning of Odysseus but seal it with an oath: and I shall claim my guerdon (make it robes of honour, within and without, glorious) the day his feet bring him home. Till then despite my need I shall accept nothing, for hateful to me as the mouth of Hell is one who tells lies out of poverty. So I call upon Zeus, God of Gods, and upon this table of my host and upon the hearth of famous Odysseus to which I have attained! Bear me witness that all things shall happen according to my word; during this very year Odysseus will arrive, between the waning of this moon and the rise of the next, to take his revenge upon those who dishonour his wife and brilliant son.'

And your reply to this, O Eumaeus? You said: 'Ancient, I shall never have to pay this guerdon of yours. Nor will Odysseus regain his house. Be at peace and drink, while we mind ourselves of other things; for I would have you spare these memories, to save me the heartache which comes whenever anyone brings back the thought of my dear lord. So we will let pass your oath. Yet how grateful would be the coming of Odysseus to me and to Penelope, as to old Laertes and Telemachus! See, that god-like young Telemachus is now grown into one of my quick griefs. When the Gods made him flourish like a young tree I said to myself "He will be his loved father's peer, of a form and features to make men marvel," and then some earthly or heavenly thing touched his wits and off he went to Pylos, seeking news of his father. Whereupon the suitor-lords set themselves in ambush against his return, that even the name of the royal race of Arcesius might be rooted out of Ithaca. However we will let pass his affair too, whether he is to be caught or to gain some refuge. Perhaps, indeed, the son of Cronos will shield him with his arm. Instead give me the history, aged one, of your ill-fortunes, first clearly explaining who you are and your city and parents, and what ship you came in and how the sailors brought you to Ithaca, or what sailors they called themselves: for I think you found no dry way hither."

Odysseus answered advisedly: 'I will be plain with you. Yet I wish we had food and good wine enough to let us sit here at our quiet entertainment all through the others' working hours. Easily could I fill a year and still not end the recital of my heart's griefs and the pains the Gods have given me. Let me admit to being a Cretan, the son of a rich man in whose house were born and brought up many other sons of his marriage – whereas my mother was a bought woman, his concubine. Still, Castor the son of Hylax, whose seed I declare myself, made no distinction in honour between me and his lawful issue. Amongst the other Cretans he was held almost divine, having such estate and fortune and splendid family. In time his fate of death came and bore him away to the House of Hades: then the sons made bold to divide his property and draw for their shares. They gave me a very meagre portion but assigned me a house; and to it I brought the wife (daughter of a leading land-owner) whom my prowess had won me: for I was no sluggard and never shirked a fight. To-day my strength has been cropped away by my too-plentiful tribulations: but perhaps from the look of the stubble you can guess what my ripeness was. Ares and Athene granted me a courage which carried me through the press of battle. When once I had determined my tactics against an enemy, no inkling of death would visit my high heart. I would post a chosen party in ambush and then thrust far beyond its leaders to bring down with my spear any opponent less nimble than myself upon his feet. That was the fighting me: but labour I never could abide, nor the husbandry which breeds healthy children. My fancies were set upon galleys and wars, pikes and burnished javelins, the deadly toys that bring shivers to men of ordinary mould. I think such tastes came to me from heaven. Each man sports the activity he enjoys.

'Before the prime of Achaea went up to battle against Troy I had nine times commanded men and warships on foreign expeditions, at great profit to myself, with the leader's first choice of the booty to increase my individual share. So my house rapidly filled with wealth and I became formidable and respected among the Cretans. Consequently, when far-seeing Zeus finally imagined this dread course which has enfeebled the knees of so many men, people clamoured for me and for famous Idomeneus to lead their fleet to Ilium: and so firmly was the popular mind made up that we had no option. Wherefore we sons of the Achaeans stayed fighting for nine years. In the tenth we sacked Priam's city and after-wards embarked for home, a God dispersing the host.

'My unhappy lot, though, was to be vexed anew by an invention of Zeus the Disposer, after only one month's enjoyment of my children and faithful wife and goods: for then my heart prompted me to take my faithful companies and sail against Egypt, after properly refitting the ships. So I commissioned nine vessels. Crews for them rallied quickly to me and to my feast which was sustained for six whole days by the many divine sacrifices I provided to furnish the tables. On the seventh day we launched out from the coast of Crete and sailed with so fair and filling a north wind that it made the sea run like a stream in our favour. We just sat there in careless ease; nor did any ship meet harm with that wind and the helmsmen to steady us. On the fifth day we made the smoothly-flowing river which is Egypt and into its stream I brought our imposing fleet, anchoring it there and ordering my trusty fellows to stand by on ship-guard while I put out watchers into picket posts about. But the men gave themselves up to their baser instincts and the prompting of their own ungovernable passions. In a trice they were ravaging the rich Egyptian countryside, killing the men and carrying off women and children. An instant alarm was given in the town: and the war-cry roused the townspeople to pour out against us at the first show of dawn. The entire valley filled with footmen and horsemen and the glint of bronze. Thunder-loving Zeus crumbled my men into shameful flight, leaving no single one of them the courage to stand firm and face it out. Disaster seemed to beset us on every side. Many of our company perished there by the Egyptians' keen weapons: many others were led living into captivity, there to labour under duress. As for me, I had an inspiration from Zeus himself – yet would rather I had then died and met my final end in Egypt there; for since that day my continued abiding has been in the house of sorrow. My well-wrought helm I hurriedly did off, and let fall the shield from my shoulders. Away went the spear from my hand, while I ran over to the King's car to embrace his knees and kiss them. He drew me to him and had mercy upon me, seating me all tearful as I was on the floor of his own war-chariot. Then he took me to his palace, through the hate-maddened throng whose blood-lust set every spear in rest against my life. But he drove them all back in his reverence for our Lord Zeus whose wrath soonest rises when strangers in his protection are outraged.

'So there for seven years I remained amassing great wealth, for all Egypt gave me gifts. But the eighth year brought in its train a very subtile Phoenician, one of those subverters who have wrought such havoc in the world. His plausibility won me to keep him company even so far as Phoenicia, where lay his house and interests. I stayed with him the round of a year: but when with the march of months and days the season returned he decoyed me into a ship bound overseas for Libya, on the pretence of my running a cargo with him: whereas really he was exporting me for sale as a slave at some incredible profit. My mind misgave me, yet my hands were tied. I had no choice but to embark with him. Our ship ran before a fair freshening wind as far as the open passage south of Crete; where Zeus had taken counsel to destroy her complement. So soon as we sank the Cretan hills and had only sea and sky in view he massed over our ship a deep purple cloud which shadowed the sea in gloom. Then Zeus thundered and at the same instant struck the ship with his lightning. She reeled from stem to stern at the divine stroke and was filled with brimstone-fumes. All fell from her and were tossed like gulls past the black hull on the huge waves. That was the end to their journey which the God gave them: but between my hands Zeus thrust the ship's mast, that despite my heart-load of misery I might yet avoid final bane. I twined myself about this mast and drifted at mercy of the savage winds for nine days: for it was not till the tenth black night that the great rolling swell approached me to the land of the Thesprotians, where the king, Pheidon, received me generously. It was his son who happened to find me lying helpless from exposure and exhaustion; and he lifted me with his own hands and bore me home to his father's palace, where they clothed me anew.

'At their place I got my news of Odysseus. The lord of the house told me he had been their honoured guest on his way home, and showed me treasures of bronze and gold and well-purified iron, laid up by Odysseus within the royal palace, in bulk to satisfy ten generations of heirs. Their owner, the King said, had gone to Dodona to hear what Zeus would counsel him out of the God's tall leafy oak, whether it were better, after so long an absence, to re-enter fertile Ithaca publicly or privily. Besides this the King swore to me, while he made libation in his house, "that the ship to take Odysseus home to his loved country was launched and her crew equipped and ready." Only a chance made him dispatch me first, because there was a Thesprotian ship clearing for granaried Dulichium. He charged her masters to convey me most surely to its King, Acastus; but they preferred to follow their own evil imaginings, which plunged me to the very depths of despair. For when the ship had put far out and was in the mid-sea they schemed to enslave me then and there, stripping me naked to exchange my good clothes against these rags of a tunic and cloak you see. In the evening they made the tilled coasts of vivid Ithaca and hurried out upon its foreshore to prepare their supper, after securing me in the well of the hull with coils of stranded rope.

'I think it was the Gods themselves who let the knots slip off me easily. I piled my clothing on top of my head, lowered myself down the slippery after-part and launched out into the sea on my breast with an arm-over-arm stroke that quickly carried me to land beyond their party. I pushed up country as far as a particularly dense thicket and there huddled into its full-leaved bushes. They were wildly distressed over my escape and beat here and there for me: but at last understood that a wider search was unprofitable and went back into their ship. Only the Gods made my hiding so easy; and by their mercy, again, I have found myself the guest of an enlightened man. It seems I am granted a new lease of life.'

And your answer, Eumaeus the pig-keeper? 'My unhappy guest, these sufferings you narrate touch me to the heart, save and except your tattle about Odysseus which is all awry and unconvincing. Why feel constrained by your plight to invent so wild a lie? My mind is definitely made up on this point of my lord's return, knowing for sure that the Gods all hated him, in that they did not grant him death at the climax of the war, in his friends' arms and amid the Trojans: for then every Achaean would have helped set up his tomb and he would have devolved great after-glory upon his son: whereas now the random winds have borne him meanly away. So it is that I hold myself withdrawn here amongst my pigs, never visiting the city except when bidden by circumspect Penelope to hear some news which has casually blown in. Then how they sit round and ply the tale-bearer with questions, not merely those who sorrow for their absent lord but also those others who are enjoying a free run of their teeth in his substance! Only I have lacked heart to query or chop questions, since that day an Aetolian cheated me with his tale. He had killed his man and wandered over the face of the earth till he reached my place. I tended him with all kindness and he told me he had seen Odysseus in Crete with Idomeneus, patching his storm-battered ships. By the summer or at harvest-time he would be back, he said, enriched and with his noble following. But you, old misery whom Fortune has brought to my door, have no need of lies to ingratiate yourself or to warm my heart: that is no road to my regard and charity, which derive from fear of Zeus, the strangers' patron, and from pity for yourself.'

Odysseus the subtle replied: 'Your heart must indeed be froward if this my sworn testimony fails with you and is discredited. See, we will make a bargain and have the Gods of Olympus as witnesses between us. If your lord regains this house you shall clothe me freshly in mantle and tunic before sending me forward to Dulichium, my goal. And if he does not return as I say, then bid your bondmen hurl me from that great crag to teach the next beggar not to invent.'

'Why,' cried the honest swineherd, 'what public name and fame should I have for ever and ever after that, if I brought you into my quarters and entertained you only to set on you and rob you of dear life? With how clean a heart, then, would I supplicate Zeus son of Cronos! See, it is the supper hour. I hope my fellows come back to time, that we may cook something choice for supper here in our place.' As they spoke of it the drovers and their swine appeared. Very shrilly the clamour went up from every sty while the beasts were being herded into their yards for the night; but kindly Eumaeus called to his men, saying, 'Pick out the best of the porkers for devoting to this my foreign guest. And we will have our share too. Over long have we put ourselves to great labour and vexation in keeping these white-tusked boars, only to see others eat for nothing the product of our pains.' While he called to them he was cleaving firewood with his trenchant axe. The others dragged in a fat boar of five years old. They set it by the flaming fire, while the swineherd's ripe understanding prompted him to fulfil his exact duty towards the Deathless Ones. He began by pulling hairs from the head of the tusker and throwing them into the fire, while he implored of all the Gods a home-coming for wise Odysseus. Then he drew himself up and with a billet of wood spared from his chopping he clubbed the beast. It died. They slit its throat, singed it and quickly quartered it for the swineherd to cut a first slice from every limb, of lean doubled in fat. These offerings he dusted with barley groats and flung into the fire, while they were cutting up the rest for threading on the spits to roast with care. Afterwards they drew away the spits and heaped the flesh upon platters. The swineherd stood up to apportion it, for his eye was just. Most precisely he divided the whole into seven helpings. With an invocation he set the first aside for the nymphs and for Hermes, son of Maia: the rest he handed round. For Odysseus he picked out the most noble part, the long back of the white-tusked beast.

The spirit of the king was so gratified thereby that he cried: 'I am praying, Eumaeus, that Father Zeus may love you even as I do, for your conferring this signal portion upon a lone man.' To which you, O Eumaeus, replied, 'Eat, my fine Sir, and be happy with what there is: the God gives and withholds at pleasure, being almighty.' So he pronounced, dedicating his first sacrings to the Eternal Gods. Then he made libation and passed the dark wine to Odysseus the waster of cities, before sitting to eat his own portion. Their bread was brought to them by Mesaulius, the swineherd's private slave, whom he had bought out of his own means from some Taphians during his master's absence, without telling his lady or old Laertes. They reached out and made play amongst the prepared dishes until their appetites for meat and drink had been assuaged: then their replete instincts veered towards bed, even as Mesaulius was clearing the remains of food away. However the night proved dirty. The moon was wrapped in clouds and Zeus rained through all the dark hours; while a powerful west wind, that wet wind, never ceased to blow.

Odysseus had in mind to prove his swineherd by seeing if he would doff his cloak to lend it him, or require a cloak of one of his fellows for the guest he had so entertained. Wherefore he said: 'Hear me now, O Eumaeus and you others, while I let myself go as your wine's intoxication tempts me. Drink will set the most solid man singing or giggling with laughter; if indeed it does not push him forward to dance or make him blurt out something better left unsaid. However now I have loosened my tongue I had best go through with it.

'I wish I were young, with the enduring vigour that was mine in the days when we imagined and took on a surprise raid against Troy. Odysseus was one of our leaders:

with him was Menelaus, son of Atreus, and for third in command (by their arranging) went myself. We worked our way round the city till we reached its massive wall and there we lay by the swamp beneath the citadel, our panoply weighing us down into the reeds and dense brake. As we waited the night turned very foul. The north wind came down and it froze hard. Then snow began to fall, chill and dry like rime, while ice plated our shields. The others all wore cloaks over their tunics and so slept well enough, hunched up with their shields over their shoulders; but I had left my cloak with my fellows before setting out, having been fool enough to think I should never feel cold. So there I was with just a gay jerkin and my shield. When the third part of the night had come and the stars were going down I nudged with my elbow against Odysseus who lay next me, and whispered to his attentive ear: 'Son of Laertes, surely I will not be counted long among the living, for this cold is more than I can bear without my cloak. Something possessed me to come out only in my vest and now there is no helping it.'

'Even as I spoke a notion flashed into his mind, for he was in a class by himself when either scheming or fighting were in question. He hissed at me sharply: "Be quiet, lest some other Achaean hear you." With that he propped his head on his bent arm and said in a low carrying voice: "Listen, friends. I fell asleep and God has sent me an important dream to show how much too far from the ships we have come. I would have someone bear warning to Agamemnon son of Atreus, the shepherd of the people, that he may move us reinforcements from the leaguer." At his word Thoas son of Andraemon leaped up nimbly, flung aside his purple cloak and broke into a run for the ships, while I snuggled into his garment till Dawn shone from her golden throne. Now, as I remarked, if only I could be young and strong again like that. For then some swineherd of the manor would lend me his cloak, from the double motives of charity to a guest and pity for a stout comrade: but as it is I look for no regard, because of these rags disfiguring my body.'

To which you replied, Eumaeus: 'Old man, that was a really good story you told of him; not one word amiss or wasted. So to-night you shall not be stinted of a coverlet, nor of anything a luckless client may reasonably expect from those with power to help him. Only for to-night, of course; in the morning you must flap away in your own rags again. We have here no store of cloaks nor changes of tunics, but just the suits in which we stand. Yet when Odysseus' darling son comes back he will present you with outer garment and under garment and speed you whither your heart's longing claims.'

He rose as he spoke and pitched a bed by the fireside, covering it with sheepskins and goatskins; and after Odysseus had lain down he drew over him a thick and ample cloak that he kept by him for change in the worst weather. So there Odysseus slept with the lads beside him. Only the swineherd had no heart to lie there apart from his swine, in comfort. Wherefore, to the joy of Odysseus who marked this diligence for the welfare of his absent lord's estate, he girded himself for going out to them, looping a sharp sword about the breadth of his shoulders and wrapping himself in a wind-defying cloak of solid weave, about which went a broad tough goat-skin. Also he took a sharp javelin as defence against dogs or men and so sallied forth to lay himself under the overhang of the crag where the white-tusked boars slept in shelter from the north wind.

BOOK 15

Meanwhile Pallas Athene had gone to Lacedaemon of the broad acres to prompt the son of Odysseus to a quick return. She found him and Nestor's noble son asleep in the porch of great Menelaus' house – or rather Nestor's son lay in gentle slumber while Telemachus stirred with anxious thoughts about his father all through the divine night.

Pallas stood by him and said: 'My Telemachus, with those bold men behind you in your house you dare not prolong your wandering abroad, to the neglect of your affairs. This journey will have been useless if during it they share out your wealth and devour it. Make stentorian Menelaus speed you homeward at once, while your mother is yet to be found there: for her father and his sons are urging her to accept Eurymachus, who has proved more lavish than any other of the suitors and has largely increased his wedding-bids. If you return she cannot carry off from the house things you would regret to lose: for you know what a woman's nature is and how an eagerness to enrich her actual husband makes her cease speaking or thinking of her once-dear lord and the children she bore him. So back with you and put your gains for safety in hand of the house-maiden you most trust, till the Gods designate some stately woman to be your consort.

'Other news I have for you, and heed it carefully. An ambush of picked men from the suitors is hiding in the gut between the reefs of Samos and Ithaca, with intent to kill you before you regain home. I do not fear it: they are likelier to die themselves, some of these suitors who batten on your livelihood. Yet give those islands a wide berth and sail day and night in your staunch ship – for that Immortal who watches over you for good will vouchsafe you a fair wind. Get ashore on the hither end of Ithaca and send your ship and company round to the city, while you make straight for where your loyal and devoted swineherd lives with his beasts. Lodge with him that night and send him to tell Penelope how you are spared to her and safely come out of Pylos.'

She departed for the peak of Olympus, while Telemachus let drive with his heel against the son of Nestor and woke him, to say: 'Up, Peisistratus, and harness your sure-stepping horses to the chariot, that we may be on our way,' but the son of Nestor replied: 'Telemachus, no matter what the urgency, there is no driving in the dead of night. See, dawn is near. I vote we stay to take the warm farewells and god-speed of the son of Atreus, that master spearsman, as also for the gifts with which this hero Menelaus will load our car. A guest should be ever considerate of the host who has lovingly entreated him.'

Thus he advised: and Dawn assumed her golden throne. Clarion-voiced Menelaus quitted fair Helen's side and came towards them. When the son of Odysseus perceived this he flung the bright tunic about his glossy body and draped his great shoulders in a cloak to go through the gates to meet him: and then he said, 'O royal Menelaus! Here and now send me home; my heart is yearning to be in my own dear country,' and to him Menelaus replied, 'Telemachus, if you so want to go I shall not hold you back. Hosts, to my mind, should be neither importunate nor abrupt. There is always the happy mean. It is as wrong to despatch a reluctant guest as to detain the impatient. Cherish the stranger in the house and speed him so soon as he has the mind. Yet wait while I display the beauty of my gifts to you, while I pack them in the chariot; and let me tell the women to set out in the hall a refection of what meats they have ready. It is a point of credit and honour with us, and of benefit for you to set out with full bellies across these boundless plains. Or would you make the tour of Hellas and mid-Argos in my company, me furnishing the horses and directing you among the towns? Verily not one man would send us away as we came, but every time there would be a gift, some tripod or tub of real bronze, some yoke of mules or golden cup.'

Tactful was the reply of Telemachus: 'Menelaus, I want to go to my own land so quickly because when I left it I did appoint no warden over my goods; and to lose some prized ancestral treasure would suit my taste no better than dying myself in quest of my glorious father.' So soon as stentorian Menelaus understood him he commanded his wife and her maids to contrive a luncheon from the victuals that lay plenteously to their hands. Then came in Etoneus the son of Boethus, all new from bed, for he lived near by. Menelaus had him light the fire and cook meat: which he obediently did. Next the king went down into his sweet-smelling treasure house; not unattended, for Helen and Megapenthes kept him company. At the treasure heap Atrides picked out a double cup and made Megapenthes his son take a mixing bowl of silver. Helen hesitated by the clothes-chests with their bright store of variegated garments of her own needle-working. Finally from them this fairest of women chose the amplest and richest vestment of all. It had been buried deeply beneath the others and glittered like a star. Then they marched back through the palace till they found Telemachus. Menelaus addressed him saying: 'O Telemachus, may Zeus the Thunderer, who is Hera's lord, allow you this return home you covet. Meanwhile I am giving you the choicest and rarest treasure in my house. Here it is: the storied mixing bowl, of pure silver but for its lip of gold, which Hephaestus made and His Majesty the King of Sidon, Phaedimus, gave me as I was sheltering under his roof on my homeward journey: it pleases me to confer it upon you.'

With such words the warrior son of Atreus presented him the double-cup. Then sturdy Megapenthes brought forward his polished silver bowl, while Helen in her beauty advanced with the robe and naming him said, 'This, dear child, is to be my gift, a keepsake from Helen's hand for your bride to wear on the day of expectation, your wedding-day; till then lay it up with your mother in the house. May gladness go with you homeward to your own place and land.' She gave it him and he was glad. Staunch Peisistratus marvelled at the sight of all the gifts, even while he was stowing them away in the chariot's locker.

Again the tawny-crested king led them within his palace, where they sat enthroned while the maid poured the cleansing water for their hands from her golden ewer over its basin and set out their polished table, which the matron bountifully spread with wheaten loaves and cooked meats. The son of Boethus carved and helped the flesh while Menelaus' son poured out their wine. So they fed till they were satisfied. Then Nestor's son and Telemachus harnessed their horses and in their brilliant chariot swept through the echoing portal and its porch. But there, full in the track of the horses, stood the son of Atreus with a golden beaker, the stirrup-cup of honeyed wine, in his right hand; calling out, 'Your healths, young men! Pledge me to Nestor the people's shepherd who was such a father to me when we young Achaeans were fighting in the Troad.' To which Telemachus properly replied: 'We will repeat him all your message as you have given it, bantling of Zeus, when we arrive; and as my setting out from you has been upon such loving usage and weighted with this wealth of gifts, even so may my return to Ithaca discover Odysseus surely in the house, to hear my tale.'

Upon the word there flew out from the right an eagle whose talons held an enormous white goose, one of their fowls from the yard. After it rushed the farm-hands and maids, yelling; but the eagle sheered again to the right, just by their horses. The sight gave them joy and excited every heart, till Peisistratus said: 'Interpret it, O royal Menelaus, if the God means this portent for us two or for you.' Fighting Menelaus fell on thought, how he should properly read it and reply; but Helen took the word from him and said, 'Hear me, while I declare the meaning (surely the true meaning) which the Gods have flashed into my mind. As that eagle from the mountain eyrie which the eagles haunt has borne off in one swoop our farm-fattened goose, so shall Odysseus come back from his sore wandering and avenge himself: unless perhaps he is already home and brooding ruin for the suitors.'

Telemachus thanked her saying, 'Zeus grant it so,

Lady; and I shall reverence you as a divinity.' He whipped up the horses and they raced through the town to the open country where day-long the yoke nodded over their steady pacing till night-fall darkened the roads. They had attained Pherae, by the house of Diocles, son of that Orsilochus whom Alpheus begot; and there they stayed the night, fitly entertained. Rosy dawn saw them harnessing the horses. They climbed into their decorated chariot and drove through the loud gateway. Telemachus laid on with the whip and the willing pair flew onward, so that soon they reached frowning Pylos. There he said to Nestor's son: 'How shall I persuade you now to promise me what I want? Friends we are by reason of our fathers' old acquaintance: also we are of an age and have had this trip together to confirm our love. So do not drive me past my ship, O favoured of Zeus, but set me down beside her, that the old man's sense of hospitality may not have power to keep me chafing in his house. I would speed homeward.'

The son of Nestor pondered if this was a thing he could properly accept and perform. Reflection showed it to be best. So he turned his team out of the way to the water's edge and transferred to the after-part of the ship all the noble gifts of Menelaus, the clothing and the gold. Then he said to Telemachus urgently: 'Now get aboard and have your crew mustered before my reaching home warns the old man. My heart and head assure me that his wilfulness will take no excuse. He will himself come here and hail you; refusing, as I say, to go back alone. This will fling him in a rage.'

With that he turned his long-maned horses back to the town of the Pylians and quickly was at home: while Telemachus was busied greeting his men and bidding them make all ready in the black ship for an instant start. They heeded him and hurriedly obeyed, climbing aboard and taking their places to row. Telemachus was ordering them and praying and sacrificing to Athene in the stern-sheets when there appeared an utter stranger, fugitive from Argos for having killed a man. He was a prophet, being indeed kin to Melampus who had had a splendid house and been rich among the people of sheep-breeding Pylos, where he lived until forced to quit his land and settle abroad for having offended Neleus over his daughter. That haughtiest of nobles laid violent hands on all Melampus' property and kept it, during the long year its owner lay painfully gyved in the house of Phylacus – a spirit-breaking penalty he suffered by decree of the grim fury and Goddess, Erinys. At length Melampus avoided his doom and avenged his wrongs upon the mighty Neleus by driving off to Pylos the loudly-lowing cattle from Phylace: with which deed he won the daughter and brought her home to be his brother's wife. Afterwards he banished himself to Argos, that land of thoroughbreds, where fortune made him, a chance-comer, acquire lordship over very many of the Argives. He built a palace there, married and had two stout sons, Antiphates and Mantius.

Antiphates' son, Oicles, was the father of Amphiaraus inspirer of peoples, who though beloved of Zeus and Apollo yet attained not the quiet of old age but died in Thebes for a woman's gifts, leaving Alcmaeon and Amphilochus as issue. Mantius, the other son of Melampus, had a child Cleitus who was so very lovely that golden-throned Dawn snatched him up to be with the Immortals: also another son, Polypheides, who by grace of Apollo succeeded Amphiaraus as the greatest prophet alive. But he fell out with his father and so transferred himself to Hyperesia where he lived and prophesied publicly. It was his son, by name Theoclymenus, who now approached Telemachus as he made prayer and libation beside the black hull of his ship, to say earnestly, 'My friend, whom I find in act of sacrifice, tell me truthfully I pray you, by that sacrifice and God, upon your head and your followers' heads – who are you? where from? what city and family?'

Telemachus replied: 'Actually I am from Ithaca and my father is Odysseus, or was Odysseus if he existed, ever. Anyway he died in misery long ago. I took these companions and sallied out to solve the mystery of his disappearance.' Then said Theoclymenus 'And I too have left my country, for manslaughter of a kinsman whose powerful family bears sway over the Achaeans of the Argive plain. I fled their dark sentence of death, thereby dooming myself to wander across the habitable world. Hear a fugitive's prayer. Admit me to your ship and save my life. I think the pursuers are not far behind.'

Said Telemachus, 'If you really wish to sail with us I shall not refuse you. Come to our home and welcome to your share of what we have.' He took the bronze spear from him and laid it on the deck, then stepped aboard himself and had Theoclymenus sit by him in the stern-sheets. As they cast off the warps he gave order to rig the boat. Zealously they raised their pine-tree mast, stepped it, trapped it in the thwart and tautened its stays. Then they hoisted the white sails by their halyards of plaited hide. Athene gave them a fair wind which sang shrilly through the cloudless firmament so that the ship scudded most quickly towards her goal across the salt sea-water. By Crouni and by Chalcis of the running brooks they went, till sunset and the darkness fell. The ship coasted Pheae in the might of Zeus' wind and raised Elis, the Epeans' strong sanctuary. As he drove thence past each jagged islet Telemachus asked himself if he would escape death or be trapped.

~

Meanwhile Odysseus was supping in their homestead with the honest shepherd and his men. When appetite had been appeased he spoke again, in wish to find out the swineherd's real mind towards him and if he would extend him longer hospitality there in the farm, or compel him city-wards. 'Now Eumaeus and you others, listen. So as not to exhaust your kindness I would go at crack of dawn to the town, where I can beg my way. Only give me hints and skilful guidance thither: for once arrived I must work by myself if I am to win bread and sup from someone. My special idea is to pass a word with wise Penelope at Odysseus' house and meet the graceless suitors. Perhaps they will fill my mouth out of their superfluity; and it is likely I may prove useful to them for I tell you – heed me and believe it well – that by help of Hermes (whose is the dignity that graces human labour) no man equals me in service, at building fires and chopping wood for them, at carving or roasting meats, at serving drink, at anything you like to mention that menials can do for their betters.'

Ah then, Eumaeus, how your heart sank while you answered him. 'Alas, my guest, that this notion should have come to your mind. You must thirst for your own destruction if you would push among that mob of suitors whose rank cruelty affronts the steely sky. Their lackeys are not men like you, but young rufflers in gay cloaks and robes, sleek-headed and blooming-cheeked. Already their tables groan with bread and meat and wine. So stay with us. No man here, not myself nor any of these my fellows, grudges your tarrying: and when Odysseus' good son returns he will clothe you newly and forward you whither your spirit bids.' To this Odysseus said: 'May Father Zeus love you, Eumaeus, as I do for your sparing me further distressful vagabondage, that saddest of human fates. For their loathly bellies' sake do men incur these pains and griefs of vagrancy. But now, if I am to settle here till the son returns, tell me about the mother of Odysseus and of the father whom his going left behind stricken in years. Are they yet living in the eye of day, or dead and in Hades' mansions?'

Said the excellent swineherd: 'I will tell it you in detail. Laertes lives: but prays ever and ever that Zeus will let the life flicker from his limbs in the hall. So bitterly does he lament his missing son and the long-proven wife whose death has been a main grief to age him before his time. Know too that she herself fell on death for grieving after her famous son. A tragic end hers was, such as I would wish to no kindly neighbour who had entreated me well. Despite her sorrow I was careful and glad to ask after her while she lived: for I was brought up by her with tall long-gowned Climene, her youngest daughter. Together we grew up, the mother honouring me almost like her own child, until both of us came to blissful adolescence. Then they parted with her (for a high wedding-price) to a man of Same, while me my lady clothed and shod fairly and put to work on the farm. Her love toward me ever grew, and it is that which I now miss, despite the Gods having prospered me in the work which is my livelihood, so that I have my food and drink and can give alms to the deserving. But since the shadow fell on the great house and ruffians beset it there is no more cheerfulness in the mistress, neither kind word nor kindly deed – whereas it is the way of servants to take great satisfaction in meeting their mistress, to pass the time of day and gossip, perchance to eat or drink somewhat and carry off to their fields a trifle which warms their loyal hearts.'

Odysseus rejoined: 'Was it as an infant, Eumaeus, that you went astray from your home and kin? Take this chance to tell me all your story. Did they sack and ruin that spacious city where your parents lived, or were you alone, herding sheep or cattle for instance, when raiders caught you and shipped you overseas for sale at a stiff price into a master's household?' The swineherd replied, 'Stranger, if you will open up that topic, settle yourself comfortably into your seat, refill your cup and listen to me closely. These nights are inordinately long and afford us time for diverting tales and for sleep too. Nor is there point in sleeping over soon: that way lies boredom. Of the others let anyone who feels like it go off to bed. At daybreak there will be a snatch-meal and then away out with our lord's swine. But we two snugly indoors here may drink and eat and revel in an interchange of sorrows – sorrows that are memories, I mean; for when a man has endured deeply and strayed far from home he can cull solace from the rehearsal of old griefs. And so I will meet your questioning.

'There is an island called Syria, if you have heard of it, beyond Ortygia where the sun has its turning. No populous place, but good, with its bounties of cattle and sheep, corn and wine; so that its people are never straitened nor made miserable by disease. When a generation has grown old Apollo of the silver bow and Artemis come with kindly darts to end their term. Politically the whole island is comprised in two cities, and my god-like father, Ctesius son of Ormenus, was king of both.

'Ours was a place where profit-seeking Phoenician

master mariners would come to chaffer the ten thousand gew-gaws in their ships: also my father had a Phoenician woman among his bond-maids. Beautiful and tall she was and an accomplished seamstress: but passion will lead astray the very best of women, and she fell, seduced by a wily fellow-countryman, actually while she did our laundry. The Phoenician who lusted and lay with her was from a near-by ship; and afterward he asked her about herself. She pointed to my father's towering roof with "Yet I swear I am from the mart of bronze, from Sidon itself, own daughter to Arybas, that source of wealth. Taphian pirates captured me as I was strolling down the country road. They brought me here and sold me into this king's establishment. No small sum he paid."

'Then the sailor who had secretly enjoyed her said, "And would you like to come back with us, to see again the tall house of your father and mother, and be with them once more? They live still and are reputed rich." The woman replied, "Let it be so, indeed, if you sailors will pledge your word to bring me honourably home." They all swore it as she wished and after the oath was taken she began again: "Be mum now and see that never a one of you speaks to me on the highway or even at the fountain, should we meet. Someone might go and tell the old man in the palace, and on the suspicion he would fetter me savagely and compass your destruction. So keep it to yourselves while you drive your cargo-bargain. Afterwards, when the ship is fully freighted, make sure that a swift word finds me in the palace: for I would bring with me every scrap of gold within reach, together with another sort of goods that I will most gladly give you for my fare. I play nurse to my master's child, a priceless boy, who toddles by my side in and out the house. If I bring him aboard he should fetch you a huge sum from some foreign buyer."

'Thus she said and returned within the mansion. The seafarers delayed amongst us for a whole year till their trading had brought together great wealth in the ship. When all the holds were filled ready for departure they sent up a messenger to warn the woman. The crafty fellow came to my father's house hawking a golden collar beaded here and there with amber. As the serving women in the hall and my lady mother were offering him bids for this, fingering it and devouring it with their eyes, he nodded silently to the woman. Then he went back towards his ship, while she took me by the hand and led me out through the hall door. In its porch she found cups and tables where the men in attendance upon my father had refreshed themselves before going out to Assembly for their debate. Swiftly she snatched up three goblets and hid them in her bosom, me tripping along meantime in all innocence. As we hurried towards our familiar harbour the sun set and the roads grew obscured. The Phoenician vessel lay ready. The crew embarked us and sailed across the waters, Zeus affording a fair wind. We sailed for six days and nights on end: but as the son of Cronos created the seventh day Artemis the archer smote the woman, who dropped with a sea-gull's headlong dive into the bilges. They flung her overboard to feed the seals and fishes, leaving me disconsolate. Wind and currents at length brought them up in Ithaca where Laertes purchased me with his wealth. So I came to see this land.'

Odysseus in his answer said: 'Eumaeus, your tale of all these haps and sorrows sadly borne touches my heart. Yet surely Zeus has given you good to set off against the evil, in bringing you at the end of your distress to this house of a gentle man who has so well provided you with meat and drink as to let you live wholesomely. While I have arrived only as a waif, errant among the haunts of men.' So they chatted, till at last they slept away the little remnant of the night. Little it was, for Dawn was soon enthroned.

~

In this same dawn the crew of Telemachus, off shore, lowered first their sails and then their mast, smartly, and rowed their ship to land. They let go the anchors and bitted their hawsers, before going out upon the margin of the sea to prepare the day-meal and mix their sparkling wine. After they had well eaten and drunken Telemachus exhorted them prudently: 'Now you must take our black ship round to the city, while I go up-country to my herdsmen. By evening I shall have checked my affairs and got back to the city: where early to-morrow I will discharge your journey-fee in a worthy feast of meat and good wine.'

Here reverend Theoclymenus broke in to say, 'And where am I to go, dear lad? Whose house should I make for, in this rugged Ithaca with all its chiefs? Or shall I go straight to your mother's house, which is yours?' Telemachus pensively replied: 'Normally I would have you come to ours, where guests are welcomed; but now it might be unsuitable, with me away and my mother invisible – for she likes not to be seen much among the suitors in the hall, but keeps her upper room, weaving. However there is one man I can commend to you as host, and that is Eurymachus, wise Polybus' distinguished son. In the eyes of the Ithacans he is rather more than mortal, being beyond cavil their greatest figure. It is his ambition to espouse my mother and succeed to the honours of Odysseus: but that only Zeus, in his Olympian firmament, can judge. The God might cause their day of wrath to come before their wedding day' and as he finished speaking a bird (one of the hawks that are Apollo's speedy messengers) swooped past upon the right hand with a dove in its claws and tearing at it so that the feathers came fluttering to earth midway between Telemachus and the ship.

Theoclymenus called him apart from the crowd, gripped his arm and said: 'Telemachus, as soon as I saw it I knew that bird was significant. Only by the God's warrant did it fly past on the right. There is no family more royal than yours in all Ithaca. To you will ever be its sovereignty.' Upon which sober Telemachus rejoined: 'Ah, stranger, if only this word come true. My love and generosity would then so light upon you in swift measure that every one who met you would pronounce you blessed.' Then he summoned Peiraeus, one of his trusted ones, and said, 'Son of Clytius, during this voyage to Pylos you have proved most heedful of my wishes. Now I would have you take this stranger home and tend him with kindly honour till I come,' and Peiraeus the doughty spearman answered, 'Telemachus, I will receive him and not pinch his entertainment, however long you tarry.' He turned to the ship and had the others embark and cast off. They hurried to their rowing stations while Telemachus was doing on his neat sandals. Then he lifted from the deck his great spear with its keen bronze tip. The crew cast off their cables, pulled out to sea and sailed for the port, as the son of Odysseus had enjoined: while his feet sped him inland to the penfold where slept his swarms of swine about their herdsman, that loyal servant of his master's weal.

BOOK 16

At dawn, after they had sent out the drovers with their pigs, Odysseus was helping the honest swineherd light the fire within their hut and prepare breakfast, when suddenly the restless noisy dogs hushed their baying to fawn about the approaching Telemachus. Odysseus, hearing foot-falls, noted this quiet welcome that the dogs were giving, and exclaimed to Eumaeus, 'Friend, here comes a mate of yours, or someone so familiar that the dogs instead of barking play round him in friendship. Now I hear his footsteps.' With the words yet in his mouth his dear son appeared at the door. The astonished swineherd let drop the jars in which he had been mixing wine and sprang to his feet. With tears of joy he met his lord, to kiss his head, his eyes, his hands, as a good father greets the darling of his heart, his only and beloved son, home after ten long anxious years. Just so the good swineherd clung to the prince and embraced him like one snatched from death, while he cried out: 'Your coming, O Telemachus, is sweetness and light. After you had sailed for Pylos I whispered to myself that I had seen you for the last time. Come in, my child, come in to the house, that my heart may be gladdened by the wanderer's return. You keep yourself so closely in the town, to the neglect of your estate and husbandmen, as if you liked to watch that swarm of suitors devouring everything in view.'

'Have it your way, father,' protested Telemachus. 'Yet here I come to see you with my own eyes and hear from your lips if my mother is still at home. Or has she yielded to another, and abandoned the bed of Odysseus for spiders to defoul with their webs?' The swineherd replied, 'She abides constantly in the house, though the nights wane for her wearily and her days are wet with tears,' and as he spoke he was ushering him over the stone threshold and relieving him of his brazen spear. Odysseus, the father, made to give him place, but Telemachus motioned him back, saying, 'No, stranger, rest where you are. This farm is ours and we will find another seat. Here is the man to arrange it.' So Odysseus sat still while the swineherd strewed green twigs and covered them with a fleece on which the dear son of Odysseus set himself. Then the swineherd brought out on platters what was left of yesterday's baked meats, busily arranging with them baskets of bread and sweet wine mixed in an ivy-bowl. He sat to face Odysseus and they made play with the cheer till appetite was stayed. Then said Telemachus to Eumaeus, 'Father, how did this stranger reach you, in what ship's company and whence their declaration? Surely he has not just tramped in?'

Then you, O swineherd Eumaeus, said, 'I will inform you, son. He calls himself a native of the Cretan coast and a wanderer through earth's cities, that being his destiny. Actually he reached the farmstead as runaway from a Thesprotian ship. To you I convey him for disposal: yet he would be your suppliant.' Telemachus replied soberly, 'This word of yours cuts deep, Eumaeus; for how can I entertain a stranger in my house? I am still young and unversed in defending myself against aggressors. My mother is in two minds, at one time wanting to stay carefully at home keeping true to her husband's bed and public opinion, and another time ready to accept whichever of her Achaean parties shows himself the most generous wooer. Yet now you have received this guest, I will clothe him fairly with robe and tunic, give him a stabbing-sword and shoes, and send him whither he wishes: or if you prefer to look after him here, I will supply you his clothes and full rations, to prevent his being a drain upon you and your fellows. Only amongst the suitors I will not have him come, lest their vile rudeness undo me by offering him insult. It is hard for one man, however eminent, to assert himself against the odds of a crowd.'

Odysseus took up the word. 'Friend, it is my place to answer that, I think. I am desolated to hear you tell how unconscionably these suitors spite you at home. Explain – do you suffer it, or have the local people heard a God bidding them turn against you? Or perhaps you have been let down by the blood-relations upon whose armed help a man naturally counts in his greatest need? Ah, if only I were your age or as young as I feel, and could be the son of Odysseus or the great man himself back from wandering, as yet might happen! Anybody might cut my head off if I failed to go to the palace of Laertes' son and visit my fury upon every soul within it. And if their numbers prevailed over my solitary self, why I would be happy to die there in my house rather than passively witness such outrages as guests insulted and serving women violated in the stately halls, my wine spilt wantonly and my food wasted, day after day.'

Telemachus gravely replied: 'Stranger, I can explain

it all. The people do not hate me, nor have I been deserted in extremity by kinsmen on whom I did rely. The son of Cronos made our house single-fruited. Arcesius had the one son, Laertes. Odysseus was the only son of his father, and his sailing to the war left me as sole heir at home – to his loss, for now his house is beset with these innumerable enemies. The pick of all the island gentry from Dulichium and Same and leafy Zacynthus (not to mention rugged Ithaca itself) are courting my mother and eating the estate bare. She cannot either reject the horrid match or get it over. So to the ruin of the house they eat and eat, till soon they will eat me too. However such things lie in the lap of the Gods. Father swineherd, I pray you hurry to Penelope and tell her I am safely arrived out of Pylos for her sake. Till you get back I shall stay here. Be sure you see her apart and let no Achaean overhear you: I have only too many ill-wishers.'

And you said, Eumaeus, 'I know. I understand. You speak to a man who thinks: but continue and direct me plainly. Shall I push my journey a little further and inform poor Laertes, who till lately through all his griefs for Odysseus kept the supervision of the property, eating and drinking whenever he thought it advisable with the house-hold staff? They tell me now that since you sailed for Pylos he has never once feasted thus nor cared for the farm-work; but sits in grief and lamentation, letting the flesh waste off his bones.'

Telemachus replied: 'Our misfortunes grow; but very sadly we must let him be: though had mankind the faculty of choice we would plump for my father's return. So just do your errand and come back, without seeking over the country-side for the aged man – yet warn my mother to send her old hand-maiden quickly and secretly across to him with the news.' So he despatched the swineherd, who picked up his sandals, put them on and struck out for the city. His departure was watched by Athene who then repaired to the farm herself, in the guise of a tall, splendidly accomplished woman. She stood before the living quarters and revealed herself to Odysseus; but Telemachus saw nothing there, the Gods having the power not to be manifested except at will. However Odysseus perceived her, and the dogs, who instead of barking slunk in whining terror to the back of the yard. She frowned biddingly towards Odysseus. He rose and went past the outer wall to stand before her.

She said, 'God-begotten, cease hiding from your son. Open yourself to him and concert a way to slaughter the suitors. Then start together for the famous town. Nor will I lag behind. I am longing for the fray.' She touched him with her golden rod and clothed his body anew in laundered robes. She restored his stature and presence. His flesh took on colour, his cheeks filled out. The dark beard bushed once more about his chin. When her work was perfected she went away, leaving Odysseus to re-enter the hut. His son, who took him for a God, was astounded and withdrew his face, saying urgently, 'Stranger, you are not what you seemed to me just now. Your clothes are different, even your flesh is changed. Surely you are a God, a denizen of heaven. Be propitious; while we set before you gold offerings beautifully wrought, and sacrifices. Spare us, Lord.'

But Odysseus said, 'I am no God: liken me not with the Immortals. In very deed I am your father, the Odysseus for whose sake you have grieved and endured adversity and suffered indignities from men.' He spoke and kissed the lad, yielding to the tears he had hitherto held back; but Telemachus could not credit that it was his father, so he said, 'You are not Odysseus, not my father, but some subtile devil plaguing me worse till I cry with pain. No mortal man can so alter his fashion by taking thought; nor may it be, unless some very God come down and arbitrarily change him between youth and eld. You were aged and degraded: and now you are like the Gods in their wide heaven.' Odysseus replied, 'My Telemachus, do not let yourself be amazed or shaken beyond measure by your father's return. No other Odysseus than I will ever come to you now. As for my state, that is how I reach my own land after twenty years of woes and wanderings. This changing me to old or young is the whim of Athene the Reiver, who can make me at one time a sorry beggar and at another a youth of fashion. It costs the Gods of high heaven no pains to exalt or to abase plain men.'

Upon this he sat down: but Telemachus with a cry folded his father in his arms and burst out weeping. The longing for tears welled up in them both at once so that their cries rose conjoined, longer drawn and more piercing than the din of vultures or hook-taloned sea hawks whose nests have been plundered of their fledgelings by country-folk. So sorrowfully did the tears rain down from their eyelids and so unstaunched that the sun might have set upon their lamentations, only for Telemachus suddenly saying to his father, 'But in what manner of ship, father, did your crew bring you to Ithaca, and whence did they avouch themselves? You cannot have come afoot.' And Odysseus answered, 'My child, in truth they were the famous Phaeacians, those stout seamen who convey all comers. I slept the quick voyage through and was yet sleeping when they landed me in Ithaca with their wonderful rich gifts of bronze and gold and clothing. By the Gods' care all these things are bestowed in caves: and

Athene's behest brings me here for us to plan the destruction of our enemies. So recite to me the sum of these suitors and let me know their quality and quantity, that my noble heart may ponder and determine if we two can take them on, alone and unsupported; or must seek allies.'

Telemachus soberly replied, 'Father, I know your reputation as a man of your hands, but shrewd. Surely you have said too much. It appals me. Two men cannot fight a company of champions. These suitors are not just ten men or twenty even, but a crowd. Listen while I count them off. From Dulichium fifty-two men of standing with six varlets. From Same twenty-four. From Zacynthus twenty noble Achaeans; while from our Ithaca there are twelve of the best men, besides Medon the usher, the inspired bard and two skilled waiters and carvers. If we come upon all these in the house, beware lest your vengeance recoil altogether too bitterly. Rack your wits for the name of some doughty one who would stand by us manfully.'

Dauntless Odysseus replied, 'Indeed I can give you a name. Heed me and mark it carefully. Will Athene, supported by Father Zeus, do for us two, or must I think of another helper?'

Telemachus said gently, 'This pair rule all mankind, with the Immortals to boot, and are indeed mighty helpers; but their seat is very far away amongst the clouds.' 'It may be,' said Odysseus, 'yet when the ordeal by Ares is staged between us and the suitors in the hall, those two will not hold back from the din and press. Our first move is for you to go home at daybreak and rejoin the haughty suitors, whither the swineherd a little later will conduct me in my beggarly guise, seeming old and broken. Should they insult me in the house, harden your heart's love for me against my pains, even if they hurl at me or drag me feet-first across the floor to cast me out. Endure all such scenes, only reasoning sweetly with them to moderate their wildness – which they will not do. Their fateful day looms near. Now remember my next words carefully. When the wisdom of Athene prompts me I will nod to you. Watch me closely for this and when you see it, carry off all the deadly weapons within reach to that recess in the solar upstairs; and when they miss them put the suitors off with some such likely excuse as "I took them away out of the smoke, for they have become so tarnished by firereek as hardly to look like the same things Odysseus left here when he went to Troy. Also the son of Cronos prompted me with this deeper reason, that iron of itself tempts man's frailty. In wine you might quarrel and a scandal of wounds follow to mar this junketing and courtship." Just leave for the pair of us where we can snatch them suddenly, two swords, two spears and two hide shields. Pallas and deepplanning Zeus will do the rest, to confound them. Only I tell you – and again pay attention – if you are my own trueblood son let no one know Odysseus is back, not Laertes nor the swineherd nor any servant; not Penelope herself. We will study the women, you and I alone: and test the serfs also, to divide those with some respect for discipline from the froward who disparage even your dignity.'

His famous son spoke up and said, 'My father, you will prove my courage by and by, I know, and find me steadfastness itself. But I would have you reconsider this plan, in which I see nothing to our joint advantage. If you run round the properties to test each serf, you will spend ever so much time during which those others sitting in our house will go on using up our wealth with the coolness of effrontery. The women I would indeed have you prove, to see which have disgraced you and which are innocent; but the men in the farms I would postpone till later; if you can truly pin your reliance on aegis-bearing Zeus.'

~

While they discussed their plans the staunch ship and company of Telemachus were putting in to Ithaca. Deep within the harbour they beached her and drew up the dark hull. Pages carried their arms proudly homeward, and took the splendid gifts to Clytius' house. They sent a herald to the palace of Odysseus to tell careful Penelope (lest the pround queen's fears set her weeping) how Telemachus had sent the ship round to the port, while he struck overland. This herald and the honest swineherd ran into one another on the same errand to their lady: but the herald, from amongst the serving-women in the room, proclaimed aloud, 'Your dear son, O Queen, has just come back to you,' while the swineherd went near to Penelope herself and privily imparted her son's message. As soon as he had said his say he quitted the house and its precincts, to regain his swine.

The news vexed and depressed the suitors who flocked out from the hall through the high-walled court to its gate where they sat in conclave; Eurymachus opening thus: 'My friends, Telemachus has made an insolent success of his difficult task, this voyage, which we decided he must not complete. Now our job is to launch as good a vessel as there is, with deep-sea oarsmen for crew, to bid our others homeward at their best speed.' Even while he spoke Amphinoumus looked aside and saw their ship in the deep harbour, with its crew striking sail and gathering up their oars. So he laughed shortly and proclaimed, 'We will send no such message. Here they are. Either some God warned them or they saw the other ship go by and could not catch her.' All rose and trooped to the sea-front where the crew were drawing the black hull quickly up the foreshore while haughty lackeys took their weapons home. Then the united body of suitors moved to the assembly-place, strictly excluding old and young from their number, for Antinous, son of Eupeithes, to make this speech: –

'It is a sad blow, the Gods' letting this man escape his predicament. Our scouts in quick reliefs crowned the windy headlands, on the look-out all day; nor did we pass one night ashore. With sunset we ever put out in the ship and lay at sea in wait for Telemachus till dawn, to catch and kill him. Yet some power has brought him home. So here and now let us determine his bloody end, and prevent his slipping through our hands: for I think we shall never achieve our purpose while he lives. The crowd grow less partial to us as he shows himself persuasive and resourceful. We must act before he can gather the Achaeans into council; for I feel sure he will not spare us or mince matters. He will get up and blurt out how we meant to murder him, but under-reached: and they will not support us when they hear our treachery. They may even turn on us and banish us to find our living in some land of strangers. Let us anticipate, by catching him somewhere apart from the city or on his way thither. Then shall we possess his livelihood and wealth for even division amongst ourselves, leaving the house itself to his mother for him who marries her. If you will not have this course, but decide to let him live and have all his father had, then must we leave off devouring his riches and disperse to our own houses, thence to woo the woman and tempt her with gifts until she weds the designated best payer.'

After his word came a stillness till Amphinomus rose amongst them and spoke – Amphinomus, the famed son of royal Nisus son of Aretias, chief suitor from grassy and grana-ried Dulichium. His company was specially agreeable to

Penelope because of his poise and judgement, which expressed themselves as he said, 'Friends, I would not kill Telemachus. It is heinous to spill royal blood. Let us first consult the Gods. If the oracles of great Zeus commend it, then will I be the executioner myself, and halloo you on: but if not, I will bid you hold.' His saying pleased them. They rose and returned to the palace and resumed their polished thrones.

The notion came to wise Penelope that she must face the suitors in all their brutal pride, for Medon the usher who knew their plans had told her of the plot to kill her son in the house. So down to the hall-full of suitors went the stately lady with her two tiring-women and stood by a pillar of the mighty roof. She held the thin head-veil before her face and by his name rebuked Antinous, saying, 'Ill-mannered trickster, do they call you prime amongst your peers of Ithaca in eloquence and resource? You show it not. Crazy, I call you, for daring to flout those who have petitioned great Zeus to have Telemachus in his care. And you would kill him? Plotting murder is a deadly sin. Have you forgotten your father's taking refuge in this house from the people who rose against him when he joined the Taphian pirates to harry our Thesprotian friends? They were set upon killing him and plundering his great wealth; but Odysseus beat down their fury. And now you rudely devour his home and court his wife and would murder his son, all to my sore hurt. I bid you hold; and hold back the rest.'

Eurymachus, son of Polybus, intervened: 'Penelope, wise daughter of Icarius, take heart. Be not so distressed. The man who would lift hand against Telemachus is not, shall not be, cannot be, while I exist in the light of day! So I proclaim and ensure it, for quickly would such a fellow's blood drip down my spear. How often has Odysseus, that breaker of cities, dandled me on his knees and put scraps of roast meat into my fingers and made me taste the ruddy wine! Wherefore to me is Telemachus particularly dear, and I bid him have no thought of death at the wooers' hands. From the Gods, of course, there is no avoiding fate.' He spoke to calm her, with death hidden in his heart: and the queen turned back to her glorious upper room where she bewailed Odysseus, her loved husband, till Athene of the grey eyes shed merciful sleep upon her.

∼

At dusk the good swineherd rejoined Odysseus and his son, to find them contriving supper from a yearling pig they had sacrificed. Again had Athene come to the son of Laertes, and with a stroke of her wand aged him anew before wrapping him in his body-rags, for fear of the swineherd's recognizing him and running to Penelope to betray his news. Said Telemachus, 'You have come, dear Eumaeus. What news in town? Are the suitor-lords back from ambush, or still waiting for me?' And to him you replied, O swineherd, 'To wander down town and gossip was no part of my duty. I thought to deliver my message and come straight home, only there met me a herald coming from your crew in haste, and he forestalled me with your mother. Yet this I do know, for I saw it from the head of Hermes' ridge above the city, on my way back – a fast ship entering our harbour, crowded, and bristling with shields and double-edged spears. I think it was them, though I cannot be sure.' His saying made great Telemachus smile and glance aside to catch his father's eye.

Now their preparations were ended and the meal was ready. So they feasted to their common content. When hunger and thirst were put away they remembered their beds and took the boon of sleep.

BOOK 17

Dawn saw Telemachus, the son Odysseus loved, binding on his rich sandals. He picked up the heavy spear that so well fitted his grasp and turned his face townwards, saying to the swineherd, 'I am for home, father, to show myself to my mother, for I think she will not stop her tearful lamenting till she has seen me in the flesh. Now for my orders. You are to bring this poor creature to the city where he can beg his bite or sup off the charitable. My heart is too distracted to care for every chance-comer. If the stranger resents my saying so, that is his misfortune. I like blurting out the truth.' But Odysseus replied composedly, 'Why, friend, I have no wish to dally here. There is better begging in a town, where those who feel inclined will give me things. I am no longer of an age to live in quarters, obedient to my superior's every nod. So go; and this man will bring me along as you have ordered, when I have warmed myself through at the fire and the day has heated up. The morning frosts might be too sharp for me, in these poor clothes: also it seems the city is quite a journey off.'

After he had heard him out Telemachus strode vigorously from the farm, maturing schemes against the suitors by the way, till he reached his substantial house and paused to prop his spear against the tall column before stepping across its stone threshold. Eurycleia his nurse was quickest to see him, from her job of spreading sheepskins over the ornate seats. She ran to him in a flurry of tears, and the other maids of the household followed her to flock about him with loving kisses for his head and shoulders. Forth from her chamber issued heedful Penelope, fair as Artemis or golden Aphrodite, to clasp her son and kiss his face and both his beautiful eyes, while she sobbed, 'Are you back, Telemachus, dear light? I thought never to see you more after you sailed secretly and without my leave to Pylos for news of your father. Quick, tell me what you saw.' He answered, 'Mother mine, I have barely missed death. Do not ruffle my heart or set me crying again, but bathe yourself and change your clothing: then go upstairs with your women into your room and vow victims by hundreds to the Gods, on the day Zeus will vouchsafe us perfect vengeance. I am for the assembly to recover a stranger who came back with me, but whom I had to send on with my devoted crew after getting Peiraeus to take him to his place and care for him honourably till I arrived.' His speech stifled the questions on her lips. She performed her libation, put on clean garments and vowed whole hecatombs to the Gods if Zeus would ever let their revenge fructify.

Telemachus left the house spear in hand, with two fleet hounds at heel, and upon him such grace from Athene that all the people adored as he came. The suitor-lords bustled up with welcomes that covered the malice in their hearts; but he avoided them, to sit by Mentor and Antiphus and Halitherses, his old family friends. They questioned him eagerly: but at the instant Peiraeus the spearsman appeared, leading his guest through the town to the assembly, Telemachus went over to be greeted thus: 'Telemachus, send your women promptly to my house and collect the gifts of Menelaus.' But he replied, 'Peiraeus, we cannot yet see how things will go. If the suitors manage to kill me traitorously in the palace and split up my heritage, I would rather you held these gifts. But if I succeed in dooming them to death, then shall I be just as glad to get them as you to let them go.'

He led the way-worn Theoclymenus to the house. Within its massy walls they threw down their cloaks upon some settle or throne and went to wash themselves in the polished baths. The ministering women bathed and anointed them and clothed them warmly. Forth they came once more to their seats, where the maid of the ewer poured for them the hand-water over its basin and drew up their table which the housekeeper hospitably spread with loaves and many dishes. But Penelope placed herself in a reclining chair against the pillar opposite, and spun fine yarn on her distaff all the while they fed themselves full.

At last she broke out, 'Telemachus, I am returning to my room; to that bed of sorrow which I have kept bedewed with tears since the day Odysseus went to Ilium with the sons of Atreus; seeing that you will not move yourself to tell me, now before the suitors come in, what the news is of your father's return – if you did hear anything.' Said Telemachus, 'Nay, mother, listen. We went to Pylos where Nestor the king welcomed me like a child who had been long abroad. He and his sons were so kind: but of Odysseus, alive or dead, he had no news at all. He found me well in chariot and horses and sent me across to Menelaus the son of Atreus, in whose house I met Helen, the cause, under God, of all the Argive-Trojan travail. Menelaus enquired why I had come, and when I explained he said, "For those cowardly suitors to aspire after Odysseus' bed is for a hind to lay her unweaned fawns in a lion's den while she ranges abroad for food. As the lion on his return makes sad work of them, so will Odysseus grimly slay the suitors. If only the Gods would bring him upon them in the might whereby he flung Philomeleides at Lesbos, to the general joy, what a short sharp issue they would have to their wedding! Your query I will best meet by telling you exactly what I learnt from the old man of the sea. He said he had seen Odysseus in an island, Nymph Calypso's prisoner, miserable in her house but unable to escape for lack of shipping and men to ferry him across the swelling sea." That is what Menelaus said. Having achieved my mission I sailed for home and the Gods gave me a fair wind which brought me quickly here.'

His tidings fluttered her heart: but godlike Theoclymenus interposed, 'Hear my word, O august consort of Odysseus. Indeed he had no certain knowledge, but I will prophesy to you most clearly and exactly. I testify by Zeus in first instance, as by this hospitable board and the hearth of Odysseus at which I stand, that already HE is in his native place, active it may be or else lying low; but surely hearing of these disorders and meditating vengeance upon all the suitors. The bird I saw by the decked ship pointed the future so plainly that then and there I declared it to Telemachus.' To him Penelope replied, 'May your word be fulfilled, stranger; then I would show you how lavish my gratitude could be, even till every passerby did praise your fortune.' While they thus talked the suitors on the flat land before the palace were heedlessly amusing themselves with the discus or spear-throwing. Supper-time came and homeward after their appointed shepherds came the flocks from the outlying pastures. Then did Medon, the favourite attendant who was always at the feasts, proclaim: 'Lordlings, now that you have played to your hearts' content, turn back to the house; and we shall feast. Nothing is better than a timely meal.' They sprang up and went as he advised into the stately house, where they piled their cloaks on the high seats and slaughtered great sheep, fat goats and pigs, even a bull from the stock, to furnish their table.

~

Odysseus and the swineherd were ready to leave the country for the town. The exemplary swineherd remarked, 'Stranger, you are keen on moving today to the city, as my prince ordained. Yet I would have left you here in charge, only for regard of my master, and in fear of the rebuke which would follow from him. Very terrible are the rebukes of kings. So let us away. More than half the day has sped and you will feel the chill towards nightfall.' Odysseus answered, 'I understand. I agree. You address an enlightened man. Indeed let us set off under your sole guidance. Yet if you have a trimmed staff give it me, to steady my steps over this road which you describe as difficult.' He slipped on his mean wallet, that tattered thing with its shoulder-cord, and Eumaeus gave him the stick he wanted. Off they went together, leaving dogs and herding-men to keep the farm. In such state, like an aged and sorry pauper hobbling on a staff and deplorably dressed, did the swineherd bring his King home.

They threaded the awkward path till hard by the town, when they found the running spring, steyned round, which Ithacus, Neritus and Polyctor had built. From this fountain the citizens drew their water. A grove of black poplars completely encircled it and the water, ever so cold, ran down thither from a crag crowned by an altar to the

Nymphs. Every wayfarer paid reverence there. Here it was they encountered Melanthius the goat-herd, son of Dolius, who with two herd-boys was bringing in the pick of all his goats for the suitors' supper. When he saw the pair he broke into abuse, calling them every vile and shameful name; which put Odysseus mightily about. 'See one beast escorting another!' he cried. 'How the God joins like with like. Whither, you rogue of a pig-keeper, will you take that hang-dog beggar, that gorbellied mar-feast? His sort hang about, scratching their backs against ever so many door-posts, and whine not for swords or cauldrons but for orts of food. If you lent him to me for helping at my place to clean stalls or fodder the kids, why he could drink much butter-milk and plump out his spindle-legs. But having acquired none but bad habits he will not attempt a job so long as he can go begging through the town and pester everyone to feed his gross paunch. Yet listen to my telling you what will surely happen if he ventures to the great palace of Odysseus: showers of foot-stools flung by manly hands will whizz round his head or crack sharply against his ribs while they pelt him through the hall.'

So he reviled; and in passing he back-heeled Odysseus savagely in the rump, but nevertheless failed to jolt him off the path, so solidly he stood. Odysseus was in two minds, if he should not lift his cudgel to bludgeon him out of his senses, or tackle him low and bang his head against the ground. However he mastered himself to take it quietly; but the swineherd with a glare of disgust lifted his hands to pray aloud: 'O fountain-nymphs who are daughters of Zeus, if ever Odysseus burned on your altar the fat-smoth-ered thighs of rams or kids, then grant my petition and let him return; let some God restore him. How he would toss to the winds all this sham splendour with which you deck yourself to parade the city; while faithless shepherds let your flock run to ruin.' Melanthius called back, 'Beshrew me, but the dog talks as if he would bewitch us. Upon a day I shall take him far from Ithaca in a fast dark ship and let his sale bring me a fat profit. O that Apollo of the silver bow would strike Telemachus today in his house, or the suitors settle his account, even so faithfully as Odysseus has died in some far land.' With that parting shot he left them to plod on, while by a short cut he gained the palace, entered it and sat amongst the suitors opposite Eurymachus who was very partial to him. The servers brought him meat and the housekeeper bread, for his eating.

Step by step Odysseus and Eumaeus were drawing near. They halted when the music of the polished harp broke on their ears as Phemius struck up his song to the company. The hero caught the swineherd's hand and said, 'Eumaeus, of a truth this dwelling of Odysseus is noble, easily picked out and recognizable amongst many. See how it rises stage beyond stage with its courts all properly walled and coped, and its double doors so securely hung. No man could reckon it cheap. And I can tell there are many men banqueting within, for the smell of roast hangs round, and loudly rings the lyre which the Gods have made to chime so well with feasts.' To which you, Eumaeus, answered, 'Well may you notice that, if you have any wit at all. But now let us think what to do. Will you go first into the great house and join the suitors, while I stay here? or you remain without and I precede you? Settle it quickly, for if they see you dawdling outside, they may smite or throw something. Weigh my words.'

Odysseus replied, 'I have you: you address a sensible man. Go in front while I wait here. I have no more to learn about beatings or stonings. With all those accidents of sea or battle my heart is grown wholly callous. Let what may be go on the reckoning. Yet it is deplorable there is no hiding humanity's chief curse, this clamorous belly which launches so many proud ships to the affliction of enemies beyond the sterile seas.' As they talked a dog lying there lifted head and pricked his ears. This was Argos whom Odysseus had bred but never worked, because he left for Ilium too soon. On a time the young fellows used to take him out to course the wild goats, the deer, the hares: but now he lay derelict and masterless on the dung-heap before the gates, on the deep bed of mule-droppings and cow-dung which collected there till the serfs of Odysseus had time to carry it off for manuring his broad acres. So lay Argos the hound, all shivering with dog-ticks. Yet the instant Odysseus approached, the beast knew him. He thumped his tail and drooped his ears forward, but lacked power to drag himself ever so little towards his master. However Odysseus saw him out of the corner of his eye and brushed away a tear, which he covered by quickly saying to Eumaeus in an off-hand way:

'Strange, that they let such a hound lie on the dung-hill! What a beauty to look at! though of course I cannot tell if he has speed to match, or is merely one of those show-dogs men prize for their points.' Eumaeus answered, 'That is the hound of a man who died far from home. If only he could recover the fire and life that were his when Odysseus left for Troy, how your eyes would open at seeing such speed and power. Put him on the trail and no quarry ever escaped him, not even in the densest thickets, so keen he was of scent. Now he has fallen low, his master having perished abroad and the heartless women caring for him not at all. Slaves, when their master's control is loosed, do not even wish to work well. Ah, the day a man's enslaved, Zeus robs him of half his virtue!' With this word he plunged into the house, going straight along the hall amidst the suitors; but Argos the dog went down into the blackness of death, that moment he saw Odysseus again after twenty years.

Telemachus, being the first to notice the swineherd come in, waved and called him forward. He peered about till he saw the trestle on which the carver would sit whenever he had much meat to divide amongst the feasting suitors. This he carried to the other side of Telemachus' table and there straddled it. The usher served him a portion, with bread from the basket. On his heels Odysseus entered, a miserable aged beggar to all seeming, halting on a stick and ragged. He sat down on the door-tread, a beam of ash, and leant against the cypress wainscot which the old-time carpenter had planed so smoothly and plumbed upright. Telemachus called up the swineherd, gave him a whole loaf from the fair basket and a double handful of meat and said, 'For the newcomer, with my instructions to go round and beg of all the suitors. Shyness and destitution are poor bed-fellows.' The swineherd on hearing this went across and said emphatically, 'These, stranger, from Telemachus, who bids you go round and beg of all the suitors. Modesty, he says, sits ill on beggars.' Odysseus for response prayed aloud: 'O royal Zeus, make Telemachus happy on earth and ensure his heart's desire.' He took the present in both hands, laid it on the sorry wallet between his feet and made his meal there, while the musician sang. When he was satisfied, the song had ended and the clamour of the suitors was loud across the hall: but then Athene's spirit visited Odysseus and prompted him to solicit hunks of bread off them, as a test to distinguish the just from the lawless – though not even so would she save one man of them all from fate.

Accordingly he set off by the right, to beg from each man in turn with outstretched palm like a trained mendicant. They had compassion and began to give, in surprise asking one another who and whence this man was. Melanthius the goat-man then gave tongue, crying, 'Hear me, suitors of our great Queen, and I will tell you about this stranger whom I have seen before. The swineherd introduced him here. As to who or what he is, that I cannot say.' The news made Antinous short with Eumaeus. 'Infamous swineherd,' he called out, 'why bring this thing to town? Have we not vagabonds enough, paupers whose pestering turns our stomachs while we feast? Do you reck so little that they swarm here and eat up your lord's substance as to add another to the list of them?' Eumaeus replied, 'An ungenerous speech, Lord Antinous, be you ever so noble. Who invites or constrains a stranger to his board, unless he happens to be some creative man, a prophet or healer or worker in wood, or perhaps some surpassing musician with power to give joy by song? Such men are asked the world over. But beggars – who invites them to prey on him? You are always harshest of the suitors against the servants of Odysseus, and especially against me. Yet I complain not while staid Penelope and god-like Telemachus remain in the palace.'

Telemachus hushed him. 'Hold your peace, Eumaeus. Never enter into discussion with Antinous, whose custom it is to rail upon us angrily and inflame the company.' Then to Antinous: 'Is it out of love, Antinous, with a father's feeling for his son that you would have me arbitrarily expel this stranger from our house? God forbid. Instead I pray you take somewhat and give it him yourself. Far from grudging this, I urge, I enjoin you so. Disregard Penelope and my great father's servants. No? Your heart prompts you this way not at all? Truly you would rather feed yourself than give a crumb away.' Antinous retorted, 'Telemachus, pride and temper run away with your tongue. If all the wooers gave him what I am going to give, this house would be quit of him for three months or so' – and as he spoke he hooked out into view from under the table and poised in his hand the footstool on which his lithe feet had rested during the feast.

But all the others were giving Odysseus presents and stuffing his wallet with bread and meat. Really it seemed he might regain his door-sill unscathed after feeling the temper of the Achaeans: only he paused facing Antinous to adjure him direct. 'Alms, my kind sir: for you seem to me not the meanest of the Achaeans but their kingliest. As such you owe me a greater hunk of bread than any, and so should I hymn your praise the length and breadth of the earth. Once I had my house and was rich, with crowds of servants and what else composes a decent life. Charity to waifs of all kinds and degrees was then my habit. But Zeus stripped me – surely it was Zeus – when he sent me roving with pirates to distant Egypt and disaster. In Egypt's mighty river I stationed my fleet and commanded my stout companions to bide by their ships, on guard while the scouts went ashore to spy. But the scouts began wantonly plundering the land, killing its people and carrying off its women and children. An alarm was raised and there came against us great hordes that filled the country-side. Panic took hold of my followers. They broke, and were slain or taken: but my lot was to be sent away by the Egyptians to Cyprus, as a gift to Dmetor, son of Iasus its valiant king, who happened to be with them. From Cyprus am I come to you so miserably.'

Antinous roared back: 'What murrain brought this

kill-joy here to curdle our feast? Leave my table. Stand away there, clear, or again you will find yourself in a bad Egypt and bitter Cyprus. The impudence of the beggar! to visit unabashed every man here and solicit alms, which they heap upon you so freely and carelessly because it happens to be another man's property, and plenty still remains!' Odysseus drew off a little and said, 'It grieves me that your breeding should not compare with your looks. If you, thus sitting in another's house, refuse me one crumb from his plenty, it follows that at your own place, with you there, no suppliant would get even a grain of salt.' At this saying fury possessed the heart of Antinous. With sinister leer he ground out, 'For your saucy speaking I shall make sure you do not get away from the hall in good order'; and upon the word he swung his footstool and hurled it to hit him on the right side, just where the arm roots into the back.

Odysseus stood up against the blow like a rock; only he wagged his head in silence, while a black rage swelled within him. He reached his doorstep, laid the bursting wallet on the floor and sat down to say, 'Listen, O suitors of the great Queen, while I unburden my mind. There is no soreness or rancour over wounds received in battle, where a man defends his neat or his grey wethers. But here Antinous assaults me in an affair of the belly, that pestilent member which everlastingly afflicts us. If there are Gods and Avengers for the poor, may the crisis of death overtake Antinous before his wedding day.' Antinous rejoined, 'Keep your place, stranger, and eat, and hold your tongue: or else quit, lest the lads punish your words by dragging you hand and foot through the house till you are torn in ribbons' – but actually he had greatly vexed the company so that in succession these reckless young lords were protesting to him and saying, 'Your striking this unhappy waif was a sin, Antinous, which will seal your fate so surely as there is a God in heaven. Not to mention that these very Gods are always disguising themselves as travellers from abroad and roaming our settlements to note human good or ill.' However he would not abide the others' remonstrances. As for Telemachus, though the anger grew within him, yet he too only shook his head dumbly at witnessing his father assaulted.

When Penelope heard of a man's having been beaten in the guest-hall she cried before her maidens, 'Oh that the great archer, Apollo, may smite you, Antinous, as you have smitten!' and matronly Eurynome observed, 'If our prayers were answered, never a one of these would see another Dawn fairly enthroned.' Penelope said to her, 'Ah, mother, every one of them is hateful and all their desires are evil: but Antinous is black doom itself. A wretched stranger under spur of necessity wanders round the house to beg, and all give him something and fill his wallet, until he comes to that one, who smites him with his stool behind the right shoulder.'

So she held forth to her handmaidens from her chair in her room, while Odysseus was eating. Then she summoned the swineherd and said, 'Good Eumaeus, bid the stranger come up to receive my hearty greeting and be asked if he has heard anything of Odysseus, or seen him, perchance; for he looks a much-travelled man.'

And your reply to that, O Eumaeus, swineherd? 'Ah, Queen, if only the Achaeans would grant you a moment's peace! How his tales would enchant your very wits. I had him for three nights and kept him three days in my home-stead: for he came straight to me when he escaped his ship. Yet he could not exhaust this history of his mishaps.

Spellbound he held me at my own fireside while I yearned for him to go on for ever, as the sight of a bard with the god-given art of entrancing song makes men yearn to hear him so long as he will sing. He claims a family acquaintance with the house of Odysseus, and to be a Cretan of Minos' race, made by misfortune to roll round the world till he reached here. He says he has heard of Odysseus near-by, in the rich Thesprotian land, alive and bringing all kinds of treasure home with him.'

Then Penelope cried, 'Bring him quickly to tell me this to my face, while those others sit in our gates or house, rejoicing to the top of their bent. Intact in their homes lies all their wealth, bread and sweet wine, with none but their house-thralls to consume it: while they haunt us day by day, sacrificing our oxen and sheep and fat goats, and bibbing our precious wine in their revels. Our entire wealth goes to wrack for need of one like Odysseus to defend it from ruin. Ah, if only he might regain his country! How very soon he and his son would repay these men their outrages!'

While the words were yet on her lips Telemachus sneezed so vehemently that the house resounded. Penelope laughed. Then she hastily repeated to Eumaeus, 'Now call the stranger instantly. Did you not hear how my son sealed all I said with that sneeze? It spells no half-measures for the suitors, but utter death and doom for every individual man. Note this too: if I find that what he says is truth I shall clothe him in tunic and cloak most handsomely.'

Off went the swineherd on his urgent errand, to say, 'Venerable stranger, Penelope the wise, the mother of Telemachus, calls you; having a mind to enquire about the lord for whose sake she has suffered so much: and if she approves your good-faith she will give you the clothing you sorely need and let you go on begging in the town, to profit your belly amongst all the well-disposed.' Odysseus replied, 'I would readily tell Penelope what I know and I have good information upon Odysseus, having endured ill-luck in his company: but I fear this horde of irritable suitors with their rude arrogance towering into the iron skies. Just now that man yonder struck me very sorely as I went inoffensively through the house; and neither Telemachus nor any other saved me. So let Penelope bridle her eagerness and wait upstairs till the sun goes down. Then let her find me a seat nearer the fire – my clothing, as you well know from my first coming to you, being threadbare – and question me upon her lord's returning home.'

Back went the swineherd with this message: but hardly had he crossed her threshold than Penelope cried, 'Not bringing him, Eumaeus? What ails the tramp? Is he too afraid of someone or does our palace scare him? A timid man makes a sorry beggar.' Eumaeus answered, 'What he says is only what everyone feels about keeping clear of these bullies' violence. He wants you to delay till sunset; and that would benefit yourself, O Queen, by letting you be alone when you question him and get his news.' Wise Penelope said, 'Perhaps the stranger's caution is right. Surely of all living men these suitors are the most outrageous and extravagant.' So the queen: but the swineherd had said all he wished.

Back he went to the suitors' gathering, to put his head close to Telemachus' ear and whisper so that none overheard: 'Beloved, I am going. I must see to the swine and all – my livelihood and yours. I leave you to manage here: but make it your first concern to guard yourself and ensure no harm befalls you. They wish you all the evil there is, this mob of Achaeans. Zeus confound them before their mischief reaches us!' Said Telemachus, 'Amen, father: go after the time of supper, but return early tomorrow with sound beasts for sacrifice. The Immortals and myself will regulate this business.'

The swineherd sat once more on his smooth trestle till contented with meat and drink. Then he forsook the courts and hall-full of banqueters. The day was ending, and their merriment broke out into dancing and singing: while he went back to the pigs.

BOOK 18

Then arrived on the scene a vulgar tout who used to cadge his living everywhere round Ithaca and had the champion gluttonous belly of the world, that put no bounds to his eating or drinking: yet he got no muscle and no vigour by it, for all his bulky look. Arnaeus, his respectable mother had called him at birth; but all the lads nicknamed him Irus, because there was never an errand he would not run. His coming now was to pick a quarrel with Odysseus and expel him from his own house. So he floutingly began, 'Outside the porch, old one, or you may be haled forth by the leg. Cannot you see how all these give me the wink to throw you out? But I should be sorry to do that. So off with you instantly, before our difference turns to blows.'

Deep, devious Odysseus eyed him hard and replied, 'Sir, I am doing you no hurt and saying nothing; nor do I resent the bounty these reserve for you, however liberal it be. The door-sill is amply wide for both of us and you have no call to be close with strangers' goods. You seem, like me, a wanderer: just as dependent on the Gods for happiness. Wherefore do not rouse me with show of fists, lest I forget my years, lose temper and sully your breast and mouth with blood. Yet thereby should I gain a calm tomorrow: for afterward, I think, you would never frequent the house of Odysseus again.' This angered Irus the tramp. He cried, 'Tut, tut! the pot-belly nags away like an old cinder-quean. I shall play on him my wicked trick, that two-handed chop; to spatter the teeth of his jaw about the ground as a boar in the crops rattles down grains of corn. Gird yourself, then, to let all these see our fight – yet how dare you stand up to a much younger man?'

Thus vigorously did each abuse the other on the polished threshold under the high entry, till the dignified Antinous became aware of them. He laughed out right musically and called to the rest, saying, 'My dears, here is such luck as we never had before; real sport from God. Irus and our stranger are challenging each other to fisticuffs. Let us make a match of it, instantly.' Then they sprang up, laughing, and pressed round the two scare-crow tramps; but Antinous called, 'Just a moment, Sir suitors. Roasting there by the fire lie those goat-paunches we stuffed with fat and blood and reserved for supper. Suppose we let the better man, after he has won this fight, go over to take his pick of them, and make him ever after free of our feasts; to be the only beggar allowed inside, begging?'

His proposal gained favour, till Odysseus, with crafty intent, said, 'But, friends, an old man worn with toil cannot fairly fight a young one. It is my mischief-making belly that eggs me on to earn this thrashing. So promise me on oath, everyone, not to foul me for Irus' sake with some heavy hand-stroke that will lay me at his mercy.' All solemnly swore as he wished; and after the oath Telemachus said, 'Stranger, if your pride and pluck move you to mate this man, have no concern for any Achaean. He who strikes you will have the crowd upon him. Witness myself, your host; and thereto agree Prince Antinous and Prince Eurymachus, men of judgement.'

All approved. Odysseus kilted up his rags like a loin-cloth, baring his massive, shapely thighs, his arching shoulders, chest and brawny arms. Attendant Athene magnified the limbs of the shepherd of the people. The suitors were startled out of their wits and stared at each other, saying, 'Such hams has the old fellow brought out from his rags that soon our tout will be outed by an evil of his own procuring.' Their boding shook Irus to the core. The workmen had to truss him forcibly: they brought him on with the flesh of his limbs quaking in panic. Antinous spoke to him sharply: 'Now, bully, you were better dead or not born, maybe, if you will start so in terror of an old man crippled with suffering. Let me tell you this, for certain. Should he best you and win, I shall thrust you into a black ship for export to the continent; to King Echetus, bane of the earth, who will hack off your nose and ears with his cruel knives and tear away your privy parts for throwing all raw to his dogs as food.' These words gave the trembling a deeper hold upon his limbs.

However they haled him into the open, and there the two squared off. Royal Odysseus was puzzling himself if it were better to smite the other so starkly that life would leave him where he fell, or to tap him gently and just stretch him out. On the whole the gentle way seemed right, to save himself from too close notice by the Achaeans. So when they put up their hands and Irus hit at his right shoulder Odysseus only hooked him to the neck under the ear and crushed the bones inward, so that blood gushed purple from his lips and with a shriek he fell in the dust, biting the ground and drumming with his feet. The suitor lords flung up their hands and died of laughing; but

Odysseus took him by the leg and dragged him through the entrance, across the yard and to the outer-gate, where he propped him with his back against the precinct-fence and his beggar's crutch between his hands, remarking bitterly, 'Sit there and play bogy to the dogs and pigs: but unless you want a worse beating never again set up your silly self as beggar-king.' Then he reassumed his sorry wallet, the poor burst thing with a mere string for strap, and walked back to the door-step where he sat once more. The suitors, still laughing merrily as they trooped past into the hall, hailed him with, 'Zeus and his Immortals grant you your ambition, stranger, and fulfil your heart's wish, for your having ended that insatiable tramp's begging up and down. Now will we trade him to the mainland, to King Echetus, mankind's worst enemy.' Odysseus rejoiced at this fair omen; and Antinous set beside him the great tripe-pudding all bubbling with its blood and fat, while Amphinomus picked him two loaves from the basket and pledged him thus in a golden loving-cup: 'Your health, venerable stranger. May there be happiness for you here-after, in place of the many woes you now endure.'

Odysseus replied, 'Amphinomus, apparently you take after your enlightened father: for I have heard how Nisus of Dulichium was decent and rich. You whom they call his son seem approachable. So now attend closely and mark what I say. Of all that creep and breathe upon her, Earth breeds no feebler thing than man. While the Gods grant him vigour and limber joints he says that evil can never overtake him: and when the blessed Gods doom him to sorrow he must harden his heart and bear that too. Man's free-will on earth is no more his than the daylight Zeus ordains. Once I might have held a place in society, only that I (with infatuate reliance upon my father and kinsmen) let my pride and strength run wild. Might everyone take example thereby to abjure lawlessness and accept God's providence evenly and without cavil! Yet here are the suitors just as lawlessly employed in spending the substance and pestering the wife of a man who, I tell you, will soon regain his friends and country. Indeed he is near. May some power waft you away home, to miss meeting him when he stands at last beneath his roof-tree – for I think he and the suitors will not be separated, then, till blood has flowed.' He ended and spilled the ritual drop before setting his lips to the honeyed wine. Then he restored his cup to that marshal of the people who went back down the hall with bowed head in distress of mind. A foreboding of evil chilled his spirit; yet it did not save him from fate, for Athene had appointed him to meet death at the hands and spear of Telemachus. For the while he sank once more upon the throne from which he had risen.

Goddess Athene now put it into the mind of Penelope, the royal daughter of Icarius, to appear before the suitors and inflame their hearts – while gaining distinction with her husband and son. So the Queen laughed mirthlessly and said, 'Eurynome, my heart urges me to visit these suitors in all their hatefulness: and I would also speak a timely word to my son, adjuring him (for his good) not to haunt the company of intolerant men whose kindly speaking is only a mask for infamy.' The old dame replied, 'Your proposal, my child, is fitting. Exhort your son and spare not: only first wash yourself and make up your cheeks, so as not to show him this tear-stained face. Unrelieved grief is not wholesome, and your son is now a man. Have you not much prayed the deathless ones to let you see him bearded?' Said Penelope, 'Your partiality, Eurynome, must not flatter me to cleanse and anoint myself with unguent.

The Gods of high Olympus took away what appeal I had the day my man embarked. Summon Antonöe and Hippodameia to support me in the hall. Unattended I go not amongst the men: modesty forbids.' The old crone went off down the house to call these women and speed them.

Another notion came to Athene, who breathed down sweet sleep upon the daughter of Icarius, so that she leaned back in slumber on the long couch, with all her joints relaxed. As she thus lay the Goddess was giving her immortal gifts to bewilder the Achaeans. First of all she refined the beauty of her face with the imperishable salve used by well-crowned Cytherea whenever she goes featly dancing with the Graces. She made her taller and fuller to the eye and whiter than ivory freshly sawn: so having worked her pleasure the Goddess departed as the white-armed maids chattered in from their room. Drowsiness left Penelope, who said, rubbing her cheeks, 'That was a pretty trance which overlaid my sorrow. Would but chaste Artemis grant me, here and now, a death as calm; and save me an eternity of heartgrief and sickness for my peerless lord, who surpassed the Achaeans in all nobility.' With this on her lips the fairest of women went down from her shining upper room (not by herself, for the two maids attended her) till she reached the suitors. She took her stand by the great column which upheld the roof; she spread her bright head-veil before her face. One to either side stood the trusted maids. The vision of such loveliness enfeebled her courtiers' knees and filched away their hearts with desire. Each man prayed that his might be the luck to lie abed with her.

She addressed her dear son: 'My Telemachus, your feelings and your reason are not so stable as they were. Your childish nature was particularly knowing: but now that you are grown of age, your instincts and judgements fail. Yet any stranger setting eyes on your tall beauty would know you for some great man's heir! Consider what has just now passed, in your letting this stranger be mishandled. What would be the outcome of a guest's suffering brutal injury in our halls? You would incur public obloquy and contempt for ever and ever.' Telemachus answered reasonably: 'My mother, I do not resent your being vexed at this. Agreed that lately I was a child; but now I can distinguish good and evil and comprehend them. Yet I cannot order all things according to reason, for these men's wicked imaginings pull me hither and thither and I get help from none. Still, this broil between Irus and our guest did not end in the least as the suitors wished, for the stranger proved the doughtier. By Zeus and Athene and Apollo! would that these suitors in our palace might every one lie vanquished in house or court with hanging head asprawl, as Irus now squats by the precinct-gates lolling his drunk-like head, not able to stand upright or make off home (wherever home may be) because his limbs are all abroad.'

So the one answered the other: but Eurymachus rose to compliment Penelope. 'O daughter of Icarius, if only the remaining Achaeans of Iasian Argos might see you, this press of suitors feasting in your halls would be augmented by tomorrow's sunrise. You outshine your sex in features, stature and intellect.' But Penelope sadly rejoined, 'My charms of face and form, Eurymachus, the Immortals reft from me, what time the Argives, with lord Odysseus, sailed for Ilium. If he were back to shelter my existence I should have a fairer and a wider fame: but now I am made sad by all these ill-fortunes God has imposed. Listen: when he left his native strand he took me by the wrist, by this right wrist, and said, "Dear wife, I fear not quite all of us mail-clad Achaeans can live through this campaign: for the

Trojans are described as fighters, good with javelin or bow, and expert managers of the swift-pacing horses that oftenest decide the issue of a well-matched fight. So I cannot tell if heaven will grant me a home-coming or retain me in the Troad. Hence you must take charge here. Study my father and mother in the house as you do now; or even more, perhaps, to replace my absence. But when you see our son a bearded man, then feel free to marry again as you will and leave your home." Thus he enjoined; and his period is accomplished. The night comes which will see me a victim of the wedlock I loathe, one more misfortune for this ill-starred soul bereft of happiness by Zeus and further harried by this new-fangled courtship. Such conscienceless devouring of another's livelihood is clean contrary to rule. Properly, when rivals compete for the hand of a lady of family and fortune they should bring their own fat flocks and beeves to feast her friends, and give her costly gifts.'

As he listened Odysseus laughed to hear her cozening gifts from them and speciously keeping their hearts' lust in play, while preserving her very different purpose: for Antinous replied, 'O discreet Penelope, take what gifts the Achaeans will willingly bring in. No decent man shirks giving. Yet understand that we are not going to our own places, or elsewhere, till you have married the worthiest Achaean.' All cried assent; and charged their attendants to collect her gifts. The page of Antinous brought a lovely ample robe, embroidered throughout. It was fitted with twelve toggles of pure gold, each pin complete with looped fasteners. From Eurymachus there arrived an elaborate chain, strung with beads of amber like golden sunshine. The attendants of Eurydamas fetched a pair of triple-drop pendants, so clear that they sparkled brilliantly: while the squire of Peisander, King Polyctor's son, brought from his place a necklace that was a choice jewel. Every Achaean contributed something. Her maids took up the precious tribute and away she went to her room upstairs.

The company whiled away the evening hours with dancing and joyous singing, very well amused; and the darkness of night came down upon their gaiety. Then three fire-stands were set out along the hall to light it, and about them piles of kindling wood, good dry stuff, long seasoned but freshly split. Into each heap were sorted firebrands and the house-maidens took turns to feed their blaze until bold Odysseus said to them: 'Maids of the long-absent King, away with you to your honoured mistress's quarters. Sit there to divert her while you twirl yarn on the distaffs or comb wool for her with your fingers. I will maintain these men's light, nor yield to weariness though they should fancy to outwear the enthroned Dawn. I have stout endurance.'

His words made them exchange glances and giggle. Only fresh-faced Melantho mocked him vilely. She was Dolius' child, reared and tended by Penelope like a daughter and indulged with every bauble she set her heart on. Yet did she have no feeling for her lady's woes, but was Eurymachus' light of love. 'O shabby guest!' she now rudely cried, 'are your wits unhinged that instead of seeking fit lodging in some smith's booth or public house, you thrust in here and impudently enlarge your mouth amongst our lords? Or perhaps drink has gone to your head; or maybe you are a natural and so talk gustily always. Or did your overcoming beggarman Irus unbalance you? If so beware lest one stronger than Irus arise and hurl you forth all bloody from great buffets on your pate.' Odysseus glared back and said, 'Bitch, I shall instantly find Telemachus to tell him your words; and he will hew you in pieces where you stand.' His fierceness appalled the women, who believed what he said and scattered through the house with terror in every shivering limb: while he took his stand beside the flaring braziers, tending them and staring round, yet with his thoughts far away, fixed on what would be.

Athene was determined to provoke the suitor lords to sharper scorning, whose sting should pierce the heart of Laertes' son; so Eurymachus began to sneer at his expense in the others' hearing, to excite their ridicule. 'Listen, O suitors of the famous queen, while I speak my mind. Surely this fellow's coming to the hall of Odysseus is a godsend. I fancy the main blaze of torchlight shines from him, from that polished head unruffled by the littlest hair!' Then he turned to the stormer of cities and asked, 'Stranger, would you enter my service if I hired you for my outlying farm, to build dykes of dry stone or plant timber trees? You should be sufficiently paid and get rations all the time, good clothes and shoe-leather. But alas! I fear you are a mere waster, through and through, who will refuse employment while you can tout round the country-side and cadge to gratify your bottomless appetite.'

Odysseus replied, 'Ah, Eurymachus, if only there might be a working match just between us two during the late springtide when the days are long: in a hay meadow, perhaps; me with a well-curved scythe and you with one like mine; our match to last all day, foodless, and far into the gloaming, with grass yet to spare! Or draught oxen of the finest, great flaming beasts lusty with feed, well matched in age and pulling-power, and fresh: also a four-team field of loam that turns cleanly from the coulter. Then should you see what a long straight furrow I would drive. Or Zeus might, this very day, stir us up one of his wars; and I get a target, two spears and a skull-cap of good bronze fitting tight to my temples. Then, when you saw me abreast the forefront of the battle, you would rant no more nor ridicule my belly. Enough of this! You are an ill-natured cad, puffed up to think yourself someone by association with these few weaklings. Ah, if Odysseus came back to his land, how quickly would those wide doors become too narrow for your rush to safety through the porch.'

The retort swelled the anger of Eurymachus, who glared at Odysseus and cried sharply, 'Wretch! I shall see that your big talk before this crowd gets you into instant trouble. Your impudence! – has that wine touched your wits? Maybe you always play the public fool; or are you above yourself through beating poor scapegrace Irus?' While shouting he snatched up his footstool; but Odysseus for fear of him ducked downward by the knees of Amphinomus of Dulichium. So the stool struck the cup-bearer's right hand. He uttered a groan and measured his length in the dust; while his spouted flagon clanged loudly as it rolled. A gasp from the suitors ran the length and breadth of the hall: they exclaimed among themselves: 'O that our foreign visitor had died before he got here, and spared us this disorder and falling out over two beggars! Now the contagion of malice will spread, to spoil our delight in the luscious feast.'

Telemachus rose in reproof. 'My lords, you are mad. Some God excites you, or do you fail to carry your food and liquor? You have feasted too well. Go home now and sleep just as soon as you like – though of course I force no man away.' As they bit their lips in astonishment at such plain speaking Amphinomus intervened: 'Friends, that is proper comment and we have no ground for offence or tart reply. Hands off the stranger and the servants of the house. Cup-bearer, fill all round that we may offer libation before going away to sleep. We can leave the stranger to Telemachus, his host.' All were pleased with this. Brave Mulius, the squire who attended Amphinomus from Dulichium, mixed them a bowl and served it. They poured to the blessed Gods and themselves drank of its sweetness: then, heart-full, they went to their rest.

BOOK 19

Odysseus lingered where he was in the hall, nursing his schemes to kill the suitors with Athene's help. Suddenly he spoke out to his son: 'My Telemachus, let us now stow away all the serviceable weapons; and for reasoned excuse, when the suitors ask you why, say, "To save them from the fire-reek: for they have become so tarnished by smoke as not to look like the same weapons Odysseus left here when he sailed for Troy. Also the graver thought came to me from above that some day in wine you might yield to anger and disgrace the hospitality of this courtship by wounds given and taken. Iron has that attraction for men."'

In furtherance of his father's words Telemachus called to Eurycleia the nurse: 'Mother, pray keep me the women in their quarters while I transfer my father's costly war-gear to the store. The things are getting so sooted, with no one to care for them since he went. I was a baby then; but now I would put them where the fumes of the fire will not reach.' Eurycleia answered, 'It would be as well, my child, if you made a habit of caring for the house and the preservation of its goods: but who is going to light you at work, if you will not have the maids whose office that is?' He replied, 'The stranger here. Though a man come to me from the ends of the earth I will not have him idle while he eats at my expense.' This saying cut off her speech: the well-fitting doors clashed behind her. Up sprang Odysseus and his noble son, to start carrying off helmets, bossed shields and sharp spears; while Pallas Athene with a golden lamp made their way beautifully bright.

Telemachus gasped out, 'Father, my eyes behold a miracle. The sides of the hall, its roof-beams and pinewood framing and the tall columns glow with lambent flame. Some God must be here in the midst; one of the heavenly host.' 'Hush,' said Odysseus, 'repress your thoughts and ask no question. This is the mode of the divinities of Olympus. To bed with you, and leave me here to probe the feelings of the serving-women and your mother. Grief will make her question me by and large.' Telemachus duly crossed the hall, under its flaring torch-light, to seek the room where he always lay when sleep's bounty visited him. Through this night, too, he rested on his couch for Dawn to come: while Odysseus waited alone in the hall, still meditating the suitors' destruction by aid of Athene.

Like Artemis or golden Aphrodite Penelope appeared from her room. In its wonted place before the fire they had set her chair, an early piece turned in ivory and silver by Ikmalius the artist, who had added an extension forward from the seat to serve as foot-rest: and this was upholstered with a great fleece. In such state Penelope sat, while from their part of the house her bare-armed maids pressed in to clear the tables of the plentiful broken bread and the cups which those haughty ones had used. They raked out the embers from the braziers and piled them high again with fresh logs, to afford light and heat.

But Melantho began again upon Odysseus: 'Hanging

about still, plaguy stranger, to prowl through the darkened house peeping at the maids? Put paid to your supper, wretch, and get outside the gate. Quickly too, or you will be chased out at the point of a fire-brand.' Odysseus, looking at her hardly, said, 'Damsel, why persecute me with such malignity? I know I am dirty. I know I am ragged. I do beg round the country-side, as I needs must. It is the way of paupers and homeless men. Once, like my fellows, I had a house and was prosperous, with crowds of freedmen and the other trappings of an easy life. In those days I often helped such-like waifs, no matter what their need or nature. Only Zeus brought me down: God's will be done. One day, woman, you too may lose this pride of place wherefrom you now dominate the maids, for your lady might fall out with you, or Odysseus return. There is still hope of that: while supposing he is really dead and gone, his son, Telemachus (like him, by grace of Apollo), is old enough now to notice it whenever a servant of the house misconducts herself.'

Penelope overheard his speech and called up the maid for reproof. 'Bold brazen piece!' she rated her, 'the great secret in your life is not hidden from me. Your head shall pay for it. Also you know perfectly (having heard me say it) that the stranger waits in the hall because I mean to question him upon my husband, so grievously lost.' She turned to Eurynome: 'Bring a bench and spread it with a sheep-skin for the stranger to sit and hear me and reply. I want all his tale.' Quickly the place was set and then Penelope opened, with, 'Stranger, my first enquiry must be – whence are you and who? What town and parents?' and Odysseus said, 'Lady, no mortal man could resent your least saying. High and wide as heaven your fame extends, pure as the glory of some god-fearing king of a populous

powerful race, by virtue of whose equity and good govern-
ance the masses prosper and the dark earth abounds with
wheat or barley and the trees bow down with fruit and the
ewes lamb infallibly and the sea yields fish. Enquire of me,
here in your house, upon every imaginable thing save only
those of my race and country. Their memories would fill
my heart too full of woe. I am a very melancholy man; but
it is unbecoming to sit in another's house sobbing and
sighing, for such promiscuous grief makes things worse.
Further, one of the maids or even yourself, Lady, losing
patience with me, might cry out that the tears in which I
wallow derive from an overload of wine.'

Penelope replied, 'Stranger, my beauty went forfeit to
the Gods the day my husband sailed with the Argives for
Troy. Should he return to cherish me my fortune and favour
would improve. As it is Heaven afflicts me too sorely. All
the island chiefs court me uninvited and ravage the estate:
while I neglect my guests, the suppliants that come and
even heralds on mission, to eat my heart out for Odysseus.
Men urge my re-marriage: but over that I lead them a fair
dance. I was inspired to build me a monster loom upstairs,
on which I set up a great, fine-threaded linen weave, telling
them by and by, "My lords and suitors, be patient with me
(however much you wish me wedded now great Odysseus
is lost) till I complete this shroud against the inevitable day
that death shall smite Laertes, the aged hero, low. I would
not have my threads idly wind-scattered, lest some Achaean
woman find me blameworthy – with good reason should
this once-wealthy man lie unhouseled." They honoured
my request. All day I would weave and after dark unravel
my work by torch-light. So for three undetected years I
fooled them, but by connivance of my traitorous and despi-
cable maids they caught me in the act as the fourth year

drew toward its close. Their wrath forced me to finish the winding-sheet incontinently, and now I can find no other excuse or means of shirking this marriage. My parents insist on it; my son resents the inroads upon his income caused by the suitors' forced entertainment and is very conscious of their expensiveness, he being now a grown man, house-proud and honourably endowed by Zeus with wits. Yet do tell me of your family, for you cannot be the fabulous child of some crag or oak-tree.'

Odysseus said to her in answer, 'O honoured wife of Odysseus, must you indeed press me about my family? Very well: you shall have it, though the telling entails great pain, as is ever the way with men who have spent years in sorry vagabondage from city to city. Hear your answer. Amidst the wine-dark sea lies Crete, a fair rich island populous beyond compute, with ninety cities of mixed speech, where several languages co-exist. Besides the Cretans proper there are Achaeans, Cydonians, Dorians of tossing crests and noble Pelasgians. The capital is Knosos, ruled by Minos, who from his ninth year talked familiarly with great Zeus. He was my grandfather, King Idomeneus and myself being the children of Deucalion, his son. I had the honour of being called Aethon but was the cadet, Idomeneus being elder and preferred. He accompanied the sons of Atreus to Ilion in the war-fleet, so giving me the chance of seeing Odysseus and playing host to him when an adverse wind forced him to leeward of Maleia and ashore in Crete, while Troy-bound. He only just escaped the storm but made the difficult port of Amnisus by the cave of Eileithyia; and there stopped. Presently he visited our city to ask after Idomeneus, claiming close and esteemed friendship. Only Idomeneus had sailed for Ilium ten or eleven dawns before; so I had the bringing of him to our palace where I could entertain him with all courtesy and nobility, because of our abundant wealth. I found him, and the troop that followed him, in barley-meal and dark wine from the public magazines; and collected all the cattle they needed for sacrifice. Twelve days these noble Achaeans passed with us while a northerly gale (excited by some wrathful God) raged so madly that they could not even stand upon the shore. On the thirteenth the wind fell and they put out.'

As he spun them, his lies took on the hue of truth; and as she listened, her tears rained down till her being utterly dissolved, as the snow laid upon the lofty peaks by the west wind melts before the breath of the south-easter and streams down to fill the water-brooks. So did her fair cheeks stream with grief for the husband who was sitting beside her in the flesh. Even Odysseus pitied his unhappy wife, but crafty purpose kept his eyes hard, with never a tremor to break their steady stare from eyelids that might have been of horn or iron. She wept her fill and ceased; to say, 'Now before everything, Stranger, I must test you to make sure it was really my husband and his glorious company you entertained, as you allege. So tell me of his dress. Describe him and the fellows in his train.'

Odysseus answered, 'Lady it is hard after so long; twenty years have passed since he came and went: but I will recite the impression he left on my mind. Odysseus himself wore a heavy purple cloak; lined self, it was. His brooch of wrought gold was double-bowed. Its flat bore the design of a hound holding down a dappled fawn with his fore-paws and watching it struggle. All admired how the dog was made (in the metal) to be eyeing his prey while gripping it by the throat; and how the fawn's feet writhed in convulsive effort to escape. Also I noted the sheen of the tunic that fitted his trunk as closely as clings the sheath to a dried onion, smooth like that and shining like the sun. The many women could not take their eyes from it. Let me recount another thing for you, as there can be no certainty that Odysseus wore these clothes at home and did not have them given him for the voyage by some friend or host, he being greatly beloved, a man almost beyond compare amongst Achaeans. Myself when re-conducting him respectfully to his ship presented to him a bronze sword, another good doubled purple cloak, and a fringed tunic. But he had a herald with him, a man rather older than himself; whom I can describe as well, for he was stooping and dark-faced, with clustering curls. His name? Eurybates. Odysseus, finding him sympathetic, prized him beyond his other men-at-arms.'

His words renewed her longing to weep, for she recognized the authentic proofs he showed. She cried herself out and said, 'Till now, stranger, you have been an object of compassion. Henceforward you shall be privileged and loved here in my house. The garments you describe I furnished from my store and packed for him; adding the burnished pin to be his ornament. Alas that I shall never have him back with me, home in his own dear land! An ill-season took Odysseus in his hollow ship to desTroy, that cursed place whose name shall not pass my lips.'

Odysseus urged her, 'Lady of Odysseus, melt not your heart nor mar your face with further grief for your lord. Though I cannot blame you, seeing how many women lament the dear dead fathers of their children, husbands not to be mentioned in the same breath with Odysseus, who all agree was godlike. Yet dry your tears, to mark what I now say frankly, and with assurance. Very recently I had news of Odysseus returning. He is alive and near-by, no further than the rich Thesprotian land; and well, for he has collected and brings with him great store of choice treasure. Only he lost all his retinue and ship in the sea this side of Thrinacia, when Zeus and Helios were wroth with him for his men's killing the cattle of the Sun. The crew perished to a man in the waves: but the currents brought him ashore riding the ship's keel, to the Phaeacians who are near-Gods by race. These almost worshipped him and gave him great gifts, offering to bring him safely here – in which case he would have been back already: but he preferred to fetch a long compass round and further enrich himself. Odysseus is wiser at profit-turning than any of us. No one matches him there. Pheidon king of the Thesprotians (my informant) swore to me in the act of libation at his house that both ship and crew to bring Odysseus home stood ready. He sent me first only because a merchantman was clearing for Dulichium. He showed me Odysseus' stored wealth; and what was there of his in the royal treasury would suffice his heirs for ten generations. The king said he had gone to Dodona to hear Zeus counsel him, out of the tall leafy oak, upon the manner of his return to Ithaca, whether it should be open or secret, after so long. I assure you, and swear to it, that he is safe, well, near and about to regain his friends and land. Bear me witness Zeus, the supreme and noblest God, as also the hearth of great Odysseus to which I have attained. As I have said, all things shall come to pass. During this cycle of the sun, between the waning of the present moon and the next, will Odysseus arrive.'

Penelope replied, 'Ah, stranger, should that come true my bounty will rain on you till all comers praise your state. But my heart warns me that the contrary will be the way of it. Odysseus will never return, nor you secure your passage hence: for today we have not in our house masterful ones like Odysseus – was there ever an Odysseus? – to greet guests of merit and speed them onward. Let be now. Women, prepare the bath and make down the stranger's bed, with quilt and rugs and glossy blankets, that he may arrive snugly before Dawn's golden throne. And be prompt in the morning to wash and anoint him, that he may sit at table within the hall beside Telemachus. Any one of these bullies who offends him shall learn to his vexation that he has done himself no good in his suit here. But tell me, stranger, how you adjudge me to transcend all women in character and resource, while I leave you sitting here weather-beaten and in tatters at your meal? Man's day is very short before the end, and the cruel man whose ways are cruel lives accursed and is a by-word after death: while the righteous man who works righteousness has his renown bruited across the wide earth by guests, until many acclaim such nobility.'

Odysseus protested, 'O great and grave spouse of Odysseus, I foreswore rugs and smooth blankets that day the snow-clad hills of Crete faded in my long-oared galley's wake. Let me lie as I have lain through many wakeful nights. How many dark hours have I not endured on rough couches till the well-throned Dawn! Baths for my feet appeal to me no more, nor shall any waiting-maid of yours lay hand on me – save you have some aged and trusty woman upon whose head have passed sorrows like mine. Of her tending I should not be jealous.' Penelope said, 'Dear stranger, among all the great travellers received in this house, never has one in speech given proof of such grateful discretion or juster insight than yourself. I have a shrewdly-conducted old dame, the nurse whose arms received my unhappy lord from his mother the day of his birth, and who tended and nourished him devotedly. She is frail now, but can wash your feet. Rise, prudent Eurycleia, to serve this man of your master's generation. Who dare say that the feet and hands of Odysseus are not, today, old like his? Hardship does so soon age its men.'

At the Queen's words the old servant covered her face with her hands and burst into scalding tears, while she bewailed Odysseus: 'My child, my child! And I cannot help. Despite that piety of yours Zeus has hated you worse than all mankind. Never were such fat thighs, such choice hecatombs consumed to the Thunder-lover as when you prayed him for calm declining years in which to educate your splendid son. Yet you alone are denied a home-coming. Is Odysseus, when seeking hospitality in some foreign palace, mocked by its women as all these curs, O stranger, mock at you? For shame of their ribald vileness you will not let them tend your feet; but in me the wisdom of Penelope has found you a glad ministrant. For her sake do I wash your feet; but for your own too, my heart being touched and thrilled. Why thrilled? Because we have had many way-worn strangers here: but never have seen such likeness as yours, I say, to Odysseus, in shape and feet and voice.'

With presence of mind Odysseus exclaimed, 'Old woman, all who have set eye on both of us remark it. They saw what you say, that we are exceedingly like.' While he spoke the hoary woman had taken the burnished foot-bath and poured in much cold water before stirring in the hot. Odysseus had been sitting towards the hearth, but now sharply turned himself to face the shadow, as his heart suddenly chilled with fear that in handling him she might notice his scar, and the truth come to light. Yet so it was, when she bent near in her washing. She knew it for the old wound of the boar's white tusk that he took years ago in Parnassus, while visiting his mother's brother and noble

Autolycus, their father, who swore falser and stole better than all the world beside. These arts were conferred upon him by Hermes the God, who lent him cheerful countenance for the gratification of his kids' and goats' thighs burned in sacrifice.

Autolycus once visited Ithaca, to find his daughter just delivered of a son. Eurycleia brought in the baby and set it in his lap at the end of supper, saying, 'Autolycus, invent a name for this your dear daughter's son – a child much prayed for,' and Autolycus had answered, 'Son-in-law and daughter, name him as I shall say. Forasmuch as I come here full of plaints against many dwellers upon earth, women as well as men, so call him Odysseus, for the odiousness: and when he is a man make him visit the palace of his mother's family at Parnassus, which is mine, and I will give him enough to send him joyfully home.' And so it came about. Young Odysseus went for his gifts and Autolycus with his sons welcomed him in open-handed courtesy, while his grandmother Amphithea embraced him to kiss his face and two lovely eyes. Autolycus told his famous sons to order food. Hastily they produced a five-year-old bull which they flayed and flensed, before jointing its limbs to piece them cunningly small for the spits. After roasting them they served the portions round; and day-long till sunset all feasted, equally content. After sunset when the darkness came they stretched out and took the boon of sleep. At dawn they were for hunting, the sons of Autolycus with their hounds. Odysseus went too. Their way climbed steep Parnassus through the zone of trees till they attained its wind-swept upper folds just as the sun, newly risen from the calm and brimming river of Ocean, touched the plough-lands. Their beaters were entering a little glen when the hounds broke away forward, hot on a scent. After them ran the sons of Autolycus, with Odysseus pressing hard upon the pack, his poised spear trembling in his eager hand. A great boar was couching there in a thicket so dense and over-grown as to be proof against all dank-breathing winds; and proof, too, against the flashing sun-heat and the soaking rain; while its ground was deep in fallen leaves. About this rolled the thunder of their chase. When the tramp of men and dogs came close the boar sprang from his lair to meet them. With bristling spine and fire-red eyes he faced their charge. Odysseus in the van eagerly rushed in to stick him, brandishing the spear in his stout hand: but the boar struck first with a sideways lift of the head that drove in his tusk above the man's knee and gashed the flesh deeply, though not to the bone. Odysseus' return thrust took the beast on the right shoulder, the spear-point flashing right through and out. Down in the dust with a grunt dropped the boar, and its life fled. Then the sons of Autolycus turned to and skilfully bound up the wound of gallant god-like Odysseus. They staunched the dark blood with a chanted rune and made back at once to their dear father's house, and then Autolycus and the sons completed his cure, made him great gifts (delighting a delightful guest) and punctually returned him to his own land of Ithaca. Laertes and his lady mother, in welcoming him home, enquired of everything and especially of how he suffered that wound: and he recounted the whole story of the boar's gleaming tusk that ripped his leg while he hunted Parnassus with the sons of Autolycus.

～

Now as the old woman took up his leg and stroked her hands gently along it she knew the scar by its feel. She let go the foot, which with his shin splashed down into the tub and upset it instantly with a noisy clatter. The water poured over the ground. In Eurycleia's heart such joy and sorrow fought for mastery that her eyes filled with tears and her voice was stifled in her throat. So she caught Odysseus by the beard to whisper, 'You are my own child, Odysseus himself, and I never knew – not till I had fondled the body of my King.' Her eyes travelled across to Penelope, meaning to signal that her beloved husband was at home: but Penelope failed to meet this glance or read its meaning, because Athene momently drew her thought away. Odysseus' right hand shot out, feeling for Eurycleia's throat, and tightened about it, while with his left he crushed her to him and muttered, 'Would you kill me, nurse, you who have so often suckled me at your breasts, when I at last return after twenty years of manifold misfortune? Now you have guessed this and the God has flashed its truth into your mind, keep it close, not to let another soul in the house suspect. Otherwise, believe me – and I mean it – if Heaven lets me beat the suitor lords I shall not spare you, my old nurse though you be, when I slaughter the other serving-women in my hall.'

Wise Eurycleia protested, 'My child, what a dreadful thing to say! You should know my close and stubborn spirit and how I carry myself with the starkness of iron or rock. Allow me, in turn, to suggest a point for your considering. If the God delivers you the bold suitors, then let me rehearse to you which women of the house disgrace you and which are innocent.' He replied, 'Nurse, why trouble? There is no need: on my own I can note them, and class each one. Keep your news to yourself and commend the issue to the Gods.' Thereupon the beldam hobbled off through the house for water to replace what had been spilled; and

Odysseus after being washed and anointed with smooth olive oil dragged his bench nearer the fire to warm himself, carefully hiding the scarred leg beneath his rags.

Then said Penelope, 'Stranger, only a trifle have I to put to you now: for soon it will be the hour of happy sleep which comes so graciously to man, however sad. But not to me; Heaven has overburdened me with griefs beyond measure. During the daytime I glut myself with sorrow and lament, having my own duties to see to, and my house-maidens' work: but night falls and the world sleeps. Then I lie in my bed and the swarming cares so assail my inmost heart that I go distraught with misery. You know how the daughter of Pandareus, the sylvan nightingale, lights when the spring is young amidst the closest sprays and sings marvellously; the trills pouring from her colourful throat in saddest memory of the son she bore King Zethus, darling Itylus, whom she unknowingly put to the sword and slew. My troubled mind quavers like her song. Must I stay by my son and firmly guard all my chattels, my maids, the towering great palace itself, out of reverence for my lord's bed and what people say? Or shall I go off with the best of these Achaeans who court me here and proffer priceless gifts? While my son was an unthinking child his tender years forbade my leaving home to take a new husband: but he, tall now and come to man's estate, prays me to leave for my father's house, so greatly does he grudge the sight of the Achaeans swallowing up his substance. Wherefore listen, and read me this dream of mine. I have twenty geese on the place, wild geese from the river, who have learned to eat my corn: and I love watching them. But a great hook-billed eagle swooped from the mountain, seized them neck by neck and killed them all. Their bodies littered the house in tumbled heaps, while he swung aloft again into

God's air. All this I tell you was a dream, of course, but in it I wept and sobbed bitterly, and the goodly-haired Achaean women thronged about me while I bewailed my geese which the eagle had killed. But suddenly he swooped back to perch on a projecting black beam of the house and bring forth a human voice that dried my tears: "Daughter of Icarius, be comforted," it said. "This is no dream but a picture of stark reality, wholly to be fulfilled. The geese are your suitors; and I, lately the eagle, am your husband come again, to launch foul death upon them all." With this in my ears I awoke from my sleep, to be aware of the geese waddling through the place or guzzling their food from the trough, just as ever."

Odysseus replied to her, 'Lady, this dream cannot be twisted to read otherwise than as Odysseus himself promised its fulfilment. Destruction is foredoomed for each and every suitor. None will escape the fatal issue.' But wise Penelope responded, 'Stranger, dreams are tricksy things and hard to unravel. By no means all in them comes true for us. Twin are the gates to the impalpable land of dreams, these made from horn and those of ivory. Dreams that pass by the pale carven ivory are irony, cheats with a burden of vain hope: but every dream which comes to man through the gate of horn forecasts the future truth. I fear my odd dream was not such a one, welcome though the event would be to me and my son. Let me tell you something to bear in mind. Presently will dawn the illfamed day which severs me from the house of Odysseus. To introduce it I am staging a contest with those axes my lord (when at home) used to set up, all twelve together, like an alley of oaken bilge-blocks, before standing well back to send an arrow through the lot. Now will I put this same feat to my suitors: and the one who easiest strings the bow with his bare hands and shoots through the twelve axes, after him will I go, forsaking this house of my marriage, this very noble, well-appointed house that surely I shall remember, after, in my dreams.'

Odysseus uttered his opinion again: 'August wife of Odysseus, do not hesitate to arrange this trial in the hall; for Odysseus of the many sleights will be here before these men, for all their pawing of the shapely bow, shall have strung it and shot the arrow through the gallery of iron.' Said Penelope, 'If only you would consent, stranger, to sit by me all night, entertaining me, sleep would not again drown my eyes. Yet mortals cannot for ever dispense with sleep, the deathless ones having appointed its due time to each thing for man upon this fertile earth. So I will away to my room and lie on its couch, the place of my groaning, which has been wet with my tears all the while since Odysseus went to desTroy that place I never name. There shall I be lying while you rest here in the hall. Either spread something on the floor, or have them arrange you a bed.'

She ceased and went off to her shining upper room; not alone, for the maids trooped after her. So she lamented Odysseus, her dear husband, till Athene's kindly sleep closed her eyelids.

BOOK 20

Eventually noble Odysseus made his bed in the entrance hall, by stretching an untanned ox-hide on the floor and piling upon it many fleeces of the sheep sacrificed to Achaean appetite. Eurynome drew a mantle over him after he had lain down. Yet sleep would not come, because his heart was too active in planning evil against the suitors: for whom, besides, after a while those women that nightly played the strumpet poured out with laughter and loud jest from the servants' quarter. His gorge rose then: impulse and reason warred within him, now wanting to charge forth and give each whore her death, now to yield them a latest and last chambering. Over this his secret self snarled like a bitch standing guard over her helpless litter, when she stiffens with a growl to fly at any approaching stranger. So the anger rumbled within Odysseus at their lechery: but he smote his breast in self-rebuke, saying, 'Be patient, heart. You stood a grimmer trial, that day the bestial Cyclops devoured my splendid fellows. Steadfastly you bore it, till your cunning had frayed you a path from that cave you thought your death-trap.'

He so conjured himself and rated his passions that his

soul's patience survived to the end: but the strain tossed his body about, like the basting paunch stuffed with blood and fat that a man who wants it immediately cooked will turn over and over before a blazing fire. In such fashion did Odysseus roll to this side and to that in the throes of wondering how his single self could get the many shameless suitors into his grasp. Upon his perplexity Athene in her woman's shape came down from Heaven, to stand above his head and say, 'Why still awake and watchful, O sorriest man of men, now you lie at last in your own house where are your wife and also your son – such a lad as everyone would wish his son to be?' And to her Odysseus replied, 'Alas, Goddess, your rebuke is justified: but my heart's debate was how one man might lay hands upon these wasters who keep the house in droves. And out of that rises the second and stiffer problem. Supposing the grace of Zeus, with yours, lets me slay them, where afterwards may I find sanctuary? Inspire me, pray.' ·

'Exigent wretch,' said the Goddess, 'others trust friends so much feebler than me, creatures all too human and not various: whereas I am very God and your buckler to the end of toil. Let me state you a naked truth. Though fifty troops of humans hemmed us round, all mad to kill outright, yet should you win through to lift their flocks and herds. So let yourself sleep. Watching all night is very wearying and presently you will be quitted of evil.' She spoke, shed a slumbering upon his eyelids and left for Olympus. Odysseus sank into the arms of sleep, a nerve-allaying sleep which ravelled out the tangles of his mind. But his loyal wife awoke and sat up in her soft couch to weep, before praying directly to Artemis: –

'Artemis, Goddess, daughter of Zeus! Only strike me through now with your dart and take my life utterly away – or

let a whirlwind hurtle me down the darkling ways and
fling me where the under-tow of Ocean joins the main!
The whirlwinds thus paid the daughters of Pandareus, who
had been orphaned in their home by the Gods' killing their
parents. Aphrodite nourished them with goat-milk cheese
and sweet honey and wholesome wine, Hera gave them
beauty and insight above all women, and Artemis made
them buxom; while Athene dowered them with every grace
and art. Yet as Aphrodite was journeying to high Olympus
to beg their crowning glory of fortunate marriages – and
beg it of Zeus the Thunder-lover, who knows what is or is
not destined for mankind – even then the Harpies of the
storm snatched the girls away and cast them to serve the
terrible Furies. O that the dwellers on Olympus would so
blot me from human sight, or well-tressed Artemis thrust
me through, that as I went to my grave under the hateful
earth I might yet carry with me the image of Odysseus
unsmirched by dalliance with some baser man! I call that
pain endurable if it makes one mourn day-long from the
heart's great ache but permits sleep of nights, the sleep
which assoils all good and ill concern, once it has lidded
the eyes. But for me even the dreams vouchsafed by the
powers are an affliction. Tonight, for example, there lay by
me the image of my man as when he left for the war; and
my heart leapt up, thinking it no dream, but truth at last.'

So ran her complaint till Dawn came, golden-throned:
but then her sobbing pierced to the ears of Odysseus and
mingled with his waking thoughts, to make him fancy she
had discovered him and was there by his side. He rose to
fold the cloak, and the sheepskins on which he had slept;
then laid them on a hall-throne: but the ox-hide he took
out of doors and spread for his praying to Zeus with uplifted
hands: 'O father Zeus, if heaven's good will has led me

safely home across the waters and the wilderness, despite terrible danger, then let the welkin yield some sign thereof from you, and waking humanity confirm it with an important word.'

This prayer Zeus the contriver heard. He pealed from out the mists veiling the radiant peak of Olympus, and made Odysseus glad; while the momentous word was uttered by a woman slaving at her quern near by, in the mill-room attached to the palace of the people's shepherd. There all day twelve women strove their hardest, grinding barley-meal and flour, the marrow of man's strength. They were sleeping now with their stint of grain well ground – all save the feeblest one, who yet laboured: but at the thunder she too let her mill run down, to sigh out the word for which her King was waiting: 'O father Zeus, ruler of gods and men, this loud peal from a star-spangled sky without one wisp of cloud – do you thereby show some sign for man? Grant it import, I pray, even for wretched me. Let today's be the final and ultimate easy feast of the suitors in Odysseus' halls. To mill groats for them must my limbs be wrung with this excruciating toil. Make it their last supper, Lord!'

She breathed this out, and great Odysseus rejoiced for its aptness and for the thunder of Zeus. He told himself he had won his revenge upon the wrong-doers. Meantime the other maids of the great palace were stirring. They rebuilt the undying fire upon the hearth. Telemachus rose from his couch, a god-like figure of a man as he put on his clothes, before slinging his sharp sword about his shoulders and binding the handsome sandals to his lissom feet. He picked up his massive bronze-tipped spear and stood by the outer door to ask Eurycleia, 'Dear nurse, about our guest – was he honourably entreated as regards bed and food or left anyhow to fend for himself, as is so much my mother's way, woman of the world though she be? She falls over herself to please some worthless fellow and leaves a worthy man in utter neglect.' Faithful Eurycleia answered back, 'Child, you find fault where no fault is found. The man sat and drank all the wine he wished: but refused food on the plea of no appetite, though she pressed him. She would have had the maids make down a bed against his wanting to sleep: but he seemed so beaten and hopeless that he would not lie between blankets on a couch. Instead he had an undressed ox-hide and fleeces in the entrance hall. We put a cloak over him, too.'

After hearing her Telemachus, carrying his spear, left the house with two swift dogs at heel, making for the assembly-ground to meet the warrior Achaeans: while the dame began to hustle her maids, calling out, 'Rally round now and fall to work, some of you, on the floor, sweeping till your breath is spent – but first put water down – and then smooth the thrones' purple housings; while you others take sponges and clean down all the tables, swilling out the mixing-bowls and the handsome double-handled cups. All the rest fetch water from the spring, briskly there and briskly back. Very soon this morning will the house see its suitors again, today being the public festival.' She rained orders upon them and freely they obeyed. Full twenty set off for the fountain where the dark water flowed, while the others skilfully did out the hall. Then the freedmen began to appear. Some of these adeptly split kindling-wood till the women should return from the spring: but when they did come Eumaeus the swineherd was of the party, with his three fattest hogs. He left these rooting in the precincts, to address Odysseus in all courtesy: 'Stranger, have the Achaeans come to look upon you with more favour, or are they yet despiteful as they were?' and Odysseus rejoined, 'Ah, Eumaeus, may the Gods punish their outrages and the way these nefarious ruffians misuse another's house.'

So far they had got when Melanthius the goat-man appeared with two herders and the finest of their goats for the suitors' table. He tied his beasts under the echoing porchway and remarked to Odysseus with a sneer, 'You still pester the household, stranger, by your begging and refusal to leave? I think our affair will not be closed without you get a taste of fist. Importunity like yours is not decent. This is not the solitary Achaean banquet.' Roundly he abused him, but crafty Odysseus made no reply, only hanging his head in silence: yet within him his enmity increased. A third party arrived, Philoetius, a man of mark, who had with him a heifer for the suitors and more prime goats. He had been brought across by the boatmen of the public ferry. After tethering his charges securely in the porch he came over to Eumaeus, asking, 'Swineherd, who is this fresh stranger in our house? What race does he claim? Where are his people and their lands? Shabby he may be but his build is royal. A man meshed in the web of the Gods' wrath and made homeless soon shows the strain, even if he have been a King.'

He turned to Odysseus and held out a right hand, saying cordially, 'Greeting, sir stranger: may the future bring you happiness; for patently you are now in the toils of misfortune. Father Zeus, you are the deadliest of all Gods, in that you make no allowance for the men you have created, but tangle them in such sad and sorry pains. I sweat only to think of it and my eyes grow moist, remembering Odysseus, who if yet alive and in the sunshine may be ragged and adrift like this. But if he is dead, and gone down to Hades' mansions, then hear me bemoan the excellent Odysseus, who while I was yet a boy promoted me over his herds in Cephallenia. Yes, and these have so increased as to be beyond number, like ears of standing corn for multitude. Never did any man's broad-fronted cattle breed better. But these outsiders, disregarding the son of the house and slighting the Gods, make me bring in my beasts ever and again for their banqueting. Their latest freak is to share out the whole fortune of our missing King. I keep on turning the affair over in my mind, well aware how wrong it would be to go off, beeves and all, to a stranger's service while the heir lives; but certain that it is worse still to sit down here under such iniquities and herd my cattle for the benefit of men who have no claim to them. My position is unbearable. Long since I should have run off and engaged myself with some other mighty King, only that I keep thinking of this unhappy man and of how he might suddenly turn up from nowhere and chase the suitors helter-skelter through his house.'

Said Odysseus in crafty reply, 'Cow-herd, you display a goodly discretion. My judgement assures me upon the rightness of your instincts: so I shall tell you a thing on my solemn and lawful oath. O Zeus, greatest of the Gods, be my witness, and the hospitable table and hearth of great Odysseus by which I stand! You shall be yet in this place when Odysseus comes home. Your eyes shall see the fate you invoke meted these officious suitors.' The cow-man replied, 'May the son of Cronos fulfil your word, Stranger, to let you see how my hands should gratify my strength.' Eumaeus echoed his prayer to all the Gods that Odysseus might return: while the suitors in their place were again conspiring a death by violence for Telemachus.

But an eagle stooped from the heights of the sky and

flew past on their left, bearing off a pitiful dove: whereupon Amphinomus rose and said, 'Friends, our plot to assassinate Telemachus is misjudged. Let us feast instead.' They accepted his verdict and marched to the palace of Odysseus, where they laid their cloaks aside upon seats before turning to slaughter the sheep, the goats, the swine and the heifer from the stock. They roasted the inwards and passed them round, then mixed wine in the bowls. The swineherd gave out the cups, stately Philoetius helped them to bread from the fair baskets and Melanthius poured wine. All set to and feasted.

With subtle intent Telemachus had brought Odysseus within the hall, arranging him a small table and plain settle by the stone entry. He helped him to the inward meats and poured him wine in a golden cup, pronouncing, 'Rest you there and drink your wine among the men. Should abuse or assault follow from the suitors I shall be your defence. This place is not a public house but the palace of Odysseus which he won for me: so you, suitors, must govern your hearts and hands, to prevent breach of the peace.' Such bold speech from Telemachus made them bite their lips in amazement; but Antinous rallied them: 'What Telemachus says is severe and he threatens us starkly, Achaeans. Yet take it quietly. Zeus was not willing – or already we should have cut off his peevish railing in the hall.' However, Telemachus paid no heed to this, for already the heralds were going in procession through the town with the long array of beasts to be slain in the Gods' honour: and the long-haired Achaeans were gathering within the shady grove of Apollo, lord of the bow. There they roasted the flesh and drew it off the spits for division. Nobly they feasted, the servers helping Odysseus to his portion just like their own or another's: for that was the ruling of Telemachus, his dear son.

However Athene did not mean to let the suitors rest from provoking Odysseus, for she wanted their contempt to make his heart ache. Among the suitors was one especial ruffian, Ctesippus of Same, whose enormous wealth had emboldened him to woo the wife of absent Odysseus, and he now bayed forth in their midst: 'Hear me, suitor-lords, hear what I suggest! The stranger has had his share like the others, as is fitting. To stint a guest of Telemachus, whatever his sort, would be unjust and indecorous. But it is quite a while since he had it: so now I am adding my guesting-gift which will let him spare his old foot-washing hag a trifle, or tip some other palace servant.' Therewith he snatched a cow's foot from the dish before him and hurled it with a strong hand: but Odysseus inclined his head lightly to one side and avoided it, with a wry smile. It crashed harmlessly against the solid wall.

Telemachus was up to rate Ctesippus soundly. He cried, 'Very profitable for your peace of mind, Ctesippus, that you missed the stranger! Had he not dodged your shot I should have thrust you through the midriff with my war-spear and given your father the pains of your funeral, not your marriage, here. Let me finally warn you all against displaying violence in my house. I used to be a child; but have now come to the knowledge of good and evil. Necessity may lead us to stand impotently by while our sheep are butchered and our wine and food wasted, for one man can scarcely make head against many. Only make sure your enmity stops short of actual crime – otherwise, if you must persist in your murderous intent against me, hear my delib-erate conviction; that death is better than longer looking upon your villainies – this outraging my guests and man-handling my servant-women all through the stately palace, to their shame.'

His outburst stilled them for a while. At last Agelaus, son of Damastor, said, 'My friends, when there has been plain speaking it is not a man's part to lose temper or complain. Let be the stranger and the servants of Odysseus' household. I would offer Telemachus a soft answer – meant for his mother too – hoping it may move them. So long as your hearts kept a vestige of hope for the return of Odysseus, your delaying and excusing the suitors vexed nobody. Clearly it was expedient, while a chance remained of his survival and return. But now it is plain that he is gone. So sit down beside your mother and put it to her that she must wed the best man and highest bidder. Then she will take over that other's house and let you comfortably assume your whole inheritance in free enjoyment of your food and drink.'

Telemachus protested, 'Indeed, Agelaus, I swear to you by Zeus and by all the pains my father suffered in dying or straying far from Ithaca, that the obstacle to my mother's marrying lies not in me. I implore her to choose whom she prefers and take him. I go so far as to offer countless presents if but she will. Only I shrink from ordering her unwillingly from the house. God forbid it should come to that.' Upon these words of Telemachus, Pallas Athene fired the suitors to a laughter that ran on and on till it crazed them out of their wits. Now they were laughing with mouths that were not their own, while blood oozed from the flesh they ate. Their eyes filled with tears and their souls were racked in agony. Godlike Theoclymenus wailed aloud, 'O unhappy men, what is this horror come upon you? A night shrouds your heads, your faces: it creeps down to your knees. Weeping and wailing flash back and forth. Cheeks stream with tears and a dew of blood beads over the smooth wall-panels. Ghostly forms throng the entrance and pack the hall itself, shuffling in long file through the murk towards hell. The sun is lost out of heaven and a dire gloom prevails.'

Laughter rang loud from the company as he unburdened himself, and Eurymachus son of Polybus rose to say, 'Our new-come visitor from alien parts has lost his senses. Quick, young men, escort him out and to the market-place. He fancies it is black night here.' Theoclymenus retorted, 'Eurymachus, I want none of your guiding. Eyes I have and ears, my two feet and a spirit not of the meanest. In their power will I pass the threshold, for I feel that evil – evil not to be shunned or avoided – looms over each single one of you suitors whose brutal and perverse imaginings pollute the house of Odysseus.' He quitted the hall, to receive honest welcome from Peiraeus in his house; while the suitors after an interchange of stares began to tease Telemachus by poking fun at his guests, repeating despitefully, 'Indeed, Telemachus, there can be no unluckier host. First you take in this lousy unknown tramp without profession and without prowess but insatiably bellied for eating and drinking, a perfect cumberer of the earth: and then your second guest stands up to play the prophet! Have my advice and make something by them. Let us pack them for sale aboard some many-oared galley bound for Sicily. You would get a good price that way.' Thus the suitors: but he ignored them, in the intensity of his silent gaze upon his father, awaiting the moment to lift hand against his tormentors.

Decorous Penelope had put her state chair just over against them and so heard all that passed. Not that their laughter had hindered the slaughter of many victims to furnish their juicy abundant meal. Though what ghastlier banquet could be dreamed of than this which the Goddess and the valiant man – trapping them after their own villainous example – were now about to provide?

BOOK 21

For Athene chose this moment to introduce the means of bloody death, by prompting wise Penelope to ordain bow and pallid iron as gages of prowess for her suitors in Odysseus' halls. With her throng of escorting women the queen stepped from her room by the tall stairway firmly carrying the curved key (a noble key, bronze forged, with ivory shank) as far as the store chamber in the depths of the house, where the treasures of her king were laid up, his bronze, his gold, his patiently-wrought iron. Among them were the recurved bow with its arrow-case that yet held many arrows, each a groan-maker.

These had been given Odysseus years ago by a fellow-guest in Lacedaemon, at the hospitable house of Ortilochus in Messene where a whim of fate threw him into the company of god-like Iphitus, son of Eurytus. Odysseus had come thither on a suit affecting the whole community, for the men of Messene had lifted in their ships three hundred Ithacan sheep with the thralls minding them: and his father and the other elders had commissioned Odysseus (still a lad in years) to make this long journey on their behalf. As for Iphitus, he was in search of strayed horses – a dozen mares with sturdy mule-foals at milk. Later, these same beasts were to be the death of him, by bringing upon him that supreme man of action, Herakles, Zeus' bold son, who flouted the Gods and stained his hospitable board by the dastardly killing of Iphitus while a guest under his roof; and after the crime Herakles kept the strong-hooved horses in his palace for himself.

While thus searching, Iphitus met Odysseus and presented him with the bow which great Eurytus had carried before his time and, dying, left to the son of his lofty house. The return gifts of Odysseus were a keen sword and formidable spear – earnests of a cherished acquaintanceship that however failed to ripen into mutual entertainment because the son of Zeus too soon murdered god-like Iphitus, the giver of the bow; which great Odysseus preserved in his house as an abiding memorial of this beloved fellow guest, and never took with him on foray in his dun vessels. He would carry it only when he went about his own lands.

The fairest of women held on her way to the treasury till she stood on its oak threshold which had been dressed so skilfully smooth by the old-time workman – squared it, he had, by rule and trued the jambs upon it and set up his gleaming doors – and there she swiftly unbound the thong from the hook of the latch and thrust the key home with such decision that the door-fastenings snapped open. The roar with which the splendid doors sprang wide at the stroke of her key resounded like the bellow of a bull afield at grass; so abruptly they opened for her. She climbed to the high stand supporting the chests in which the clothing was laid away in spices. She reached up to its peg and unhooked the bow, all proper in its shining case, and sat herself there with it across her knees; and taking out her lord's bow cried bitterly a while. Then after her tearful sorrow had exhausted itself she proceeded again to the hall of the proud suitors, holding the recurved bow in one hand and also bearing its quiver-load of woeful arrows. Her women brought along in its chest the iron and bronze gear used by the king when he would play.

Once more in the suitors' presence the queen stood by the roof-pillar with her gauzy veil before her face and two trusty women flanking her. She called to her suitors and said, 'Hear me, my lords and courtiers that have haunted and beset this house and eaten and drunk here all the long time the master has been away, with only excuse and burden of talk your lustful desire to wed me and possess me for wife. Now, my suitors, see your test plain. Here I set the huge bow of god-like Odysseus. Whoso easiest strings the bow with bare hands and shoots an arrow through the twelve axes – after him will I follow, forsaking this house, my husband's home, a house so goodly and stocked with all life's comforts that remembrance thereof will come back to me, I think, hereafter in my dreams.'

Upon that she bade Eumaeus, the master swineherd, arrange the bow and the grey iron axes for the suitors: but Eumaeus burst into tears as he received them for handing over, and the cowherd in his place wept too at sight of the royal bow. They brought upon themselves the rebuke of Antinous who called out, 'You silly yokels with day-cribbed imaginations, twin fools, how dare you by floods of tears further distress that womanly heart which already lies prostrate in agony at losing a beloved husband? Sit you down and eat in silence or take your lamenting out of doors, being careful, however, to leave us that bow, the suitors' dire and infallible test. Not easily, I think, will that smooth bow be strung. In all this crowd there is never a match for the

Odysseus I remember. How that peep at him sticks with me, child though I was.' This was what he said aloud: but in his heart of hearts he fancied his own chance of notching the string and shooting through the irons. Yet his actual destiny was to get the first taste of arrow from great Odysseus whom now he was himself contemning and egging on his fellows to contemn, there where he sat in his own hall.

Princely Telemachus cut across them with the cry, 'Alas and woe is me! Zeus drives me crazy. My beloved mother in her wisdom proclaims that she will forsake this house and cleave to a stranger – and I laugh out and go gay in my heart's folly. Step up, you suitors, with this prize in view. The lady has no peer in the Achaean country: not in Pylos the holy nor in Argos nor Mycenae: nowhere in our Ithaca or on the dark mainland. You know it all. What have I to do, praising my mother? Up with you; let us see what we shall see. Away with excuses for hanging back or putting off the bow-bending. Stay, why should I not try it myself? If I can string it and shoot through the iron I shall not so regret my mother's leaving home in some stranger's train, for I shall at least be living here and man enough to bear my father's arms.'

With this he slipped the keen sword and blood-red cloak from his shoulders, to heave himself upright. He began to set up the axes, hollowing one long trench for them all, getting them exactly in line and firming the earth about them with his foot. Every onlooker was amazed at how regularly he set them, despite his never having seen it done before. Then he took his stand by the main threshold and essayed the bow. Three times it quivered under his frantic efforts to string it, and three times he had to rest his muscles, though still the hope buoyed him of notching the cord and sending a shaft between the irons. Perhaps he might have summoned all his forces and succeeded at the fourth try, only Odysseus frowned him off it and checked his zeal. Whereupon Telemachus sighed that all could hear, 'Alas, must I go on being a feeble failure, or am I still too young to trust to my own hands for safety against attack? However, to it you with the stouter thews. Attempt the bow and let us get this contest over.' With this he laid aside the bow, propping it between the floor and the close-joined door frame: while the keen shaft he leaned against the showy crook of the latch.

As he resumed his throne Antinous the son of Eupeithes called out, 'Up with you in turn from left to right, fellows, the way our wine goes round.' His notion pleased them and so Leodes the son of Oenopus was the first to rise. As their augurer he had the end seat beside the splendid mixing bowl: but their violence so repelled him that he kept by himself in solitary loathing of the suitors. Yet now he led off by picking up the bow and its sharp arrow, over there by the threshold, where he felt the bow's stiffness but could not string it. Before ever it bent his hands gave way; his soft, untried hands. So he cried to the suitors, 'I cannot bend it, friends: let some other try. Indeed this bow will break many princes, body and soul: yet how much better is it that we die, than live in the failure of that ideal which holds us yearning here, day after day! Doubtless some one aspires with his whole heart's strength to marry Penelope, the bedmate of Odysseus. Let such a one try this bow and learn its lesson; and then divert his gifts to winning another of the well-robed Achaean women, while this one weds her fated best-bidder.' He, also, put down the bow to lean against the smooth doors, with the arrow against the door-handle, before going straight back to sit on the seat he had left; but Antinous named him in sharpest rebuke and said:

'Leodes, it shocks me to hear this dismal judgement escape your lips. Merely because you fail to bend it must this bow cost our bravest ones their lives or souls? In very truth your lady mother, when she conceived you, was not making a master-bowman: yet there are some amongst the distinguished suitors who will soon manage the stringing.' He turned to Melanthius the herder of goats, saying, 'Bestir yourself, Melanthius, and quicken the hall-fire. Put before it a broad trestle with sheepskin a-top, and fetch that great ball of tallow from within. Then after it has been warmed through and well greased we young men can prove this bow to conclude our test.' At his bidding Melanthius quickened the never-dying fire and brought near it the trestle with its sheepskin and the big ball of tallow from inside the house. The young men warmed the bow and did their best to string it, but failed. They showed themselves not nearly strong enough; but Antinous and Eurymachus kept themselves out of it – and they were the leading suitors, their best in general merit.

While this was happening the neatherd and swineherd of royal Odysseus had quitted the palace together. Odysseus himself followed them out through the courtyard and its gates, where he cleared his throat and said to them ever so smoothly, 'O herder of cattle and you, swineherd, am I to tell you something or keep it to myself? My impulse is to say it out. If Odysseus were to appear, somehow, suddenly – shall we say a God bringing him – how far would you help? Would you be for the suitors or for Odysseus? Show me the working of your hearts and minds.'

The keeper of his cattle then burst out: 'Ah, Father Zeus, only let that hope come true and him return, led by the spirit. So shall you witness how my hands would serve my might,' and Eumaeus echoed him in praying to all the Gods for the home-coming of resourceful Odysseus. Thus assured of their hearts he quickly replied. 'But I am back again, my own true self, here at home after twenty years of hardship: to realise that of all my servants only you two long for my coming. From the rest I have not heard one prayer breathed for my return. So let me lay down to you what will follow upon God's giving me the victory over the haughty suitors. I shall find you a wife each and an endowment of chattels and houses built next mine: and you shall rank with me hereafter as the fellows and blood-brothers of Telemachus. Now I will show you a sure and certain sign, to make you credit me from the bottom of your hearts. See my scar, given me by the boar's white tusk so long ago, as I went upon Parnassus with the sons of Autolycus.'

As he spoke he opened his rags to betray the great scar: and when the pair of them had studied it and knew it for sure, they wept and flung their arms about Odysseus, with most loving kisses for his head and shoulders. Odysseus had answering kisses for their heads and hands, so that truly the sun might have gone down upon their emotion, only for Odysseus pulling himself together to say: 'Now stop this sorrow and weeping, lest some one coming from the house espy us and report it within. Instead, go you back, not together but one by one, me first and you afterward, with a procedure fixed up between us. Understand that those suitor lords will one and all refuse me a loan of the bow and quiver: so you, Eumaeus, as you carry it up and down the hall must put it into my hands and then go tell the women to close the stout doors of their quarters, and should they hear men's voices from our side groaning or in dispute, let there be no running out of doors but a steady holding to their work within. While you, noble Philoetius, I tell off to shut and bar the gates of the court, lashing them together as quickly as you can.' Upon which he turned back into the stately house, to resume the seat he had left. Then the two serfs came in.

Eurymachus' hands still held the bow and turned it every way before the blazing fire to warm it; but nevertheless he utterly failed at the stringing. Deeply he groaned in his pride of heart and woefully he exclaimed, 'Alas, I sorrow for my own sake and for the general! It is bitter to forfeit this marriage, yet that is not the worst. There are plenty more Achaean women here in sea-girt Ithaca, and others in other cities. What I chiefly regret is our appearing to fall so short of god-like Odysseus in strength as not to be able even to bend his bow. The tale will disgrace us generations hence.'

Antinous the son of Eupeithes protested: 'Not so, Eurymachus, and you know why. To-day is sacred to the Archergod and his public feast. On it who will be bending bows? Put it down and leave it, and the axes too. We can let them stand. I fancy no one will venture into the great hall of Odysseus, son of Laertes, to lift them. Come on, have the server fill once more our cups that we may offer libation before the bow as it lies there in a hoop. To-morrow morning we will have Melanthius the goat-keeper fetch in the best goats of his whole flock, for us to offer thigh-pieces to the mighty archer Apollo before our trial of the bow and the ending of this contest.' Thus Antinous, and his advice pleased. The heralds poured water on their hands and their squires brimmed the bowls with wine all round; everyone offered and afterwards drank his fill.

But then craftily and subtly Odysseus spoke out, saying,

'Hear me, suitors of the famous queen, while I retail the promptings of my heart, making my main appeal to Eurymachus, and to god-like Antinous for his fitting counsel just now to leave the bow to the Gods' reference. In the morning the God will give mastery to whom he wills. Yet for the moment pass me this polished bow that I may test my hands and strength while you watch, to see whether there yet lies in me the virtue that once inhabited my supple limbs, or if the privations of a wandering life have wasted it right away.'

His words enraged them all and instantly, for fear lest he string the polished bow. Loudly Antinous rebuked him, 'Foreign wretch, are you utterly devoid of sense? Is this dining in our high company not enough for you? We let you eat your full share unmolested and hear our debate and conversation, which no other beggared stranger overhears. It is wine that plays the mischief with you, the sweet wine which ruins all who drink with deep and greedy gullet. It was the downfall of Eurytion the famous Centaur, in the house of brave Peirithous, during his visit to the Lapithae. The wine took away his senses and maddened him so that he did terrible things in Peirithous' house. The heroes went wild with rage and flung him out of doors after slicing his ears and nose with their cruel weapons; and away with shattered wits he went, hag-ridden by the burden of his folly. So began the feud between the Centaurs and mankind, the original injury being self-inflicted by immoderacy in wine. Wherefore let me warn you against the painful consequences of your stringing that bow. You will find no grace from anyone in this country, but we shall ship you promptly in a dark hull to King Echetus, that mutilator of the human race; and once with him you are doomed beyond hope. So drink up in all quietness and avoid challenging the younger generation.'

Decorous Penelope complained to him, 'Antinous, it is neither fair nor seemly to browbeat in this house any visiting guest of Telemachus, whatever his quality. Do you really envisage the stranger's taking me home and lying with me, if by prowess and sleight of hand he strings the great bow of Odysseus? Why he, in his own heart of hearts, has no hope of that. Let not a thought so ugly vex the soul of any one of you feasters. It would never, never do!' Eurymachus the son of Polybus replied to her, 'Wise Penelope, we do not contemplate his carrying you off. That is unthinkable: only we shrink from what some low-down Achaean – man or woman – might later say; such as "Poor creatures, these courtiers of the hero's widow, with their efforts and failures to string his polished bow until a beggarman came wandering by and strung it easily and shot through the iron." They will gossip so, to our shame.'

Penelope retorted, 'Eurymachus, the men who devour and dishonour a nobleman's house will not anyhow be accorded public respect: so why thus nice upon a detail? Our guest, this tall personable figure, claims that his father was a man of breeding. Up with you, therefore, and hand him the polished bow, to let us see. I tell you, I will make a firm offer. If he (by the ordering of Apollo) bends it I shall clothe him fairly in tunic and cloak, and give him a sharp spear and double-edged sword for defence against dogs and men; and also shoes for his feet and passage withersoever his spirit bids.'

Telemachus thus answered her: 'My mother, in the disposal of the bow there lives not an Achaean with more rights than I; to grant it or refuse, at my pleasure. If it so pleases me no chief from this craggy Ithaca, or from any other island right down to Elis of the stud-farms, shall prevent my giving these arms outright to the stranger, for his taking away. Off with you, then, to your quarters and your duties, the weaving and the spinning and the ordering of your maids' work. The bow is man's business and especially my business, as I am master here.' She turned, bewildered, into the house with this pregnant phrase of her son's laid up in her heart, and when upstairs again with her serving women she bewailed Odysseus, her sweet husband, till Athene shed a balm of sleep upon her eyes.

The worthy swineherd took up the bow; but then the whole crowd of suitors in the hall roared against him, stuttering in their young pride: 'Miserable half-wit of a pig-keeper, where would you carry that recurved bow? Let but Apollo and the other Immortal Gods hear our petition and soon shall those swift hounds you breed eat you alive amongst your swine, far from man's help.' Their threats so frightened him that he dropped his burden where he stood, all mazed with their many-voiced clamouring in the hall: but now Telemachus menaced him loudly from the opposite part, shouting, 'Carry on with the bow, ancient; if you obey all these you will be instantly sorry, when I take advantage of my youth and greater strength to chase you into the open country with volleys of flung stones. There is someone else I would as soon send sorrily packing from the house for their evil designs, had I only a like margin of power over the suitors.'

His outburst made them laugh so merrily together that their anger against Telemachus passed: and the swineherd went along through the hall with the bow till he reached Odysseus and put it into his hands. Then he called Eurycleia the nurse aside and charged her: 'Telemachus orders you, wise Eurycleia, to shut tight the stout doors of your quarter; and if any one of the women inside should hear the sound of groaning men from our part of the house, see that she comes not out but keeps quietly at work.' These words made her speech flutter and fall. She fastened the doors of the stately place, while Philoetius slipped stealthily out-doors to secure the gates of the courtyard. In its loggia there chanced to be lying the grass hawser of a merchantman. This he used to make all fast before he went in again to sit as he had sat, on his settle; watching Odysseus who still felt the bow, turning it round and round and testing it throughout, to make sure that worms had not riddled the tips during its lord's absence. Men turned to their neighbours and muttered, 'The fellow is a bow-fancier or expert, what? Perhaps he has something of the kind laid by at home; or is the ill-conditioned beggar planning to make one, by the way he twists it over and over in his hands?' – to which the next young scoffer might reply, 'May his luck, in that, end like his bow-stringing effort.'

Thus the suitors: but Odysseus the master of craft had by now handled and surveyed the great bow up and down. Calmly he stretched it out with the effortless ease of a skilled musician who makes fast both ends of a piece of twined cat-gut and strains it to a new peg in his lyre. Changing the bow to his right hand he proved the string, which sang to his pluck, sharp like a swallow's cry. Distress overwhelmed the suitors and they changed colour. Zeus declared himself in a loud thunder-peal; and long-suffering royal Odysseus rejoiced that the son of devious-counselled Cronos should make him a sign. He snatched up the keen arrow which lay naked there upon his table – all the others which the Achaeans were so soon to feel being yet stored in their quiver – and set it firmly upon the grip of the bow. He notched it to the string and drew; and from his place upon his settle, just as he sat, sent the arrow with so straight an aim that he did not foul one single axe. The bronze-headed shaft threaded them clean, from the leading helve onward till it issued through the portal of the last ones.

Then he cried to Telemachus, 'Telemachus, the guest sitting in your hall does you no disgrace. My aim went true and my drawing the bow was no long struggle. See, my strength stands unimpaired to disprove the suitors' slandering. In this very hour, while daylight lasts, is the Achaeans' supper to be contrived: and after it we must make them a different play, with the dancing and music that garnish any feast.' He frowned to him in warning: and Telemachus his loved son belted the sharp sword to him and tightened grip upon his spear before he rose, gleamingcrested, to stand by Odysseus, beside the throne.

BOOK 22

Therewith the wily Odysseus shed his rags, grasped the bow with its filled quiver and made one leap to the doorsill, where he tumbled out the swift shafts at his feet before calling in a great voice to the suitors, 'At last, at last the ending of this fearful strain! Before me, by favour of Apollo if my luck holds, stands a virgin target never yet hit.' He levelled the bitter arrow at Antinous whose two hands were raising the splendid golden wine-cup to his lips, without suspicion of death in his heart – for who, at a thronged banquet, could conceive of any single man being bold enough to dare compass his violent death and bloody destruction? However Odysseus shot, and took him with the shaft full in the throat. Right through his graceful neck and out again went the point. He rolled over sideways, letting the cup fall from his stricken grasp and thrusting back the table with a jerk of the foot that threw his food, the bread and the cooked meats, to pollution on the floor. The life-blood spurted thickly from his nostrils.

One outcry broke through the house from the suitors when they saw the man fall. They sprang in terror from their thrones, and gaped all about the smooth walls, to find never a shield or great spear they could snatch up. They rained abuse upon Odysseus – 'Stranger, your wicked shooting at people makes this the last trial of strength in which you compete. It seals your doom. You go as carrion to the vultures, for having slain the crown of all Ithaca's young manhood.' They clamoured so, because they were persuaded his killing was not deliberate, their infatuation hiding from them the toils of death that enlaced each and every one: but Odysseus glaring at them cried, 'Dogs that you are, you kept harping on your conviction that I would never return from the Troad, and in that strong belief let yourselves ravage my house, ravish my house-maidens and woo my wife, while I was yet alive. You have flouted the Gods of high heaven and the consequent wrath of men: so now you are all trapped in death's toils.'

His words chased the pallor of fear from man to man, and wildly each one stared round for escape from this brink of disaster. Only Eurymachus found tongue, and he said, 'If you are indeed Odysseus of Ithaca come back to us, then you have substance for protest against the many offences committed by the Achaeans in your palace and estates. But the begetter of all your hurt lies there – Antinous, whose true spring of action was no great need or necessity for marriage, but a very different motive, ambition, which entailed the waylaying and killing of your son to make himself king over the whole of prosperous Ithaca. Cronos prevented him, and now he has met the death he deserved: wherefore your part should be one of forbearance towards this people who are your people, and a chance for us to make good publicly all that has been eaten and drunk in your guest-rooms, each of us subscribing as much as twenty oxen to recoup you with bronze and gold till your heart warms toward us. Meanwhile no man can make a stricture upon your rage.'

There was no softening of that glare as Odysseus rejoined, 'Eurymachus, not if you gave away to me your whole inheritance, all that you now own and yet may earn, would I relax my hands from slaughtering until the suitors have paid the last jot for their presumptions. Only flight or fight confront you now as escapes from ultimate death: and some of you, I think, will find no way of avoiding doom's abyss.'

The menace of him shook their hearts and knees; but Eurymachus had yet a word for them. 'O my friends,' he said, 'this man will not curb his ruthless hands. He would shoot us down from the polished threshold with that goodly bow and quiver that he has until we all be slain. Wherefore let us whip up the thrill of battle. Out swords, and hold the tables up as bulwark against his deadly arrows. Let us have at him in one rush to drive him off his doorstep, maybe: that way we can attain the city and raise an instant alarm, to ensure this man's never bending bow again.' Upon the word he bared his keen, two-edged bronze sword and sprang forward with an awful cry: but instantly Odysseus launched at him a flying arrow which struck him by the nipple of his chest and lodged deep in his liver. The sword fell from his hand and he went down doubled and writhing over his table, to spill the food and loving-cup upon the floor. His heart's agony made him hammer his brow against the ground and flail his two legs about till the throne rocked: then dimness veiled his eyes.

Amphinomus, naked sharp sword in hand, followed him in the rush to edge glorious Odysseus off the doors; but for him Telemachus was too quick, catching him behind the shoulders so fair and square that the bronze spear-point transfixed his breast. He crashed earthward full on his face, while Telemachus abandoning his weapon sprang away in fear that some Achaean might stab him whilst he was tugging at the long shaft, or cut him down while he stooped for it. So he ran off quickly to his father and paused by him to say excitedly, 'Father, now let me fetch you a shield and pair of spears and a bronze skull-cap with cheek-pieces. At the same time I can equip myself and provide for the swineherd and cowman. We had best be properly armed'; and Odysseus the man of judgement replied, 'Run for them, then, while I still have arrows; or they will force my unsupported self off from the doors.'

To obey his dear father's word Telemachus raced to the side chamber where the famous weapons lay. He snatched up four shields and eight spears and four of the bronze helmets with their heavy horse-hair crests, and came running with them back to his father. There he first arrayed his own person in the brazen arms; then the two freedmen put on the like noble panoply; and they all lined up by wary, cunning Odysseus who made great shooting whilst the arrows held out for his defence, each time bringing down an enemy until they lay in swathes; but when the royal archer had no arrows left he put the bow aside against a polished return of the massive hall-entrance, while he passed a four-ply shield over his shoulders and dressed his great head in a close-fitting helmet, grim under the towering menace of its nodding horse-hair crest. He took up two brave bronze-pointed spears.

It chanced that through the main wall had been contrived a hatch with a shutter of framed boards, opening into a narrow passage beyond the top landing. Odysseus had ordered the trusty swineherd to take post there on guard, it being but a one-man approach: and now Agelaus spoke up, suggesting generally, 'Comrades, might not someone clamber through the hatch and thence warn the world outside, to get the alarm immediately raised? So this fellow will have shot his last.' But Melanthius the goatherd answered, 'That will not do, high-born Agelaus. The main gates to the court are dangerously near and the alley-way too narrow. One man of courage could hold it against all comers. Yet I think I can find you body-armour from the inner chamber: for surely there, and nowhere else, did Odysseus and his high-born son hide away their arms.'

Whereupon up went goatherd Melanthius through the smoke-vents of the hall, into the back chambers, whence he picked twelve shields with spears and crested bronze helms to match, and was soon back amongst the suitors, issuing them out. When Odysseus saw his enemies doing-on hauberks and brandishing spears he shook at the heart and knees, realising how heavy his task grew. He called to Telemachus in a sharp quick tone, 'My Telemachus, evidently one of those women inside is weighting the odds against us – or is it Melanthius?' And Telemachus answered from what he knew, 'O my father, the real blame for this lies on me and wholly on me. My faulty hand left the store-chamber's stout door unfastened, and they have spied after me too well. Now, good Eumaeus, go close it; and note if the meddler in our business is one of the women or that son of Dolius, Melanthius, as I guess.'

While they settled the plan, Melanthius the goatherd made his second journey to the chamber after other useful arms. The stout swineherd recognising him reported at once to Odysseus who stood close by. 'Royal son of Laertes, the villain is the man we suspected, and he is once again on his way to the store. Tell me plainly – shall I kill him if I can better him in fight; or bring him here, to pay for all the wickedness he has committed in your house?' Odysseus weighed his reply and concluded, 'However fiercely they attack, Telemachus and I can hold the raging suitors at bay inside the hall. So away with both of you and fling him down amidst the store-room, pinion his hands and feet behind him and lash him, back down, on a plank. Then make fast a twisted cord about him and hoist him up the pillar high into the roof-beams, where leave him to ebb out his life in lingering torture.'

They heard these orders eagerly and obeyed. They reached the chamber without the man inside it knowing, for he was right at the far end groping after more weapons. The two of them took stand either side the doorway and waited for Melanthius, who at last made to cross the threshold with a noble casque in the one hand and in the other a great old shield, now all warped with mildew, for it had belonged to the hero Laertes in his prime and the stitching of its straps had given from lying by so long. Then they leapt at once upon him, gripping his hair and haling him back into the room; where they cast him in terror upon the floor and bound him tightly, hand and foot, twisting the joints painfully behind him just as great Odysseus ordered, before they passed the stranded rope about his body and hauled him up the pillar to the rafters. And then how you baited him, O Eumaeus the swineherd! You said, 'There you are, Melanthius, fixed in the soft bed you deserve, where you can stretch out on watch all night long, sure to see golden Dawn ascend her throne from out the ocean streams, in warning that you must now drive your goats to the palace for the suitors' feasting.' So they left him, racked in bonds of agony.

They armed themselves again, fastened the shining door and came back to wary Odysseus; and then from the threshold these four men, breathing battle, faced the many champions that held the body of the hall. To them came

Athene the daughter of Zeus, but like Mentor in form and voice: and Odysseus in his gladness at the sight of her cried out, 'Mentor, remember we were friends who grew up together, and I helped you often. Rescue me from ruin.' Though he spoke thus, he felt sure it was Athene, the inspirer of peoples; but the suitors booed from down the hall, especially Agelaus the son of Damastor, who threatened, 'Mentor, I warn you against letting Odysseus' smooth tongue lure you into helping him fight the suitors; for I think that will not in the long run defeat our aim to kill them both, father and son. After which we shall put an end to you, taking your head in payment for your foolish dream that you can affect things here. And when our swords have lopped away your strength we shall treat all your possessions, indoor and outdoor, as one with the wealth of Odysseus; forbidding your sons and daughters the use of your mansion, and your devoted wife any longer abiding in the town of Ithaca.'

That they should so threaten her made Athene's heart swell with rage into angry words, wherewith she turned and rent Odysseus, saying, 'How are your strength and manhood fallen, O Odysseus, since those nine years on end you battled with the Trojans for white-armed gentle Helen's sake, and slaughtered them by heaps in the deadly struggle, till Priam's spacious city bowed to your design! Dare you appeal for pity before the suitors' faces and let your courage fail you amidst your home and chattels? Hither, dear heart; stand by me and watch my work, to see how Mentor the son of Alcimus requites, even into the teeth of the enemy, the kindnesses he has received.' She gave him only words like these, and not unchallenged victory, because she had it in her mind yet to prove the force and fervour of Odysseus and his aspiring son. Away she flitted in the guise of a swallow to the smoke-dimmed rafters of the hall, and there perched.

So heavily had the arrows rained down that very many had fallen; but Agelaus the son of Damastor, Eurynomus, Amphimedon, Demoptolemus, Peisander (Polyctor's son) and wise Polybus still survived and stood out as natural leaders to hearten those suitors yet fighting for dear life. Now Agelaus exclaimed so that all his fellows heard, 'Aha, my friends, those peerless hands are ceasing to avail him any. Mentor has mouthed some empty words and gone. They are left by themselves up there on the landing before the doors. So be careful not to volley your long spears at random, but begin hurling, six at a time, and maybe Zeus will grant that Odysseus is hit and glory won. The rest amount to nothing, once he goes down.'

So he said; and they regulated their throwing according to his orders: but Athene made everything miscarry. One hit the massive door-jamb, another the great door itself, while the heavy bronze head of yet another's ashen shaft crashed upon the wall-face; and after his party had lived through this volley all unhurt, stout Odysseus prompted them, 'My friends, I say it is now our turn to fling into the thick of these suitors who deepen their former wickedness by such lust to spoil us.' They took careful aim and let fly their sharp spears. Odysseus killed Demoptolemus, Telemachus Euryades, the swine-herd Elatus and the cowman Peisander. As all these tumbled to the immense floor and bit its dust the suitors fell back to the rear of the hall, while the others ran down and recovered their spears from the corpses. Then came the suitors' second critical cast of spears, most of which Athene again made to fall idly against door-post, door or wall: but Amphimedon's shot caught Telemachus on the wrist (only a graze, the blade just breaking the outer skin) while the long spear of Ctesippus ripped Eumaeus across the shoulder above the rim of his shield and glanced upward before falling to the ground.

The party led by wary Odysseus then threw back into the crowd, the waster of cities himself striking Eurydamas, Telemachus killing Amphimedon and the swineherd Poly-bus: while after them the herdsman flung, to hit Ctesippus in the heart and vaunt himself, saying, 'You loved your jibe, son of Polytherses, but the Gods are greatest: wherefore another time give them the word and let not your folly talk so big. This gift squares the neats-foot hospitality you gave divine Odysseus lately, while he was begging through his house.' As the keeper of the screw-horned herds declaimed, the others were stemming the rush hand to hand, the long shaft of Odysseus stabbing the son of Damastor; and Telemachus thrusting Leocritus, son of Euenor, in the pit of the stomach so shrewdly that the bronze spear-point went right through and he tipped headlong to earth, face down: while at that moment Athene from the high roof brandished her death-dealing Aegis. Their souls were terrified and they stamped down the long hall like a herd of cattle distracted and put to flight by some dancing gad-fly in the rush of the year when the days grow long: but the onslaught the four made upon them was a stooping from the mountains of crook-taloned, hook-billed vultures upon small birds, forcing them out of the skies to cower along a plain which yet affords no cover and no escape; so there they are harried to death, and men love the sport of it. Like that were the suitors buffetted every way up and down the hall, while the dismal crunch of cracking skulls increased and the whole floor seeped with blood.

Leodes in his extremity caught at the knees of Odysseus,

loudly imploring, 'By your clasped knees, O Odysseus, pity me and show mercy. Never once, I swear, did I offend any woman in your house by word or deed. Rather would I give pause to the other suitors with such intent, though they would not be persuaded to restrain their hands from evil and therefore has this shameful death caught them amidst their sins. But am I, their wholly guiltless sacrificing priest, to be confounded in their number and perish with them, the good which I have done not being counted to me for charity?' Odysseus scowled down at him and cried, 'If you admit yourself these men's sacrificing priest, then how often have you not prayed in my own house for the happy issue of a homecoming to be removed from me, that my dear wife might follow you and bear you children? For that you shall not escape the grave's strait couch.' As Odysseus cried it, one powerful hand grasped the sword that still lay where Agelaus had dropped it, dying, and swung it free at his throat. So his head, yet praying for mercy, was confounded in the dust.

The bard, Phemius son of Terpes, who had sung for the suitors by constraint, had thus far escaped black fate. He was hesitating – and still fingering his loud lyre – near the hatch, in doubt whether he had best spring in and conjure Odysseus by his knees or flee the house to sit by the altar, so fairly builded outside to great Zeus of the Court, upon which Laertes and Odysseus had burnt many thigh pieces of oxen. As he turned it over, the better way seemed to clasp the knees of Laertes' son: so he set down the fragile lyre between the mixing bowl and his silver-mounted chair and himself darted forward to embrace the knees of Odysseus and beseech him with fluttering words: 'At your knees, Odysseus, I seek consideration and mercy. Remorse will overtake you hereafter should you kill, in me, a bard fit to sing to Gods as well as men: and from innate genius I do it, God having sown in me the seeds of every mode. I am like to hymn you divinely: wherefore curb your rage to cut off my head. Also Telemachus, your loved son, can vouch that in my case neither good-will nor avarice kept me in your house as musician for the suitors' feasts. They were so many and so violent that they could compel my attendance.'

God-fearing Telemachus who had heard his protestation called quickly to the father by his side, 'Let be, indeed, and keep your sword off this one: for he is truly innocent. Let us save our usher Medon, too, the guardian of my boyhood in the house; unless he has already fallen before Philoetius or the swineherd or met you raging through the house.' His word reached the ears of Medon, that discreet man, where he lay beneath a throne with the hide of a freshly-flayed ox wrapped round him to ward off the darkness of death. At once he crawled from under the throne, flung the ox-skin aside and darted forward to embrace the knees of Telemachus with the fervent prayer, 'O my dear, here I am. Master yourself and keep exhorting your father, lest he destroy me with that sharp sword in his excessive strength and rage against these suitors who wasted his worldly goods and ignored you in their recklessness.'

Odysseus smiled then and said to him, 'Take heart; Telemachus has redeemed you and preserved you for this time to learn in your heart of hearts and testify aloud the advantage of virtue over vice: but see that you and the full-throated bard leave the house and sit outside in the court away from the killing, till I have ended all that yet lies for me to do within'; and as he said it they were out of the hall and sitting by the altar of great Zeus, their eyes yet staring wildly with the instant sense of death;

while the gaze of Odysseus went ranging the house, on the chance that some living man still hid there, to dodge his fate. However he found them all weltering in dust and blood, many as the fish dragged forth by sailors from the grey sea in seine nets up the beach of some bay, where they lie heaped on the sand and languishing for the briny waves, while the sun's shining saps their life away. Just so were the suitors heaped together.

Then said the guileful Odysseus to Telemachus, 'Go now and call nurse Eurycleia: for I have a word near my heart to speak with her.' Telemachus obeyed his dear father's orders and rattled at the door to summon the nurse, crying, 'Up with you now, aged dame and supervisor of our house-women. Come hither. My father calls you for somewhat he has to say.' Not a word could she launch in reply. She opened the doors of the stately hall and paced in (Telemachus ushering her) to where Odysseus stood in a slaver of blood and muck amidst the corpses of his victims, like some lion that has devoured an ox at grass and prowls forth, terrible to the eye, with gory breast and chaps. So was Odysseus bedabbled from his hands right down to his feet. She, when she saw the corpses and the pools of blood, knew how great was the achievement and opened her mouth to raise the woman's battle-wail: but Odysseus checked her excitement and stilled her with these trenchant words, 'Rejoice within yourself, beldam, and quietly. Keep back that throbbing cry. To make very glad over men's deaths is not proper. These fell by doom of the Gods and through the wickedness themselves had wrought, in disregarding good and bad alike amongst their earthly visitors. To such infatuation they owe their ignominious death. Now, instead, name me the full roll of house-women, those that disgrace me and the innocent ones.'

Then his good nurse Eurycleia said to him, 'Indeed, my child, I will tell you the very truth. In the palace you have fifty serving women whom we have broken to your service and taught such duties as carding wool. Of them just twelve ran to shamelessness, despite me and the orders of the Queen: – not of Telemachus, for his growing to account is a new thing; never did his mother let him touch the women servants. But now let me mount to that bright upper room and bear tidings to your wife where she lies plunged in a god-given sleep.' But cunning Odysseus forbade her. 'By no means call her yet. Bid me in those women who have been disorderly'; and away at his word went the old dame through the house, warning the women and hustling them forward: while Odysseus called to Telemachus, to the stockman and to the swineherd, saying with energy, 'Start to clear away the dead, making the women do the work; and then swill down the rich seats and tables with water and fibrous sponges. Afterwards, when you have restored the whole house to order, take these servants outside the stately hall to that spot between the round vault and the courtyard's strong boundary wall and there slaughter them with your long swords till the last life is spent and their love-passages with the suitors are wholly out of mind.'

So he bade them, and the erring women trailed in, all huddled together and crying great bitter tears of woe. First they bore out the dead and laid them in heaps along the portico of the walled court – Odysseus directing that work himself and driving them, for it took force to make them do it – and then they cleaned down the noble thrones and tables with water and soft sponges, while Telemachus with the swineherd and cattle-man scraped down the floor of the strong house with hoes, the maids carrying for them to a dump out of doors. When the house was tidy they led the women servants beyond the great hall and penned them in that blind place between vault and boundary wall, whence escape was impossible; and then Telemachus began to speak thoughtfully. 'It irks me,' he said, 'to give any sort of clean death to women who have heaped shame on my head and my mother's, and have wantoned with the suitors.' That was what he said. He made fast a dark-prowed ship's hawser to a pillar and strained it round the great spiral of the vault, at too great a height for anyone to touch the floor with her feet. Sometimes in a shrubbery men so stretch out nets, upon which long-winged thrushes or doves alight on their way to roost: and fatal the perch proves. Exactly thus were the women's heads all held a-row with a bight of cord drawn round each throat, to suffer their caitiff's death. A little while they twittered with their feet – only a little. It was not long.

Melanthius they dragged through the entry and the court, sliced his nose and ears with their cruel swords and tore out his privates, which they fed raw to the dogs. Their spite made them also cut off his hands and feet, after which they rinsed their own feet and hands and rejoined Odysseus in the house, all their achievement perfected. Wherefore he called to Eurycleia the beloved nurse, 'Bring me purifying brimstone, dame, and bring fire, for me to smoke the place through: also summon Penelope with her handmaidens. Have all the women of the house in here at once.' Devoted Eurycleia answered him, 'In this, my child, you follow precisely the right course: yet suffer me to bring you tunic and cloak for covering. You lower your dignity by standing in your hall with mere rags about your broad shoulders.' To which Odysseus only said, 'Light me the fire in the hall first . . .' and Eurycleia had no choice but to obey. Whereupon Odysseus carefully purged the hall, the private rooms and the court, with the fire and brimstone of her furnishing.

Afterwards the old woman went through the noble house to notify the women and bid them hastily attend. They came forth from their quarters, torch in hand, poured round Odysseus and embraced him with kisses and loving handclasps for his head, shoulders and hands: and, as his heart recalled each one of them, sorely his temptation grew to burst out weeping and wailing.

BOOK 23

But it was with a cackle of laughter that the old dame climbed towards the upper room, to warn her mistress of the beloved husband's return. Her knees moved nimbly and her feet tripped along to the lady's bed-head where she stood and spoke her part. 'Awake dear child, Penelope: open your eyes upon the sight you have yearned for all these days. Odysseus has appeared, at this end of time. He has reached his home and in it slaughtered the recalcitrant suitors who for so long vexed the house, ate his stored wealth and outfaced his son.'

Circumspect Penelope replied to this: 'Dear mother, the Gods have driven you frantic. They turn to foolishness the ripest judgements and the flighty into sober ways. From them comes this derangement of your old true under-standing: – but why tease with fantasies a heart already brimmed with grief? Why wake me from this sleep whose sweetness held me in thrall and veiled my eyelids; the best sleep I have enjoyed since Odysseus went away to view that ill city never-to-be-named. Off with you below, instantly, to the women's quarters. Had any other of my housemaidens roused me with news of this sort I should have sent her smartingly back into her place. Just for this once your great age shall excuse you.'

Eurycleia persisted. 'Dear child, I am in very earnest with you. Odysseus, I say, is here. He came back to the house as that stranger who met such scurvy treatment at all hands. Telemachus long since learnt his identity but very properly hid the knowledge, to let his father's revenge take shape against those proud rough men.'

This time her word transported Penelope who leaped from the couch and clasped the old woman, crying shrilly through the tears that rained from her eyes: 'Ah, dear mother, but tell me, tell me truly – if as you say he is really come home, how has he coped single-handed with the shameless suitors, who mobbed our house continually?' And the good nurse told her, 'I did not see, I do not know: but I heard the groans of their slaying. We all shrank trembling into a corner of our safe room – its doors wedged fast – until your son Telemachus came and called me forth at his father's bidding. There in the hall I found Odysseus, stalking amidst the bodies of his slain that littered the beaten floor. Your heart would have glowed to see him so lion-like, all battle-stained and steeped in blood. Now the corpses are piled up outside, by the courtyard gates, while he has had a great fire lighted and purges the lovely house. He sent me to summon you; so come, that at the end of all the sorrow you two may enter your hearts' gladness hand in hand. Surely your lingering hope is now fulfilled. He reaches his fireside alive and finds you and your son still there; while upon each and every one of those suitors who served him ill in the house he has wreaked revenge.'

'Hush, mother,' said Penelope the decorous. 'Do not sing too loud or soon. You know how grateful his reappearance in the house would be to everybody, particularly to me and to his son and mine: but what you proclaim does not ring true. This massacre of the overbearing suitors has been the work of some Immortal, inflamed by their heart-breaking wanton insolence which had regard for no soul they met, neither the bad nor the good: so they have been punished according to their sins. But meantime Odysseus in some far land has lost his way to Achaea – yea, lost himself.' Nurse Eurycleia replied: 'My child, why let fall that dull word of your husband's never coming home, when he is here already and by his fireside? Your heart was always stubborn in unbelief. Why I can quote you a sure proof, that scar from the boar's white tusk long years ago, which I noted as I washed him. I wanted to tell you upon the instant; but he, careful for his own interests put his hand over my jaw and silenced me. Come with me now – and I pledge my life on it. If I mislead you, then slay me by the meanest death you know.'

Penelope responded: 'Even your storied wisdom, mother dear, hardly equips you to interpret the designs of the eternal Gods. Howbeit let us away to my son, for I would see the suitors lying in death; and their slayer.' She was going down as she spoke, her heart in a turmoil of debate whether to keep her distance while she examined her dear lord, or go straight up at once to kiss his head and clasp his hand. So when at length she came in across the stone threshold it was to take a seat in the fire-light facing Odysseus, but over against the further wall. He sat at the base of a tall pillar, waiting with drooping eyelids to hear his stately consort cry out when she caught sight of him. But she sat there in a long silence, with bewildered heart. One moment she would look and see him in his face; and the next moment fail to see him there, by reason of the foul rags he wore – till Telemachus named her in disapproval. 'Mother mine,' he cried, 'unmotherly mother and cruel-hearted, how dare you hold aloof from father, instead of running to sit by his side and ply him with questions? No other woman could in cold blood keep herself apart, when her man got home after twenty years of toil and sorrow. Your heart remains harder than a stone.'

But Penelope explained: 'Child, my heart is dazed. I have no force to speak, or ask, or even stare upon his face. If this is Odysseus in truth and at last, then shall we soon know each other better than well by certain private signs between us two, hidden from the rest of the world.' At which the glorious long-suffering Odysseus smiled and said hastily to Telemachus, 'After that, leave your mother alone for the test in her room with me presently. Soon she will come to fuller understanding. The filth of my body, these shabby clothes – such things make her overlook me and deny it can be myself. Meanwhile you and I must discuss our best policy. In a community the slaying of even a single man with few surviving connections to avenge him entails outlawry from home and family; and we have been killing best part of the young men of Ithaca, its pillars of state. I would have you ponder it' – but Telemachus rejoined, 'Let that be your business, father dear. They call you the clearest-headed man alive, supreme in your generation. We others will support you whole-heartedly: and I fancy whatever our strength may be, courage at least will not fail us.'

Said Odysseus, 'Then hear what I think best. Wash now and dress, and have the house-women deck themselves. Then let the inspired minstrel with his resounding lyre lead off for us in a dance so merry that all hearing it from outside the walls, neighbours or passers-by, will say, "There is a wedding toward." Thus rumour of the suitors' deaths will not spread across the city before we have got away to our tree-clad country place, there to weigh what means of advantage the Olympian may offer to our hands.' They had all listened intently and moved to do his bidding. They washed and put on tunics: the women were arrayed: the revered musician took his hollow lyre and awoke their appetite for rhythm and the gay dance, till the great house around them rang with the measured foot-falls of men and well-gowned women. Outside the house one and another hearing the harmony did say, 'I swear someone has wedded the much-courted queen! Callous she was, and lacked the fortitude and constancy to keep the house of her lawful husband until he came.' Such was the gossip, in ignorance of the real event.

Meanwhile, within, old Eurynome washed and anointed Odysseus, draping upon him a fair tunic and cloak, while Athene crowned him with an especial splendour that filled the eye; she made the hair of his head curl downward floridly, like bloom of hyacinth. As a craftsman lavishly endowed with skill by Hephaestus and Pallas washes his silver-work with fine gold until its mastery shines out, so the grace from Athene glorified his head and shoulders and made his figure, when he left the bath-chamber, seem divine. He retook his former throne opposite his wife and declared, 'Proud lady, the heart that the lords of Olympus gave you is harder than any true woman's. None but you would pitilessly repulse the husband who had won his way home after twenty years of toil. Old dame, favour me now by arranging my bed somewhere apart, that I may lie solitary: for the heart in her breast has turned to iron.'

Said Penelope with reserve, 'Proud lord, I neither set myself too high nor esteem you too low: nor am I confused out of mind. It is that I remember only too well how you were when you sailed from Ithaca in your long-oared ship.

So Eurycleia, when you make up his great bed for him, move it outside the bridal chamber that he built so firmly. Have forth the heavy bed-frame and pile it high with fleeces and rugs and glossy blankets.' This she said to draw her husband out; and indeed Odysseus was ruffled into protesting to his wife, 'Woman, this order pains my heart. Who has changed my bed? It would task the cunningest man – forbye no God happened to shift it in whim – for not the stoutest wight alive could heave it up directly. That bed's design held a marvellous feature of my own contriving. Within our court had sprung a stem of olive, bushy, long in the leaf, vigorous; the bole of it column-thick. Round it I plotted my bed-chamber, walled entire with fine-jointed ashlar and soundly roofed. After adding joinery doors, fitting very close, I then polled the olive's spreading top and trimmed its stump from the root up, dressing it so smooth with my tools and so knowingly that I got it plumb, to serve for bed-post just as it stood. With this for main member (boring it with my auger wherever required) I went on to frame up the bed, complete; inlaying it with gold, silver and ivory and lacing it across with ox-hide thongs, dyed blood-purple. That was the style of it, woman, as I explain: but of course I do not know whether the bed stands as it did; or has someone sawn through the olive stem and altered it?'

As Odysseus had run on, furnishing her with proof too solid for rejection, her knees trembled, and her heart. She burst into tears, she ran to him, she flung her arms about his neck and kissed his head and cried, 'My Odysseus, forgive me this time too, you who were of old more comprehending than any man of men. The Gods gave us sorrow for our portion, and in envy denied us the happiness of being together throughout our days, from the heat of youth to the shadow of old age. Be not angry with me, therefore, nor resentful, because at first sight I failed to fondle you thus. The heart within me ever shook for terror of being cheated by some man's lie, so innumerable are those who plot to serve greedy ends. See, it was that way our life's sorrow first began. Argive Helen, the daughter of Zeus, did not in her own imagination invent the ruinous folly that let a strange man lie with her in love and intercourse. A God it was that tempted her astray. Never would she have done it had she known how the warrior sons of the Achaeans would fetch her back once more to her native land. But now with those authentic details of our bed, seen by no human eye but yours, mine and my maid's (Actor's daughter, given me by my father before I came here and ever the sole keeper of our closed bed-chamber-door) you have convinced my heart, slow though you may think it to believe.'

This word increased by so much his inclination to tears that he wept, even with his arms about his faithful, lovely wife. So at sea when Poseidon has swamped a good ship by making her the target of his winds and mighty waves, the sight of land appears wonderfully kind to the few men of her crew who have escaped by swimming. How they swarm ashore from the grey sea, their bodies all crusted with salt spume, but happy, happy, for the evil overpassed! Just so was she happy to have her husband once more in sight and clasped in her white arms which lingered round his neck, unable to let him go. Rosy dawn might have found them thus, still weeping, only that grey-eyed Athene otherwise ordained. She retarded the night a long while in transit and made Dawn, the golden-throned, tarry by the eastern Ocean's edge; not harnessing Lampus and Phaethon, the sharp-hooved young horses that carry her and bring daylight to the world.

At last provident Odysseus said to his wife: 'My dear

one, we have not yet reached the issue of our trials. In store for us is immeasurable toil prescribed, and needs must I fulfil it to the end. The day I went down into Hades' realm, the ghost of Teiresias warned me of everything when I asked after my home-coming and my company's. Wherefore let us to bed, dear wife, there at long last to renew ourselves with the sweet meed of sleep.' To which Penelope answered, 'Bed is yours the instant your heart wills, for have not the Gods restored you to your own great house and native land? But now that Heaven has put it in your mind, tell me of this ordeal remaining. Later I must know; and forewarned is forearmed.'

Odysseus in reply assured her, 'Brave spirit, I shall tell you, hiding nothing: but why press me insistently for knowledge that will no more please you than me? He gave me word that I must take my shapely oar and wander through many places of men, until I find a people that know not the sea and have no salt to season their food, a people for whom purple-prowed ships are unknown things, as too the shaped oars which wing their flight. An infallible token of them he told me, and I make you wise to it. When another wayfarer passes me and says I have a winnowing fan on my stout shoulder, even there am I to strike my oar into the ground and offer for rich sacrifice to King Poseidon a ram, a bull and a ramping boar. Thence I may turn homeward, to celebrate the Gods of high heaven with heca-tombs of victims, and all things else in order due. While death shall come for me from the sea, very mildly, ending me amidst a contented people after failing years have brought me low. He assured me all this would be fulfilled.' And Penelope's wise comment was, 'If the Gods will make old age your happier time, then there is prospect of your ill-luck passing.'

Thus they chatted while Eurynome and the nurse under the flaring torchlight arranged the soft coverlets upon the bed. When they had busily made it comfortable and deep, the old nurse returned to her sleeping-place, while Eurynome the chambermaid conducted them bedward with her torch. She ushered them to their chamber and withdrew; and gladsomely they performed their bed-rites in the old fashion: Telemachus and the herdsmen staying their feet from the dance and staying the women, so that all slept in the darkling halls.

After the first thrill of love had passed, the pair began to exchange histories for mutual entertainment, the fairest of women telling what she had put up with in the house, watching the suitors' greedy swarming, and the multitudinous sheep and cattle they slew for sake of her, and all the broached jars of wine: while heaven-born Odysseus told of every hurt he had done to others and the woes himself had suffered, detailing thing by thing; and eagerly she heard him, slumber never weighing down her eyelids until all was told. He began with the conquest of the Cicones, thence to Lotos-land, and of what Cyclops did and the price exacted for his cruelly-devoured friends: then how he got welcome and help from Aeolus, but unavailingly, for further storms drove him sadly adrift: also of Telepylus, where the Laestrygonians destroyed all the ships and crews except his own: next of Circe's wiles and of his ship's voyaging to Hades to consult Teiresias, where he saw all his dead company and the mother who had cherished him when young: then of the Sirens' song, the clashers, Scylla and Charybdis those fatal ones: of his crew's killing the cattle of the Sun wherefore Zeus's lightning destroyed the ship and all aboard but himself: of Ogygia and his kindly durance in the cave with Calypso whose promised immortality did not seduce his love: of his pains to reach Phaeacia where he got worshipful hospitality, gifts and transport home: – and as the tale ended sleep fell gently upon him, relaxing his limbs and delivering his mind from care.

Athene was not at the end of her plans: the instant she judged Odysseus satisfied with love and sleeping she let golden Dawn rise from the Ocean to light mankind. With her rose Odysseus and held forth to his wife: 'Lady mine, hitherto we have both travailed exhaustively, you in lamenting the hindrances to my return, I in the sorrows wherewith Zeus and the other Gods afflicted me, homesick, far away: but now that we have both reached the bed of our desire, do you take my indoor interests under your especial care. As for the sheep butchered by the impudent suitors, I shall go raid a-many, and more will the Achaeans give me till the sheep-folds are full. But my first journey must be to the plantations of our farm where I shall see the good father who has been in grief for me. One prior consideration, however, I would put to your most subtle mind, Lady. Upon the sunrise rumour will run abroad of the suitors I slew within. So get above stairs with all your women and sit there, seeing and questioning none.'

He braced the splendid arms about his shoulders, called Telemachus, the neatherd and the swineherd, and had them all take weapons of war in their hands – not that they required urging. They did on their brazen breast-pieces, opened the doors and marched out, Odysseus in the van. Day lay wide upon the face of the earth, but Athene hid them in obscurity and led them swiftly from the town.

BOOK 24

Hermes the Cyllenian bade forth those ghosts of men that had been suitors. In his hand was the rod of pure gold with which at will he charms men's eyes to rest or stirs them from sleep. By a wave of it he had them afoot and following him with such thin cries as bats use in the fastnesses of their mysterious cave, whenever one falls squeaking from the clustered swarms that hang downward from the rocky roof. So they flocked after, weakly piping, while gentle Hermes led them down the dank, dark passage – by the Ocean Stream and the White Crag, past the portal of the Sun and the land of Dreams – till soon they entered the asphodel meadows where harbour the shadowy ghosts of those that have passed away.

There was to be found the soul of Achilles, son of Peleus, with that of Aias, next after him of all the Greeks for splendid face and figure; also the souls of Patroclus and of brave Antilochus. As these were grouped round Achilles the woe-begone spirit of Agamemnon son of Atreus approached amidst a concourse of those who fell with him in the house of Aegisthus and there miserably died. To him Achilles' ghost began: 'Why, Atrides, we used to fancy you more continually beloved of Zeus the Thunderer than any earthly hero, because you commanded the hosts of brave men in that Trojan land so costly to us Achaeans. Yet was it decreed that the doom of death (which no son of man avoids) must come to you so soon! If only you could have met it in the Troad while your sovranty endured – for then the Concert of Achaea would have raised your tomb and a great glory been earned for your son – instead of this piteous fate which has been your lot.'

The ghost of Atrides answered: 'You happy son of Peleus, god-like Achilles, to have found death near Troy and not near Argos! Some of the noblest youths, both Trojan and Achaean, died about you, furiously contending for your body whose grandeur lay so grandly in the whirling dust, forgetful of its chivalry. Through the long day we battled, and should not even then have ceased but for the storm with which Zeus halted us. Afterward we bore you from the field to our ships, where we set you on a couch and cleansed your beautiful body with warmed water and unguents. Round you the Danaans pressed, shedding hot tears and shearing their love-tresses. Your mother, when she heard, came forth from the waves with her deathless sea-maidens, the cry of them ringing across Ocean so marvellously that a thrill of fear passed over the Achaean host, which would have risen and fled to the ships but for Nestor's stemming them with his rich, rare wisdom, so often tested and approved. Because he knew, he called to them and said, 'Be still, Argives: flee not, you young Achaeans. This is his mother coming from the sea and with her the immortal maidens of the sea, to encounter her dead son.' When they heard him the Achaeans bravely contained their fear, while the daughters of the ancient of the sea circled about you with bitter lamentations and wound your body in imperishable robes. The nine Muses joined to sing your dirge, voice answering sweet voice in harmony; and so movingly rose and fell their clear chant that you would not have found one Argive there dry-eyed. Through seventeen days and seventeen nights we mourned you, deathless Gods and mortal men alike; and on the eighteenth, having sacrificed many good sheep and screw-horned kine, we gave you to the flames and you were consumed, in those divine robes and lapped with a plenty of spices and sweet honey; while panoplied companies of Achaean warriors, mounted or on foot, tramped round your burning pyre with a loud clashing of arms. Then after the fire of Hephaestus had had its way with you, very early in the morning we disposed your white bones, Achilles, in neat wine and unguent. Your mother offered a gold two-handled urn, saying it was Dionysus' gift and a work of famed Hephaestus. In it, brilliant Achilles, rest your white bones with the bones of dead Patroclus the son of Menoetias; while apart but near lie the ashes of Antilochus whom you admired above all your other friends, the fallen Patroclus only excepted. Over you we, the army of devoted Argive spearsmen, piled a great tomb that towers on its jutting headland far over the Hellespont, a mark for seafaring men of our day and days to come. Your mother went to the Gods and begged of them noble trophies which she exhibited in an arena for the Achaean athletes. In your time you have attended the obsequies of many champions, or seen the young men, when some king has died, gird themselves to compete for prizes: but had you seen these treasures your mind would have been astonished, so wonderful were the gages offered in your honour by that fair Goddess, Thetis of the silver foot. The Gods loved you out of measure, Achilles, and even death has not robbed you of your name.

Everywhere and for ever you will inherit glory. But for me, what satisfaction did I gain in winding up my war's coil, when Zeus had plotted me so dismal a fate at the hands of Aegisthus and my accursed wife, upon my coming home?'

Thus they communed as the slayer of Argus, the messenger, drew near conducting the ghosts of the suitors Odysseus killed. Amazement at the throng of them led the two forward to watch, and so the spirit of Agamemnon recognized famous Amphimedon, the dear son of Melaneus, by whom he had been entertained in Ithaca. Atrides' spirit called across to him asking, 'Amphimedon, what disaster brings all you picked men in your prime down to this land of shades? Almost might someone have chosen out and gathered the best men of your city. Did Poseidon's harsh winds raise running seas and overwhelm you in your ships? Or did enemies destroy you on some shore while you were busied rounding up their cattle or great flocks of sheep? Or perhaps the fighting was to protect their wives and towns? Tell it me, for I ask as your intimate. Do you not recollect great Menelaus and me coming to your place when we wanted Odysseus to follow with his fleet to Ilium? A full month we were, before we got across the wide gulf, so hard to persuade was the spoiler of cities, Odysseus.'

'Most renowned son of Atreus, Agamemnon, King of Kings,' answered the spirit of Amphimedon, 'Indeed, Majesty, I do remember it. So here I will give you the full, exact account of our death's deplorable chance. Odysseus was missing: wherefore we fell to courting his wife. She never admitted that our proposals were abhorrent, any more than she would determine upon one of us: nevertheless her heart of hearts kept plotting our black death and doom. For the moment she imagined another device, by setting up a very broad, fine warp on a great loom in her chamber; and pleading to us regarding it, "My lords and courtiers, as great Odysseus is dead, can you not bridle your haste to have me wedded, until I finish this winding-sheet against hero Laertes' burial on the fateful day that all-conquering death lays him low? I would not have my yarns rot unused, lest some Achaean woman of the district censure me for letting a man who had broad possessions lie unshrouded." This was her petition and we lords accepted it. Day-long she wove at her great task but after dark, by torchlight, would unpick it. For three years she maintained this deceit and fooled the Achaeans; but when a fourth year came with its days passing and its months, in seasonal progression, then one of her women (who knew) told on her and we surprised her unravelling the splendid fabric. That forced her, very unwillingly, to finish it. When the immense sheet was washed and displayed, its brilliance was like the sun or moon – but on that very day somehow some unfriendly power led Odysseus back to the isolated homestead where his swineherd lived. Thither also came his son, returned from Pylos after a sea voyage; and the two of them, before ever setting out thence for town, concerted the suitors' murder. Telemachus started first, followed by Odysseus under guidance of the swineherd, like a worn-out wretched beggar, tattered and limping on a crutch. On his sudden appearance in such rags none of us could guess what he was: even our seniors failed to know him. We gave him the rough of our tongues, not to mention blows; and for a time he endured this abuse and pelting in his own halls stolidly enough; but at last inspiration came to him from Zeus, lord of the Aegis. With the help of Telemachus he collected all the house-weapons, hid them in the store-chamber and bolted the doors. Then he ingeniously prompted his wife to set out his bow and irons as

test of the suitors' prowess – and also to provide means
for our fatal undoing. None of us had strength enough,
not by a long way, to notch the string: yet when the bow
came round to Odysseus' hands we all vehemently
protested against his having it, despite his pleading.
However Telemachus stood out and made him try it.
When mighty Odysseus got the bow he strung it easily
and flashed an arrow through the irons: then he leaped
to the threshold, poised himself firmly, tipped the arrows
out all ready, glared round him and shot royal Antinous.
Afterwards he rained his murderous shafts upon the
crowd, shooting so accurately that men fell dead in rows.
Evidently some God was aiding his party for they raged
at will through the house, slaughtering right and left.
Awful was the screaming as the brains were beaten out,
while the floor ran with blood. That was the manner of
our perishing, Atrides, and our neglected bodies still strew
the house of Odysseus, for tidings have not yet reached
the friends in our houses who would wash the clotted
gore from our wounds, lay out our bodies and raise dirges
as the dead deserve.'

The shade of Agamemnon loudly intoned: 'Blessed
have you been O son of Laertes, ingenious Odysseus, in
winning a wife of such surpassing virtue! So upright in
disposition was Penelope the daughter of Icarius that she
never forgot Odysseus the husband of her youth: and there-
fore shall the fame of her goodness be conserved in the
splendid poem wherewith the Immortals shall celebrate
the constancy of Penelope for all the dwellers upon earth.
How unlike the wickedness of that daughter of Tyndareus
who slew her husband! In the poem that men sing of her
she shall seem abominable, a blot upon even the honest
women among her sex.' Things like this the two said to

one another where they stood in Hades' mansions, under the hidden places of the world.

~

Meanwhile Odysseus and his men had passed the town. Soon they reached the flourishing estate of Laertes, acquired by him years before, after great effort. There stood his place, ringed with the hovels in which the slaves who served his purposes ate and sat and slept: while in the house proper he kept an old Sicilian woman who diligently tended her aged master in this farm so far from the town. Now Odysseus had a word for his son and the serfs. 'In with you smartly to the well-built house,' he said, 'and there devote the finest of their hogs to making our dinner; meanwhile, in view of my long absence abroad I shall go to test if my father knows me again by sight, or not.' He handed his arms to the two thralls who went straight in, as Odysseus proceeded through the rich fruit-farm, on his quest.

He went down the great garden, but did not meet Dolius, nor any other of the serfs or serfs' sons. Everybody had gone under that old man's guidance to collect stones for walling up the vines. So what he found was his father alone in the neat vineyard, hoeing round a vinestock. The greasy tunic upon him was patched and mean. His shins were cross-gartered in botched leggings of cowhide, to save their being scratched, and he wore hedging gloves against the brambles, with a goat-skin cap for his head: all of which made plain his despondency. When Odysseus knew for his father this out-worn old man, lined with heart-sickness, he paused beneath a tall pear-tree to drop a tear, while his heart asked his head if he might not kiss and clasp this father and blurt out how he had returned and regained his native land – instead of catechising him first and trying him every way – but upon reflection he deemed it still expedient to rake him with searching enquiries.

In this mood Odysseus marched up to him: only he had his head down and so went on working carefully about his vine till his famous son was beside him and said: 'Old man, you prove yourself no fool at looking after trees. What a return they make! In all the garden there is not one plant – no fig, vine, olive, pear or vegetable plot – without its contribution to the whole. Yet one remark I would offer, and take it not amiss. Your own state seems less considered. Old age presses ruinously upon you, yet you go wasted and pitifully clad. No idleness gives the master grounds for this neglect: nor do your carriage and demeanour betray the slave. You have a royal air like one who can take his ease abed, after bath and refreshment, as befits great age. So tell me now plainly and well whose serf you are and whose fruit garden is this you tend? I require the truth particularly to satisfy myself that this is really Ithaca, as a fellow just now told me when I met him in my way. A boorish fellow, lacking the manners to answer me fully or hear out my enquiries after a friend of whom I wished to know if he were yet here, alive, or dead and in Hades' domain. Wherefore let me enlarge upon this to your attentive ear. Once in my own dear land I played host to a man that happened along: and never among all the wayfaring creatures that visited me was one more welcome. He acknowledged himself an Ithacan by race: his father Laertes son of Arcesius. I brought him to my home and entertained him lavishly, as I well could from the plenty I possessed. Also I gave him gifts of hospitality agreeable to the event. Seven talents of refined gold I gave, and a petal-bowl of solid silver; twelve cloaks of a piece, so many carpets, over-mantles, tunics: and beside all these four women superbly trained in handicraft and very buxom, those which his own taste chose.'

The father wept as he answered him, 'Stranger, you are in the land you seek, but alas it has fallen into the hands of coarse and ungodly ruffians. Vain have been the gifts you generously gave, your many splendid gifts. Had you found that man living here in his land of Ithaca he would have received you with noble hospitality, as is the due of the prime benefactor, and sent you on with a goodly return of gifts. But tell me this, precisely: – how many years is it since you entertained your guest, your unhappy guest, my son – had I a son? – that ill-starred one whom the fishes of the deep sea may have swallowed, or birds and beasts of the field devoured, far from his friends and country? His mother and his father, we his parents, have not shrouded his body or raised his dirge. His well-dowered wife, faithful Penelope, never wailed as a wife should over her husband's bier, or closed his eyes in pious duty to the dead. Tell me all the truth of what you are: your city and people? Where lies the swift ship with capable crew that brought you? Or did you ferry here in another's ship which landed you and sailed away?'

Devious Odysseus answered and said: 'Yea, hear the truth. I am from Alybas, where my house is famous. My father is Apheidas, son of Polypemon, and royal. My own name is Eperitus. Some involuntary urge drove me hither from Sicania. My ship stands off the open shore beyond the town. As for Odysseus, this is the fifth year since he took leave and left my country. Unhappy man – and yet the bird-omens were favourable, wholly on his right, as he went away. That made me glad to speed him, and him glad to go. Both of us in our hearts were hoping for another meeting to seal our friendship with rich gifts.'

The news shrouded the old man in a black misery. He groaned deep and long and gathered cupped palm-fulls of dust which he poured over his grey head. This touched Odysseus to the heart; there stabbed through his nostrils a spasm of pain, to see his dear father thus. He leaped forward and caught him in his arms and kissed him, crying, 'I, my father, I myself am the one you ask after, arrived in this twentieth year at home. Cease your sighs and sobs – for let me tell you, quickly as the need is, that I have killed all those suitors in my house, to punish their burning insolence and iniquity.'

Laertes wailed, 'If you are my son Odysseus returned, then show me some clear sign that I may believe,' and the ready Odysseus answered, 'Set your eyes first on this scar, given me by the boar's white tusk that time I was on Parnassus, when you and my mother had sent me to her father, Autolycus, after the presents which he proposed and promised for me while he stayed in our house. Next I shall repeat to you the tale of trees all down the formal garden – trees which you gave me once when I was but a child following you about and asking for every thing I saw. We were walking amongst these very trees when you told me each one's name and sort. Thirteen pear-trees you gave me, ten apples, forty fig-trees: also you described the fifty rows of vines you would give, each ripening in its time, so that bunches of grapes there would be continually, as the seasons of Zeus swelled them from on high.'

At these words Laertes' knees and heart gave way, for he recognized the manifest proofs furnished by his son. He caught at the great Odysseus who drew the old man, fainting, to his breast and held him thus till the breath came back and the spirit quickened in him once more. Then Laertes called, 'Father Zeus, still there are Gods on tall Olympus, if truly the suitors have paid the penalty of their shocking pride. Yet terribly the fear takes my soul that now all the men of Ithaca will mass against us here, while they send hue and cry through the cities of the Cephallenians.'

'Never fear it,' replied Odysseus, 'nor let it concern your mind. Off with us to the near-by garden house whither I despatched Telemachus with the cowman and swineherd, to prepare a hasty meal:' and away the two strolled, chatting, to the pleasant house, within whose stout walls laboured Telemachus and the herdsmen carving the abundant flesh and mixing rich wine. There his Sicilian dame washed honest Laertes and anointed him, before putting upon him a handsome cloak: while Athene came down, to enhance the stature and build of this shepherd of the people, so dignifying his limbs that the figure which issued from the bath was like an immortal. His amazed son put his wonder into words. 'Father,' he said, 'surely one of the Eternal Gods has made you taller and more impressive to the eye,' to which the wise old man replied, 'Ah, if but Zeus and Athene and Apollo would make me the man I was when as King of my Cephallenians I led them to the capture of Nericus, that great fortress of the mainland! Had that old fighting self of mine been with you yesterday in our house to help you repulse the suitors, I should have made many a one give at the knees, and delighted your heart of hearts.'

They talked till the others, having ended their work of getting the meal, sat down in order upon their thrones or chairs. They were helping themselves to the food when old man Dolius arrived and with him his sons, panting from their toil. Their mother, the old Sicilian, whose zealous cherishing of her age-crippled master yet let her care for them, had run outdoors and hailed them in. When they saw Odysseus and minded him again they stood dumbstruck in the hall: but Odysseus fastened upon them with honeyed words, saying: 'Forget your surprise, aged man, and sit down to eat. For quite a while we have been in the house eager to begin; but we hung about, momently expecting you.' Dolius heard him and ran forward openarmed to take Odysseus' hand and kiss his wrist while he cried excitedly, 'My dear, now you have come back to those who loved and longed and despaired for you – now the Gods bring you home – all hail and very welcome! Heaven grant you happiness. But do assure me that Penelope knows of your return. Else must we send a messenger.' To which Odysseus: 'Ancient man, she knows already; you have no call to meddle there,' and back went venerable Dolius to his polished bench, while the sons pressed round famous Odysseus, greeting him and clasping his hands. Then they sat properly beside their father and were busied on their dinner in the house.

Meanwhile in the city rumour had coursed far and fast, proclaiming the destruction of the suitors by death. When the people heard of it they gathered from all sides to Odysseus' house with wailing and lamentation. Thence party after party bore out the corpses of their dead to burial: while those that came from outlying cities were loaded into swift ships and sent by boatmen home. Afterward the entire populace trooped in deepest mourning to their debatingground; and when all were in place Eupeithes rose, heartburdened with inconsolate misery for sake of his son Antinous, the first victim of kingly Odysseus. Tears rained from his eyes as he harangued them, saying, 'O my friends,

the vast mischief this man has worked against the Achaeans!
Think of the many stout warriors he took aboard with him,
only to cast away his ships and all their crews; while he
returns only to butcher the very best leaders of the
Cephallenians that remained. You must act before he takes
swift flight to Pylos or to sacred Elis, the Epeian sanctuary.
Let us forward, or our faces will be for ever bowed with
shame. The disgrace of it will echo down the generations,
should we fail to punish the murderers of our sons and
kinsmen. For me, there would remain no sweetness in life.
Rather would I choose death and the company of these
dead. Up and strike, before they steal from us oversea.'

This and his tears awoke pity in every Achaean; but
now Medon appeared, coming with the inspired bard from
the palace of Odysseus where they had just awaked. They
strode to the heart of the gaping crowd, and there Medon
halted to say temperately, 'O men of Ithaca, hear me. What
Odysseus has done was not of his own design, unsupported
by the Immortal Gods. With my own eyes I saw a deathless
form, in exact guise of Mentor, stand next Odysseus and
manifest divinity by thrusting forward to embolden him;
and again by an onslaught which drove the suitors in terror
about the hall, till they fell side by side.' His words turned
them pale with fear, and then old Halitherses, Mastor's
stately son, struck in to exhort them, out of his unequalled
knowledge of things past and things to be. Very candidly
he spoke, saying, 'And now listen to me, men of Ithaca,
and to what I say. These disasters have followed upon your
negligence, my friends. You would not be persuaded by
me, or by Mentor the people's shepherd, to make your sons
cease their insensate ways. Wilfully and wantonly they
were led to waste the property and insult the wife of a man
of virtue, through believing him gone beyond return. But

take my advice now and let things be. If we make another move, maybe some will find that evil recoils.' Thus he counselled and a few stayed in their place; but the rest, the majority, preferred Eupeithes' advice and leaped to their feet crying the war-cry. They ran to arms and arrayed their bodies in shining bronze, before assembling in their multitudes outside the broad town. Eupeithes led them, frantic at the slaying of his son and thinking to avenge him: whereas in the event he was to find his own death and never return.

~

In heaven Athene appealed to Zeus, son of Cronos. 'O Father of us all and King of Kings, answer what I ask and make plain the secret working of your mind. Will you provoke a new cruel war, more din of battle? Or turn them again to loving one another?' Then the Cloud-compellor replied, 'Daughter, why put to Me this question? The affair is of your creating. Did you not plan for the coming of Odysseus to be with vengeance upon the suitors? Now work it as you please, though I will tell you the fitting way. Great Odysseus has revenged himself. Let the parties compose a binding treaty, by virtue of which he shall remain their king: while we will expunge from memory this slaughter of the people's kith and kin. So shall they love one another as of yore and peace abound, with wealth.' His words exalted Athene, already eager. Down she went hurtling from the crest of Olympus.

At the farm the men had glutted their desire for the honey-sweet food. Odysseus began directing them. 'One of you had better look if any enemy approaches,' he said, and accordingly out went a son of Dolius to the threshold:

whence he saw the mob quite near at hand. So he cried in haste to Odysseus, 'They are on top of us. Our arms! Quick!' They leaped to their feet and armed. Besides the four with Odysseus, Dolius had six of his sons; while even the hoary-headed Laertes and Dolius harnessed themselves once again to become men of war at the need. They flung wide the gate and marched out, all corseleted in shining bronze, Odysseus leading. Athene, talking and looking like Mentor, joined them, to the delight of Odysseus who admonished his son: 'My Telemachus, you are taking part with men in battle where the best will win. Learn instantly not to disgrace your lineage: ours has had a world-reputation for courage and skill' – and to this Telemachus appositely replied, 'Dear Father, if it pleases you to watch, you will see me in such form as will indeed not disgrace my forbears, the way you put it.' Laertes, who had overheard them, gleefully cried out, 'Dear Gods, what a day for me! O joy, to have my son and my son's son vying on the point of valour!'

Athene came to Laertes' elbow and whispered, 'Son of Arcesius, whom I love best of all my friends, offer a prayer to the grey-eyed Goddess and to Father Zeus, then poise your long-shafted spear and let fly.' With her words she breathed vigour into him. He invoked the daughter of great Zeus, balanced the weapon a moment and hurled it to strike Eupeithes on his helmet's bronze cheek-piece, which did not resist the spear. The point went through and with a clang of armour the man crashed down.

Odysseus and his brave son fell upon the leading rank, hacking with their swords and thrusting with their spears. They would have cut them off and destroyed every one had not Athene, the daughter of aegis-bearing Zeus, shouted with such force as to halt the array. 'Let be your deadly battle, men of Ithaca,' she cried. 'Without bloodshed is the affair best arranged.' The voice of the Goddess blenched them with fear. In their panic the weapons slipped from their grasp and fell together to the ground, as the Goddess called. They turned their faces toward the town for dear life, while with a roar the great long-suffering Odysseus gathered himself for the spring and launched after them, like an eagle in free air.

But instantly the son of Cronos flung his lurid levin which fell before the grey-eyed Goddess, the dread Father's own child; then did Athene cry to Odysseus, 'Back with you, heaven-nourished son of Laertes, Odysseus of the many wiles. Hold back. Cease this arbitrament of civil war. Move not far-sighted Zeus to wrath.'

So Athene said, she the daughter of aegis-bearing Zeus. Odysseus obeyed, inwardly glad: and Pallas, still with Mentor's form and voice, set a pact between them for ever and ever.

CLASSIC LITERATURE: WORDS AND PHRASES
adapted from the *Collins English Dictionary*

Accoucheur NOUN a male midwife or doctor ❑ *I think my sister must have had some general idea that I was a young offender whom an Accoucheur Policemen had taken up (on my birthday) and delivered over to her* (*Great Expectations* by Charles Dickens)

addled ADJ confused and unable to think properly ❑ *But she counted and counted till she got that addled* (*The Adventures of Huckleberry Finn* by Mark Twain)

admiration NOUN amazement or wonder ❑ *lifting up his hands and eyes by way of admiration* (*Gulliver's Travels* by Jonathan Swift)

afeard ADJ afeard means afraid ❑ *shake it – and don't be afeard* (*The Adventures of Huckleberry Finn* by Mark Twain)

affected VERB affected means followed ❑ *Hadst thou affected sweet divinity* (*Doctor Faustus 5.2* by Christopher Marlowe)

aground ADV when a boat runs aground, it touches the ground in a shallow part of the water and gets stuck ❑ *what kep' you? – boat get aground?* (*The Adventures of Huckleberry Finn* by Mark Twain)

ague NOUN a fever in which the patient has alternate hot and cold shivering fits ❑ *his exposure to the wet and cold had brought on fever and ague* (*Oliver Twist* by Charles Dickens)

alchemy ADJ false or worthless ❑ *all wealth alchemy* (*The Sun Rising* by John Donne)

all alike PHRASE the same all the time ❑ *Love, all alike* (*The Sun Rising* by John Donne)

alow and aloft PHRASE alow means in the lower part or bottom, and aloft means on the top, so alow and aloft means on the top and in the bottom or throughout ❑ *Someone's turned the chest out alow and aloft* (*Treasure Island* by Robert Louis Stevenson)

ambuscade NOUN ambuscade is not a proper word. Tom means an ambush, which is when a group of people attack their enemies, after hiding and waiting for them ❑ *and so we would lie in ambuscade, as he called it* (*The Adventures of Huckleberry Finn* by Mark Twain)

amiable ADJ likeable or pleasant ❑ *Such amiable qualities must speak for themselves* (*Pride and Prejudice* by Jane Austen)

amulet NOUN an amulet is a charm thought to drive away evil spirits. ❑ *uttered phrases at once occult and familiar, like the amulet worn on the heart* (*Silas Marner* by George Eliot)

amusement NOUN here amusement means a strange and disturbing puzzle ❑ *this was an amusement the other way* (*Robinson Crusoe* by Daniel Defoe)

ancient NOUN an ancient was the flag displayed on a ship to show which country it belongs to. It is also called the ensign ❑ *her ancient and pendants out* (*Robinson Crusoe* by Daniel Defoe)

antic ADJ here antic means horrible or grotesque ❑ *armed and dressed after a very antic manner* (*Gulliver's Travels* by Jonathan Swift)

antics NOUN antics is an old word meaning clowns, or people who do silly things to make other people laugh ❑ *And point like antics at his triple crown* (*Doctor Faustus 3.2* by Christopher Marlowe)

appanage NOUN an appanage is a living allowance ❏ *As if loveliness were not the special prerogative of woman – her legitimate appanage and heritage!* (Jane Eyre by Charlotte Brontë)

appended VERB appended means attached or added to ❏ *and these words appended* (Treasure Island by Robert Louis Stevenson)

approver NOUN an approver is someone who gives evidence against someone he used to work with ❏ *Mr. Noah Claypole: receiving a free pardon from the Crown in consequence of being admitted approver against Fagin* (Oliver Twist by Charles Dickens)

areas NOUN the areas is the space, below street level, in front of the basement of a house ❏ *The Dodger had a vicious propensity, too, of pulling the caps from the heads of small boys and tossing them down areas* (Oliver Twist by Charles Dickens)

argument NOUN theme or important idea or subject which runs through a piece of writing ❏ *Thrice needful to the argument which now* (The Prelude by William Wordsworth) .

artificially ADJ artfully or cleverly ❏ *and he with a sharp flint sharpened very artificially* (Gulliver's Travels by Jonathan Swift)

artist NOUN here artist means a skilled workman ❏ *This man was a most ingenious artist* (Gulliver's Travels by Jonathan Swift)

assizes NOUN assizes were regular court sessions which a visiting judge was in charge of ❏ *you shall hang at the next assizes* (Treasure Island by Robert Louis Stevenson)

attraction NOUN gravitation, or Newton's theory of gravitation ❏ *he predicted the same fate to attraction* (Gulliver's Travels by Jonathan Swift)

aver VERB to aver is to claim something strongly ❏ *for Jem Rodney,* the mole catcher, averred that one evening as he was returning homeward (Silas Marner by George Eliot)

baby NOUN here baby means doll, which is a child's toy that looks like a small person ❏ *and skilful dressing her baby* (Gulliver's Travels by Jonathan Swift)

bagatelle NOUN bagatelle is a game rather like billiards and pool ❏ *Breakfast had been ordered at a pleasant little tavern, a mile or so away upon the rising ground beyond the green; and there was a bagatelle board in the room, in case we should desire to unbend our minds after the solemnity.* (Great Expectations by Charles Dickens)

bah EXCLAM Bah is an exclamation of frustration or anger ❏ *"Bah," said Scrooge.* (A Christmas Carol by Charles Dickens)

bairn NOUN a northern word for child ❏ *Who has taught you those fine words, my bairn?* (Wuthering Heights by Emily Brontë)

bait VERB to bait means to stop on a journey to take refreshment ❏ *So, when they stopped to bait the horse, and ate and drank and enjoyed themselves, I could touch nothing that they touched, but kept my fast unbroken.* (David Copperfield by Charles Dickens)

balustrade NOUN a balustrade is a row of vertical columns that form railings ❏ *but I mean to say you might have got a hearse up that staircase, and taken it broadwise, with the splinter-bar towards the wall, and the door towards the balustrades: and done it easy* (A Christmas Carol by Charles Dickens)

bandbox NOUN a large lightweight box for carrying bonnets or hats ❏ *I am glad I bought my bonnet, if it is only for the fun of having another bandbox* (Pride and Prejudice by Jane Austen)

barren NOUN a barren here is a stretch or expanse of barren land ❏ *a line* *of upright stones, continued the length of the barren* (Wuthering Heights by Emily Brontë)

basin NOUN a basin was a cup without a handle ❑ *who is drinking his tea out of a basin* (Wuthering Heights by Emily Brontë)

battalia NOUN the order of battle ❑ *till I saw part of his army in battalia* (Gulliver's Travels by Jonathan Swift)

battery NOUN a Battery is a fort or a place where guns are positioned ❑ *You bring the lot to me, at that old Battery over yonder* (Great Expectations by Charles Dickens)

battledore and shuttlecock NOUN The game battledore and shuttlecock was an early version of the game now known as badminton. The aim of the early game was simply to keep the shuttlecock from hitting the ground. ❑ *Battledore and shuttlecock's a wery good game vhen you an't the shuttlecock and two lawyers the battledores, in which case it gets too excitin' to be pleasant* (Pickwick Papers by Charles Dickens)

beadle NOUN a beadle was a local official who had power over the poor ❑ *But these impertinences were speedily checked by the evidence of the surgeon, and the testimony of the beadle* (Oliver Twist by Charles Dickens)

bearings NOUN the bearings of a place are the measurements or directions that are used to find or locate it ❑ *the bearings of the island* (Treasure Island by Robert Louis Stevenson)

beaufet NOUN a beaufet was a sideboard ❑ *and sweet-cake from the beaufet* (Emma by Jane Austen)

beck NOUN a beck is a small stream ❑ *a beck which follows the bend of the glen* (Wuthering Heights by Emily Brontë)

bedight VERB decorated ❑ *and bedight with Christmas holly stuck into the top.* (A Christmas Carol by Charles Dickens)

Bedlam NOUN Bedlam was a lunatic asylum in London which had statues carved by Caius Gabriel Cibber at its entrance ❑ *Bedlam, and those carved maniacs at the gates* (The Prelude by William Wordsworth)

beeves NOUN oxen or castrated bulls which are animals used for pulling vehicles or carrying things ❑ *to deliver in every morning six beeves* (Gulliver's Travels by Jonathan Swift)

begot VERB created or caused ❑ *Begot in thee* (On His Mistress by John Donne)

behoof NOUN behoof means benefit ❑ *"Yes, young man," said he, releasing the handle of the article in question, retiring a step or two from my table, and speaking for the behoof of the landlord and waiter at the door* (Great Expectations by Charles Dickens)

berth NOUN a berth is a bed on a boat ❑ *this is the berth for me* (Treasure Island by Robert Louis Stevenson)

bevers NOUN a bever was a snack, or small portion of food, eaten between main meals ❑ *that buys me thirty meals a day and ten bevers* (Doctor Faustus 2.1 by Christopher Marlowe)

bilge water NOUN the bilge is the widest part of a ship's bottom, and the bilge water is the dirty water that collects there ❑ *no gush of bilge-water had turned it to fetid puddle* (Jane Eyre by Charlotte Brontë)

bills NOUN bills is an old term meaning prescription. A prescription is the piece of paper on which your doctor writes an order for medicine and which you give to a chemist to get the medicine ❑ *Are not thy bills hung up as monuments* (Doctor Faustus 1.1 by Christopher Marlowe)

black cap NOUN a judge wore a black cap when he was about to sentence a prisoner to death ❑ *The judge* assumed the black cap, and the prisoner still stood with the same air and gesture. (*Oliver Twist* by Charles Dickens)

boot-jack NOUN a wooden device to help take boots off ❑ *The speaker appeared to throw a boot-jack, or some such article, at the person he addressed* (*Oliver Twist* by Charles Dickens)

booty NOUN booty means treasure or prizes ❑ *would be inclined to give up their booty in payment of the dead man's debts* (*Treasure Island* by Robert Louis Stevenson)

Bow Street runner PHRASE Bow Street runners were the first British police force, set up by the author Henry Fielding in the eighteenth century ❑ *as would have convinced a judge or a Bow Street runner* (*Treasure Island* by Robert Louis Stevenson)

brawn NOUN brawn is a dish of meat which is set in jelly ❑ *Heaped up upon the floor, to form a kind of throne, were turkeys, geese, game, poultry, brawn, great joints of meat, sucking-pigs* (*A Christmas Carol* by Charles Dickens)

bray VERB when a donkey brays, it makes a loud, harsh sound ❑ *and she doesn't bray like a jackass* (*The Adventures of Huckleberry Finn* by Mark Twain)

break VERB in order to train a horse you first have to break it ❑ *"If a high-mettled creature like this," said he, "can't be broken by fair means, she will never be good for anything"* (*Black Beauty* by Anna Sewell)

bullyragging VERB bullyragging is an old word which means bullying. To bullyrag someone is to threaten or force someone to do something they don't want to do ❑ *and a lot of loafers bullyragging him for sport* (*The Adventures of Huckleberry Finn* by Mark Twain)

but PREP except for (this) ❑ *but this, all pleasures fancies be* (*The Good-Morrow* by John Donne)

by hand PHRASE by hand was a common expression of the time meaning that baby had been fed either using a spoon or a bottle rather than by breast-feeding ❑ *My sister, Mrs. Joe Gargery, was more than twenty years older than I, and had established a great reputation with herself . . . because she had bought me up 'by hand'* (*Great Expectations* by Charles Dickens)

bye-spots NOUN bye-spots are lonely places ❑ *and bye-spots of tales rich with indigenous produce* (*The Prelude* by William Wordsworth)

calico NOUN calico is plain white fabric made from cotton ❑ *There was two old dirty calico dresses* (*The Adventures of Huckleberry Finn* by Mark Twain)

camp-fever NOUN camp-fever was another word for the disease typhus ❑ *during a severe camp-fever* (*Emma* by Jane Austen)

cant NOUN cant is insincere or empty talk ❑ *"Man," said the Ghost, "if man you be in heart, not adamant, forbear that wicked cant until you have discovered What the surplus is, and Where it is."* (*A Christmas Carol* by Charles Dickens)

canty ADJ canty means lively, full of life ❑ *My mother lived til eighty, a canty dame to the last* (*Wuthering Heights* by Emily Brontë)

canvas VERB to canvas is to discuss ❑ *We think so very differently on this point Mr Knightley, that there can be no use in canvassing it* (*Emma* by Jane Austen)

capital ADJ capital means excellent or extremely good ❑ *for it's capital, so shady, light, and big* (*Little Women* by Louisa May Alcott)

capstan NOUN a capstan is a device used on a ship to lift sails and anchors ❑ *capstans going, ships going out to sea, and unintelligible sea creatures* roaring curses over the bulwarks at respondent lightermen (*Great Expectations* by Charles Dickens)

case-bottle NOUN a square bottle designed to fit with others into a case ❑ *The spirit being set before him in a huge case-bottle, which had originally come out of some ship's locker* (*The Old Curiosity Shop* by Charles Dickens)

casement NOUN casement is a word meaning window. The teacher in Nicholas Nickleby misspells window showing what a bad teacher he is ❑ *W-i-n, win, d-e-r, der, winder, a casement.'* (*Nicholas Nickleby* by Charles Dickens)

cataleptic ADJ a cataleptic fit is one in which the victim goes into a trance-like state and remains still for a long time ❑ *It was at this point in their history that Silas's cataleptic fit occurred during the prayer-meeting* (*Silas Marner* by George Eliot)

cauldron NOUN a cauldron is a large cooking pot made of metal ❑ *stirring a large cauldron which seemed to be full of soup* (*Alice's Adventures in Wonderland* by Lewis Carroll)

cephalic ADJ cephalic means to do with the head ❑ *with ink composed of a cephalic tincture* (*Gulliver's Travels* by Jonathan Swift)

chaise and four NOUN a closed four-wheel carriage pulled by four horses ❑ *he came down on Monday in a chaise and four to see the place* (*Pride and Prejudice* by Jane Austen)

chamberlain NOUN the main servant in a household ❑ *In those times a bed was always to be got there at any hour of the night, and the chamberlain, letting me in at his ready wicket, lighted the candle next in order on his shelf* (*Great Expectations* by Charles Dickens)

characters NOUN distinguishing marks ❑ *Impressed upon all forms the characters* (*The Prelude* by William Wordsworth)

chary ADJ cautious ❑ *I should have been chary of discussing my guardian too freely even with her* (*Great Expectations* by Charles Dickens)

cherishes VERB here cherishes means cheers or brightens ❑ *some philosophic song of Truth that cherishes our daily life* (*The Prelude* by William Wordsworth)

chickens' meat PHRASE chickens' meat is an old term which means chickens' feed or food ❑ *I had shook a bag of chickens' meat out in that place* (*Robinson Crusoe* by Daniel Defoe)

chimeras NOUN a chimera is an unrealistic idea or a wish which is unlikely to be fulfilled ❑ *with many other wild impossible chimeras* (*Gulliver's Travels* by Jonathan Swift)

chines NOUN chine is a cut of meat that includes part or all of the backbone of the animal ❑ *and they found hams and chines uncut* (*Silas Marner* by George Eliot)

chits NOUN chits is a slang word which means girls ❑ *I hate affected, niminy-piminy chits!* (*Little Women* by Louisa May Alcott)

chopped VERB chopped means come suddenly or accidentally ❑ *if I had chopped upon them* (*Robinson Crusoe* by Daniel Defoe)

chute NOUN a narrow channel ❑ *One morning about day-break, I found a canoe and crossed over a chute to the main shore* (*The Adventures of Huckleberry Finn* by Mark Twain)

circumspection NOUN careful observation of events and circumstances; caution ❑ *I honour your circumspection* (*Pride and Prejudice* by Jane Austen)

clambered VERB clambered means to climb somewhere with difficulty, usually using your hands and your feet ❑ *he clambered up and down stairs* (*Treasure Island* by Robert Louis Stevenson)

clime NOUN climate ❑ *no season knows nor clime* (*The Sun Rising* by John Donne)

clinched VERB clenched ❑ *the tops whereof I could but just reach with my fist clinched* (*Gulliver's Travels* by Jonathan Swift)

close chair NOUN a close chair is a sedan chair, which is an covered chair which has room for one person. The sedan chair is carried on two poles by two men, one in front and one behind ❑ *persuaded even the Empress herself to let me hold her in her close chair* (*Gulliver's Travels* by Jonathan Swift)

clown NOUN clown here means peasant or person who lives off the land ❑ *In ancient days by emperor and clown* (*Ode on a Nightingale* by John Keats)

coalheaver NOUN a coalheaver loaded coal onto ships using a spade ❑ *Good, strong, wholesome medicine, as was given with great success to two Irish labourers and a coalheaver* (*Oliver Twist* by Charles Dickens)

coal-whippers NOUN men who worked at docks using machines to load coal onto ships ❑ *here, were colliers by the score and score, with the coalwhippers plunging off stages on deck* (*Great Expectations* by Charles Dickens)

cobweb NOUN a cobweb is the net which a spider makes for catching insects ❑ *the walls and ceilings were all hung round with cobwebs* (*Gulliver's Travels* by Jonathan Swift)

coddling VERB coddling means to treat someone too kindly or protect them too much ❑ *and I've been coddling the fellow as if I'd been his grandmother* (*Little Women* by Louisa May Alcott)

coil NOUN coil means noise or fuss or disturbance ❑ *What a coil is there?* (*Doctor Faustus 4.7* by Christopher Marlowe)

collared VERB to collar something is a slang term which means to capture. In this sentence, it means he stole it [the money] ❑ *he collared it* (*The Adventures of Huckleberry Finn* by Mark Twain)

colling VERB colling is an old word which means to embrace and kiss ❑ *and no clasping and colling at all* (*Tess of the D'Urbervilles* by Thomas Hardy)

colloquies NOUN colloquy is a formal conversation or dialogue ❑ *Such colloquies have occupied many a pair of pale-faced weavers* (*Silas Marner* by George Eliot)

comfit NOUN sugar-covered pieces of fruit or nut eaten as sweets ❑ *and pulled out a box of comfits* (*Alice's Adventures in Wonderland* by Lewis Carroll)

coming out VERB when a girl came out in society it meant she was of marriageable age. In order to 'come out' girls were expecting to attend balls and other parties during a season ❑ *The younger girls formed hopes of coming out a year or two sooner than they might otherwise have done* (*Pride and Prejudice* by Jane Austen)

commit VERB commit means arrest or stop ❑ *Commit the rascals* (*Doctor Faustus 4.7* by Christopher Marlowe)

commodious ADJ commodious means convenient ❑ *the most commodious and effectual ways* (*Gulliver's Travels* by Jonathan Swift)

commons NOUN commons is an old term meaning food shared with others ❑ *his pauper assistants ranged themselves behind him; the gruel was served out; and a long grace was said over the short commons.* (*Oliver Twist* by Charles Dickens)

complacency NOUN here complacency means a desire to please others. Today complacency means feeling pleased with oneself without good reason. ❑ *Twas thy power that raised the first complacency in me* (*The Prelude* by William Wordsworth)

complaisance NOUN complaisance was eagerness to please ❑ *we cannot wonder at his complaisance* (*Pride and Prejudice* by Jane Austen)

complaisant ADJ complaisant means polite ❑ *extremely cheerful and complaisant to their guest* (*Gulliver's Travels* by Jonathan Swift)

conning VERB conning means learning by heart ❑ *Or conning more* (*The Prelude* by William Wordsworth)

consequent NOUN consequence ❑ *as avarice is the necessary consequent of old age* (*Gulliver's Travels* by Jonathan Swift)

consorts NOUN concerts ❑ *The King, who delighted in music, had frequent consorts at Court* (*Gulliver's Travels* by Jonathan Swift)

conversible ADJ conversible meant easy to talk to, companionably ❑ *He can be a conversible companion* (*Pride and Prejudice* by Jane Austen)

copper NOUN a copper is a large pot that can be heated directly over a fire ❑ *He gazed in stupefied astonishment on the small rebel for some seconds, and then clung for support to the copper* (*Oliver Twist* by Charles Dickens)

copper-stick NOUN a copper-stick is the long piece of wood used to stir washing in the copper (or boiler) which was usually the biggest cooking pot in the house ❑ *It was Christmas Eve, and I had to stir the pudding for next day, with a copper-stick, from seven to eight by the Dutch clock* (*Great Expectations* by Charles Dickens)

counting-house NOUN a counting house is a place where accountants work ❑ *Once upon a time – of all the good days in the year, on Christmas Eve – old Scrooge sat busy in his countinghouse* (*A Christmas Carol* by Charles Dickens)

courtier NOUN a courtier is someone who attends the king or queen – a member of the court ❑ *next the ten courtiers;* (*Alice's Adventures in Wonderland* by Lewis Carroll)

covies NOUN covies were flocks of partridges ❑ *and will save all of the best covies for you* (*Pride and Prejudice* by Jane Austen)

cowed VERB cowed means frightened or intimidated ❑ *it cowed me more than the pain* (*Treasure Island* by Robert Louis Stevenson)

cozened VERB cozened means tricked or deceived ❑ *Do you remember, sir, how you cozened me* (*Doctor Faustus* 4.7 by Christopher Marlowe)

cravats NOUN a cravat is a folded cloth that a man wears wrapped around his neck as a decorative item of clothing ❑ *we'd'a' slept in our cravats to-night* (*The Adventures of Huckleberry Finn* by Mark Twain)

crock and dirt PHRASE crock and dirt is an old expression meaning soot and dirt ❑ *and the mare catching cold at the door, and the boy grimed with crock and dirt* (*Great Expectations* by Charles Dickens)

crockery NOUN here crockery means pottery ❑ *By one of the parrots was a cat made of crockery* (*The Adventures of Huckleberry Finn* by Mark Twain)

crooked sixpence PHRASE it was considered unlucky to have a bent sixpence ❑ *You've got the beauty, you see, and I've got the luck, so you must keep me by you for your crooked sixpence* (*Silas Marner* by George Eliot)

croquet NOUN croquet is a traditional English summer game in which players try to hit wooden balls through hoops ❑ *and once she remembered trying to box her own ears for having cheated herself in a game of croquet* (*Alice's Adventures in Wonderland* by Lewis Carroll)

cross PREP across ❑ *The two great streets, which run cross and divide it into four quarters* (*Gulliver's Travels* by Jonathan Swift)

culpable ADJ if you are culpable for something it means you are to blame ❏ *deep are the sorrows that spring from false ideas for which no man is culpable.* (*Silas Marner* by George Eliot)

cultured ADJ cultivated ❏ *Nor less when spring had warmed the cultured Vale* (*The Prelude* by William Wordsworth)

cupidity NOUN cupidity is greed ❏ *These people hated me with the hatred of cupidity and disappointment.* (*Great Expectations* by Charles Dickens)

curricle NOUN an open two-wheeled carriage with one seat for the driver and space for a single passenger ❏ *and they saw a lady and a gentleman in a curricle* (*Pride and Prejudice* by Jane Austen)

cynosure NOUN a cynosure is something that strongly attracts attention or admiration ❏ *Then I thought of Eliza and Georgiana; I beheld one the cynosure of a ballroom, the other the inmate of a convent cell* (*Jane Eyre* by Charlotte Brontë)

dalliance NOUN someone's dalliance with something is a brief involvement with it ❏ *nor sporting in the dalliance of love* (*Doctor Faustus Chorus* by Christopher Marlowe)

darkling ADV darkling is an archaic way of saying in the dark ❏ *Darkling I listen* (*Ode on a Nightingale* by John Keats)

delf-case NOUN a sideboard for holding dishes and crockery ❏ *at the pewter dishes and delf-case* (*Wuthering Heights* by Emily Brontë)

determined ■ VERB here determined means ended ❏ *and be out of vogue when that was determined* (*Gulliver's Travels* by Jonathan Swift) ■ VERB determined can mean to have been learned or found especially by investigation or experience ❏ *All the sensitive feelings it wounded so cruelly, all the shame and misery it kept alive within my breast, became more poignant as I thought of this; and I determined that the life was unendurable* (*David Copperfield* by Charles Dickens)

Deuce NOUN a slang term for the Devil ❏ *Ah, I dare say I did. Deuce take me, he added suddenly, I know I did. I find I am not quite unscrewed yet.* (*Great Expectations* by Charles Dickens)

diabolical ADJ diabolical means devilish or evil ❏ *and with a thousand diabolical expressions* (*Treasure Island* by Robert Louis Stevenson)

direction NOUN here direction means address ❏ *Elizabeth was not surprised at it, as Jane had written the direction remarkably ill* (*Pride and Prejudice* by Jane Austen)

discover VERB to make known or announce ❏ *the Emperor would discover the secret while I was out of his power* (*Gulliver's Travels* by Jonathan Swift)

dissemble VERB hide or conceal ❏ *Dissemble nothing* (*On His Mistress* by John Donne)

dissolve VERB dissolve here means to release from life, to die ❏ *Fade far away, dissolve, and quite forget* (*Ode on a Nightingale* by John Keats)

distrain VERB to distrain is to seize the property of someone who is in debt in compensation for the money owed ❏ *for he's threatening to distrain for it* (*Silas Marner* by George Eliot)

Divan NOUN a Divan was originally a Turkish council of state – the name was transferred to the couches they sat on and is used to mean this in English ❏ *Mr Brass applauded this picture very much, and the bed being soft and comfortable, Mr Quilp determined to use it, both as a sleeping place by night and as a kind of Divan by day.* (*The Old Curiosity Shop* by Charles Dickens)

divorcement NOUN separation ❏ *By all pains which want and* divorcement hath (*On His Mistress* by John Donne)

dog in the manger, PHRASE this phrase describes someone who prevents you from enjoying something that they themselves have no need for ❑ *You are a dog in the manger, Cathy, and desire no one to be loved but yourself* (*Wuthering Heights* by Emily Brontë)

dolorifuge NOUN dolorifuge is a word which Thomas Hardy invented. It means pain-killer or comfort ❑ *as a species of dolorifuge* (*Tess of the D'Urbervilles* by Thomas Hardy)

dome NOUN building ❑ *that river and that mouldering dome* (*The Prelude* by William Wordsworth)

domestic PHRASE here domestic means a person's management of the house ❑ *to give some account of my domestic* (*Gulliver's Travels* by Jonathan Swift)

dunce NOUN a dunce is another word for idiot ❑ *Do you take me for a dunce? Go on?* (*Alice's Adventures in Wonderland* by Lewis Carroll)

Ecod EXCLAM a slang exclamation meaning 'oh God!' ❑ *"Ecod," replied Wemmick, shaking his head, "that's not my trade."* (*Great Expectations* by Charles Dickens)

egg-hot NOUN an egg-hot (see also 'flip' and 'negus') was a hot drink made from beer and eggs, sweetened with nutmeg ❑ *She fainted when she saw me return, and made a little jug of egg-hot afterwards to console us while we talked it over.* (*David Copperfield* by Charles Dickens)

encores NOUN an encore is a short extra performance at the end of a longer one, which the entertainer gives because the audience has enthusiastically asked for it ❑ *we want a little something to answer encores with, anyway* (*The Adventures of Huckleberry Finn* by Mark Twain)

equipage NOUN an elegant and impressive carriage ❑ *and besides, the equipage did not answer to any of*

their neighbours (*Pride and Prejudice* by Jane Austen)

exordium NOUN an exordium is the opening part of a speech ❑ *"Now, Handel," as if it were the grave beginning of a portentous business exordium, he had suddenly given up that tone* (*Great Expectations* by Charles Dickens)

expect VERB here expect means to wait for ❑ *to expect his farther commands* (*Gulliver's Travels* by Jonathan Swift)

familiars NOUN familiars means spirits or devils who come to someone when they are called ❑ *I'll turn all the lice about thee into familiars* (*Doctor Faustus* 1.4 by Christopher Marlowe)

fantods NOUN a fantod is a person who fidgets or can't stop moving nervously ❑ *It most give me the fantods* (*The Adventures of Huckleberry Finn* by Mark Twain)

farthing NOUN a farthing is an old unit of British currency which was worth a quarter of a penny ❑ *Not a farthing less. A great many back-payments are included in it, I assure you.* (*A Christmas Carol* by Charles Dickens)

farthingale NOUN a hoop worn under a skirt to extend it ❑ *A bell with an old voice – which I dare say in its time had often said to the house, Here is the green farthingale* (*Great Expectations* by Charles Dickens)

favours NOUN here favours is an old word which means ribbons ❑ *A group of humble mourners entered the gate: wearing white favours* (*Oliver Twist* by Charles Dickens)

feigned VERB pretend or pretending ❑ *not my feigned page* (*On His Mistress* by John Donne)

fence ■ NOUN a fence is someone who receives and sells stolen goods ❑ *What are you up to? Ill-treating the boys, you covetous, avaricious, in-sa-ti-a-ble old fence?* (*Oliver Twist* by

Charles Dickens) ■ NOUN defence or protection ❑ *but honesty hath no fence against superior cunning* (*Gulliver's Travels* by Jonathan Swift)

fess ADJ fess is an old word which means pleased or proud ❑ *You'll be fess enough, my poppet* (*Tess of the D'Urbervilles* by Thomas Hardy)

fettered ADJ fettered means bound in chains or chained ❑ *"You are fettered," said Scrooge, trembling. "Tell me why?"* (*A Christmas Carol* by Charles Dickens)

fidges VERB fidges means fidgets, which is to keep moving your hands slightly because you are nervous or excited ❑ *Look, Jim, how my fingers fidges* (*Treasure Island* by Robert Louis Stevenson)

finger-post NOUN a finger-post is a sign-post showing the direction to different places ❑ *"The gallows," continued Fagin, "the gallows, my dear, is an ugly finger-post, which points out a very short and sharp turning that has stopped many a bold fellow's career on the broad highway."* (*Oliver Twist* by Charles Dickens)

fire-irons NOUN fire-irons are tools kept by the side of the fire to either cook with or look after the fire ❑ *the fire-irons came first* (*Alice's Adventures in Wonderland* by Lewis Carroll)

fire-plug NOUN a fire-plug is another word for a fire hydrant ❑ *The pony looked with great attention into a fire-plug, which was near him, and appeared to be quite absorbed in contemplating it* (*The Old Curiosity Shop* by Charles Dickens)

flank NOUN flank is the side of an animal ❑ *And all her silken flanks with garlands dressed* (*Ode on a Grecian Urn* by John Keats)

flip NOUN a flip is a drink made from warmed ale, sugar, spice and beaten egg ❑ *The events of the day, in combination with the twins, if not with the flip, had made Mrs. Micawber hysterical, and she shed tears as she replied* (*David Copperfield* by Charles Dickens)

flit VERB flit means to move quickly ❑ *and if he had meant to flit to Thrushcross Grange* (*Wuthering Heights* by Emily Brontë)

floorcloth NOUN a floorcloth was a hard-wearing piece of canvas used instead of carpet ❑ *This avenging phantom was ordered to be on duty at eight on Tuesday morning in the hall (it was two feet square, as charged for floorcloth)* (*Great Expectations* by Charles Dickens)

fly-driver NOUN a fly-driver is a carriage drawn by a single horse ❑ *The fly-drivers, among whom I inquired next, were equally jocose and equally disrespectful* (*David Copperfield* by Charles Dickens)

fob NOUN a small pocket in which a watch is kept ❑ *"Certain," replied the man, drawing a gold watch from his fob* (*Oliver Twist* by Charles Dickens)

folly NOUN folly means foolishness or stupidity ❑ *the folly of beginning a work* (*Robinson Crusoe* by Daniel Defoe)

fond ADJ fond means foolish ❑ *Fond worldling* (*Doctor Faustus 5.2* by Christopher Marlowe)

fondness NOUN silly or foolish affection ❑ *They have no fondness for their colts or foals* (*Gulliver's Travels* by Jonathan Swift)

for his fancy PHRASE for his fancy means for his liking or as he wanted ❑ *and as I did not obey quick enough for his fancy* (*Treasure Island* by Robert Louis Stevenson)

forlorn ADJ lost or very upset ❑ *you are from that day forlorn* (*Gulliver's Travels* by Jonathan Swift)

foster-sister NOUN a foster-sister was someone brought up by the same nurse or in the same household ❑ *I had been his foster-sister* (*Wuthering Heights* by Emily Brontë)

fox-fire NOUN fox-fire is a weak glow that is given off by decaying, rotten wood ❑ *what we must have was a lot of them rotten chunks* *that's called fox-fire (The Adventures of Huckleberry Finn by Mark Twain)*

frozen sea PHRASE the Arctic Ocean ❑ *into the frozen sea (Gulliver's Travels by Jonathan Swift)*

gainsay VERB to gainsay something is to say it isn't true or to deny it ❑ *"So she had," cried Scrooge. "You're right. I'll not gainsay it, Spirit. God forbid!" (A Christmas Carol by Charles Dickens)*

gaiters NOUN gaiters were leggings made of a cloth or piece of leather which covered the leg from the knee to the ankle ❑ *Mr Knightley was hard at work upon the lower buttons of his thick leather gaiters (Emma by Jane Austen)*

galluses NOUN galluses is an old spelling of gallows, and here means suspenders. Suspenders are straps worn over someone's shoulders and fastened to their trousers to prevent the trousers falling down ❑ *and home-knit galluses (The Adventures of Huckleberry Finn by Mark Twain)*

galoot NOUN a sailor but also a clumsy person ❑ *and maybe a galoot on it chopping (The Adventures of Huckleberry Finn by Mark Twain)*

gayest ADJ gayest means the most lively and bright or merry ❑ *Beth played her gayest march (Little Women by Louisa May Alcott)*

gem NOUN here gem means jewellery ❑ *the mountain shook off turf and flower, had only heath for raiment and crag for gem (Jane Eyre by Charlotte Brontë)*

giddy ADJ giddy means dizzy ❑ *and I wish you wouldn't keep appearing and vanishing so suddenly; you make one quite giddy. (Alice's Adventures in Wonderland by Lewis Carroll)*

gig NOUN a light two-wheeled carriage ❑ *when a gig drove up to the garden gate: out of which there jumped a fat gentleman (Oliver Twist by Charles Dickens)*

gladsome ADJ gladsome is an old word meaning glad or happy ❑ *Nobody ever stopped him in the street to say, with gladsome looks (A Christmas Carol by Charles Dickens)*

glen NOUN a glen is a small valley; the word is used commonly in Scotland ❑ *a beck which follows the bend of the glen (Wuthering Heights by Emily Brontë)*

gravelled VERB gravelled is an old term which means to baffle or defeat someone ❑ *Gravelled the pastors of the German Church (Doctor Faustus 1.1 by Christopher Marlowe)*

grinder NOUN a grinder was a private tutor ❑ *but that when he had had the happiness of marrying Mrs Pocket very early in his life, he had impaired his prospects and taken up the calling of a Grinder (Great Expectations by Charles Dickens)*

gruel NOUN gruel is a thin, watery corn-meal or oatmeal soup ❑ *and the little saucepan of gruel (Scrooge had a cold in his head) upon the hob. (A Christmas Carol by Charles Dickens)*

guinea, half a NOUN a half guinea was ten shillings and sixpence ❑ *but lay out half a guinea at Ford's (Emma by Jane Austen)*

gull VERB gull is an old term which means to fool or deceive someone ❑ *Hush, I'll gull him supernaturally (Doctor Faustus 3.4 by Christopher Marlowe)*

gunnel NOUN the gunnel, or gunwhale, is the upper edge of a boat's side ❑ *But he put his foot on the gunnel and rocked her (The Adventures of Huckleberry Finn by Mark Twain)*

gunwale NOUN the side of a ship ❑ *He dipped his hand in the water over the boat's gunwale (Great Expectations by Charles Dickens)*

Gytrash NOUN a Gytrash is an omen of misfortune to the superstitious, usually taking the form of a hound ❑ *I remembered certain of Bessie's tales, wherein figured a*

North-of-England spirit, called a 'Gytrash' (*Jane Eyre* by Charlotte Brontë)

hackney-cabriolet NOUN a two-wheeled carriage with four seats for hire and pulled by a horse ❏ *A hackney-cabriolet was in waiting; with the same vehemence which she had exhibited in addressing Oliver, the girl pulled him in with her, and drew the curtains close.* (*Oliver Twist* by Charles Dickens)

hackney-coach NOUN a four-wheeled horse-drawn vehicle for hire ❏ *The twilight was beginning to close in, when Mr. Brownlow alighted from a hackney-coach at his own door, and knocked softly.* (*Oliver Twist* by Charles Dickens)

haggler NOUN a haggler is someone who travels from place to place selling small goods and items ❏ *when I be plain Jack Durbeyfield, the haggler* (*Tess of the D'Urbervilles* by Thomas Hardy)

halter NOUN a halter is a rope or strap used to lead an animal or to tie it up ❏ *I had of course long been used to a halter and a headstall* (*Black Beauty* by Anna Sewell)

hamlet NOUN a hamlet is a small village or a group of houses in the countryside ❏ *down from the hamlet* (*Treasure Island* by Robert Louis Stevenson)

hand-barrow NOUN a hand-barrow is a device for carrying heavy objects. It is like a wheelbarrow except that it has handles, rather than wheels, for moving the barrow ❏ *his sea chest following behind him in a hand-barrow* (*Treasure Island* by Robert Louis Stevenson)

handspike NOUN a handspike was a stick which was used as a lever ❏ *a bit of stick like a handspike* (*Treasure Island* by Robert Louis Stevenson)

haply ADV haply means by chance or perhaps ❏ *And haply the Queen-Moon is on her throne* (*Ode on a Nightingale* by John Keats)

harem NOUN the harem was the part of the house where the women lived ❏ *mostly they hang round the harem* (*The Adventures of Huckleberry Finn* by Mark Twain)

hautboys NOUN hautboys are oboes ❏ *sausages and puddings resembling flutes and hautboys* (*Gulliver's Travels* by Jonathan Swift)

hawker NOUN a hawker is someone who sells goods to people as he travels rather than from a fixed place like a shop ❏ *to buy some stockings from a hawker* (*Treasure Island* by Robert Louis Stevenson)

hawser NOUN a hawser is a rope used to tie up or tow a ship or boat ❏ *Again among the tiers of shipping, in and out, avoiding rusty chain-cables, frayed hempen hawsers* (*Great Expectations* by Charles Dickens)

headstall NOUN the headstall is the part of the bridle or halter that goes around a horse's head ❏ *I had of course long been used to a halter and a headstall* (*Black Beauty* by Anna Sewell)

hearken VERB hearken means to listen ❏ *though we sometimes stopped to lay hold of each other and hearken* (*Treasure Island* by Robert Louis Stevenson)

heartless ADJ here heartless means without heart or dejected ❏ *I am not heartless* (*The Prelude* by William Wordsworth)

hebdomadal ADJ hebdomadal means weekly ❏ *It was the hebdomadal treat to which we all looked forward from Sabbath to Sabbath* (*Jane Eyre* by Charlotte Brontë)

highwaymen NOUN highwaymen were people who stopped travellers and robbed them ❏ *We are highwaymen* (*The Adventures of Huckleberry Finn* by Mark Twain)

hinds NOUN hinds means farm hands, or people who work on a farm ❏ *He called his hinds about him* (*Gulliver's Travels* by Jonathan Swift)

histrionic ADJ if you refer to someone's behaviour as histrionic, you are being critical of it because it is dramatic and exaggerated ❑ *But the histrionic muse is the darling* (*The Adventures of Huckleberry Finn* by Mark Twain)

hogs NOUN hogs is another word for pigs ❑ *Tom called the hogs 'ingots'* (*The Adventures of Huckleberry Finn* by Mark Twain)

horrors NOUN the horrors are a fit, called delirium tremens, which is caused by drinking too much alcohol ❑ *I'll have the horrors* (*Treasure Island* by Robert Louis Stevenson)

huffy ADJ huffy means to be obviously annoyed or offended about something ❑ *They will feel that more than angry speeches or huffy actions* (*Little Women* by Louisa May Alcott)

hulks NOUN hulks were prison-ships ❑ *The miserable companion of thieves and ruffians, the fallen outcast of low haunts, the associate of the scourings of the jails and hulks* (*Oliver Twist* by Charles Dickens)

humbug NOUN humbug means nonsense or rubbish ❑ *"Bah," said Scrooge. "Humbug!"* (*A Christmas Carol* by Charles Dickens)

humours NOUN it was believed that there were four fluids in the body called humours which decided the temperament of a person depending on how much of each fluid was present ❑ *other peccant humours* (*Gulliver's Travels* by Jonathan Swift)

husbandry NOUN husbandry is farming animals ❑ *bad husbandry were plentifully anointing their wheels* (*Silas Marner* by George Eliot)

huswife NOUN a huswife was a small sewing kit ❑ *but I had put my huswife on it* (*Emma* by Jane Austen)

ideal ADJ ideal in this context means imaginary ❑ *I discovered the yell was not ideal* (*Wuthering Heights* by Emily Brontë)

If our two PHRASE if both our ❑ *If our two loves be one* (*The Good-Morrow* by John Donne)

ignis-fatuus NOUN ignis-fatuus is the light given out by burning marsh gases, which lead careless travellers into danger ❑ *it is madness in all women to let a secret love kindle within them, which, if unreturned and unknown, must devour the life that feeds it; and, if discovered and responded to, must lead ignis-fatuus-like, into miry wilds whence there is no extrication.* (*Jane Eyre* by Charlotte Brontë)

imaginations NOUN here imaginations means schemes or plans ❑ *soon drove out those imaginations* (*Gulliver's Travels* by Jonathan Swift)

impressible ADJ impressible means open or impressionable ❑ *for Marner had one of those impressible, self-doubting natures* (*Silas Marner* by George Eliot)

in good intelligence PHRASE friendly with each other ❑ *that these two persons were in good intelligence with each other* (*Gulliver's Travels* by Jonathan Swift)

inanity NOUN inanity is sillyness or dull stupidity ❑ *Do we not wile away moments of inanity* (*Silas Marner* by George Eliot)

incivility NOUN incivility means rudeness or impoliteness ❑ *if it's only for a piece of incivility like to-night's* (*Treasure Island* by Robert Louis Stevenson)

indigenae NOUN indigenae means natives or people from that area ❑ *an exotic that the surly indigenae will not recognise for kin* (*Wuthering Heights* by Emily Brontë)

indocible ADJ unteachable ❑ *so they were the most restive and indocible* (*Gulliver's Travels* by Jonathan Swift)

ingenuity NOUN inventiveness ❑ *entreated me to give him something as an encouragement to ingenuity*

(*Gulliver's Travels* by Jonathan Swift)

ingots NOUN an ingot is a lump of a valuable metal like gold, usually shaped like a brick ❏ *Tom called the hogs 'ingots'* (*The Adventures of Huckleberry Finn* by Mark Twain)

inkstand NOUN an inkstand is a pot which was put on a desk to contain either ink or pencils and pens ❏ *throwing an inkstand at the Lizard as she spoke* (*Alice's Adventures in Wonderland* by Lewis Carroll)

inordinate ADJ without order. Today inordinate means 'excessive'. ❏ *Though yet untutored and inordinate* (*The Prelude* by William Wordsworth)

intellectuals NOUN here intellectuals means the minds (of the workmen) ❏ *those instructions they give being too refined for the intellectuals of their workmen* (*Gulliver's Travels* by Jonathan Swift)

interview NOUN meeting ❏ *By our first strange and fatal interview* (*On His Mistress* by John Donne)

jacks NOUN jacks are rods for turning a spit over a fire ❏ *It was a small bit of pork suspended from the kettle hanger by a string passed through a large door key, in a way known to primitive housekeepers unpossessed of jacks* (*Silas Marner* by George Eliot)

jews-harp NOUN a jews-harp is a small, metal, musical instrument that is played by the mouth ❏ *A jews-harp's plenty good enough for a rat* (*The Adventures of Huckleberry Finn* by Mark Twain)

jorum NOUN a large bowl ❏ *while Miss Skiffins brewed such a jorum of tea, that the pig in the back premises became strongly excited* (*Great Expectations* by Charles Dickens)

jostled VERB jostled means bumped or pushed by someone or some people ❏ *being jostled himself into the kennel* (*Gulliver's Travels* by Jonathan Swift)

keepsake NOUN a keepsake is a gift which reminds someone of an event or of the person who gave it to them. ❏ *books and ornaments they had in their boudoirs at home: keepsakes that different relations had presented to them* (*Jane Eyre* by Charlotte Brontë)

kenned VERB kenned means knew ❏ *though little kenned the lamplighter that he had any company but Christmas!* (*A Christmas Carol* by Charles Dickens)

kennel NOUN kennel means gutter, which is the edge of a road next to the pavement, where rain water collects and flows away ❏ *being jostled himself into the kennel* (*Gulliver's Travels* by Jonathan Swift)

knock-knee ADJ knock-knee means slanted, at an angle. ❏ *LOT 1 was marked in whitewashed knock-knee letters on the brewhouse* (*Great Expectations* by Charles Dickens)

ladylike ADJ to be ladylike is to behave in a polite, dignified and graceful way ❏ *No, winking isn't ladylike* (*Little Women* by Louisa May Alcott)

lapse NOUN flow ❏ *Stealing with silent lapse to join the brook* (*The Prelude* by William Wordsworth)

larry NOUN larry is an old word which means commotion or noisy celebration ❏ *That was all a part of the larry!* (*Tess of the D'Urbervilles* by Thomas Hardy)

laths NOUN laths are strips of wood ❏ *The panels shrunk, the windows cracked; fragments of plaster fell out of the ceiling, and the naked laths were shown instead* (*A Christmas Carol* by Charles Dickens)

leer NOUN a leer is an unpleasant smile ❏ *with a kind of leer* (*Treasure Island* by Robert Louis Stevenson)

lenitives NOUN these are different kinds of drugs or medicines: lenitives and palliatives were pain relievers; aperitives were laxatives;

abstersives caused vomiting; corrosives destroyed human tissue; restringents caused constipation; cephalalgics stopped headaches; icterics were used as medicine for jaundice; apophlegmatics were cough medicine, and acoustics were cures for the loss of hearing ❑ *lenitives, aperitives, abstersives, corrosives, restringents, palliatives, laxatives, cephalalgics, icterics, apophlegmatics, acoustics* (*Gulliver's Travels* by Jonathan Swift)

lest CONJ in case. If you do something lest something (usually) unpleasant happens you do it to try to prevent it happening ❑ *She went in without knocking, and hurried upstairs, in great fear lest she should meet the real Mary Ann* (*Alice's Adventures in Wonderland* by Lewis Carroll)

levee NOUN a levee is an old term for a meeting held in the morning, shortly after the person holding the meeting has got out of bed ❑ *I used to attend the King's levee once or twice a week* (*Gulliver's Travels* by Jonathan Swift)

life-preserver NOUN a club which had lead inside it to make it heavier and therefore more dangerous ❑ *and with no more suspicious articles displayed to view than two or three heavy bludgeons which stood in a corner, and a 'life-preserver' that hung over the chimney-piece.* (*Oliver Twist* by Charles Dickens)

lighterman NOUN a lighterman is another word for sailor ❑ *in and out, hammers going in ship-builders' yards, saws going at timber, clashing engines going at things unknown, pumps going in leaky ships, capstans going, ships going out to sea, and unintelligible sea creatures roaring curses over the bulwarks at respondent lightermen* (*Great Expectations* by Charles Dickens)

livery NOUN servants often wore a uniform known as a livery ❑ *suddenly a footman in livery came running out of the wood* (*Alice's Adventures in Wonderland* by Lewis Carroll)

livid ADJ livid means pale or ash coloured. Livid also means very angry ❑ *a dirty, livid white* (*Treasure Island* by Robert Louis Stevenson)

lottery-tickets NOUN a popular card game ❑ *and Mrs. Philips protested that they would have a nice comfortable noisy game of lottery tickets* (*Pride and Prejudice* by Jane Austen)

lower and upper world PHRASE the earth and the heavens are the lower and upper worlds ❑ *the changes in the lower and upper world* (*Gulliver's Travels* by Jonathan Swift)

lustres NOUN lustres are chandeliers. A chandelier is a large, decorative frame which holds light bulbs or candles and hangs from the ceiling ❑ *the lustres, lights, the carving and the guilding* (*The Prelude* by William Wordsworth)

lynched VERB killed without a criminal trial by a crowd of people ❑ *He'll never know how nigh he come to getting lynched* (*The Adventures of Huckleberry Finn* by Mark Twain)

malingering VERB if someone is malingering they are pretending to be ill to avoid working ❑ *And you stand there malingering* (*Treasure Island* by Robert Louis Stevenson)

managing PHRASE treating with consideration ❑ *to think the honour of my own kind not worth managing* (*Gulliver's Travels* by Jonathan Swift)

manhood PHRASE manhood means human nature ❑ *concerning the nature of manhood* (*Gulliver's Travels* by Jonathan Swift)

man-trap NOUN a man-trap is a set of steel jaws that snap shut when trodden on and trap a person's leg ❑ *"Don't go to him," I called out of the window, "he's an assassin! A* man-trap!" (*Oliver Twist* by Charles Dickens)

maps NOUN charts of the night sky ❑ *Let maps to others, worlds on worlds have shown* (*The Good-Morrow* by John Donne)

mark VERB look at or notice ❑ *Mark but this flea, and mark in this* (*The Flea* by John Donne)

maroons NOUN A maroon is someone who has been left in a place which it is difficult for them to escape from, like a small island ❑ *if schooners, islands, and maroons* (*Treasure Island* by Robert Louis Stevenson)

mast NOUN here mast means the fruit of forest trees ❑ *a quantity of acorns, dates, chestnuts, and other mast* (*Gulliver's Travels* by Jonathan Swift)

mate VERB defeat ❑ *Where Mars did mate the warlike Carthigens* (*Doctor Faustus Chorus* by Christopher Marlowe)

mealy ADJ Mealy when used to describe a face meant palid, pale or colourless ❑ *I only know two sorts of boys. Mealy boys, and beef-faced boys* (*Oliver Twist* by Charles Dickens)

middling ADJ fairly or moderately ❑ *she worked me middling hard for about an hour* (*The Adventures of Huckleberry Finn* by Mark Twain)

mill NOUN a mill, or treadmill, was a device for hard labour or punishment in prison ❑ *Was you never on the mill?* (*Oliver Twist* by Charles Dickens)

milliner's shop NOUN a milliner's sold fabrics, clothing, lace and accessories; as time went on they specialized more and more in hats ❑ *to pay their duty to their aunt and to a milliner's shop just over the way* (*Pride and Prejudice* by Jane Austen)

minching un' munching PHRASE how people in the north of England used to describe the way people from the south speak ❑ *Minching*

un' munching! (*Wuthering Heights* by Emily Brontë)

mine NOUN gold ❑ *Whether both th'Indias of spice and mine* (*The Sun Rising* by John Donne)

mire NOUN mud ❑ *Tis my fate to be always ground into the mire under the iron heel of oppression* (*The Adventures of Huckleberry Finn* by Mark Twain)

miscellany NOUN a miscellany is a collection of many different kinds of things ❑ *under that, the miscellany began* (*Treasure Island* by Robert Louis Stevenson)

mistarshers NOUN mistarshers means moustache, which is the hair that grows on a man's upper lip ❑ *when he put his hand up to his mistarshers* (*Tess of the D'Urbervilles* by Thomas Hardy)

morrow NOUN here good-morrow means tomorrow and a new and better life ❑ *And now good-morrow to our waking souls* (*The Good-Morrow* by John Donne)

mortification NOUN mortification is an old word for gangrene which is when part of the body decays or 'dies' because of disease ❑ *Yes, it was a mortification – that was it* (*The Adventures of Huckleberry Finn* by Mark Twain)

mought PARTICIPLE mought is an old spelling of might ❑ *what you mought call me? You mought call me captain* (*Treasure Island* by Robert Louis Stevenson)

move VERB move me not means do not make me angry ❑ *Move me not, Faustus* (*Doctor Faustus 2.1* by Christopher Marlowe)

muffin-cap NOUN a muffin cap is a flat cap made from wool ❑ *the old one, remained stationary in the muffin-cap and leathers* (*Oliver Twist* by Charles Dickens)

mulatter NOUN a mulatter was another word for mulatto, which is a person with parents who are from different races ❑ *a mulatter, most as white as* a white man (*The Adventures of Huckleberry Finn* by Mark Twain)

mummery NOUN mummery is an old word that meant meaningless (or pretentious) ceremony ❑ *When they were all gone, and when Trabb and his men – but not his boy: I looked for him – had crammed their mummery into bags, and were gone too, the house felt wholesomer.* (*Great Expectations* by Charles Dickens)

nap NOUN the nap is the woolly surface on a new item of clothing. Here the surface has been worn away so it looks bare ❑ *like an old hat with the nap rubbed off* (*The Adventures of Huckleberry Finn* by Mark Twain)

natural ■ NOUN a natural is a person born with learning difficulties ❑ *though he had been left to his particular care by their deceased father, who thought him almost a natural.* (*David Copperfield* by Charles Dickens) ■ ADJ natural meant illegitimate ❑ *Harriet Smith was the natural daughter of somebody* (*Emma* by Jane Austen)

navigator NOUN a navigator was originally someone employed to dig canals. It is the origin of the word 'navvy' meaning a labourer ❑ *She ascertained from me in a few words what it was all about, comforted Dora, and gradually convinced her that I was not a labourer – from my manner of stating the case I believe Dora concluded that I was a navigator, and went balancing myself up and down a plank all day with a wheelbarrow – and so brought us together in peace.* (*David Copperfield* by Charles Dickens)

necromancy NOUN necromancy means a kind of magic where the magician speaks to spirits or ghosts to find out what will happen in the future ❑ *He surfeits upon cursed necromancy* (*Doctor Faustus chorus* by Christopher Marlowe)

negus NOUN a negus is a hot drink made from sweetened wine and

water ❑ *He sat placidly perusing the newspaper, with his little head on one side, and a glass of warm sherry negus at his elbow.* (*David Copperfield* by Charles Dickens)

nice ADJ discriminating. Able to make good judgements or choices ❑ *consequently a claim to be nice* (*Emma* by Jane Austen)

nigh ADV nigh means near ❑ *He'll never know how nigh he come to getting lynched* (*The Adventures of Huckleberry Finn* by Mark Twain)

nimbleness NOUN nimbleness means being able to move very quickly or skillfully ❑ *and with incredible accuracy and nimbleness* (*Treasure Island* by Robert Louis Stevenson)

noggin NOUN a noggin is a small mug or a wooden cup ❑ *you'll bring me one noggin of rum* (*Treasure Island* by Robert Louis Stevenson)

none ADJ neither ❑ *none can die* (*The Good-Morrow* by John Donne)

notices NOUN observations ❑ *Arch are his notices* (*The Prelude* by William Wordsworth)

occiput NOUN occiput means the back of the head ❑ *saw off the occiput of each couple* (*Gulliver's Travels* by Jonathan Swift)

officiously ADJ kindly ❑ *the governess who attended Glumdalclitch very officiously lifted me up* (*Gulliver's Travels* by Jonathan Swift)

old salt PHRASE old salt is a slang term for an experienced sailor ❑ *a 'true sea-dog', and a 'real old salt'* (*Treasure Island* by Robert Louis Stevenson)

or ere PHRASE before ❑ *or ere the Hall was built* (*The Prelude* by William Wordsworth)

ostler NOUN one who looks after horses at an inn ❑ *The bill paid, and the waiter remembered, and the ostler not forgotten, and the chambermaid taken into consideration* (*Great Expectations* by Charles Dickens)

ostry NOUN an ostry is an old word for a pub or hotel ❑ *lest I send you into the ostry with a vengeance* (Doctor Faustus 2.2 by Christopher Marlowe)

outrunning the constable PHRASE outrunning the constable meant spending more than you earn ❑ *but I shall by this means be able to check your bills and to pull you up if I find you outrunning the constable.* (Great Expectations by Charles Dickens)

over ADJ across ❑ *It is in length six yards, and in the thickest part at least three yards over* (Gulliver's Travels by Jonathan Swift)

over the broomstick PHRASE this is a phrase meaning 'getting married without a formal ceremony' ❑ *They both led tramping lives, and this woman in Gerrard-street here, had been married very young, over the broomstick (as we say), to a tramping man, and was a perfect fury in point of jealousy.* (Great Expectations by Charles Dickens)

own VERB own means to admit or to acknowledge ❑ *It's my old girl that advises. She has the head. But I never own to it before her. Discipline must be maintained* (Bleak House by Charles Dickens)

page NOUN here page means a boy employed to run errands ❑ *not my feigned page* (On His Mistress by John Donne)

paid pretty dear PHRASE paid pretty dear means paid a high price or suffered quite a lot ❑ *I paid pretty dear for my monthly fourpenny piece* (Treasure Island by Robert Louis Stevenson)

pannikins NOUN pannikins were small tin cups ❑ *of lifting light glasses and cups to his lips, as if they were clumsy pannikins* (Great Expectations by Charles Dickens)

pards NOUN pards are leopards ❑ *Not charioted by Bacchus and his pards* (Ode on a Nightingale by John Keats)

parlour boarder NOUN a pupil who lived with the family ❑ *and somebody had lately raised her from the condition of scholar to parlour boarder* (Emma by Jane Austen)

particular, a London PHRASE London in Victorian times and up to the 1950s was famous for having very dense fog – which was a combination of real fog and the smog of pollution from factories ❑ *This is a London particular . . . A fog, miss'* (Bleak House by Charles Dickens)

patten NOUN pattens were wooden soles which were fixed to shoes by straps to protect the shoes in wet weather ❑ *carrying a basket like the Great Seal of England in plaited straw, a pair of pattens, a spare shawl, and an umbrella, though it was a fine bright day* (Great Expectations by Charles Dickens)

paviour NOUN a paviour was a labourer who worked on the street pavement ❑ *the paviour his pickaxe* (Oliver Twist by Charles Dickens)

peccant ADJ peccant means unhealthy ❑ *other peccant humours* (Gulliver's Travels by Jonathan Swift)

penetralium NOUN penetralium is a word used to describe the inner rooms of the house ❑ *and I had no desire to aggravate his impatience previous to inspecting the penetralium* (Wuthering Heights by Emily Brontë)

pensive ADV pensive means deep in thought or thinking seriously about something ❑ *and she was leaning pensive on a tomb-stone on her right elbow* (The Adventures of Huckleberry Finn by Mark Twain)

penury NOUN penury is the state of being extremely poor ❑ *Distress, if not penury, loomed in the distance* (Tess of the D'Urbervilles by Thomas Hardy)

perspective NOUN telescope ❑ *a pocket perspective* (Gulliver's Travels by Jonathan Swift)

phaeton NOUN a phaeton was an open carriage for four people ❑ *often* condescends to drive by my humble abode in her little phaeton and ponies (*Pride and Prejudice* by Jane Austen)

phantasm NOUN a phantasm is an illusion, something that is not real. It is sometimes used to mean ghost ❑ *Experience had bred no fancies in him that could raise the phantasm of appetite* (*Silas Marner* by George Eliot)

physic NOUN here physic means medicine ❑ *there I studied physic two years and seven months* (*Gulliver's Travels* by Jonathan Swift)

pinioned VERB to pinion is to hold both arms so that a person cannot move them ❑ *But the relentless Ghost pinioned him in both his arms, and forced him to observe what happened next.* (*A Christmas Carol* by Charles Dickens)

piquet NOUN piquet was a popular card game in the C18th ❑ *Mr Hurst and Mr Bingley were at piquet* (*Pride and Prejudice* by Jane Austen)

plaister NOUN a plaister is a piece of cloth on which an apothecary (or pharmacist) would spread ointment. The cloth is then applied to wounds or bruises to treat them ❑ *Then, she gave the knife a final smart wipe on the edge of the plaister, and then sawed a very thick round off the loaf: which she finally, before separating from the loaf, hewed into two halves, of which Joe got one, and I the other.* (*Great Expectations* by Charles Dickens)

plantations NOUN here plantations means colonies, which are countries controlled by a more powerful country ❑ *besides our plantations in America* (*Gulliver's Travels* by Jonathan Swift)

plastic ADV here plastic is an old term meaning shaping or a power that was forming ❑ *A plastic power abode with me* (*The Prelude* by William Wordsworth)

players NOUN actors ❑ *of players which*

upon the world's stage be (*On His Mistress* by John Donne)

plump ADV all at once, suddenly ❑ *But it took a bit of time to get it well round, the change come so uncommon plump, didn't it? (Great Expectations* by Charles Dickens)

plundered VERB to plunder is to rob or steal from ❑ *These crosses stand for the names of ships or towns that they sank or plundered* (*Treasure Island* by Robert Louis Stevenson)

pommel ■ VERB to pommel someone is to hit them repeatedly with your fists ❑ *hug him round the neck, pommel his back, and kick his legs in irrepressible affection! (A Christmas Carol* by Charles Dickens) ■ NOUN a pommel is the part of a saddle that rises up at the front ❑ *He had his gun across his pommel* (*The Adventures of Huckleberry Finn* by Mark Twain)

poor's rates NOUN poor's rates were property taxes which were used to support the poor ❑ *"Oh!" replied the undertaker; "why, you know, Mr. Bumble, I pay a good deal towards the poor's rates." (Oliver Twist* by Charles Dickens)

popular ADJ popular means ruled by the people, or Republican, rather than ruled by a monarch ❑ *With those of Greece compared and popular Rome* (*The Prelude* by William Wordsworth)

porringer NOUN a porringer is a small bowl ❑ *Of this festive composition each boy had one porringer, and no more* (*Oliver Twist* by Charles Dickens)

postboy NOUN a postboy was the driver of a horse-drawn carriage ❑ *He spoke to a postboy who was dozing under the gateway* (*Oliver Twist* by Charles Dickens)

post-chaise NOUN a fast carriage for two or four passengers ❑ *Looking round, he saw that it was a post-chaise, driven at great speed* (*Oliver Twist* by Charles Dickens)

postern NOUN a small gate usually at the back of a building ❑ *The little servant happening to be entering the fortress with two hot rolls, I passed through the postern and crossed the drawbridge, in her company* (*Great Expectations* by Charles Dickens)

pottle NOUN a pottle was a small basket ❑ *He had a paper-bag under each arm and a pottle of strawberries in one hand . . .* (*Great Expectations* by Charles Dickens)

pounce NOUN pounce is a fine powder used to prevent ink spreading on untreated paper ❑ *in that grim atmosphere of pounce and parchment, red-tape, dusty wafers, ink-jars, brief and draft paper, law reports, writs, declarations, and bills of costs* (*David Copperfield* by Charles Dickens)

pox NOUN pox means sexually transmitted diseases like syphilis ❑ *how the pox in all its consequences and denominations* (*Gulliver's Travels* by Jonathan Swift)

prelibation NOUN prelibation means a foretaste of or an example of something to come ❑ *A prelibation to the mower's scythe* (*The Prelude* by William Wordsworth)

prentice NOUN an apprentice ❑ *and Joe, sitting on an old gun, had told me that when I was 'prentice to him regularly bound, we would have such Larks there!* (*Great Expectations* by Charles Dickens)

presently ADV immediately ❑ *I presently knew what they meant* (*Gulliver's Travels* by Jonathan Swift)

pumpion NOUN pumpkin ❑ *for it was almost as large as a small pumpion* (*Gulliver's Travels* by Jonathan Swift)

punctual ADJ kept in one place ❑ *was not a punctual presence, but a spirit* (*The Prelude* by William Wordsworth)

quadrille ■ NOUN a quadrille is a dance invented in France which is usually performed by four couples ❑ *However, Mr Swiveller had Miss Sophy's hand for the first quadrille (country-dances being low, were utterly proscribed)* (*The Old Curiosity Shop* by Charles Dickens) ■ NOUN quadrille was a card game for four people ❑ *to make up her pool of quadrille in the evening* (*Pride and Prejudice* by Jane Austen)

quality NOUN gentry or upper-class people ❑ *if you are with the quality* (*The Adventures of Huckleberry Finn* by Mark Twain)

quick parts PHRASE quick-witted ❑ *Mr Bennet was so odd a mixture of quick parts* (*Pride and Prejudice* by Jane Austen)

quid NOUN a quid is something chewed or kept in the mouth, like a piece of tobacco ❑ *rolling his quid* (*Treasure Island* by Robert Louis Stevenson)

quit VERB quit means to avenge or to make even ❑ *But Faustus's death shall quit my infamy* (*Doctor Faustus 4.3* by Christopher Marlowe)

rags NOUN divisions ❑ *Nor hours, days, months, which are the rags of time* (*The Sun Rising* by John Donne)

raiment NOUN raiment means clothing ❑ *the mountain shook off turf and flower, had only heath for raiment and crag for gem* (*Jane Eyre* by Charlotte Brontë)

rain cats and dogs PHRASE an expression meaning rain heavily. The origin of the expression is unclear ❑ *But it'll perhaps rain cats and dogs to-morrow* (*Silas Marner* by George Eliot)

raised Cain PHRASE raised Cain means caused a lot of trouble. Cain is a character in the Bible who killed his brother Abel ❑ *and every time he got drunk he raised Cain around town* (*The Adventures of Huckleberry Finn* by Mark Twain)

rambling ADJ rambling means confused and not very clear ❑ *my* *head began to be filled very early with rambling thoughts* (*Robinson Crusoe* by Daniel Defoe)

raree-show NOUN a raree-show is an old term for a peep-show or a fairground entertainment ❑ *A raree-show is here, with children gathered round* (*The Prelude* by William Wordsworth)

recusants NOUN people who resisted authority ❑ *hardy recusants* (*The Prelude* by William Wordsworth)

redounding VERB eddying. An eddy is a movement in water or air which goes round and round instead of flowing in one direction ❑ *mists and steam-like fogs redounding everywhere* (*The Prelude* by William Wordsworth)

redundant ADJ here redundant means overflowing but Wordsworth also uses it to mean excessively large or too big ❑ *A tempest, a redundant energy* (*The Prelude* by William Wordsworth)

reflex NOUN reflex is a shortened version of reflexion, which is an alternative spelling of reflection ❑ *To cut across the reflex of a star* (*The Prelude* by William Wordsworth)

Reformatory NOUN a prison for young offenders/criminals ❑ *Even when I was taken to have a new suit of clothes, the tailor had orders to make them like a kind of Reformatory, and on no account to let me have the free use of my limbs.* (*Great Expectations* by Charles Dickens)

remorse NOUN pity or compassion ❑ *by that remorse* (*On His Mistress* by John Donne)

render VERB in this context render means give. ❑ *and Sarah could render no reason that would be sanctioned by the feeling of the community.* (*Silas Marner* by George Eliot)

repeater NOUN a repeater was a watch that chimed the last hour when a button was pressed – as a result it

was useful in the dark ❑ *And his watch is a gold repeater, and worth a hundred pound if it's worth a penny.* (*Great Expectations* by Charles Dickens)

repugnance NOUN repugnance means a strong dislike of something or someone ❑ *overcoming a strong repugnance* (*Treasure Island* by Robert Louis Stevenson)

reverence NOUN reverence means bow. When you bow to someone, you briefly bend your body towards them as a formal way of showing them respect ❑ *made my reverence* (*Gulliver's Travels* by Jonathan Swift)

reverie NOUN a reverie is a day dream ❑ *I can guess the subject of your reverie* (*Pride and Prejudice* by Jane Austen)

revival NOUN a religious meeting held in public ❑ *well I'd ben a-running' a little temperance revival thar' bout a week* (*The Adventures of Huckleberry Finn* by Mark Twain)

revolt VERB revolt means turn back or stop your present course of action and go back to what you were doing before ❑ *Revolt, or I'll in piecemeal tear thy flesh* (*Doctor Faustus 5.1* by Christopher Marlowe)

rheumatics/rheumatism NOUN rheumatics [rheumatism] is an illness that makes your joints or muscles stiff and painful ❑ *a new cure for the rheumatics* (*Treasure Island* by Robert Louis Stevenson)

riddance NOUN riddance is usually used in the form good riddance which you say when you are pleased that something has gone or been left behind ❑ *I'd better go into the house, and die and be a riddance* (*David Copperfield* by Charles Dickens)

rimy ADJ rimy is an ADJECTIVE which means covered in ice or frost ❑ *It was a rimy morning, and very damp* (*Great Expectations* by Charles Dickens)

riper ADJ riper means more mature or older ❑ *At riper years to Wittenberg he went* (*Doctor Faustus chorus* by Christopher Marlowe)

rubber NOUN a set of games in whist or backgammon ❑ *her father was sure of his rubber* (*Emma* by Jane Austen)

ruffian NOUN a ruffian is a person who behaves violently ❑ *and when the ruffian had told him* (*Treasure Island* by Robert Louis Stevenson)

sadness NOUN sadness is an old term meaning seriousness ❑ *But I prithee tell me, in good sadness* (*Doctor Faustus 2.2* by Christopher Marlowe)

sailed before the mast PHRASE this phrase meant someone who did not look like a sailor ❑ *he had none of the appearance of a man that sailed before the mast* (*Treasure Island* by Robert Louis Stevenson)

scabbard NOUN a scabbard is the covering for a sword or dagger ❑ *Girded round its middle was an antique scabbard; but no sword was in it, and the ancient sheath was eaten up with rust* (*A Christmas Carol* by Charles Dickens)

schooners NOUN A schooner is a fast, medium-sized sailing ship ❑ *if schooners, islands, and maroons* (*Treasure Island* by Robert Louis Stevenson)

science NOUN learning or knowledge ❑ *Even Science, too, at hand* (*The Prelude* by William Wordsworth)

scrouge VERB to scrouge means to squeeze or to crowd ❑ *to scrouge in and get a sight* (*The Adventures of Huckleberry Finn* by Mark Twain)

scrutore NOUN a scrutore, or escritoire, was a writing table ❑ *set me gently on my feet upon the scrutore* (*Gulliver's Travels* by Jonathan Swift)

scutcheon/escutcheon NOUN an escutcheon is a shield with a coat of arms, or the symbols of a family name, engraved on it ❑ *On the*

scutcheon we'll have a bend (*The Adventures of Huckleberry Finn* by Mark Twain)

sea-dog PHRASE sea-dog is a slang term for an experienced sailor or pirate ❑ *a 'true sea-dog', and a 'real old salt,'* (*Treasure Island* by Robert Louis Stevenson)

see the lions PHRASE to see the lions was to go and see the sights of London. Originally the phrase referred to the menagerie in the Tower of London and later in Regent's Park ❑ *We will go and see the lions for an hour or two – it's something to have a fresh fellow like you to show them to, Copperfield* (*David Copperfield* by Charles Dickens)

self-conceit NOUN self-conceit is an old term which means having too high an opinion of oneself, or deceiving yourself ❑ *Till swollen with cunning, of a self-conceit* (*Doctor Faustus chorus* by Christopher Marlowe)

seneschal NOUN a steward ❑ *where a grey-headed seneschal sings a funny chorus with a funnier body of vassals* (*Oliver Twist* by Charles Dickens)

sensible ADJ if you were sensible of something you are aware or conscious of something ❑ *If my children are silly I must hope to be always sensible of it* (*Pride and Prejudice* by Jane Austen)

sessions NOUN court cases were heard at specific times of the year called sessions ❑ *He lay in prison very ill, during the whole interval between his committal for trial, and the coming round of the Sessions.* (*Great Expectations* by Charles Dickens)

shabby ADJ shabby places look old and in bad condition ❑ *a little bit of a shabby village named Pikesville* (*The Adventures of Huckleberry Finn* by Mark Twain)

shay-cart NOUN a shay-cart was a small cart drawn by one horse ❑ *"I were at the Bargemen t'other night, Pip;"*

whenever he subsided into affection, he called me Pip, and whenever he relapsed into politeness he called me Sir; "when there come up in his shay-cart Pumblechook." (*Great Expectations* by Charles Dickens)

shilling NOUN a shilling is an old unit of currency. There were twenty shillings in every British pound ❑ *"Ten shillings too much," said the gentleman in the white waistcoat.* (*Oliver Twist* by Charles Dickens)

shines NOUN tricks or games ❑ *well, it would make a cow laugh to see the shines that old idiot cut* (*The Adventures of Huckleberry Finn* by Mark Twain)

shirking VERB shirking means not doing what you are meant to be doing, or evading your duties ❑ *some of you shirking lubbers* (*Treasure Island* by Robert Louis Stevenson)

shiver my timbers PHRASE shiver my timbers is an expression which was used by sailors and pirates to express surprise ❑ *why, shiver my timbers, if I hadn't forgotten my score!* (*Treasure Island* by Robert Louis Stevenson)

shoe-roses NOUN shoe-roses were roses made from ribbons which were stuck on to shoes as decoration ❑ *the very shoe-roses for Netherfield were got by proxy* (*Pride and Prejudice* by Jane Austen)

singular ADJ singular means very great and remarkable or strange ❑ *"Singular dream," he says* (*The Adventures of Huckleberry Finn* by Mark Twain)

sire NOUN sire is an old word which means lord or master or elder ❑ *She also defied her sire* (*Little Women* by Louisa May Alcott)

sixpence NOUN a sixpence was half of a shilling ❑ *if she had only a shilling in the world, she would be very lilkely to give away sixpence of it* (*Emma* by Jane Austen)

slavey NOUN the word slavey was used when there was only one servant in a house or boarding-house – so she had to perform all the duties of a larger staff ❑ *Two distinct knocks, sir, will produce the slavey at any time* (*The Old Curiosity Shop* by Charles Dickens)

slender ADJ weak ❑ *In slender accents of sweet verse* (*The Prelude* by William Wordsworth)

slop-shops NOUN slop-shops were shops where cheap ready-made clothes were sold. They mainly sold clothes to sailors ❑ *Accordingly, I took the jacket off, that I might learn to do without it; and carrying it under my arm, began a tour of inspection of the various slop-shops.* (*David Copperfield* by Charles Dickens)

sluggard NOUN a lazy person ❑ *"Stand up and repeat 'Tis the voice of the sluggard,'" said the Gryphon.* (*Alice's Adventures in Wonderland* by Lewis Carroll)

smallpox NOUN smallpox is a serious infectious disease ❑ *by telling the men we had smallpox aboard* (*The Adventures of Huckleberry Finn* by Mark Twain)

smalls NOUN smalls are short trousers ❑ *It is difficult for a large-headed, small-eyed youth, of lumbering make and heavy countenance, to look dignified under any circumstances; but it is more especially so, when superadded to these personal attractions are a red nose and yellow smalls* (*Oliver Twist* by Charles Dickens)

sneeze-box NOUN a box for snuff was called a sneeze-box because sniffing snuff makes the user sneeze ❑ *To think of Jack Dawkins — lummy Jack — the Dodger — the Artful Dodger — going abroad for a common twopenny-halfpenny sneeze-box!* (*Oliver Twist* by Charles Dickens)

snorted VERB slept ❑ *Or snorted we in the Seven Sleepers' den?* (*The Good-Morrow* by John Donne)

snuff NOUN snuff is tobacco in powder form which is taken by sniffing ❑

as he thrust his thumb and fore-finger into the proffered snuff-box of the undertaker: which was an ingenious little model of a patent coffin. (*Oliver Twist* by Charles Dickens)

soliloquized VERB to soliloquize is when an actor in a play speaks to himself or herself rather than to another actor ❑ *"A new servitude! There is something in that," I soliloquized (mentally, be it understood; I did not talk aloud)* (*Jane Eyre* by Charlotte Brontë)

sough NOUN a sough is a drain or a ditch ❑ *as you may have noticed the sough that runs from the marshes* (*Wuthering Heights* by Emily Brontë)

spirits NOUN a spirit is the nonphysical part of a person which is believed to remain alive after their death ❑ *that I might raise up spirits when I please* (*Doctor Faustus 1.5* by Christopher Marlowe)

spleen ■ NOUN here spleen means a type of sadness or depression which was thought to only affect the wealthy ❑ *yet here I could plainly discover the true seeds of spleen* (*Gulliver's Travels* by Jonathan Swift) ■ NOUN irritability and low spirits ❑ *Adieu to disappointment and spleen* (*Pride and Prejudice* by Jane Austen)

spondulicks NOUN spondulicks is a slang word which means money ❑ *not for all his spondulicks and as much more on top of it* (*The Adventures of Huckleberry Finn* by Mark Twain)

stalled of VERB to be stalled of something is to be bored with it ❑ *I'm stalled of doing naught* (*Wuthering Heights* by Emily Brontë)

stanchion NOUN a stanchion is a pole or bar that stands upright and is used as a buidling support ❑ *and slid down a stanchion* (*The Adventures of Huckleberry Finn* by Mark Twain)

stang NOUN stang is another word for pole which was an old measurement ❑ *These fields were intermingled*

with woods of half a stang (*Gulliver's Travels* by Jonathan Swift)

starlings NOUN a starling is a wall built around the pillars that support a bridge to protect the pillars ❑ *There were states of the tide when, having been down the river, I could not get back through the eddy-chafed arches and starlings of old London Bridge* (*Great Expectations* by Charles Dickens)

startings NOUN twitching or night-time movements of the body ❑ *with midnight's startings* (*On His Mistress* by John Donne)

stomacher NOUN a panel at the front of a dress ❑ *but send her aunt the pattern of a stomacher* (*Emma* by Jane Austen)

stoop VERB swoop ❑ *Once a kite hovering over the garden made a swoop at me* (*Gulliver's Travels* by Jonathan Swift)

succedaneum NOUN a succedaneum is a substitute ❑ *But as a succedaneum* (*The Prelude* by William Wordsworth)

suet NOUN a hard animal fat used in cooking ❑ *and your jaws are too weak For anything tougher than suet* (*Alice's Adventures in Wonderland* by Lewis Carroll)

sultry ADJ sultry weather is hot and damp. Here sultry means unpleasant or risky ❑ *for it was getting pretty sultry for us* (*The Adventures of Huckleberry Finn* by Mark Twain)

summerset NOUN summerset is an old spelling of somersault. If someone does a somersault, they turn over completely in the air ❑ *I have seen him do the summerset* (*Gulliver's Travels* by Jonathan Swift)

supper NOUN supper was a light meal taken late in the evening. The main meal was dinner which was eaten at four or five in the afternoon ❑ *and the supper table was all set out* (*Emma* by Jane Austen)

surfeits VERB to surfeit in something is to have far too much of it, or to overindulge in it to an unhealthy degree ❑ *He surfeits upon cursed necromancy* (*Doctor Faustus chorus* by Christopher Marlowe)

surtout NOUN a surtout is a long close-fitting overcoat ❑ *He wore a long black surtout reaching nearly to his ankles* (*The Old Curiosity Shop* by Charles Dickens)

swath NOUN swath is the width of corn cut by a scythe ❑ *while thy hook Spares the next swath* (*Ode to Autumn* by John Keats)

sylvan ADJ sylvan means belonging to the woods ❑ *Sylvan historian* (*Ode on a Grecian Urn* by John Keats)

taction NOUN taction means touch. This means that the people had to be touched on the mouth or the ears to get their attention ❑ *without being roused by some external taction upon the organs of speech and hearing* (*Gulliver's Travels* by Jonathan Swift)

Tag and Rag and Bobtail PHRASE the riff-raff, or lower classes. Used in an insulting way ❑ *"No," said he; "not till it got about that there was no protection on the premises, and it come to be considered dangerous, with convicts and Tag and Rag and Bobtail going up and down."* (*Great Expectations* by Charles Dickens)

tallow NOUN tallow is hard animal fat that is used to make candles and soap ❑ *and a lot of tallow candles* (*The Adventures of Huckleberry Finn* by Mark Twain)

tan VERB to tan means to beat or whip ❑ *and if I catch you about that school I'll tan you good* (*The Adventures of Huckleberry Finn* by Mark Twain)

tanyard NOUN the tanyard is part of a tannery, which is a place where leather is made from animal skins ❑ *hid in the old tanyard* (*The Adventures of Huckleberry Finn* by Mark Twain)

tarry ADJ tarry means the colour of tar or black ❑ *his tarry pig-tail* (*Treasure Island* by Robert Louis Stevenson)

thereof PHRASE from there ❑ *By all desires which thereof did ensue* (*On His Mistress* by John Donne)

thick with, be PHRASE if you are 'thick with someone' you are very close, sharing secrets – it is often used to describe people who are planning something secret ❑ *Hasn't he been thick with Mr Heathcliff lately?* (*Wuthering Heights* by Emily Brontë)

thimble NOUN a thimble is a small cover used to protect the finger while sewing ❑ *The paper had been sealed in several places by a thimble* (*Treasure Island* by Robert Louis Stevenson)

thirtover ADJ thirtover is an old word which means obstinate or that someone is very determined to do want they want and can not be persuaded to do something in another way ❑ *I have been living on in a thirtover, lackadaisical way* (*Tess of the D'Urbervilles* by Thomas Hardy)

timbrel NOUN timbrel is a tambourine ❑ *What pipes and timbrels?* (*Ode on a Grecian Urn* by John Keats)

tin NOUN tin is slang for money/cash ❑ *Then the plain question is, an't it a pity that this state of things should continue, and how much better would it be for the old gentleman to hand over a reasonable amount of tin, and make it all right and comfortable* (*The Old Curiosity Shop* by Charles Dickens)

tincture NOUN a tincture is a medicine made with alcohol and a small amount of a drug ❑ *with ink composed of a cephalic tincture* (*Gulliver's Travels* by Jonathan Swift)

tithe NOUN a tithe is a tax paid to the church ❑ *and held farms which, speaking from a spiritual point of view, paid highly-desirable tithes* (*Silas Marner* by George Eliot)

towardly ADJ a towardly child is dutiful or obedient ❑ *and a towardly child* (*Gulliver's Travels* by Jonathan Swift)

toys NOUN trifles are things which are considered to have little importance, value, or significance ❑ *purchase my life from them bysome bracelets, glass rings, and other toys* (*Gulliver's Travels* by Jonathan Swift)

tract NOUN a tract is a religious pamphlet or leaflet ❑ *and Joe Harper got a hymn-book and a tract* (*The Adventures of Huckleberry Finn* by Mark Twain)

train-oil NOUN train-oil is oil from whale blubber ❑ *The train-oil and gunpowder were shoved out of sight in a minute* (*Wuthering Heights* by Emily Brontë)

tribulation NOUN tribulation means the suffering or difficulty you experience in a particular situation ❑ *Amy was learning this distinction through much tribulation* (*Little Women* by Louisa May Alcott)

trivet NOUN a trivet is a three-legged stand for resting a pot or kettle ❑ *a pocket-knife in his right; and a pewter pot on the trivet* (*Oliver Twist* by Charles Dickens)

trot line NOUN a trot line is a fishing line to which a row of smaller fishing lines are attached ❑ *when he got along I was hard at it taking up a trot line* (*The Adventures of Huckleberry Finn* by Mark Twain)

troth NOUN oath or pledge ❑ *I wonder, by my troth* (*The Good-Morrow* by John Donne)

truckle NOUN a truckle bedstead is a bed that is on wheels and can be slid under another bed to save space ❑ *It rose under my hand, and the door yielded. Looking in, I saw a lighted candle on a table, a bench, and a mattress on a truckle bedstead.* (*Great Expectations* by Charles Dickens)

trump NOUN a trump is a good, reliable person wo can be trusted ❑ *This lad Hawkins is a trump, I*

perceive (*Treasure Island* by Robert Louis Stevenson)

tucker NOUN a tucker is a frilly lace collar which is worn around the neck ❑ *Whereat Scrooge's niece's sister⌐the plump one with the lace tucker: not the one with the roses⌐blushed.* (*A Christmas Carol* by Charles Dickens)

tureen NOUN a large bowl with a lid from which soup or vegetables are served ❑ *Waiting in a hot tureen!* (*Alice's Adventures in Wonderland* by Lewis Carroll)

turnkey NOUN a prison officer; jailer ❑ *As we came out of the prison through the lodge, I found that the great importance of my guardian was appreciated by the turnkeys, no less than by those whom they held in charge.* (*Great Expectations* by Charles Dickens)

turnpike NOUN the upkeep of many roads of the time was paid for by tolls (fees) collected at posts along the road. There was a gate to prevent people travelling further along the road until the toll had been paid. ❑ *Traddles, whom I have taken up by appointment at the turnpike, presents a dazzling combination of cream colour and light blue; and both he and Mr. Dick have a general effect about them of being all gloves.* (*David Copperfield* by Charles Dickens)

twas PHRASE it was ❑ *twas but a dream of thee* (*The Good-Morrow* by John Donne)

tyrannized VERB tyrannized means bullied or forced to do things against their will ❑ *for people would soon cease coming there to be tyrannized over and put down* (*Treasure Island* by Robert Louis Stevenson)

'un NOUN 'un is a slang term for one — usually used to refer to a person ❑ *She's been thinking the old 'un* (*David Copperfield* by Charles Dickens)

undistinguished ADJ undiscriminating or incapable of making a distinction between good and bad things ❏ *their undistinguished appetite to devour everything* (Gulliver's Travels by Jonathan Swift)

use NOUN habit ❏ *Though use make you apt to kill me* (The Flea by John Donne)

vacant ADJ vacant usually means empty, but here Wordsworth uses it to mean carefree ❏ *To vacant musing, unreproved neglect* (The Prelude by William Wordsworth)

valetudinarian NOUN one too concerned with his or her own health. ❏ *for having been a valetudinarian all his life* (Emma by Jane Austen)

vamp VERB vamp means to walk or tramp to somewhere ❏ *Well, vamp on to Marlott, will 'ee* (Tess of the D'Urbervilles by Thomas Hardy)

vapours NOUN the vapours is an old term which means unpleasant and strange thoughts, which make the person feel nervous and unhappy ❏ *and my head was full of vapours* (Robinson Crusoe by Daniel Defoe)

vegetables NOUN here vegetables means plants ❏ *the other vegetables are in the same proportion* (Gulliver's Travels by Jonathan Swift)

venturesome ADJ if you are venturesome you are willing to take risks ❏ *he must be either hopelessly stupid or a venturesome fool* (Wuthering Heights by Emily Brontë)

verily ADJ verily means really or truly ❏ *though I believe verily* (Robinson Crusoe by Daniel Defoe)

vicinage NOUN vicinage is an area or the residents of an area ❏ *and to his thought the whole vicinage was haunted by her.* (Silas Marner by George Eliot)

victuals NOUN victuals means food ❏ *grumble a little over the victuals* (The Adventures of Huckleberry Finn by Mark Twain)

vintage NOUN vintage in this context means wine ❏ *Oh, for a draught of*

vintage! (Ode on a Nightingale by John Keats)

virtual ADJ here virtual means powerful or strong ❏ *had virtual faith* (The Prelude by William Wordsworth)

vittles NOUN vittles is a slang word which means food ❏ *There never was such a woman for givin' away vittles and drink* (Little Women by Louisa May Alcott)

voided straight PHRASE voided straight is an old expression which means emptied immediately ❏ *see the rooms be voided straight* (Doctor Faustus 4.1 by Christopher Marlowe)

wainscot NOUN wainscot is wood panel lining in a room so wainscoted means a room lined with wooden panels ❏ *in the dark wainscoted parlor* (Silas Marner by George Eliot)

walking the plank PHRASE walking the plank was a punishment in which a prisoner would be made to walk along a plank on the side of the ship and fall into the sea, where they would be abandoned ❏ *about hanging, and walking the plank* (Treasure Island by Robert Louis Stevenson)

want VERB want means to be lacking or short of ❏ *The next thing wanted was to get the picture framed* (Emma by Jane Austen)

wanting ADJ wanting means lacking or missing ❏ *wanting two fingers of the left hand* (Treasure Island by Robert Louis Stevenson)

wanting, I was not PHRASE I was not wanting means I did not fail ❏ *I was not wanting to lay a foundation of religious knowledge in his mind* (Robinson Crusoe by Daniel Defoe)

ward NOUN a ward is, usually, a child who has been put under the protection of the court or a guardian for his or her protection ❏ *I call the Wards in Jarndcye. The*

are caged up with all the others.
(*Bleak House* by Charles Dickens)

waylay VERB to waylay someone is to
lie in wait for them or to intercept
them ❑ *I must go up the road and
waylay him* (*The Adventures of
Huckleberry Finn* by Mark Twain)

weazen NOUN weazen is a slang word for
throat. It actually means shrivelled ❑
*You with a uncle too! Why, I knowed
you at Gargery's when you was so
small a wolf that I could have took your
weazen betwixt this finger and thumb
and chucked you away dead* (*Great
Expectations* by Charles Dickens)

wery ▉ ADV very ❑ *Be wery careful o'
vidders all your life* (*Pickwick
Papers* by Charles Dickens) ▉ *See*
wibrated

wherry NOUN wherry is a small swift
rowing boat for one person ❑ *It
was flood tide when Daniel Quilp
sat himself down in the wherry to
cross to the opposite shore.* (*The Old
Curiosity Shop* by Charles Dickens)

whether PREP whether means which
of the two in this example ❑ *we
came in full view of a great island
or continent (for we knew not
whether)* (*Gulliver's Travels* by
Jonathan Swift)

whetstone NOUN a whetstone is a
stone used to sharpen knives and
other tools ❑ *I dropped pap's whet-
stone there too* (*The Adventures of
Huckleberry Finn* by Mark Twain)

wibrated VERB in Dickens's use of the
English language 'w' often replaces
'v' when he is reporting speech. So
here 'wibrated' means 'vibrated'. In
Pickwick Papers a judge asks Sam
Weller (who constantly confuses the
two letters) 'Do you spell is with a
'v' or a 'w'?' to which Weller replies
'That depends upon the taste and
fancy of the speller, my Lord' ❑
*There are strings . . . in the human
heart that had better not be wibrated*'
(*Barnaby Rudge* by Charles Dickens)

wicket NOUN a wicket is a little door in
a larger entrance ❑ *Having rested
here, for a minute or so, to collect a*

good burst of sobs and an imposing
show of tears and terror, he knocked
loudly at the wicket; (*Oliver Twist*
by Charles Dickens)

without CONJ without means unless ❑
*You don't know about me, without
you have read a book by the name of
The Adventures of Tom Sawyer* (*The
Adventures of Huckleberry Finn* by
Mark Twain)

wittles ▉ NOUN vittles is a slang word
which means food ❑ *I live on
broken wittles – and I sleep on the
coals* (*David Copperfield* by Charles
Dickens) ▉ *See* wibrated

woo VERB courts or forms a proper
relationship with ❑ *before it woo*
(*The Flea* by John Donne)

words, to have PHRASE if you have
words with someone you have a
disagreement or an argument ❑ *I
do not want to have words with a
young thing like you.* (*Black Beauty*
by Emily Brontë)

workhouse NOUN workhouses were
places where the homeless were
given food and a place to live in
return for doing very hard work ❑
*And the Union workhouses?
demanded Scrooge. Are they still in
operation?* (*A Christmas Carol* by
Charles Dickens)

yawl NOUN a yawl is a small boat kept
on a bigger boat for short trips.
Yawl is also the name for a small
fishing boat ❑ *She sent out her
yawl, and we went aboard* (*The
Adventures of Huckleberry Finn* by
Mark Twain)

yeomanry NOUN the yeomanry was a
collective term for the middle
classes involved in agriculture ❑
*The yeomanry are precisely the
order of people with whom I feel I
can have nothing to do* (*Emma* by
Jane Austen)

yonder ADV yonder means over there
❑ *all in the same second we seem to
hear low voices in yonder!* (*The
Adventures of Huckleberry Finn* by
Mark Twain)